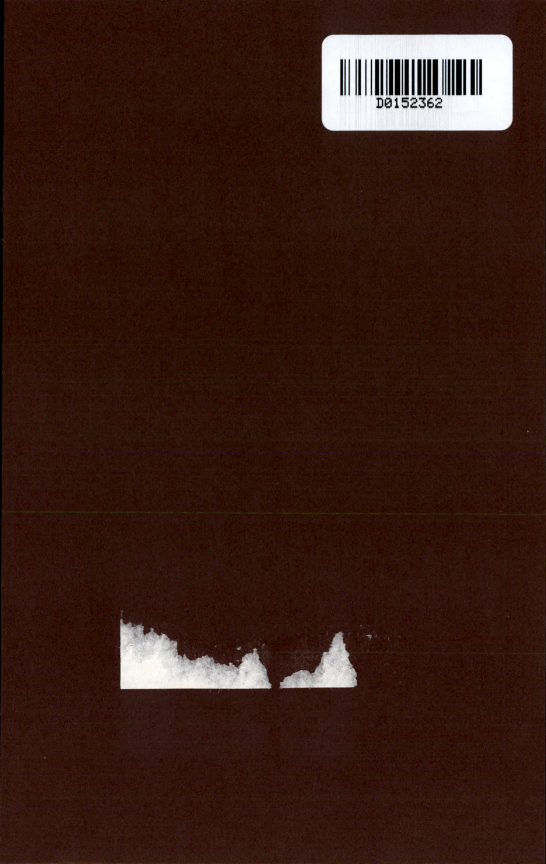

SCOTTISH COMMON SENSE IN GERMANY, 1768–1800
A Contribution to the History of Critical Philosophy

Proponents of Scottish common-sense philosophy, especially Thomas
Reid, James Oswald, and James Beattie, had a substantial influence on
late enlightenment German philosophy. In this illuminating study
Manfred Kuehn explores the nature and extent of that influence. He
finds that the work of these philosophers was widely discussed in
German philosophical journals and translated into German soon after
its publication in Britain. Important German philosophers such as
Mendelssohn, Lossius, Feder, Hamann, and Jacobi, representing the
full range of philosophical positions, read the Scots and found valuable
philosophical insights in their thought.

Most important, suggests Kuehn, was the perception of Scottish
common-sense philosophers as opposing Hume's scepticism while
complementing his positive teaching. Their views gave considerable
impetus to those developments in German thought that ultimately led
to Kant's critical philosophy. In fact Kant, whose devastating criticism
of the Scottish common-sense philosophers is often cited, learned
much from the Scots as his "exposition of Hume's problem in its widest
extent"—the *Critique of Pure Reason*—reveals.

Kuehn's analysis of the Scottish influence provides a new perspective
on the German enlightenment and Kant's role within it, revealing the
importance of problems of idealism versus realism and of philosophical justification versus mere descriptive metaphysics.

Manfred Kuehn is a member of the Department of Philosophy,
Purdue University.

McGILL-QUEEN'S STUDIES IN THE HISTORY OF IDEAS

SCOTTISH COMMON SENSE IN GERMANY, 1768–1800
A Contribution to the History of Critical Philosophy

Manfred Kuehn

Foreword by
Lewis White Beck

McGill-Queen's University Press
Kingston and Montreal

©McGill-Queen's University Press 1987
ISBN 0-7735-1009-5
Legal deposit first quarter 1987
Bibliothèque nationale du Québec

Printed in Canada

∞

Printed on acid free paper

This book has been published with the help of a grant from the
Canadian Federation for the Humanities, using funds provided by the
Social Sciences and Humanities Research Council of Canada.

Canadian Cataloguing in Publication Data

Kuehn, Manfred
Scottish common sense in Germany, 1768–1800

(McGill-Queen's studies in the history of ideas,
ISSN 0711-0995 ; 11)
Bibliography: p.
Includes index.
ISBN 0-7735-1009-5

1. Philosophy, German – 18th century – Scottish
influences. 2. Philosophy, Scottish – 18th
century. 3. Criticism (Philosophy). I. Title.
II. Series.
B2615.K84 1987   193   c86-094475-1

To the Memory of
Margarete Kühn
1920–1985

"The science of common sense is critique."
(Immanuel Kant)

"We have long been engaged in a
critique of reason; I would wish for a critique
of common sense. It would be a true blessing
for humanity, if we could demonstrate to the
complete satisfaction of common sense how far
it can reach. For this is precisely what it
needs for perfection on this earth."
(Johann Wolfgang von Goethe)

Contents

Foreword

When I accepted McGill University's invitation to participate in the *examen rigorosum* of Manfred Kuehn, I did not expect that as a consequence I was going to have to change my mind about important issues in the history of German philosophy.

Dr. Kuehn opened what he calls in this book "a new perspective on the German enlightenment." He found a pervasive knowledge of and interest in Scottish common-sense philosophy among German philosophers of the last third of the eighteenth century, and saw ramifications of this system as its teachings were assimilated into the doctrines of several native schools of philosophy.

Once he opens the eyes of his readers to the Scottish connection, they see it as unmistakably as he does, but before he opened their eyes they were generally blind to it. Hegel knew about it, and there were occasionally German monographs on some specific instances of it. But even Cassirer in his classical history of the enlightenment does not mention Reid a single time, and only once in *Das Erkenntnisproblem* does he connect Reid with any German thinker. Most historians of the German enlightenment emphasize French, English, or domestic German influences; and though Hume, Hutcheson, Kames, Ferguson, and Adam Smith had recognized roles in German intellectual life little or nothing has been said about widespread importance of the common-sense philosophers Reid, Beattie, and Oswald. Since reading Kuehn's dissertation, I have thanked heaven that I did at least mention Reid and Beattie several times in my *Early German Philosophy*, but I must confess that I saw them mostly through Kant's jaundiced eye, and had no conception of the magnitude of their influence on his fellow philosophers.

Kuehn sees a richness in the common-sense philosophy which is usually hidden from us nowadays because we tend to think of Reid alone in the company of Locke, Berkeley, and Hume. He points out significant differences among the Scottish triumvirate which explain how it came about that what appealed to one German philosopher might be wholly different from what, under precisely the same name, appealed to another. However much they differed from one another, German philosophers appear to have been anxious to affiliate themselves with the Scottish critics of Hume, though their differences among themselves caused them to embrace diverse features and interpretations of the common-sense philosophy.

Thus, for example, Kuehn shows that Wolffians emphasized the near-identity of common sense with reason; the philosophers of faith insisted that common sense was like feeling; the naturalists accepted common sense as a kind of instinct; the sceptics stressed its opposition to high-flown speculations of the kind ascribed to Berkeley; and so on. Few followed Reid in his theory of direct perceptual realism, and most combined some theory of common sense with the quite alien "way of ideas" which Reid had rejected. This explains why no stable orthodox Scottish school was established in Germany.

The most interesting and important, but also the most controversial, chapter in this book is the one on Kant. It is commonly accepted that there were two important answers to Hume, the Scots' and Kant's. Involved in this conception is the belief that Kant knew little of the Scots' writings, and that the importance they had for him was as a source of knowledge of Hume's *Treatise*, which he could not read. The common view is that the Scottish philosophers deserved Kant's censure because of their misunderstanding of "Hume's problem" and their attempting to make a sense fill the office of reason.

Kuehn rejects every part of this common belief. He makes a convincing case for Kant's having extensive knowledge of the important Scottish writings. He then maintains that Kant (in spite of several memorable outbursts) was not entirely hostile to the Scottish philosophy. In interpreting these passages Kuehn makes discreet use of Collingwood's hazardous hermeneutic maxim that a philosopher's intense polemic against a theory may be a sign that the theory has a strong attraction for him. Proceeding then to a deeper conceptual level, Kuehn argues for Windelband's statement that "Kant begins at the point at which the Scots had stopped."

These are challenges that Kant scholars must deal with. Professor

Kuehn admits with regret that an adequate treatment of these topics would require more space than a single chapter in a book. This gives us reason to hope that his next book will fully examine the case for the new interpretation of Kant which he offers here. In the meantime let us enjoy and learn from what is an impressive work of philosophical scholarship.

Lewis White Beck

Acknowledgments

The following work has taken a long time to write. It started out as a dissertation for the doctoral degree at McGill University and in that form was completed in 1980. But the research upon which it is based began in 1976. Since that time I have incurred a number of debts to institutions and individuals.

The book could not have been written without the financial assistance I received from the Canada Council (now the Social Sciences and Humanities Research Council of Canada) in the form of two doctoral fellowships, and from McGill University in the form of a Dow Hickson Fellowship. Without the services of the Departments of Inter-Library Loans at McGill University and the Westfälische Wilhelms-Universität in Münster this work would rest on an insecure foundation. Further, I am also grateful to the Philosophisches Seminar of the Westfälische Wilhelms-Universität for making available to me their library and their collection of *libri rari*.

I have learned a great deal from discussions with teachers, colleagues, and friends. Special thanks go to the late Guy Desautels for making several useful suggestions with regard to my earliest research; to my friends Pastor Hartwig Schulte and his wife Elke, with whom I had many discussions during the early stages of researching and writing; and to Professor Giorgio di Giovanni, who made important criticisms and suggestions of details. Werner Stark (Marburg) made available to me a photocopy of the review of Reid's *Inquiry* in the *Neue Zeitungen von gelehrten Sachen* of 1764, which was very useful. I am also grateful to the two anonymous referees of the book for McGill-Queen's University Press for their helpful comments.

But I owe the greatest professional debts to Professor Lewis White Beck, Professor Rolf George, and Professor David Fate Norton.

Professor Beck read this work in its dissertation format and offered most valuable criticisms and suggestions. I have learned as much from his published writings as from the discussion of some aspects of the book carried on by correspondence. His great interest in my work was the source of constant encouragement during the last few years. My former teacher at the University of Waterloo, Professor George, not only read and commented on a very early version of the Introduction, but also offered important suggestions for this version. Professor Norton supervised and directed my early research and patiently read through most drafts. In fact, the very conception of the problem derives from suggestions made by him in a seminar on Hume and the Scottish enlightenment. The work—and I—owe more to him than I can remember. I am, of course, the only one responsible for any lapses that may remain.

For help in preparing the manuscript I would like to thank especially Miriam Catellier, who introduced me to the secrets of "word processing," and my daughter Sabine, who typed onto the word processor large portions of the final version.

All quotations from books whose titles are given in German have been translated by me.

Finally, I would like to call attention to some papers of mine that either go over the same ground in a different way, or are dealing with closely related issues, and which therefore might be helpful:

"Dating Kant's 'Vorlesungen über Philosophische Enzyklopädie,'" *Kant-Studien* 74 (1983): 302-13

"Kant's Conception of Hume's Problem," *Journal of the History of Philosophy* 21 (1983): 175-93

"The Early Reception of Reid, Oswald and Beattie in Germany," *Journal of the History of Philosophy* 21 (1983): 479-95

"Hume's Antinomies," *Hume Studies* 9 (1983): 25-45

"The Context of Kant's 'Refutation of Idealism' in Eighteenth-Century Philosophy," in *God, Man and Nature in the Enlightenment* (forthcoming)

"Kant's Transcendental Deduction: A Limited *Defense* of Hume," *New Essays on Kant*, ed. Bernard den Ouden (New York and Bern: Peter F. Lang Publishing Company, forthcoming)

SCOTTISH COMMON SENSE IN GERMANY, 1768–1800

Introduction

DURING the last two decades Thomas Reid has been rediscovered as one of the most important British philosophers. His works are being read and discussed again more widely as having something of philosophical importance to say.[1] At the same time, philosophical scholars have increasingly come to realize that his philosophy has had a substantial, though often unrecognized, influence upon the development of philosophy not only in Scotland, but also in a number of other countries. The extent and importance of the influence of Reid and his followers James Oswald and James Beattie in America, France, England, Belgium, and Italy are widely acknowledged, and significant research has already been done.[2] With regard to Germany, however,

---

1. Brody, "Reid and Hamilton on Perception," p. 423. Since that time two collections of essays as well as a number of important books on Reid have appeared. The most important of these are perhaps *Thomas Reid: Critical Interpretations*, ed. Barker and Beauchamp; *The Philosophy of Thomas Reid*, ed. Beck, *The Monist*; Daniels, *Thomas Reid's Inquiry*; Marcil Lacoste, *Claude Buffier and Thomas Reid*. Bibliographies to further literature can be found especially in the collections edited by Barker and Beauchamp and Beck as well as in Lacoste's book.

2. With regard to America see, for instance, McCosh, *The Scottish Philosophy*; Martin, *The Instructed Vision*; Petersen, *Scottish Common Sense in America 1768–1850*; see also Hoeveler, Jr., *James McCosh and the Scottish Intellectual Tradition*. For more recent developments see Lehrer, "The Scottish Influences on Contemporary American Philosophy." For France see Boutroux, "De l'influence de la philosophie écossaise sur la philosophie française." For Belgium see Henry, "Le traditionalisme et l'ontologisme à Université de Louvain 1835–1865." For Italy see the various works of M. F. Sciacca, as for instance his "Reid, e Gallupi." For more general accounts see Beanblossom, Introduction to Thomas Reid, *Inquiry and Essays*, who gives a succinct and helpful account of the major influences, as does Grave, *Scottish Philosophy of Common Sense*.

matters are quite different. It is not generally known that the Scottish philosophy of common sense played a highly significant role in that country during the last third of the eighteenth century. If Germany is mentioned in the context of a discussion of Reid and Scottish common sense, then it is only in order to say that the Scots were "much less influential" there.[3]

The only widely known effect of Reid, Oswald, and Beattie in Germany appears to be the devastating criticism they received from Immanuel Kant in the *Prolegomena*:

[i]t is positively painful to see how utterly his [Hume's] opponents Reid, Oswald, Beattie, and lastly Priestley, missed the point of the problem; for while they were ever taking for granted that which he doubted, and demonstrating with zeal and often with impudence that which he never thought of doubting, they so misconstrued his valuable suggestion that everything remained in its old condition, as if nothing had happened.[4]

This critique has come to be taken at face value. No one appears to have asked *why* Kant bothered to disqualify Reid and his followers so thoroughly. Was it only the disinterested attempt to save Hume's good name? Or did he write on the spur of the moment, casually, or make a cavalier judgment based exclusively on a reading of Beattie (and perhaps Oswald)? Or was Kant aiming at something more important, or, at least, at something different?

If Collingwood's suggestion that "an intense polemic against a certain doctrine is a certain sign that the doctrine in question figures largely in a writer's environment and even has a strong attraction for himself" is correct—and I believe it is correct—then Kant's vehement

---

3. This lack of knowledge can be seen to go back as far as McCosh. While Hamilton in his edition of Reid's works, *The Philosophical Works of Thomas Reid*, calls attention to various German philosophers (most notably Tetens) as having written *against* the Scots, and notes that Jacobi was influenced by Reid, McCosh just says that the Germans mention Reid only in order to disparage him (*Scottish Philosophy*, pp. 303f.). Johnston, *Selections from the Scottish Philosophy of Common Sense*, p. 23, notes simply that the Scots have "never been appreciated" in England and Germany. Brody, Introduction to Reid's *Essays on the Intellectual Powers of Man*, p. xxiv finds: "Reid was much less influential in Germany." Grave, *Scottish Philosophy*, does not mention Germany, nor does Beanblossom in his Introduction to *Inquiry and Essays*. King's "James Beattie's *Essay on Truth* (1770)" does not discuss Beattie's effect in Germany and mentions only Kant's attack in the *Prolegomena*.

4. Kant, *Prolegomena*, ed. Beck, pp. 6–8.

rejection bespeaks the importance of the Scots.[5] At the very least, it suggests that *their* misconstrual thwarted Hume, and that *they* might have made a difference.

I shall try to show that this is actually so. Scottish common sense figured largely in Kant's intellectual environment both in Königsberg and in the German republic of letters as a whole, and the Scottish doctrine had—at least at times—the strongest attraction for him. I think that this is one of the reasons why he found it so "positively painful" when Reid, Oswald, and Beattie missed the point of his other Scottish forebear David Hume. When Kant referred to his reading of the works of the Scots in this way, he may also be understood as characterizing the labour-pains he experienced at the birth of his critical philosophy.

There was a time when this had—almost—come to be realized by philosophical scholars of Kant. Thus H. Vaihinger observed in his monumental *Commentary* to Kant's first *Critique* of 1881 that "Kant's relation to the Scottish school, the internal and systematic one as well as the external and historical one, would deserve a thorough monographic treatment."[6] And another well-known Kant scholar, Wilhelm Windelband, noted a few years later that

Kant characterized as 'dogmatic' not only the rationalism, but also the empiricism of earlier theories of knowledge, and . . . the classical passage in the Introduction of the *Prolegomena* . . . does not at all oppose Hume to Wolff, but, as a matter of fact, to Locke, Reid and Beattie. The dogmatism from which Kant declared himself freed was the *empirical* dogmatism.[7]

Indeed, in another context Windelband suggested that Reid's theory of common sense and original judgment is of great importance for the discussion of *a priori* judgments, and that Kant "begins at the very point at which the Scots had ceased [inquiry]."[8]

Others again had already begun a closer examination of Kant's relation to the Scots. Thus Julius Janitsch had argued in his *Kants Urteile über Berkeley* that Kant in all likelihood did not know Berkeley's works first hand, and that Beattie's *Essay on the Nature and Immutability of Truth* was probably the source of most of his judgments about Berkeley.

5. Collingwood, *The Idea of History*, p. 204.
6. Vaihinger, *Commentar zu Kants Kritik der reinen Vernunft*, vol. 1, p. 342.
7. Windelband and Heimsoeth, *Lehrbuch der Geschichte der Philosophie*, p. 461n.
8. Windelband, *Geschichte der neueren Philosophie*, vol. 2, p. 54.

Benno Erdmann tried to show that the same held also for Kant's knowledge of the contents of Hume's *Treatise*. Since the latter was not translated into German until well after the appearance of the first *Critique*, Kant must have relied on a secondary source. Beattie's *Essay*, which appeared in German translation in 1772 and included long passages of translations and summaries of Hume's first work, seemed to him the best candidate for this.[9]

But, in spite of these promising beginnings, the "thorough monographic treatment" of Kant's Scottish relations was never written. Instead, the prejudice that Kant and the Scots could not possibly have anything in common gained more and more acceptance during the last century. Today, neither the historians of German philosophy nor the commentators on Reid are aware of any possible fundamental significance of "Reid, Oswald, and Beattie" for Kant.

In any case, a study limited to Kant's Scottish relations would have faced insurmountable difficulties. In view of the fact that there are only two explicit references to Reid, Oswald, and Beattie in all the Kantian texts published thus far, and those two are extremely negative, the exact historical connections would have had to remain uncertain. The analysis of Kant's texts must be supplemented by external evidence. It must be shown that Kant could not have avoided knowing the Scots in much greater detail than most historians have been willing to admit. This task can only be accomplished by means of a broad survey of the philosophical developments in Germany during the period when Kant worked on his three *Critiques*. Only if we can establish the role of Scottish common sense in the thought of Kant's contemporaries, and the way in which these contemporaries were important for him, can we hope to see clearly the historical and systematic relations of Kant and the Scots. Because such a broad survey of the Scottish influence in Germany and its effects upon Kant has never been undertaken, I propose to supply it with this work.

The Scottish influence in Germany, which extends over exactly the same period as the development, success, and first demise of Kant's philosophical criticism, namely from 1768 to about 1800, was, as I shall show, inextricably bound up with all the important philosophical developments of the time. The works of the Scots were reviewed in the major philosophical journals almost immediately after they appeared. They were soon translated, and were then often reviewed again by the

9. Janitsch, *Kants Urteile über Berkeley*, and Erdmann, "Kant and Hume um 1762."

same journals. In this way Scottish thought was quickly given a wide audience in Germany.[10] As I will show, it was also assimilated by a number of German philosophers.

Reid, Oswald, and Beattie were frequently quoted and referred to. Almost every important philosopher mentions their names typically as "Reid, Oswald and Beattie" at one time or another and can be shown to have been affected by the Scottish influence. Whether sensationist or materialist, whether rationalist or empiricist, the Germans had read the Scots and most could accept certain aspects of their thought.[11] And since the reliance upon common sense provided the ground upon which the most diverse philosophical views could meet, the Scottish philosophy of common sense may be seen to have been at the centre of many philosophical debates. Thus Moses Mendelssohn, an open-minded rationalist of the Leibniz-Wolffian tradition, valued Reid and Beattie highly, since they were "not confused by sophistry and did not trust any speculation in contradiction to common sense." He believed that common sense was needed to provide us with orientation in speculative philosophy. Johann Christian Lossius, a convinced materialist, used Beattie's conception of truth extensively and believed that common sense was "the touchstone of truth in so far as it can be known by man." Johann Nicolaus Tetens, a critical empiricist, whose work was highly regarded by Kant, maintained that "the cognitions of common sense are the field which has to be worked by speculative philosophy," and can be shown to have understood his own philosophy as the proper continuation of work begun by Reid, Oswald, and Beattie.[12]

But the Scots were not only important for Kant's predecessors and

10. This can be seen from Zart, *Einfluss der englischen Philosophie*. A mere scanning of the register will show that the influence of Reid, Oswald, and Beattie was not inconsiderable. Though Reid's influence started much later than Berkeley's, both are listed 22 times. Beattie is listed 15 times (compared to Newton's 13 times) and Oswald 4 times. Locke and Hume lead in this statistical account (Locke: 157 and Hume: 91). These figures do not prove the relative importance of these philosophers in Germany, but they do show that a discussion of their influence is not inappropriate.

11. This has not so far been realized. Some of the reviews are noted in the following works: Price, *The Reception of English Literature in Germany*; Price and Price, "The Publication of English Humanioria in Germany in the Eighteenth Century"; Kloth and Fabian, "James Beattie: Contributions Towards a Bibliography." These bibliographies are supplemented by Kuehn, "The Early Reception of Reid, Oswald and Beattie."

12. Mendelssohn, "Die Bildsäule," in *Schriften zur Philosophie, Aesthetik und Apologetik*, p. 242; Lossius, *Physische Ursachen des Wahren*, p. 238; [Tetens], *Über die allgemeine speculativische Philosophie*, 1775, p. 17.

Kant himself. Their arguments were also used by those who criticized the enlightenment. Thus Hamann, Herder, Jacobi, and Goethe found the Scots very useful in their fight against faculty psychology and for a holistic conception of man. Jacobi, especially, used Reid as the source for his realism, which, strange as it may sound, was of the greatest importance for the development of German idealism.

Accordingly, it *should not* come as a surprise that Goethe noted towards the end of his life that the Germans had "fully understood the merits of worthy Scottish men for many years," and that Arthur Schopenhauer characterized Reid's *Inquiry into the Human Mind* as "very instructive and well worth reading—ten times more so than all the philosophical works written after Kant taken together."[13] That it may come as a surprise to us is an effect of the more recent historiography of German and Scottish philosophy.[14]

II

This work must not be understood as being *primarily* about the Scottish contribution to Kant's thought. It is about the role which Scottish common sense played in the broader development of German thought between 1768 and 1800. Nevertheless, since Kant's critical philosophy is of central importance in this development, the Scottish influence will be very important for the understanding of Kant as well. It exhibits the "*geistesgeschichtliche Ort*" of his thought. The *Critique* fell neither from the sky, as it were, nor was it addressed to some faceless posterity. It was firmly rooted in the philosophical discussion of the time and has its "*Sitz im Leben*" in this discussion with his contemporaries. Kant's

13. Goethe, *Sämtliche Werke*, vol. 38, p. 382; Schopenhauer, *Die Welt als Wille und Vorstellung*, vol. 2, p. 28.

14. For some of the older historians see Buhle, *Geschichte der neueren Philosophie*, vol. 5; von Eberstein, *Versuch einer Geschichte*. Both deal much more extensively with the Scots than any recent account. See also Hegel, *Vorlesungen über die Geschichte der Philosophie, Theorie Werkausgabe*, vol. 20, pp. 257–87. More recently there have been signs of a greater appreciation of the importance of the Scots for German philosophy. See, for instance, Wolf, "General Introduction: Scottish Philosophy and the Rise of Capitalist Society" in Beattie, *The Philosophical Works*, vol. 1: *An Essay on the Nature and Immutability of Truth* [reprint of the 1st ed.; subsequently referred to as "Beattie, *Essay*"]), pp. 5f. Wolf thinks Beattie is of interest because "the antithesis between the Kantian and the Humean position which would be illuminated by such an historical analysis still determines the present state of philosophical discussion in more essential ways than is often realized" (p. 5).

criticism represents a specific response to a fundamental problem common to all philosophers of his time. His proposed solution was without doubt revolutionary. But, as with all revolutions, it cannot be properly understood apart from the developments leading up to it.

Yet I shall not argue that Kant's "critical problem" in its entirety is already to be found in the works of one or several of his contemporaries.[15] Nor shall I try to show that Kant's philosophy is a mere variation on theories that can already be found in the works of his predecessors, as Lovejoy, for instance, tried to do.[16] The critical problem is to be found in Kant alone. But it cannot properly be understood without its historical background, namely the works of his contemporaries, who were all greatly influenced by Scottish common sense.

What I shall argue is that the Scottish influence opens up a new perspective on the German enlightenment—a perspective that will show many of the received opinions on what actually happened and what is important and unimportant to be little more than prejudices. And I hope that in this way the present study will contribute to a discovery of Kant's contemporaries as philosophers who are more significant than has thus far been thought.

The study presented here consists of this Introduction, followed by ten chapters, a conclusion and an appendix.[17] The first two chapters offer essential background information. Thus Chapter I consists of a relatively short sketch of the Scottish view, in which I attempt to bring out the characteristic features of this theory. Chapter II characterizes the philosophical situation in Germany after 1770, and is an attempt to show what made the Germans so receptive to the Scottish view.

15. Members of the so-called "ontological school" of Kant interpretation claim to have found Kant's critical problem in the works of various predecessors of Kant. For a critical *Auseinandersetzung* with this approach to the interpretation of Kant see the Appendix.

16. Lovejoy in "Kant and the English Platonists" and "Kant's Antithesis of Dogmatism and Criticism" argued that Kant had been anticipated by certain British writers as well as by Leibniz. For a careful criticism of Lovejoy, see Beck, "Lovejoy as a Critic of Kant" in his *Essays on Kant and Hume*, pp. 61–79. While Beck rejects Lovejoy's claims concerning the relationship of Kant and Eberhard, he finds the former's "insistence that the student of Kant be also a student of those to whom Kant himself was a student" very fruitful (p. 79). The study presented here has grown out of the recognition of this very circumstance.

17. Readers who can postpone briefly their reading of my discussion of the Scottish influence itself may want to read this appendix after Chapter I, and before Chapter II. On the other hand, those well acquainted with Reid's philosophy may want to skip Chapter I.

Chapter III gives a short account of the earliest reception of Reid, Oswald, and Beattie in Germany. In this chapter I will show that no philosophically interested thinker of the period—including Kant —could have avoided knowing a lot more about the Scots than has been traditionally assumed.

The remainder of the work will explore some of the more significant effects of the Scottish view in Germany. I shall argue that they concerned exactly those issues which were at the centre of the philosophical discussion, namely those connected with Kant's critical philosophy. Chapters IV-VIII deal with the period preceding the appearance of Kant's first *Critique* and *Prolegomena*. They explore more or less uncharted territory, as philosophical histories mention only in passing the names of the philosophers discussed there. And even those who are somewhat better known should appear in a different light.[18] In these chapters the central importance of Scottish common sense for the German attempt to create an "empirical rationalism" is shown. I shall argue that the Scottish influence was of importance especially with regard to the theory of common sense and the theory of ideas, and thus also with regard to the German views of scepticism and idealism. The Germans, like the Scots, were aiming at some sort of common-sense realism. But they could not accept the Scottish theory without modifications.

The Scots argued that the theory of ideas, which they saw as underlying all of modern philosophy, necessarily leads to scepticism concerning the reality of external objects, and thus to idealism. Representationalism, or the view that we do not perceive objects directly or immediately, but only indirectly by means of certain mediating mental entities, was for them an untenable hypothesis. The Germans felt, however, that representationalism could be saved, and they set out to do just that. The Germans also believed that they could go further in the theory of common sense than did the Scots. While Reid and his followers insisted that common sense neither needed justification nor could be justified and defended in any strict sense, the Germans felt that some form of defence or justification of common sense was both possible and desirable from a philosophical point of view. This can be seen in the thought of Christoph Meiners and Johann

18. The study presented here is not meant to be exhaustive. The Scottish influence on other thinkers, who are only mentioned here, is also of interest. Rather than attempting to discuss every German philosopher influenced by the Scots, I have tried to deal with representative thinkers for each of the various schools of thought. In general, the thinkers discussed here are the most important ones.

Georg Heinrich Feder in Göttingen (Chapter IV); in the attempt to give a materialistic foundation of common sense by Christian Lossius (Chapter V); and in the discussions of the relationship of common sense and rational metaphysical speculation found in Moses Mendelssohn and Johann August Eberhard (Chapter VI).

Chapter VII deals with Johann Nicolaus Tetens, perhaps the most important philosopher in Germany during the seventies of the eighteenth century. He pressed the German criticism of the Scots by developing an elaborate theory of representation, and by trying to justify the principles of common sense as *subjective* expressions of basic and *objective* laws of *thought*. In doing so he anticipated and influenced Kant's critical philosophy, thus opening up a very important indirect avenue of Scottish influence upon Kant.

At the same time there was a group of thinkers usually referred to as the "Counter-Enlightenment." The most important thinkers of this group were Hamann, Herder, and Jacobi. They used the Scottish common-sense doctrines for a fundamental critique of the entire enlightenment project. As I show in Chapter VIII, these so-called "philosophers of faith" agreed with the Scots in arguing that representationalism necessarily leads to nihilism, and in advocating a "radical realism." They were also close to the Scots in rejecting justification and choosing common sense, whose principles, they said, must be believed blindly.

Chapter IX deals with Kant and his relationship to the Scots. I shall argue that, starting from Tetens, Kant came to believe that our principles of thought and knowledge cannot be justified by means of a descriptive and psychological analysis of the contents of our minds. His transcendental philosophy was, at least in part, a response to this problem. He explained why common sense, as itself giving rise to natural illusions and necessary contradictions (the antinomies), was in need of justification, and he made clear that the theory of representation allowed only an empirical realism, while necessarily implying a transcendental idealism. Though his contemporaries were most unwilling to accept Kant's conclusions, what they considered to be Kant's scepticism (the doctrines developed in the Transcendental Dialectic) as well as what they tried to discredit as idealism (the conclusions of the Transcendental Analytic) were consequences of their own basic position as well.

As Chapter X will show, Kant's thought represented only a very unstable balance of the tenets of common sense versus justification, on the one hand, and of the theory of ideas versus realism, on the other.

This becomes very clear in the thought of Kant's successors. A number of philosophers gave up any attempt at a justification of knowledge. They became radical sceptics and/or followed the so-called philosophers of faith, rejecting any form of representationalism. The so-called idealists, Fichte, Schelling and Hegel and their followers, rejected Kant's understanding of philosophy as a clarification and justification of common sense and advocated the view that philosophy can only exist as the "inversion" (*Verkehrung*) of it. For these idealists philosophy is no longer justification and piecemeal revision of common sense, but a radical displacement of it. They also rejected the theory of representation, arguing that it is inconsistent to speak of "representations" which require "things in themselves" that are unknowable.

The history of German philosophy in the late eighteenth century is in this way shown to have been a struggle for a solution of the problem of knowledge, or, more exactly, as an attempt to exhibit and justify the structures of thought that enable us to know the world. It was a battle against empirical idealism and empirical scepticism; and this battle was fought more fiercely in Germany than in either the France or the Britain of that time. But it was fought with weapons forged in these two countries. Kant's contemporaries, who are usually dismissed as unoriginal and shallow, had a greater part in this struggle than they have been given credit for. They developed the framework in which the problems were seen: namely, the theory of common sense and the theory of representation.

There is no pretence that the Scottish influence was *the* major force in these developments, or that it "caused" them in some way. There were many other important philosophical forces at work.[19] But the Scottish influence was closely connected with these other developments, and is therefore extremely relevant to a proper understanding of the period. Since the conception of a common sense was a central guiding concept for all the German enlightenment thinkers, this strand of their thought can be used to unravel much of the complex problem that confronted them.

19. As Bäumler observed, "the eighteenth century is a historical organism of such delicate and rich structure as will hardly be found again." *Das Irrationalitätsproblem*, p. viii. But Bäumler himself does not proceed in accordance with his own insight and discounts the British influence on this "delicate and rich structure" almost entirely, arguing for an isolated German development with incidental French influences (see, for instance, p. 162). For an incisive criticism of this aspect of Bäumler's work see Cassirer, *The Philosophy of the Enlightenment*, pp. 319–20n.

I

The Nature of Scottish Common-Sense
Philosophy

BECAUSE I want to show how the Scottish common-sense philosophy of Thomas Reid, as propagated by Reid himself as well as by Oswald and Beattie, influenced German thought during the last third of the eighteenth century, it is necessary to state clearly what this philosophy consists of. This chapter is meant to provide this statement. It should not be viewed as an attempt to defend Reid's philosophy. For, though I find it difficult to hide my sympathy for certain aspects of Reid's position, none of the following should be construed as an argument for their philosophical validity. I am only concerned to give a short and fairly literal reading of Reid, so that we can see what the Germans could have taken from him and what they actually did take from him.[1]

Though the roots of Scottish common-sense philosophy go back to Shaftesbury, Hutcheson, and Lord Kames, and though even Hume's mitigated scepticism shares many of the characteristic doctrines of these moral and common sense philosophers, the thought of Reid and his followers arose mainly as a reaction to the sceptical philosophy of Hume's *Treatise*.[2] While the earlier common-sense philosophers were

1. Consequently, this chapter should not be taken as a full-scale assessment and discussion of Reid and Scottish common-sense philosophy. Though I neither can nor want to hide a certain degree of sympathy with Reid's views, I do not address the question of whether his analysis of perception and the history of philosophy is correct. Yolton, *Perceptual Acquaintance*, raises a number of important and most interesting objections to Reid—objections that need to be discussed in much greater detail than is possible or necessary here.

2. For the connections of Reid to Shaftesbury, Hutcheson, Lord Kames, and David Hume see David Fate Norton, *From Moral Sense to Common Sense*. For a characterization of Hume's sceptical metaphysics and his common-sense ethics see Norton, *David Hume, Common Sense Moralist, Skeptical Metaphysician*.

not very much concerned with epistemological scepticism, and felt that only moral scepticism (as found in the works of Hobbes and Mandeville, for instance) was dangerous and in need of refutation, Reid, Oswald, and Beattie found themselves unable to maintain such a distinction between (merely) epistemological and moral scepticism. They were convinced that Hume's scepticism in matters epistemological also undermined morality and religion.[3] Therefore they set out to answer or refute Hume.

But it would be a mistake to consider their philosophy merely as "the Scottish answer to Hume." As Professor Beck has pointed out with regard to the other great respondent of Hume, "what is a good answer to Hume may be a very inadequate system of philosophy."[4] And if Scottish common sense was merely the attempt to disprove Hume's specific conclusions, it would perhaps deserve the general lack of interest with which it has been treated for a long time. Yet it is clearly more than that.

Reid's theory may have the appearance of being very straightforward and simple. But this appearance is deceptive. As older and more recent studies of his thought amply demonstrate, the simplicity vanishes as soon as attention is given to the details. The points he makes are very subtle, and a proper understanding of his thought depends upon an exact understanding of his language. He is no more easily understood than any other philosopher who had anything of great interest to say; and to convey a sense of this will be at least part of this relatively brief account of his epistemology.

I

Reid's philosophy has two distinct, though closely connected, aspects. The one is negative and concerns his criticism of the theory of ideas, while the second is positive and consists of his alternative account of perception. He himself does not clearly distinguish these two aspects of his thought, but for the purpose of representing his thought clearly they are best kept apart.

3. There is, however, a difference between Reid on the one hand, and Beattie and Oswald on the other. Reid does not vilify Hume to the same extent as the other two. Beattie does not appear to have appreciated Reid's "leniency" with regard to Hume. See Mossner, "Beattie's 'The Castle of Scepticism.'"
4. Beck, "Towards a Meta-Critique of Pure Reason," in *Essays on Kant and Hume*, pp. 20–37, 24.

For Reid, the logical outcome of modern philosophy, whose most distinctive characteristic he saw in what he called the "ideal theory," is Hume's epistemological scepticism. And while he traces the ideal theory back to Plato and Aristotle, he describes it in greater detail only in the form which he thought it had acquired in the works of Descartes, Malebranche, Locke, Berkeley, and Hume.[5]

His critique of the ideal theory involves both a historical and a systematic claim. Thus he maintains not only that the history of (modern) European philosophy up to Hume constitutes the gradual working out of the consequences of the ideal theory and amounts in fact to a *reductio ad absurdum* of this theory, but also that any form of the ideal theory or representationalism necessarily leads to a denial of the existence of an external world and the self. Reid confounds these two claims. If he had differentiated clearly between the historical and the systematic claims, he might have avoided a great deal of criticism. Both claims are highly interesting in themselves and would deserve further discussion. But I will here concentrate mainly upon the systematic one.[6]

The theory of ideas is founded for Reid upon three distinct premises: (i) We do not perceive things directly, but only by means of mediating mental entities, ideas, images, etc.; (ii) these ideas are literally images of the objects (if not all, at least some fundamental class of them); (iii) the ideas enter our mind simple and uncompounded; complexity is only the result of (more or less conscious) reflection. He contests the theory of ideas on all three counts. Each of the claims necessarily leads us to deny certain facts about the human mind, facts that prove, on inspection, to be undeniable. None of the claims is

5. Reid, *Works*, vol. 1, pp. 99–101, 108–10, 201–18 (Reid, *Inquiry*, ed. Duggan, pp. 9–12, 32–36, and especially 252–72). Since Reid's influence upon German thought between 1768 and 1800 is first and foremost the result of the *Inquiry*—the *Essays on the Intellectual Powers of Man* appeared only in 1785 and the *Essays on the Active Powers of the Human Mind* in 1788 (that is, after Kant's first *Critique*)—I shall concentrate on the *Inquiry*. The *Essays* are taken into consideration only in so far as they further illustrate or clarify points made in the *Inquiry*. Whether or not there are such basic differences between Reid's earlier and later works as Immerwahr, in his "The Development of Reid's Realism," notes, I do not want to decide here. But I must point out that Immerwahr's argument depends greatly upon his identification of Reid's "sensation" with Berkeley's "ideas," an identification I think is indefensible.

6. Most commentators follow Reid in confounding the two claims. For a recent treatment of this topic see Grave, "The 'Theory of Ideas,'" in *Thomas Reid: Critical Interpretations*, pp. 55–61.

specifically argued for or defended by those who subscribe to the theory of ideas. Indeed, all three amount to nothing more than mere hypotheses, hypotheses not only not supported by fact, but actually contrary to fact.[7] According to Reid:

(i) The assertion of the existence of mediating mental entities between objects and the perceiving subject is based upon a confusion of language. There are always two meanings for the particular terms of sensation in their ordinary usage. First of all, they are thought to refer to something actually to be found in the external world, and secondly, they are also used to refer to the particular activity we are engaged in when sensing. He discusses this most fully with regard to "smell," but it is clear that the general conclusions reached about smelling are also supposed to hold for all other species of sensation.[8] Thus when we speak of the smell of a rose or the stench of a sewer, we clearly have something in mind that is quite independent of ourselves, something that confronts us whether we will or not. We expose ourselves to it or extract ourselves from it by means of locomotion of some sort and not by manipulating "pictures" in our mind.

But we can also mean by "smell" or "smelling" what we do when we smell something. Reid expresses this by saying that we can also refer by "smell" to "an act of the mind." This act of smelling has a beginning and an end. It is not a permanent characteristic or quality of ourselves. As an act of feeling it can "have no existence but when . . . felt." There is nothing in sensation over and above the act of sensing or feeling. Philosophers have failed to attend to this distinction carefully and have in fact "confounded" the two meanings of "sensation" in various ways and thus created such mediating entities as ideas. "All the systems of philosophers about our senses and their objects have split upon this rock, of not distinguishing properly sensations which can have no existence but when they are felt, from the things suggested by them." But in saying that what we sense are not the objects but (ideal) sensations the philosopher

puts a different meaning upon the word, without observing it himself, or giving warning to others, he abuses language and disgraces philosophy, without doing any service to truth: as if a man should exchange the meaning of the

---

7. Reid, *Works*, vol. 1, pp. 106, 128–32, 203–11 (Reid, *Inquiry*, ed. Duggan, pp. 26, 81f., 84–87, 256–72).

8. Reid, *Works*, vol. 1, pp. 112, 114 (Reid, *Inquiry*, ed. Duggan, pp. 39–41, and 45) where he applies the results obtained with regard to smell to sensations in general.

words *daughter* and *cow*, and the endeavour to prove to his plain neighbour, that his cow is his daughter, and his daughter his cow.[9]

(ii) One of the most characteristic doctrines of modern philosophy since Descartes is, according to Reid, that of the distinction between primary and secondary qualities. It is argued by the Cartesians (i.e. all modern philosophers) that while the secondary qualities are purely subjective and have no similarity to the external objects, the primary qualities reveal in some sense the "real" qualities of objects. Reid argues that we have no reason to believe that our sensations "resemble" the real objects in any way whatsoever. This has been shown by Berkeley, who has clearly established that "the qualities of an inanimate thing, such as matter is conceived to be, cannot resemble any sensation; that it is impossible to conceive anything like the sensations of our minds, but the sensations of other minds."[10]

But, since Berkeley also holds "that we can have no conception of anything but what resembles some sensation or idea in our minds," he must conclude from the fact that sensations and ideas of our mind can only resemble sensations and ideas in other minds that we can have no conception of an inanimate substance.[11] Reid argues now that, if we can show that we are in possession of notions that do not have any resemblance to sensations, Berkeley's idealistic conclusion is not warranted and there is nothing illegitimate about our conception of, and belief in, inanimate substances.[12]

Reid discusses this most thoroughly with regard to our notion of

9. Reid, *Works*, vol. 1, pp. 112, 114, 130f. (Reid, *Inquiry*, pp. 39f., 44f., 83, 40). It appears to me that most recent interpretations of Reid have "split upon this rock" as well. Timothy Duggan, in his Introduction to Reid's *Inquiry*, for instance, reformulates Reid's statement that "it is essential to a sensation to be felt, and it can be nothing more than we feel it to be" as "a sensation . . . cannot have characteristics that it is not sensed as having" (ibid., p. xiii). But if we take Reid's claim that sensation is an *action* seriously we should not talk this way. Duggan talks of sensation in very much the same way as we would talk of sense data. They are things we "have," or which "pass through the mind," etc. Immerwahr's use of "sensation" (see note 5 above) is similar.

10. Reid, *Works*, vol. 1, p. 131 (Reid, *Inquiry*, ed. Duggan, p. 85).

11. For this and other agreements between Berkeley and Reid see Bracken, "Thomas Reid: A Philosopher of Un-Common Common Sense," Introduction to Reid, *Philosophical Works*, vol. 1, pp. xvii–xxix. For the theory of vision see especially Silver, "A Note on Berkeley's *New Theory of Vision*."

12. But note that Reid does not offer a positive argument to show that they are legitimate.

extension.[13] For him, extension is a good example for two reasons: (a) it is the most basic of all the primary qualities, (b) the adherents of the theory of ideas have always taken it for granted that our notion of extension is indeed derived from sensation.[14] By means of an extended series of experiments he tries to show that touch, all by itself, cannot be the source of our notion of extension, nor that of space and motion. But he does not appear to take these experiments as conclusive evidence, for he closes this discussion with a challenge:

This I would, therefore, humbly propose, as an *experimentum crucis*, by which the ideal system must stand or fall; and it brings the matter to a short issue: Extension, figure, motion, may, any one, or all of them, be taken for the subject of this experiment. Either they are ideas of sensation, or they are not. If any one of them can be shown to be an idea of sensation, or to have the least resemblance to any sensation, I lay my hand upon my mouth, and give up all pretence to reconcile reason to common sense in this matter, and must suffer the ideal scepticism to triumph.[15]

Clearly, Reid does not think that this is possible. He has his own account of the origin of the notions of space and extension, as we shall see in the following.

(iii) His most important criticism of the theory of ideas concerns the assumption that we perceive simple and isolated ideas or sense data, and that complexity is created by our reflection upon these simple constituents of all knowledge. The ideal system

teaches us that the first operation of the mind about its ideas, is simple apprehension—that is, the bare conception of a thing without any belief about it; and that, after we have got simple apprehensions, by comparing them together, we perceive agreements or disagreements between them; and that this perception of the agreement or disagreement of ideas, is all that we call belief, judgment, or knowledge.[16]

13. Reid clearly wants this to hold for all other sensible qualities as well. See especially Norton, "Reid's Abstract of the *Inquiry into the Human Mind*," in *Thomas Reid: Critical Interpretations*, pp. 125–32; see also Rome, "The Scottish Refutation of Berkeley's Immaterialism."

14. Reid, *Works*, vol. 1, pp. 123f. (Reid, *Inquiry*, ed. Duggan, pp. 70f.).

15. Reid, *Works*, vol. 1, p. 128 (Reid, *Inquiry*, ed. Duggan, p. 80). See also Norton, "Reid's Abstract," p. 129.

16. Reid, *Works*, vol. 1, p. 106 (Reid, *Inquiry*, ed. Duggan, p. 27).

But this view of belief is just false. We do not first apprehend something brown, then perceive "four-leggedness" and several other characteristics, and then make a judgment to the effect that there is a table. We first perceive the table and attend only afterwards (if at all) to its particular features. For Reid "nature presents no object to the senses, or to consciousness, that is not complex."[17] The notion that simple apprehension is the most basic activity of the human mind is "all fiction, without any foundation in nature."[18] Instead of saying that belief or judgment arises from the comparison and connection of ideas simply apprehended, we should say that "the simple apprehension is performed by resolving and analyzing a natural and original judgment."[19]

Thus for Reid perceptions are no longer simple, basic, or atomic mental data which cannot be analysed further. They are not the unproblematic elements by means of which all problems concerning perception and thought can be solved. For Reid, perception, though remaining the starting point of the analysis, is the problem to be solved, the complex to be analysed. It is the perceptual process which needs explanation more than anything else.

Locke, Berkeley, and Hume began their analysis at too advanced a stage, and hence they overlooked the problem hidden in sensation. And in this they are, according to Reid, no different from Descartes and his rationalistic followers on the Continent. Thus, though it is not entirely false to say that "Reid . . . reverses the whole epistemological procedure of empiricism" and thereby "undermines the foundation of many of the most characteristic doctrines of Hume," this tells not even half the story.[20] Reid means to criticize Descartes (and therefore also Leibniz and Wolff) as much as the so-called empiricists.[21]

Perhaps we can go still further, for Reid's critique of the theory of ideas is designed as a fundamental objection to Western philosophy

17. Reid, *Essays on the Intellectual Powers of Man, Works*, vol. 1, p. 376.
18. Reid, *Works*, vol. 1, p. 106 (Reid, *Inquiry*, ed. Duggan, p. 27).
19. Ibid.
20. Raphael, *The Moral Sense*, p. 151.
21. According to Reid, Leibniz also advances a theory of idealism. He treats Leibniz specifically in the *Essays on the Intellectual Powers of Man*. Essay II, section 15: "Account of the System of Leibnitz." See also Vaihinger, "Zu Kants Widerlegung des Idealismus, pp. 104–11. Erdmann, under Hamilton's influence, calls Leibniz's philosophical system a "*Halbidealismus*." See also Kuehn, "The Context of Kant's 'Refutation of Idealism.'"

from Plato onwards. And if Reid had only attempted to do this and managed to make a number of telling points in this regard, he would deserve to be remembered as a significant philosopher. However, since his critique of the ideal system is inextricably bound up with an interesting theory of perception of his own, he has still more to offer.

II

Before I turn to the representation of Reid's alternative account of perception, I think it best to take a look at his philosophical methodology. Because for Reid all of modern philosophy is founded upon a false hypothesis concerning the workings of the human mind in perception, he thinks what is needed is a thorough re-examination of the "various powers and faculties we possess."[22] Hypotheses are to be rejected in this process. In fact, he believes that the reform of philosophy can only succeed along the same lines taken by the reformers of natural philosophy. We must apply Newton's *"regula philosophandi,"* which, according to Reid, are maxims of common sense anyway. They "are practised in common life; and he who philosophizes by other rules, either concerning the material system, or concerning the mind, mistakes his aim." As in physics, in philosophy of mind "a just interpretation of nature is the only sound and orthodox philosophy; whatever we add of our own, is apocryphal, and of no authority."[23]

Moreover, psychology or philosophy, by means of the analysis of the phenomena, aim, as do the natural sciences, at the establishment of the powers and principles or laws which govern them. For Locke, Berkeley, and Hume the description of the powers and principles in themselves was not the primary aim of investigation. Their aim was first and foremost the *explanation* (and particularly the genealogical explanation) of these laws and powers. Though they thought that this explanation had to come from experiment and observation, and not from deductive inference, as the Cartesian rationalists on the Continent believed, they are in their intention to explain these laws and powers perhaps closer to Descartes than to Newton.[24]

Reid believes himself the first who consistently follows the descrip-

22. Reid, *Works*, vol. 1, p. 98 (Reid, *Inquiry*, ed. Duggan, p. 6).
23. Reid, *Works*, vol. 1, pp. 97f., 133 (Reid, *Inquiry*, ed. Duggan, pp. 4f., 89).
24. That these philosophers are, in a quite general sense, "Cartesian" has been argued by Gilbert Ryle. But more recently it has also been claimed that they are quite

tive method in the philosophy of mind, and he thinks the philosopher cannot rest

till he find out the simple and original principles of his constitution, of which no account can be given but the will of the Maker. This may be truly called an *analysis* of the human faculties; and, till this is performed, it is in vain we expect any just *system* of the mind—that is, an enumeration of the original powers and laws of our constitution, and an explication from them of the various phenomena of human nature.[25]

These basic principles or laws of the mind are for Reid the principles of common sense.

His aim in philosophy is accordingly a much more modest one than that of the British Cartesians, the empiricists, or that of the Continental Cartesians, the rationalists. Whereas they wanted to analyse and explain, or even derive, the principles of the mind from more basic ones, he sets out to "find" them in order to "enumerate" them perhaps at some later time.

But, he finds, the anatomy of the mind is much more difficult than the anatomy of the body. While the natural philosopher has a great variety of different samples to investigate, the psychologist has really only his own mind to "look at." He must use introspection. While he may also find the observation of the behaviour of other people helpful, it is only this careful introspective analysis of his *own* mind that can explain the behaviour of others to him.

It should be emphasized that Reid does not think that his psychological and introspective analysis *justifies* or *explains* the principles he finds in any way. For him these principles cannot be justified; they are themselves the basis of all justification and explanation. Even his emphasis on the "will of the Maker" is not primarily intended as a final

------

close to Descartes in many of the particulars of their thought. With regard to Locke see Schouls, "The Cartesian Method of Locke's *Essay Concerning Human Understanding*"; see also the discussion between Schouls, Yolton and Duchesneau in the same issue of this journal pp. 603–21). For Berkeley's Cartesianism see Bracken, *Berkeley*. On Reid's anti-Cartesianism see Vernier, "Reid on Foundations of Knowledge," *Thomas Reid: Critical Interpretations*, pp. 14–24. However, Vernier sees Reid as "justifying" and "founding" knowledge.

25. Reid, *Works*, vol. 1, p. 99 (Reid, *Inquiry*, ed. Duggan, p. 8). Hume says as much, of course. But though the intentions of Hume and Reid may be very similar, the ways in which they execute their respective programs are very different. For Hume's Newtonianism see Noxon, *Hume's Philosophical Development*, as well as Barry Stroud, *Hume*.

justification of the principles of common sense. It is, rather, an emphasizing of the factual and ultimate character of these laws for us. They play the same role as do the axioms in mathematics. In this way, Reid's reference to God is not greatly different from that of Newton and other Newtonians.[26] Only when we see Reid as being engaged in justification does God assume in his thought the role of great importance that has commonly been ascribed to it.

Reid is scrupulous in his efforts to provide an anatomy or physiology of the human mind. He notes that "the labyrinth may be too intricate and the thread too fine, to be traced through all its windings," and he is resolved to stop where he "can trace it no further, and secure the ground [he has] gained," for a "quicker eye may in time trace it further."[27] And he exhibits caution and humility in this attempt to avoid error and delusion. It seems safe to say that it is this careful and modest approach that produced views that had great influence (though they were not always recognized as Reidian), and that are even now of philosophical interest.

III

Reid's positive theory of perception, consciously developed as the alternative to accounts involving one or the other version of the theory of ideas, is characterized by the following doctrines: (i) the theory of immediate perception, (ii) the doctrine of natural suggestion or belief, and (iii) a theory of common sense. These three elements of Reid's thought are welded into one organic whole by means of the language metaphor. While none of these elements or the language metaphor is a completely new or original creation of Reid, and while the elements can be traced to his immediate predecessors (most notably Berkeley and Hume), he succeeds in giving a novel account of perception by means of them. And this theory is not an eclectic synthesis or a "critique of books and systems," but a critique of our faculty of knowledge.

(i) Reid holds that we perceive the objects themselves and not some

26. See, for instance, Cote's Preface to the second edition of Newton's *Principia Mathematica*: "The business of true philosophy is to derive the natures of things from causes truly existent, and to inquire after those laws which the Great Creator actually chose to found his most beautiful Frame of the world, not those by which he might have done the same, had he so pleased." Newton's *Mathematical Principles of Natural Philosophy*, p. xxvii.

27. Reid, *Works*, vol. 1, p. 99 (Reid, *Inquiry*, ed. Duggan, pp. 8–9).

sort of mental entities which somehow have reference to objects that, in themselves, are unknowable for us. In this sense, we perceive the objects "immediately," that is, without a third kind of object "mediating" between ourselves and the world of objects.

The latter observation does not mean, of course, that we know objects without any form of mediation whatsoever, or that objects somehow enter "directly" into our mind. Perception is in some sense always dependent upon mediation; and Reid is very much aware of this. In fact, the act of perception is for him the outcome of a complicated process, involving "certain means and interests, which, by the appointment of nature must intervene between the object and our perception of it; and by these our perceptions are limited and regulated."[28]

The means and interest are: (1) the medium which intervenes between objects and bodily organs (rays of light, vibrating air, effluvia), (2) an impression or acting upon our organs, (3) a transmission of these to the brain, (4) a following sensation, and (5) a perception. According to Reid, some of these operations affect the body only, others the mind. By introspection we learn nothing of the first three steps in the process. They are investigated in the domain of the natural sciences. Nor can we know anything at all of how step three follows step two. We are conscious only of the last two means, but of them we are necessarily conscious.[29] They are the proper subjects of investigation by philosophers.

But the question remains: what are sensation and perception for Reid, and how does he think they are related? This much is certain: neither sensation nor perception is a "mediating *entity*."[30] "Sensation" is entirely different from "idea" in that the latter refers to some fictitious entity or quality in the mind that has a kind of permanent existence, while Reid's "sensation" is not thought to have had any sort of permanence. The term refers to an action or operation of the mind which has a definite beginning and a definite end in time. Thus smelling, for instance, "is an act of the mind, but is never imagined to be a quality of the mind." A sensation "can have no existence but when it is

28. Reid, *Works*, vol. 1, p. 186 (Reid, *Inquiry*, ed. Duggan, p. 214).

29. Reid, *Works*, vol. 1, p. 187 (Reid, *Inquiry*, ed. Duggan, p. 216).

30. This should hardly be necessary to emphasize. But there are several commentators of Reid who have been confused about it. The oldest one is perhaps Hamilton. More recent interpretations in this vein are given by Duggan and Immerwahr (see notes 5, 9, and 32 of this chapter).

perceived."—In fact, "this is common to all sensations, that, as they cannot exist but in being perceived, so they cannot be perceived but they must exist."—"It is essential to a sensation to be felt and it can be nothing more than we feel it to be."[31] In short, with regard to sensation we may say "its *esse* is *sentire*, and nothing can be in it that is not felt."[32]

This shows two things. First of all, Reid's "sensation" refers to a mental act, something that we do and something that is nothing over and above this action. We sense, i.e. feel pain or smell, or hear at one moment or other. But when this action has run its course, nothing remains of it. And just as it makes no sense to suppose that the action of scratching one's head has a continued existence, so it makes no sense to suppose that the act of sensation has a continued existence. Secondly, sensation is essentially related to perception. In fact, for Reid it exists only in so far as it is perceived. To speak of an "unperceived sensation" makes absolutely no sense in Reid's terminology.

The last characteristic of sensation shows that there is something very wrong in the attempt to explain Reid's theory of perception primarily by means of his account of sensation. Sensations in themselves, that is sensations in isolation from perception, would be nothing to us. They are accessible to us only because they are present within the complex process of perception. Consequently, it is through Reid's account of perception that we can make sense of sensation and not the other way around.

This has the closest connection with Reid's methodological principle,

31. Reid, *Works*, vol. 1, p. 114, 105, 87 (Reid, *Inquiry*, ed. Duggan, p. 44, 45, 24, 216).
32. Norton, "Reid's Abstract," p. 128. Duggan fails to see the importance of this characteristic. He says: (1) a sensation has no object, (2) a sensation cannot have characteristics it is not sensed as having, (3) sensation is a "natural principle of belief," and (4) we usually do not notice or attend to sensations. (See Introduction to Reid's *Inquiry*, pp. xii–xiv, as well as "Thomas Reid's Theory of Sensation.") Duggan's (1) and (2) could have led him to see the fundamental characterization of sensation as an action in Reid. In fact, he refers to *Inquiry*, pp. 150f., which makes this point very clearly. But, instead of taking note of it, he uses a quotation of H. H. Price, a sense-datum theorist, to elucidate what Reid meant (Introduction, p. xiii, and "Theory of Sensation," p. 90). Immerwahr, who sees a difference between the *Inquiry* and the *Intellectual Powers*, wants to show that Reid held a theory of indirect realism, i.e. a theory which holds "that we are directly aware only of certain mental entities (call them *sensa*) from which the mind makes some kind of inference or other mental transition to the existence of an external world." Indeed, he finds, it "should be obvious . . . that the theory of perception as suggestion in the *Inquiry* is best characterized as indirect realism" (Immerwahr, "The Development," p. 247). I find it difficult to imagine a theory more radically different from the one proposed by Reid than the one ascribed to him by Immerwahr.

never to consider nature as presenting anything simple to the human mind. Thus, though sensation, according to him, is "a simple act of the mind," it is given only as part of the complex act of perception. In this way, sensation, although in the order of nature "simple," is arrived at only by abstraction, or is separated "by art and chemical analysis."[33]

As such simple acts of the mind, "considered abstractly," sensations do not have reference to objects. So sensation may well be characterized as that act of the mind which "hath no object distinct from the act itself" and can thus be differentiated from all other acts of mind.[34]

But our actual sensations—sensations as experienced, that is—are quite different from these simple acts, for they are "necessarily accompanied" with certain beliefs.[35] Sensation compels us to believe not only in "the present existence of the thing" sensed by us, but also in "a mind, or something that has the power of smelling, of which it is called a sensation, an operation or feeling," as well as in a certain "faculty" by means of which we are capable of sensing and in certain other notions such as cause, extension, solidity, and motion. All these things "are nowise like to sensations, although they have been hitherto confounded with them." In fact, Reid takes great pride in being the first to have established this.[36]

These sensations, when considered together with the beliefs which "necessarily accompany" them, *are* the perceptions for Reid. Thus, while sensations in themselves do not have any object, but are nothing distinct from what they are felt to be, perception "hath always an object distinct from the act by which it is perceived."[37] But this object is not our sensation, it is

an object which may exist whether it be perceived or not. I perceive a tree that grows before my window; there is here an object which is perceived, and an act of the mind by which it is perceived; and these two are not only distinguishable, but they are extremely unlike in their natures. The object is made up of a trunk, branches, and leaves; but the act of the mind, by which it is perceived, hath neither trunk, branches, nor leaves. I am conscious of this act of the mind, and I

33. Reid, *Works*, vol. 1, pp. 107, 113f. (Reid, *Inquiry*, ed. Duggan, pp. 27, 43ff.).

34. Reid, *Intellectual Powers, Works*, vol. 1, p. 299. See also vol. 1, pp. 182f. (Reid, *Inquiry*, ed. Duggan, pp. 205f.).

35. Reid, *Works*, vol. 1, p. 105 (Reid, *Inquiry*, ed. Duggan, p. 25).

36. Reid, *Works*, vol. 1, p. 111 (Reid, *Inquiry*, ed. Duggan, p. 39).

37. See, for instance, the chapter "Of Extension" in the *Inquiry*, as well as Norton, "Reid's Abstract," pp. 128f. See also Rome, "The Scottish Refutation."

can reflect upon it; but it is too simple to admit of an analysis, and I cannot find proper words to describe it.[38]

Reid is too modest here. For, to some extent, he has actually analysed the act of perception already in the *Inquiry*.[39] He has shown that it is not a simple act of the mind, but consists of several elements, namely a simple act of sensation and certain beliefs which necessarily accompany this act and which lead us to a conception of an object different from the act of perception.

(ii) Like acts of sensation, beliefs, which necessarily accompany them, are simple. For this reason, belief cannot be defined logically. "Every man knows what it is, but no man can define it."[40] Belief is "like seeing and hearing which can never be so defined as to be understood by those who have not these faculties; and to such as have them, no definitions can make these operations more clear than they are already."[41] But just as this impossibility of logical definition did not stop Reid from saying interesting and new things about sensation, so it does not stop him with regard to belief.

He tries to elucidate the relation of belief to sensation by means of the "language analogy." His main reason for this seems to be his belief

38. Reid, *Works*, vol. 1, p. 183 (Reid, *Inquiry*, ed. Duggan, p. 206). Because our sensations are so intimately related to perception, "sensation and the perception of external objects by the senses, though very different in nature, have commonly been considered as one and the same thing. The purposes of common life do not make it necessary to distinguish them, and the received opinions of the philosophers tend rather to confound them; but without attending carefully to this distinction, it is impossible to have any just conception of the operations of our senses" (Reid, *Inquiry*, ed. Duggan, p. 205, *Works*, vol. 1, p. 182). Nor, we may add, is it possible to have a just conception of Reid's theory of perception without this distinction.

39. Reid, *Works*, vol. 1, p. 183 (Reid, *Inquiry*, ed. Duggan, p. 206). I do not want to deny that there is a development in Reid's thought, and that, for instance, his later account is more detailed. But the differences are not as "interesting" and basic as Immerwahr argues. For an account of Reid's theory of perception, relying mainly upon the *Intellectual Powers*, see Baruch Brody's Introduction to his edition of the work, as well as his "Reid and Hamilton on Perception," and Cummins, "Reid's Realism."

40. Reid, *Works*, vol. 1, p. 107 (Reid, *Inquiry*, ed. Duggan, p. 28). See also the following: "Does any man pretend to define consciousness? It is happy indeed that no man does. And if no philosopher had attempted to define and explain belief, some paradoxes in philosophy, more incredible than ever were brought forth by the most abject superstition or the most frantic enthusiasm, had never seen the light."

41. Reid, *Works*, vol. 1, pp. 108, 105f. Reid, *Inquiry*, ed. Duggan, pp. 30, 25).

that there is a close natural analogy between language and perception, anyway. For

the objects of human knowledge are unnumerable; but the channels by which it is conveyed to the mind are few. Among these, the perception of the external things by our senses, and the informations which we receive upon human testimony, are not the least considerable: and so remarkable is the analogy between these two, and the analogy between the principles of the mind and, those which are subservient to the other, without further apology we shall consider them together.

This analogy is then spelled out in greater detail as follows:

In the testimony given by the senses, as well as in human testimony given by language, things are signified to us by signs: and in one, as well as the other, the mind, either by original principles or by custom, passes from the sign to the conception and belief of the things signified.[42]

Thus Reid differentiates two kinds of relationship between the sign and the thing signified by it. The relation can either be based upon experience or upon principles of the mind. When "a certain kind of sound suggests immediately to the mind, a coach passing in the street," we are clearly concerned with a belief based upon experience or custom. But, as we have seen already, there are also for Reid many beliefs which "necessarily accompany" certain sensations. "We cannot get rid of the vulgar notion and belief of an external world," for instance, and even if "Reason should stomach and fret ever so much at this yoke, she cannot throw it off."[43] These beliefs are obviously the ones of greatest interest to Reid, and their description is one of his most fundamental concerns.

But Reid makes quite clear that he does not believe that it is in our power to give an account of why and how these beliefs follow upon, or better, accompany our sensations. These necessary beliefs are "instinctual."—"We are inspired with the sensation, and we are inspired with the corresponding perception, by means unknown." All he will say is that the language analogy is of help here as well. Just as there is a sort of natural language, i.e. the one consisting of "features of

---

42. Reid, *Works*, vol. 1, p. 194 (Reid, *Inquiry*, ed. Duggan, pp. 234f.). For a more extensive discussion of natural language see Reid, *Inquiry*, ed. Duggan, pp. 54–58.
43. Reid, *Works*, vol. 1, pp. 127, 183f. (Reid, *Inquiry*, ed. Duggan, pp. 78, 207f.).

the face, gestures of the body, and modulations of the voice," which conveys to us what the other person thinks or feels, so there are certain sensations which conjure up these original principles.[44]

He calls the perceptions in which these sensations occur "original perceptions," and differentiates them from "acquired perceptions" in which the relation between the sign and the thing signified depends upon experience or custom. Since he cannot explain or define the way in which this happens, he "beg[s] leave to make of the use of the word *suggestion*, because [he] know[s] not one more proper, to express a power of the mind, which seems entirely to have escaped the notice of philosophers, and to which we owe many of our simple notions which are neither impressions, nor ideas, as well as many original principles of belief."[45] Thus the sensations "suggest" to us these basic principles and notions not to be found in sensation itself.

Reid exploits the language analogy even further when he observes that, as there is in artificial signs usually no similarity between the sign and the thing signified, so there is none between the sensation and the things suggested by it. We cannot speak of a necessary relationship between the sensation and those things suggested by it either. Thus he thinks "a sensation of hardness . . . hath neither similitude to hardness, nor, as far as we can perceive, any necessary connection with it."

There are three classes of natural signs which have to be distinguished, according to Reid, so that we may "more distinctly conceive the relation between our sensations and the things they suggest, and what we mean by calling sensations signs of external things." The first class consists of those natural signs "whose connections with the thing signified is established by nature but is discovered only by experience." All natural sciences are based upon such signs.

The second class is constituted by signs "wherein the connection between the sign and the thing signified is not only established by nature, but discovered to us by a natural principle without reasoning or experience." These are the natural signs of our thought, purpose, and

44. Reid, *Works*, vol. 1, pp. 105f., 108, 184, 188, 195 (Reid, *Inquiry*, ed. Duggan, pp. 26, 30, 209, 218, 236).

45. Reid, *Works*, vol. 1, p. 111 (Reid, *Inquiry*, ed. Duggan, p. 38). It is impossible to discuss here all or even most of the implications of Reid's theory of natural suggestion. But see also Winch, "The Notion of 'Suggestion' in Thomas Reid's Theory of Perception," Daniels, "On Having Concepts 'By our Constitution,'" especially pp. 40f. For a more positive account see Rollin, "Thomas Reid and the Semiotics of Perception."

desire, or the ones that make up what Reid calls the natural language of mankind.

The "third class of natural signs comprehends those which, though we never before had any notion or conception of the things signified, do suggest it or conjure it up, as it were, by a natural kind of magic, and at once give us a conception, and create a belief in it." Thus our sensations suggest to us a mind or an identical self to which they belong, as well as such notions as those of hardness and extension, or our belief in the existence of objects.

It may be observed, that as the first class of natural signs . . . is the foundation of true philosophy, and the second, the foundation of the fine arts, or of taste; so the last is the foundation of common sense; a part of human nature which hath never been explained.[46]

(iii) Whether Reid succeeds in giving a satisfactory explanation of these matters is very much in question. Thus he is not at all clear with regard to the number and the characteristics of the principles of common sense.[47] About the only thing he is certain of is that

there are certain principles . . . which the constitution of our nature leads us to believe, and which we are under a necessity to take for granted in the common concerns of life . . . these are what we call the principles of common sense; and what is manifestly contrary to them, is what we call absurd."[48]

The principles of common sense have therefore for him the characteristics of natural necessity and indispensability. They are at the root of our ability to reason and can thus not be themselves rationally explained.

Further, they cannot be contradicted without falling into contradiction and absurdity. But Reid does not understand "absurdity" in a purely logical sense, as Kant does, for instance. He uses it to justify the irony and ridicule with which he is treating Hume and his predeces-

46. Reid, *Works*, vol. 1, pp. 121f. (Reid, *Inquiry*, ed. Duggan, pp. 66–68).

47. He is much more definite on the number of basic principles in the *Essays*. In this work there is also greater emphasis on principles leading to merely probable knowledge. But the basic difficulties still remain.

48. Reid, *Works*, vol. 1, pp. 108, 130, 209f. (Reid, *Inquiry*, ed. Duggan, pp. 32, 268f., p. 82).

sors. As Shaftesbury had already proposed in his essay, on the *Sensus Communis*, a "test of ridicule" for even the most serious and solemn opinions, so Reid (and Beattie, who in most respects resembles the zealot rejected by Shaftesbury) may be considered to apply such a test of ridicule. Yet, whatever else may be said with regard to such a test as a philosophical criterion, it clearly is not a good tool for differentiating between original principles and other generally held beliefs.

This should not be taken to mean that Reid makes no contribution to philosophical thought in developing his view on the first principles of common sense. By insisting that we can neither abstract them from sense perception nor establish them by reasoning, he also argues for them as *a priori* presuppositions for sensation and thought. Thus he claims

all reasoning must be from first principles; and for first principles no other reason can be given but this, that, by the constitution of our nature, we are under a necessity of assenting to them. Such principles are parts of our constitution, no less than the power of thinking; reason can neither make nor destroy them; nor can it do any thing without them.[49]

The necessity of an *a priori* component in all knowledge claims has been quite clearly acknowledged by Reid. Together with his closely related analysis of the act of perception as a complex phenomenon, involving certain judgment-like operations of the mind, this may be regarded as one of his most important contributions to the development of philosophy.

One of the consequences of this view is that Reid can differentiate clearly between a sensation and the things that are suggested by this sensation, but which, themselves, are not *of* sensation in the sense that they can be reduced to it.[50] Sensation and thought are different, yet united in the act of perception. For Reid, sensation is neither a sort of confused thinking, as it was for most of the rationalists, nor are our abstract notions of space, etc. rarified sensations, as they were to most of the empiricists. The principles of common sense are radically different from particular sensations, yet they are known to us only through perceptions.

49. Reid, *Works*, vol. 1, p. 185, 130 (Reid, *Inquiry*, ed. Duggan, p. 212, 82).
50. Reid appears to have been proud of this discovery; see the "Abstract" as edited and published by Norton.

At the very same time, these principles do allow Reid to bridge any gulf between thought and sensation that could have arisen when the empiricist or rationalist continuum of thought and sensation was broken. Both thought and reflection equally depend upon them, and they are therefore necessarily related. Though there is no thought in sensation and perception, as he insists, and though thought is radically different from anything found in sensation, the two share the same basic principles.

Reid does not believe he has said the last word on these matters, and he makes very clear that "a clear explication and enumeration of the principles of common sense, is [*still*] one of the chief *desiderata* in logic."[51] But he has made a beginning in this regard, a beginning that could lead to a new understanding of the human mind and its workings.

IV

Oswald and Beattie were neither the only nor the most important of Reid's followers. But they were the ones who were most closely associated with him. In fact, the expression "Reid, Oswald, and Beattie" was used very often as a reference to what was taken to be one unified theory, as we shall see. To speak of a "contribution" of Oswald and Beattie to the theory of common sense is perhaps also somewhat misleading, for they contributed very little of substance. They were indeed not much more than popularizers, with the consequence that they did not follow Reid's method of meticulous psychological analysis, but fastened on his results. Their main aim was the defence of morality and religion and the refutation of Hume.

Oswald, whose influential *An Appeal to Common Sense in Behalf of Religion* appeared in two volumes (1766 and 1772), multiplied the principles of common sense to the extent that they included even certain theological dogmas. His arguments against philosophical proofs in religious matters do not amount to more than the preaching of what he considered to be the truth and the exhortation that everybody should follow it. But, whatever the weaknesses resulting from Oswald's dislike of philosophy, the *Appeal* points towards a real shortcoming of Reid's theory, namely the insufficient characterization of his principles of common sense. Because he had not succeeded in

51. Reid, *Works*, vol. 1, p. 209 (Reid, *Inquiry*, ed. Duggan, p. 269).

giving a clear criterion of these principles, Oswald could include among them such doctrines as the existence of God. Nevertheless, the *Appeal* has one merit: Oswald emphasizes again and again that the principles of common sense cannot be proved and have to be accepted as *facts* of the constitution of our mind. As such facts they neither need rational justification, nor can be further elucidated or rationally explained, but have to be accepted. All we can do is describe them. Because our mind is constituted in the way it is, we cannot think in any other way.[52] But since he has no clear criterion of the principles of common sense, and since he is venturing into the realm of theology and morality, which had not been investigated by Reid in the *Inquiry*, his careless approach allows the appeal to common sense to deteriorate into an appeal to "the judgment of the crowd," as Kant quite correctly noted.

Beattie's works were more significant, and they were much more successful than either Oswald's *Appeal* or Reid's *Inquiry*. Of greatest philosophical interest is his *An Essay on the Nature and Immutability of Truth in Opposition to Sophistry and Scepticism*, which appeared first in 1770, and quickly went through several editions.[53] Today it is regarded by historians of philosophy as mediocre, shallow, and rightly forgotten. But the *Essay* is actually not quite as bad as it is made out to be, especially when seen in its eighteenth-century context. While Beattie does not advance beyond anything said by Reid, he also does not seriously misrepresent Reid's theory. His talent as a writer and literary critic allows him to spread Reid's thought further than Reid himself could have hoped.[54]

While the *Essay* is not a philosophical work of the first order, it is still readable, and Beattie's criticisms of Hume (usually adapted from Reid) are often well taken. Elmer Sprague notes, for instance, that Beattie

challenged the doctrine that ideas are distinguished from impressions only by their weakness or faintness. He found the meanings of "copy" and "resemble" unclear in the doctrine that ideas copy or resemble impressions. He found Hume's denial of the distinction between objects and perceptions untenable,

52. The same point is also emphasized by Adam Ferguson in his *Institutes of Moral Philosophy*. For an extensive and fairly reliable account of Oswald's philosophy see Gavin Ardley, *The Common Sense Philosophy of James Oswald*.

53. For a recent account of Beattie's popularity in the English-speaking world, see King, "James Beattie's *Essay on Truth* (1770)."

54. King speaks of Beattie's "excellent Addisonian prose-style" as his greatest asset (ibid., p. 395).

because ordinary discourse tells against it. He was dubious of the scope to be allowed the doctrine that the meaning of words must be accounted for as ideas . . . Finally, he pointed out that by defining the self as a bundle of perceptions, Hume is at a loss to account for a percipient being to perceive.[55]

Beattie also tries to explicate the meaning of "common sense" to a greater extent than had Reid in his *Inquiry*. He does this by means of a historical discussion of "common sense" and related concepts, and comes to the conclusion that it represents a special "sense of truth," different from, though connected with, reason.

This last aspect of Beattie's work points towards a certain shift in emphasis that has taken place between Reid's early work and the works of Oswald, and Beattie. While Reid's emphasis is upon original principles and the constitution of the human mind, which are then (often quite incidentally) identified with the common sense of mankind, Beattie and Oswald are stressing "common sense."[56] This does not just appear to be a shift in emphasis, but indicates a basic difference between Reid and his popularizers. Whereas for Reid "common sense" is put forward not only as a solution to philosophical puzzles but also as a subject to be analysed by philosophers, for Oswald and Beattie common sense does not appear to need any further analysis. Accordingly, they are much more dogmatic than Reid himself, while lacking his originality. They were first and foremost vehicles for the transmission of *Reidian* (and, to some extent also Humean) ideas.

v

To sum up: Scottish common-sense philosophy as developed by Reid and propagated by Oswald, and Beattie has these basic features: its intention is the refutation of scepticism and idealism (which are understood as being most closely connected), its method is that of psychological observation and introspection, its subject matter consciousness, and its systematic position is characterized negatively by the refusal of any sort of representationalism and positively by the affirmation of principles which are prior to and independent of experience, but presupposed in all knowledge whatsoever.

55. Sprague, "James Beattie."
56. Beattie, *Essay*, p. 318. Beattie also places more emphasis on the instinctual and "sense-like" character of common sense. Reid may have invited such a view in his *Inquiry*, but in the *Essays* he approximates common sense more to reason.

The Scots reject classical empiricism as much as they reject classical rationalism. Both are seen to involve representationalism or reliance upon some sort of theory of ideas, and neither follows a scientifically strict method of observation and induction. Scottish common sense offers a "critique of all preceding philosophy," as it were. Yet this critique also shares several characteristics with the theories of those criticized. As had the empiricists, the Scots begin with experience and use observation and induction, thus reducing philosophy almost completely to psychology. On the other hand, like the rationalists, they affirm certain *a priori* principles. But in contrast to the empiricists and the rationalists, they have completely given up justification.[57] And they are quite unlike the rationalists in not beginning from *a priori* principles. For them, these principles are established, or more precisely, found, by means of an inductive account of the human mind.

This last characteristic of Scottish common sense has often been taken as indicative of a certain dualism in the theory, a dualism consisting of an interesting connection of radical empiricism with a kind of intuitionism or rationalism.[58] The principles of common sense, even though they are discovered by the method of observation and induction, are not thought to be established or justified by this procedure. They are in themselves innate, or better, *a priori* and constitutive of the human mind. All the evidence they carry is a result of this.

Because of this dualism Scottish philosophy may quite appropriately be considered as a synthesis of tenets of the empiricist and the rationalist traditions. It could even be called an "empirical rationalism" or a "rational empiricism." Whether or not such a theory is best described by what may appear a philosophical oxymoron, or whether the dualism involved in it led to the dissolution of the Scottish school, need not be decided here. The fact is that these philosophers did indeed make the most original and most important attempt at such a philosophy in the period between 1764 and 1781. And this was perhaps what interested the Germans most in Scottish common sense.

That Reid's philosophy constitutes such a break with the past and the

57. This, I believe, is due to Hume's influence. Reid realized, under the influence of the *Treatise*, that *philosophical* justification is impossible.

58. This is the position of Segerstedt. He argues that Scottish common sense is "conditioned by the struggle to reconcile these two points of view" (see Segerstedt, *The Problem of Knowledge in Scottish Philosophy*, especially pp. 47ff., and pp. 150ff.). See also Jones, *Empiricism and Intuitionism in Reid's Common Sense Philosophy*.

beginning of something new, though largely ignored in recent years, was acknowledged by many important German philosophers until early this century. Thus J. F. Fries, an early follower of Kant, classifies Reid's thought together with that of Kant (and his own, of course) as "speculative speculation" as opposed to mere "speculation." In this way he meant to indicate that with Reid philosophy had become self-reflexive and thus gained a new understanding of itself.[59] G. W. F. Hegel speaks of a "third turn" of philosophy in the works of Reid, Oswald, and Beattie. This third turn consists in their attempt to "indicate also the principle of cognition exactly," and he acknowledges that the Scots had made "quite a number of subtle observations in this way."[60]

In a similar vein, Eduard von Hartmann emphasized that in Reid's relatively exact psychological observations, "beside the purely immanent sensationism, the transcendental rationalistic factor also comes into its own." Reid is a genuine predecessor of Kant in this regard. Another historian, Ernst von Aster, noted the close relationship of Reid's "phenomenological description" of the *a priori* component of all perception with Edmund Husserl's investigations.[61] So all these philosophers characterized Reid as being most important for the history of the developments that ultimately led to Kant's critical philosophy and beyond.

I find it difficult to disagree with those thinkers who emphasize the philosophical proximity of Kant and Reid. Further, it appears quite clear to me that between 1764 and 1781, the year of the appearance of the first *Critique*, there was scarcely anyone, Kant included, who could not have learned from the Scots. And I shall try to show that many Germans, Kant included, did learn from them. But in order to be able to evaluate and understand what the Germans learned from them it is necessary to take a closer look at the German background and the philosophical situation in Germany when the Scottish influence began.

59. Fries, *Tradition, Mysticismus und gesunde Logik, oder über die Geschichte der Philosophie*.
60. Hegel, *Vorlesungen über die Geschichte der Philosophie*, pp. 281–86; see also p. 283. Hegel compares the Scots with Kant and finds them similar in many respects.
61. von Hartmann, *Geschichte der Metaphysik*, vol. 2, p. 308; von Aster, *Geschichte der neueren Erkenntnistheorie*, pp. 389–97.

II

The Philosophical Situation in Germany after 1755

WHEN Christian Wolff died in 1754, his philosophy, which had dominated German schools and universities for the preceding three decades, had already begun to decline in influence. He no longer possessed the binding authority of his earlier years. But no new philosopher of similar stature or authority had arisen and the philosophical situation at the time of his death may very well be described as representing "the cognitive crisis of the Enlightenment."[1] Moses Mendelssohn, one of the best known and most important philosophical talents of this period, described the philosophical situation as one of "general anarchy." Philosophy, "the poor matron," who according to Shaftesbury had been "banished from high society and put into the schools and colleges . . . had to leave even this dusty corner. Descartes expelled the scholastics, Wolff expelled Descartes, and the contempt for all philosophy finally also expelled Wolff; and it appears that Crusius will soon be the philosopher in fashion."[2]

While it may not prove fruitful to speculate about the causes for this breakdown of all the old philosophical authorities (without the immediate emergence of any new ones), it can certainly be useful to consider some of the characteristics of this breakdown, and of certain circumstances that accompanied it, if only because it will make clear why the Scots could be found relevant by the German philosophers of this period.

---

1. Wessell, *G. E. Lessing's Theology; A Reinterpretation*, pp. 79ff. Wessell speaks of such a cognitive crisis as well, and he suggests that Thomas Kuhn's conception of a crisis phase in a scientific revolution may be used to describe what went on.

2. Mendelssohn, *Briefe, die neueste Literatur betreffend* 1 (1 March 1759): 129–34.

First of all, it has to be noted that this crisis did not represent a special German phenomenon, but one of European thought in general. While in Britain empiricism and rejection of ambitious all-inclusive speculative systems could already look back on a long tradition, during the 1740s most French and German philosophers were still engaged in the development and working out of such systems. But in the late forties and the early fifties this mood changed dramatically. Condillac, in his *Treatise on Systems* (1749), differentiated sharply between the "*esprit systématique*" and "*esprit de système*," rejecting the latter, while finding the former useful. In fact, he went so far as to ask for a synthesis of the positive or empiricistic approach and the systematic or rationalistic one. Voltaire had previously published his *Lettres philosophiques* (1743) and his *Éléments de la philosophie de Newton* (1738), in which he attacked Cartesianism and argued for Newton's approach. Diderot, in his *On the Interpretation of Nature* (1754), advocated the experimental method and gave expression to his belief that mathematics had run its course and could not develop further. Rousseau's *Discourse on the Arts and Sciences* was published in 1750, and Buffon began to exert great influence when the first volume of his *Natural History* came out in 1749. To sum up, the number of significant works which opposed "the spirit of systems" and advocated a more empiricistic approach, as being scientifically more promising and more useful for the common man, was so great that we cannot even begin to do justice to them in this context.[3]

Given the close relationship of French and German thought in this period, it was inevitable that these developments would also have profound effects upon Germany. And, since for France this empiricistic turn was closely connected with a new appreciation of British natural science and British philosophy (indeed with an enthusiasm for anything British), the same also happened in Germany. As one of the earliest historians of this period put it:

Around the middle of the century which has just passed, the German scholars familiarized themselves more and more with the languages and especially with the beautiful and philosophical literatures of the French and the English. This more familiar knowledge did not only make them aware of the deficiencies and imperfections of the German language and the German national taste in the

---

3. The best account of this decisive phase of the European Enlightenment can still be found in Cassirer, *Enlightenment*, pp. 3–36.

sciences and fine arts; it created not only the most lively passion to educate, to refine the sciences and the arts, and to compete with the foreigners in all kinds of beautiful representation, but it also made the Leibniz-Wolffian method of the school hitherto followed distasteful to the better talents. The strict systematic form, which the Wolffians had accepted, appeared to put oppressing chains upon the free flight of philosophical genius. Moreover, in a number of philosophical works by foreigners there was also thoroughness and systematic spirit, but without betraying pedantry and coercion . . . even the textbooks of foreign philosophers were much more readable than those of the Germans.[4]

The new generation of philosophers finally addressed the public directly. Fewer and fewer works were written in Latin. Philosophical treatises were not designed for the professors and students at the universities and high schools only, but were devised with the general public in mind. Even the most difficult and abstruse philosophical problems were held to be susceptible to this treatment, and in a certain sense "popularity" became a *de facto* test for the meaningfulness of philosophical theories.[5] There were many philosophers for whom style was more important than philosophical content, and for whom aesthetics came to represent the most important part of philosophy.[6]

Those more serious about philosophy as a science were most dissatisfied with this state. In 1765 J. H. Lambert, for instance, wrote to Kant, regretting that in Berlin "one philosophizes exclusively about the

4. See Buhle, *Geschichte*, vol. 4, pp. 503f., see also vol. 5, pp. i–x, and von Eberstein, *Versuch*, vol. 1, p. 289. All contemporaries were very much aware of this British influence. Above all, Shaftesbury, Hutcheson, Lord Kames, Hume, and Ferguson were found to be extremely important by the Germans. For Shaftesbury, see Weiser, *Shaftesbury und das deutsche Geistesleben*, and the older but more important essay of Walzel, "Shaftesbury und das deutsche Geistesleben." For Henry Home, Lord of Kames, see Wohlgemuth, *Henry Homes Asthetik und ihr Einfluss auf deutsche Ästhetiker*, and Neumann, *Die Bedeutung Homes für die Ästhetik* and Shaw, "Henry Home of Kames: Precursor of Herder." For a general account of the state of discussion concerning Home's influence in Germany see Randall, *The Critical Theory of Lord Kames*. On Ferguson not very much work has been done. But see, for instance, Flajole, "Lessing's Retrieval of Lost Truths." See also Pascal, "Herder and the Scottish Historical School."

5. Here there is perhaps a similarity to some aspects of the early "ordinary language philosophy." But one difference is that most philosophers of the eighteenth century were concerned with the truth and falsity of particular philosophical theories and principles, while the ordinary language philosophers were concerned with their meaningfulness.

6. The clearest example of such a philosopher is perhaps Friedrich Justus Riedel, who is briefly discussed in the Appendix.

so-called belles-lettres." Kant, who himself had just published a book on aesthetic matters, wrote back:

You complain with reason, dear sir, of the eternal trifling of punsters and the wearying chatter of today's reputed writers, with whom the only evidence of taste is that they talk about taste. I think, though, that this is the euthanasia of false philosophy, that it is perishing amid these foolish pranks, and it would be far worse to have it carried to the grave ceremoniously, with serious but dishonest hair-splitting. Before true philosophy can come to life, the old one must destroy itself; and just as putrefaction signifies the total dissolution that always precedes the start of a new creation, so the current crisis in learning magnifies my hopes that the great, long-awaited revolution in the sciences is not too far off. *For there is no shortage of good minds.*[7]

It appears that Kant was right and that Mendelssohn's fears were unfounded. The Germans did not abandon philosophy in favour of literary criticism, and Crusius's philosophy never appears to have become the powerful force that Mendelssohn feared it might become. The preoccupation with aesthetic matters did not, at least in the long run, prevent serious philosophical work in Germany.[8]

Kant, Mendelssohn, and their contemporaries tried in various ways to effect a synthesis of "British empiricism" and "German rationalism."[9] This shows, among other things, that the foreign, and especially British, influence extended much farther than to mere matters of style. Thus the Germans until this time had been occupied mainly with the rational side of man, or with logic and metaphysics, and they had neglected almost completely his sensitive aspects (or simply treated it "in analogy to reason"). But the works of the British philosophers brought the importance of man's sensitive nature most forcefully home to them. Accordingly, the younger German philosophers tried to supplement the Wolffian theory by relying on British observations, or they simply rejected Wolffianism altogether. Psychology and anthropology, aesthetic and educational theories based upon more empirical

7. Kant, *Philosophical Correspondence*, p. 49; see also p. 45.
8. I say more about aestheticism and Crusius in the Appendix.
9. It is common to accuse Kant's contemporaries (but not Kant) of uncritically mixing empiricist and rationalist doctrines. But this is not really fair. They were, like Kant, trying to find a "middle road." And much that can be found in Kant can already be found in their works. Clearly, they did fall short of Kant's achievements and many of them never understood the radically new elements in Kant's thought. But they deserve to be remembered and discussed, if only because of their importance to Kant.

methods began to replace logic and metaphysics as the key disciplines for an understanding of the world and man's place in it.

The philosopher who played one of the most important, if not the most important, role in this process was clearly David Hume.[10] When his first *Enquiry* appeared in German as the second volume of the *Vermischte Schriften* in 1755 (the year during which Kant began to teach at the University of Königsberg), Johann Georg Sulzer, in his Preface to the work, called attention to the importance of Hume as a writer and as a philosopher. Sulzer praises Hume as a model for a genuinely popular philosopher, and he expresses his hope that the Germans will imitate him. But most of all he hopes that "the publication of this work will interrupt their leisurely slumber and give them a new occupation."[11]

It appears that this is exactly what Hume did for the Germans—and he did this well before the first *Critique* by Kant appeared. In fact, most Germans were responding to Hume and/or continuing his investigations either directly or indirectly, and what Kant calls "Hume's problem" cannot really be understood without taking into account the discussions of his contemporaries.[12] In these discussions, "Reid, Oswald, and Beattie," as *the* enemies of Hume, and as the "popular" philosophers *par excellence*, played a role that is not to be underestimated. But before their exact role is discussed it is perhaps best to take a closer look at the different schools of thought among Kant's contemporaries, and how Reid, Oswald, and Beattie were first received in Germany.

II

For the purposes of this discussion it is sufficient roughly to differentiate between five different groups: the "Berlin enlightenment," the "Göttingen common sense school," the "sensationists," the "critical empiricists," and, more or less radically opposed to all of these, the "counter enlightenment." Though it is at times difficult to classify a certain thinker as belonging clearly to the one or the other group

10. His influence on the entire period has not yet been recognized and adequately discussed. See also my "Kant's Conception of Hume's Problem."

11. Hume, *Philosophische Versuche*, Vorrede.

12. Thus "Hume's problem" for Kant is not simply identical with what can be found in Hume's writings. Most discussions of Kant's relation to Hume fail to take this into account.

—some have characteristics of two or more of these—the distinction will aid the discussion.

A. The Berlin philosophers are perhaps the best known among all of these thinkers. They include such names as Gotthold Ephraim Lessing and Mendelssohn. But there are also such lesser known figures as Sulzer, Johann August Eberhard, Friedrich Nicolai, Thomas Abbt, Friedrich Gabriel Resewitz, and a number of even more minor thinkers. Because they all remained to a significant degree Wolffians they have also been called "neo-Wolffians" by some historians.[13] But this characterization is not quite fair. First of all, "*neo*-Wolffian" suggests that they had no direct historical link with the older Wolffians. But this is not true. They were part of one continuous tradition and were carrying on the work begun by their teachers. Secondly, they were not so much philosophical antiquarians, looking back to Wolff or simply following the beaten track, as they were exploring new avenues for Wolffian philosophy and trying to open up new fields of inquiry for it. They were attempting to achieve a genuine synthesis of the rationalistic elements of Wolff with what they considered to be the valuable results of a more empiricistic approach thus far engaged in mostly by British philosophers.

Apart from Lessing, who will not be discussed in this work because he was not so much a philosopher as a theologian and a man of letters, Mendelssohn was clearly the greatest thinker of the group. In his *Philosophische Gespräche* and his *Briefe über die Empfindungen*, both of which appeared in 1755, he laid the foundation for much of the work to be done in German philosophy and psychology during the sixties and seventies of the 18th century, defending Leibniz and calling attention to the necessity of a careful analysis of man's sensationally based knowledge.[14]

Mendelssohn was firmly rooted in the German enlightenment, and never ceased to admire Wolff and Baumgarten, whose work he thought he was continuing. But he can also be seen to be deeply influenced by Shaftesbury, Hutcheson, and other British writers.[15]

13. Dessoir, *Geschichte der neueren Psychologie*, pp. 74ff.

14. It is impossible in this context to deal in greater detail with these important works of Mendelssohn. See especially Altmann, *Moses Mendelssohns Frühschriften* and his *Moses Mendelssohn*. For a shorter account see Beck, *Early German Philosophy*, pp. 324–39.

15. The *Philosophische Gespräche*, for instance, are patterned after a dialogue of Shaftesbury (see Altmann, *Frühschriften*, pp. 1f. and *Biography*, pp. 37ff.). His "Briefe

This shows itself in his discussion of "*bon sens*." Thus in his short essay "Verwandtschaft des Schönen und Guten," which appeared first in the *Bibliothek der schönen Wissenschaften und der freyen Künste* in 1757, he draws a parallel between *bon sens* and Hutcheson's moral sense, and he argues in a somewhat Baumgartian fashion that both, though apparently independent faculties of the mind, have to be reduced to reason itself. All the judgments of *bon sens* "can be reduced to correct inferences of reason."[16] This reduction to reason may appear more difficult in the case of moral judgments, since our moral judgments "as they represent themselves in the soul are completely different from the effects of distinct rational principles,"[17] but that does not mean that they cannot be analysed into rational and distinct principles. Our moral sentiments are "phenomena which are related to rational principles in the same way as the colours are related to the angles of refraction of the light. Apparently they are of completely different nature, yet they are basically one and the same."[18] In this way Mendelssohn is able to accept almost everything said by Shaftesbury, Hutcheson, and Lord Kames in their analysis of moral and aesthetic knowledge, while not having to renounce any of the basic tenets of Wolffianism.

But he also set for himself another very important task, namely the explication of *how* the rational principles are related to the completely different moral sentiments. The colour analogy is very suggestive, of course, but it does not explain anything about the actual relation between rational principles and moral judgments (or aesthetic ones,

---

über die Empfindungen" are even more indebted to Shaftesbury's style (Altmann, *Frühschriften*, pp. 86–90). Mendelssohn also began a translation of Shaftesbury's essay on the *sensus communis* because he liked that work so much. What he seems to have appreciated the most was Shaftesbury's suggestion that ridicule could serve as a test of truth (Altmann, *Biography*, pp. 109–12).—Hume's *Enquiries* also played a large (though mainly negative) role in Mendelssohn's thought. In fact, his essay "Über die Wahrscheinlichkeit" is, at least in part, an attempt to answer Hume's doubts about experiential judgments and their basis in analogy and induction (see Beck, *Early German Philosophy*, p. 321n. and Altmann, *Frühschriften*, p. 233).

16. Mendelssohn, *Schriften*, ed. Brasch, vol. 2, p. 288.
17. Ibid., p. 289. His discussion of moral sense is clearly dependent upon Hutcheson. "Hutcheson says God has given us a sense with which we know and love the good, a sense, completely different from the understanding and all other faculties. Just as we cannot perceive the *qualitate sensibiles* through the understanding, so we differentiate the agreeable from the disagreeable, the beautiful from the ugly, through an independent *sense*, whose expressions cannot be analysed into more simple concepts." Mendelssohn believes "this theory has good reason, but it needs explanation" (p. 288).
18. Ibid., pp. 289f.

for that matter). Even the relationship between *bon sens* or common sense and reason is not as clear as Mendelssohn appears to believe in this early period of his thought, and it will, as we shall see, trouble him greatly even in his latest works.

B. The problem resulting from the attempt to find a balance between a more empiricistic approach and the traditional rationalistic one determines not only the further development of the thought of Mendelssohn and his Berlin friends but may also be seen as the problem facing the Göttingen philosophers Johann Georg Heinrich Feder and Christian Meiners. While their philosophical approach is usually characterized as "eclecticism" or "syncretism," it is perhaps better to call it "indifferentism" or "methodical scepticism." "Eclecticism" and "syncretism" not only imply a negative value judgment, they are also more characterizations of the final outcome of their thinking than of their endeavours. For the Göttingers did not set out simply to give a collection of different philosophical opinions, but tried to develop a consistent philosophical system. Their study of different philosophical theories was no end in itself, but a methodological tool. As Feder put it, for instance: "In order to protect myself from the delusions of one-sided representations and to reach well-founded insights it is necessary to compare different ways of representation and to study several systems."[19]

He thought that in this approach sceptical reserve was just as necessary as a sound common sense, and all the arguments against radical scepticism should not obscure the fact that both Feder and Meiners considered themselves as moderate sceptics. In fact, Feder described himself as having "wavered between Wolffian dogmatism and scepticism" early in his life. And he further characterized this scepticism as having been "unrefined," "unchecked" and "without system." His later thought consists exactly of a refined or checked scepticism, or a scepticism with a system.

The same may also be said of Meiners. His *Revision der Philosophie* of 1772 relies mostly on the "wise Locke" and the "brave and good-natured Hume," and in it he finds that for strict or "esoteric" philosophy "no other method is as favourable as the sceptical method."[20]

---

19. Feder, *Leben*, p. 60. See also Platner, *Aphorismen*, I (1793), pp. iv/v and Meiners *Revision*, pp. 61, 64, 75. Meiners sees a close connection between scepticism and eclecticism.

20. Meiners, *Revision*, pp. 161, 202; see also p. 153f.

It appears to have been this scepticism towards all philosophical theories which brought Feder and Meiners to common sense. They felt that philosophers aimed too high in their conception of philosophy, attempted to obtain knowledge out of reach for human beings, and believed that "whatever else man may try, he can only think with *his own* understanding" and not with some superhuman faculty of thought which grants absolute certain knowledge. Our understanding is very limited and not the best we can imagine, but it is all we have: "to despise it for this reason, or not to be satisfied with it . . . would be neither philosophy nor wisdom."[21] According to the Göttingers, philosophy has to become more modest. It must learn from common sense, which is stronger than philosophical speculation. Indeed, the circumstance that common sense and the principles of morals, upon which human happiness depends most, have been conserved in spite of all the many artificial webs of error shows the beneficial frame of nature, which does not allow us to drift too far from these wholesome truths in the course of exaggerated speculation. Dark feelings indicate them for us and instinct leads us always back to them.[22] Accordingly, for the Göttingers the real task of philosophy could only be to establish these principles of common sense and morality more clearly and to defend them against the exaggerated speculations of certain philosophers.[23]

They tried to show that the world which common sense represents to us is the real world, and they did so in conscious opposition to "idealism," "radical scepticism," and "rationalism." But in the end they escaped none of these, and their attempt at the development of a rational empiricism failed. Though Feder and Meiners tried to be better empiricists than the philosophers close to the Berlin enlightenment, they also remained within the basic framework of Wolffianism, as we shall see.

21. Feder, *Leben*, p. 249; Platner, *Aphorismen*, pp. v/vi: "Experience, common sense and morality—these are the best things in all the wisdom of this world." Christian Garve, *Eigene Betrachtungen über die allgemeinsten Grundsätze der Sittenlehre* (Breslau, 1798), pp. 2–3; idem, "Von der Popularität" in *Popularphilosophische Schriften über literarische, ästhetische und gesellschaftliche Gegenstände*, 2 vols., ed. Kurt Wölfel (Stuttgart, 1974), vol. 2, pp. 1064–66. For the entire problem see especially Wölfel's Nachwort to this edition (vol. 2, pp. 1–76).
22. Feder, *Logik und Metaphysik*, 2nd ed. (1770), pp. 57f. See also Meiners, *Revision*, pp. 87ff.
23. This may be said to have been *the* task of all the philosophers of that period. See, for instance, Tetens, *Über die allgemeine speculativische Philosophie*, pp. 11–13.

C. The same can, to a lesser extent, be said of the third group of philosophers to be considered here, namely the "sensationists." The most important philosophers in this group are Dietrich Tiedemann, Karl Franz von Irwing, Christian Lossius, and Ernst Platner.[24] Their theories are in many ways not much more than the stricter application of the principles of Feder and Meiners. In fact, some of them, like Dietrich Tiedemann, for instance, actually studied in Göttingen.[25] Others, like Platner, Irwing and Lossius, were more independent.[26] But in general, it may be said that while the Göttingers were content with a careful consideration of various theories and often suspended final judgment, the sensationists had a strong bias towards physiological explanations.[27] They were convinced that sensation and its basis in human physiology was the key for understanding human nature and thus for putting philosophy on a scientific basis. They all rejected Wolffian rationalism as being fundamentally mistaken and leading to a form of idealism.[28] But they were by no means radical materialists. For

24. For a thorough, though somewhat one-sided, discussion of the German materialists in the eighteenth century see Finger, *Von der Materialität der Seele*. Finger acknowledges the Scottish influence upon these philosophers (and especially Lossius), but he declines to discuss it, since it is not part of his topic (p. 9). See also Zart, *Einfluss*, pp. 154–56; Dessoir, *Geschichte der neueren Psychologie*, pp. 103–7; Beck, *Early German Philosophy*, p. 332n.; Cassirer, *Enlightenment*, pp. 116f.; and especially Cassirer, *Das Erkenntnisproblem*, vol. 2, pp. 448–56.

25. See Zart, *Einfluss*, pp. 154–69. For Tiedemann see Wundt, *Aufklärung*, p. 300 and Überweg, *Geschichte*, vol. 3, p. 474.

26. Apart from Lossius, Platner is clearly the most important thinker. His views changed greatly during his life. These changes were mainly occasioned by the works of Tetens, Kant, and Aenesidemus Schulze. Because of them he rewrote several times his major work, the *Philosophische Aphorismen*. The first volume, which appeared in 1776, and still advocated a mild form of materialism, reappeared greatly changed in 1784. Under the influence of Tetens and Kant, Platner had become a critical empiricist. In 1793 he published another completely rewritten version, in which he showed himself as a sceptic. The second volume, concerned with practical philosophy, appeared first in 1782 and was also rewritten for a second publication in 1800. The different conversions of Platner have been investigated by Wreschner, *Ernst Platners und Kants Erkenntnistheorie*.

27. But, in so far as the Göttingers had a bias towards a Lockean form of sensationism, they were rather close to these materialists.

28. In fact, Tiedemann, for instance, is better characterized as an "anti-idealist" than as a materialist. He offers arguments against both theories, but seems to consider materialism the lesser evil. His biographer characterizes his main work, the *Untersuchungen über den Menschen* (Leipzig, 1777–78) as "a product of antagonism towards the idealistic system" and notes that "this polemic tendency against idealism gives the entire work a strange outlook" (Dietrich Tiedemann, *Handbuch der Psychologie*).

they denied neither the existence and immortality of the soul nor the existence of God. Though they tended even further towards empiricism and sensationism than either the Berliners or the Göttingers, their general aim may still be described as the attempt to achieve a synthesis of British and German thought. And no matter how far they go in the direction of empiricism, they still remain deeply influenced by Wolffianism.

D. The last group of enlightenment philosophers, i.e. that of critical empiricists, is less coherent than any of the other three groups previously mentioned. In fact, it is not really a group at all. Because these philosophers are even more independent than any of the others, they are difficult to classify. The most important among them are Christian Garve, Johann Heinrich Lambert, Nicolaus Tetens, and the pre-critical Kant. They are among the most popular and successful writers of the period, and also among the most important ones. It is in their works that the "rational empiricism" aimed at by most of the thinkers of the period actually comes closest to being realized. Garve, Lambert, Tetens, and the early Kant appear to have had a much greater appreciation of the fundamental difficulty involved in a synthesis of British empiricism and German rationalism. They all saw that such a synthesis could not be achieved by a mere "critique of books and systems," but that it involved a critique of the very foundations of our faculties of knowledge.[29]

Garve's translations and essays were of seminal importance for the further development of German thought. And the two main works of Tetens, his *Über die allgemeine speculativische Philosophie* of 1775 and his *Philosophische Versuche über die menschliche Natur und ihre Entwicklung* of 1776-77, were not only most influential, but also of the greatest philosophical importance.[30] Garve and Tetens not only deal with very

29. Kant, *Critique of Pure Reason*, Axiin.
30. For some details concerning Tetens's life and thought in general, as well as an interesting discussion of his theory in relation to Kant, see Beck, *Early German Philosophy*, pp. 412–25. See also Giorgio Tonelli's article on Tetens in *Encyclopedia of Philosophy* (ed. Paul Edwards). The standard work on Tetens is still Uebele's *Johann Nicolaus Tetens*. See also Uebele's "Herder and Tetens," his "Johann Nicolaus Tetens zum 100jährigen Todestag," and Barnouw, "The Philosophical Achievement and Historical Significance of Johann Nicolaus Tetens." Of fundamental importance are still Max Dessoir "Des Johann Nicolaus Tetens Stellung in der Geschichte der Philosophie," and his *Geschichte der neueren Psychologie*, pp. 120–31. But one only has to look through the works of Kant's contemporaries to see how important he was. See, for instance, Platner, *Aphorismen*, vol. 1 (1793), pp. vii/viii.

much the same topics as does Kant in his first *Critique*, but they also approach them in a comparable way.[31]

It may even be argued that Kant wrote his critical work with these two philosophers (as well as Mendelssohn) in mind.[32] They were the

31. See Uebele, *Tetens*; H. J. Vleeshouwer, *The Development of Kantian Thought*, pp. 82–88. Beck, *Early German Philosophy*, pp. 412ff., rejects any fundamental influence of Tetens upon Kant. But perhaps he views Tetens too much from the point of view of the mature Kant. In 1775 and 1777 Tetens might have meant more to Kant than his position after 1781 suggests. In any case, Kant's contemporaries were still capable of recognizing themselves in his criticism. Platner and Eberhard clearly believed that his critical philosophy was only an extension of their own researches. Feder claimed: "what Kant calls the critique of pure reason has always been the only kind of metaphysics I could appreciate and the one I have tried to teach" (Feder, *Raum and Caussalität*, pp. vii/viii). Feder could not understand why Kant objected when his criticism was called "scepticism," asking "is it not just as much in accordance with the original etymological meaning of the term as with the usage common among philosophers until today to understand by mitigated scepticism exactly what Kant calls criticism? . . . And why should we not be allowed to call the examination of principles, either examination, or investigation, or enlightenment, or skepsis, simply because Kant calls it criticism?" (ibid., pp. xxiv/xxxi; see also the Preface to the third volume of his *Über den menschlichen Willen*, p. xvi). That Tetens did not think too highly of Kant's originality is known from a remark by Feder to the effect that Tetens's view on Kant's originality differed very much from that of Kant himself (Feder, *Leben*, p. 108).

32. When the *Critique of Pure Reason* first appeared he expected much from his contemporaries. Thus he was anxious to hear Mendelssohn's judgment about it, and he was "very uncomfortable at Mr. Mendelssohn's putting [his] book aside." He hoped that it would "not be forever." He also made clear why Mendelssohn was so important for him: "He is the most important of all the people who could explain this theory to the world; it was on him, on Mr. *Tetens* and you [Herz], dearest man, that I counted most" (Kant, *Correspondence*, ed. Zweig, p. 96). But he also hoped to enlist Garve "to use [his] position and influence to encourage . . . the enemies of [his] book . . . to consider the work in its proper order" and to make his problem understood. "*Garve, Mendelssohn*, and *Tetens*, are the only men I know through whose co-operation this subject could have been brought to a successful conclusion before too long, even though centuries before this one have not seen it done" (pp. 102f.). In the same vein he writes to Mendelssohn "to encourage an examination of [his] theses," since in this way "the critical philosophy would gain acceptability and become a promenade through a labyrinth, but with a reliable guide book to help us find our way out as often as we get lost." But Kant was far too optimistic. For, as he realized somewhat later, "Mendelssohn, Garve and Tetens have apparently declined to occupy themselves with work of this sort, and where else can anyone of sufficient talent and good will be found?" (p. 107). Thus Kant expected not only to be understood by the foremost philosophers of the time, but he also expected that they would help him spread his critical philosophy. It is difficult—but interesting—to speculate what the philosophical situation in Germany would be like even now, if his hopes had been fulfilled.

thinkers by whom he wanted (and expected) to be understood. And they were also the contemporaries in Germany who had perhaps the greatest effect on him.[33] But the suggestions of Garve and Tetens influenced not only Kant, but also most of the other German thinkers of the period; and their philosophy is also important in its own right as a sustained attempt to base metaphysics upon a careful analysis of human nature.

Kant was born approximately twenty years earlier (in 1724) than most of the philosophers mentioned so far. The beginnings of his career as a philosopher coincide exactly with the beginnings of the so-called cognitive crisis of the enlightenment. As a sensitive thinker, he could not escape this crisis, and it is no surprise that its effects upon him can be found throughout his early works. Above all, his *Dreams of a Ghost-Seer Explained by Dreams of Metaphysics* of 1766 clearly shows how greatly he was affected by the intellectual climate of the period.

For him, as for Mendelssohn and Tetens, the cognitive crisis of the enlightenment was first and foremost a crisis of the "science of metaphysics." Like Feder, Meiners, Lichtenberg, Mendelssohn, Lossius, Tetens, and Garve, he came to believe that metaphysics needed to be revised, reformed, or newly founded. In his early, or pre-critical, period, he also agreed with most of these thinkers that a moderate scepticism was the best method available "to pull off the dogmatic dress of metaphysics."[34] Accordingly, some of his most critical remarks about metaphysics are to be found in his earlier works.[35] Kant, the *elegante Magister*, shares not only the same *Weltanschauung* as his younger colleagues and friends in Königsberg, Berlin, Göttingen, Erfurt, Kiel and Leipzig; he is one of them and considered by them and others to be one of them.[36]

33. This, of course, remains to be shown in detail. But I hope that this book will go at least some way towards making such a project plausible. See also the Appendix.

34. Kant to Mendelssohn, 8 April 1766, in Kant, *Philosophical Correspondence*, p. 55. The entire letter is interesting for Kant's position at the time when he wrote the *Dreams of a Ghost-Seer*.

35. See Kant, *Werke*, ed. Weischedel, vol. 1, pp. 621, 630, 959, 974, 982, for instance. Kant compares metaphysics with a "bottomless abyss," a "slippery ground," a "land of milk and honey" (*Schlaraffenland*), an "airship," and he shows something approaching contempt for it. This speaks against the ontological school, whose members argue that Kant carried over into the critical period his (positive) "metaphysical motives" of the pre-critical period.

36. See Kant, *Critique of Pure Reason*, Axiin. It is also clear from Mendelssohn's correspondence with Kant. Kant's student and friend, Krauss, seems to have remained

All these different sets of thinkers were united in their acceptance of the ideals of enlightenment. They all believed that the way of progress for the human race consisted in the increase and clarification of knowledge. Prejudices and blind faith had to be overcome—and they were convinced that the only way to overcome them was by means of a free discussion among reasonable men. As such reasonable men they did not believe themselves to be in the possession of the truth. Nor did they think that any of the philosophical theories advanced before them could claim to have all the answers. This was also the most important reason why they did not accept any one system, and they did not so much strive to be systematic thinkers as to find truth wherever it could be found.

Because they were such eclectic thinkers, they could also talk to each other and appreciate their different points of view. And because of this they could appear to be not very different from one another. The Berliners, the Göttingers, the sensationists, and the critical empiricists, who very often knew each other not only through their writings but also on a more personal basis, formed a philosophical republic of sorts—a republic in whose forum all new philosophical ideas were given as fair a hearing as was possible.

This forum of German enlightenment philosophers consisted of their many philosophical journals. Some of the most important of these were the four journals that were published by the Berliners: The *Briefe die neueste Literatur betreffend* (1759-65), the *Bibliothek der schönen Wissenschaften und der freyen Künste* (1757-65) and, especially important for the purposes of our discussion, the *Allgemeine deutsche Bibliothek* (1765 until well after 1800) and the *Neue Bibliothek der schönen Wissenschaften und der freyen Künste*. They were equalled in importance

---

always at the stage of development at which Kant was in the late sixties. Feder and Meiners appear to have considered Kant somewhat of a "dilettante" in philosophy, as an anecdote of Krauss shows: when Krauss visited Göttingen in the seventies and told Feder and Meiners that Kant had a philosophical treatise in his desk that would some day "make them sweat," they reportedly responded by laughing (see Vorländer, *Immanuel Kants Leben*, p. 118). They probably considered Kant to belong to the same group as Lichtenberg, a physicist who also dabbled in philosophy. Goethe mentions Kant in immediate connection with Sulzer, Mendelssohn, and Garve in the *Frankfurter gelehrte Anzeigen* of 1772 (see Hettner, *Geschichte der deutschen Literatur im 18. Jahrhundert*, vol. 3, ii, p. 238). For Kant's *Weltanschauung* see especially Beck's excellent discussion in *Early German Philosophy*, pp. 426–30. Beck comes to the conclusion that it is esssentially identical to that of the popular philosophers and the professors of the Berlin enlightenment.

by the journal published by the University of Göttingen: the *Göttin-gische Anzeigen von gelehrten Sachen*. These five journals reviewed almost every important German and foreign publication in literature, theology, and philosophy and thus commented upon every intellectual development in Europe. They were feared and hated by certain people just as much as they were admired by others. Their great influence is still not sufficiently appreciated. For they shaped the course of the late German enlightenment to the greatest extent.[37]

E. There were also voices of opposition. These were the so called "counter-enlighteners," who, during the early seventies, were closely allied with the literary movement of "Storm and Stress." The most important thinkers among these figures were Johann Georg Hamann, Johann Gottfried Herder, and Friedrich Heinrich Jacobi.[38] They understood themselves first and foremost as Christian thinkers, and, as such, were fundamentally opposed to the very ideals of the enlightenment. Faith and Christian traditions were more important to them than rational investigation and secular progress.

Hamann and Jacobi specifically rejected "the spirit of *Gründlichkeit*," arguing that philosophy could not and need not supply human knowledge with any sort of foundation. For them philosophical justification was impossible. The principles of knowledge have to be believed blindly. They must be accepted on faith in much the same way as religious doctrines. Since the principles governing the testimony of the senses are identical to those governing religious testimony, philosophical justification, far from securing it, will only undermine it and necessarily lead to scepticism and nihilism—or so they believed.

In this fundamental criticism of the enlightenment, Hamann, Herder, and Jacobi found British sources very helpful. Because they were not aiming at any kind of philosophical system and were really only interested in using the British arguments against the doctrines of German and French enlightenment philosophers, their understand-ing of the texts by British thinkers is often rather peculiar. But it does reveal dimensions of thought that *are* present, though not clearly revealed, in British thought. In some ways, Hamann, Herder, and

37. These were not the only important journals. But none of the others achieved their wide distribution.

38. Though Jacobi began to exert a great influence only after 1785, he also played a minor role during the early seventies.

Jacobi are closer to British philosophy than any of the enlightenment philosophers.

But the term "counter-enlightenment" can also be misleading. For it suggests, on the one hand, that Hamann, Herder, and Jacobi have little in common with the enlightenment, and, on the other, that their philosophy is exhausted by their criticisms of the prevailing theories. Both suggestions are false. They were deeply influenced by the climate of opinion of the late German enlightenment. Nevertheless, their thought went far beyond any of the suggestions of their contemporaries and may very well be characterized as defining "the aims of a new epoch."[39]

It was in this philosophical situation that Kant first conceived of his critical problem and began to work towards his *Critique of Pure Reason*. But it was also in this period that Scottish common-sense philosophy entered the philosophical scene in Germany.

39. This is argued with special reference to Herder by Taylor, *Hegel*, pp. 1–50; see also Berlin, *Vico and Herder*, and his "The Counter-Enlightenment," as well as "Hume and the Sources of German Anti-Rationalism," in *Against the Current*.

III

The First Reception of "Reid, Oswald, and Beattie" in Germany

THE PREVIOUS CHAPTER has shown how after the middle of the eighteenth century, in the midst of what has been called the cognitive crisis of the enlightenment, the Germans began to show deep interest in British philosophy. It is not really surprising, therefore, that the Scottish philosophy of common sense came to be closely scrutinized in continental Europe. But, given the sheer volume of this critical discussion, it is surprising that the traditional account of eighteenth-century German philosophy virtually omits consideration of the Scottish influence.

I

French and German journals began to review the works of Reid, Oswald, and Beattie almost immediately after their first appearance in English. Thus the *Journal Encyclopédique* published in December 1764 a summary of the *Inquiry* in which the reviewer called attention to Reid's critique of the "theory of ideas," suggesting that it is an important work, and well worth careful study.[1] The *Journal de Trévoux* of March 1765 pointed out that the "principal goal of the author is to combat scepticism," and it mentioned as Reid's primary targets both Berkeley and "a modern author" who has written a book entitled "*Traité de la Nature humaine*" that has been published in 1739.[2] It closed by noting that

Sans prétendre admettre tous les sentiments de l'Auteur, nous croyons que son

1. *Journal Encyclopédique*, December 1764, pp. 20–27, 20f.
2. *Journal de Trévoux*, March 1765, pp. 721–31, 721 and 726.

Ouvrage renferme beaucoup d'idées neuves, intéressantes, & capables de répandre beaucoup de lumiere sur la nature & les facultés de l'entendement humain.[3]

The *Bibliothèque des sciences et des beaux arts* reviewed Reid's *Inquiry* in 1767, one year before the appearance of the French translation of this work. And the *Journal Encyclopédique* published a most favourable review of the translation in November of 1768.[4] So by 1768 the most important work by the Scottish common-sense philosophers was available in French, and thus easily accessible to German philosophers. And given its favourable reviews in major French journals, many of those Germans most interested in developing philosophy along more empiricistic lines would very likely have made an effort to obtain the work.

One of the first notices in German of Reid's *Inquiry* can be found in the Leipzig *Neue Zeitungen von gelehrten Sachen* of 14 June 1764. It is not much longer than a page, and the reviewer is, on the whole, content to summarize Reid's chapter headings. But he introduces Reid as a

learned and clear-sighted author, who, in the beautiful work here advertised, has tried to refute the irrational system of the sceptics in a very thorough fashion, and to defend with many new and incontrovertible proofs the certainty of the cognition which we obtain through the mediation of the external senses. He contests especially the *Treatise of human Nature* [sic] which first appeared in 1739 and contains the most obvious defence of scepticism.[5]

The notice concludes, somewhat surprisingly, perhaps, by pointing out that the "book is available at Wendler's in Leipzig," thus showing that even Reid's English text was available in Germany in the year of publication.

The first review of a work by Reid, Oswald, or Beattie in the *Göttingische*

3. Ibid., p. 731.

4. *Journal Encyclopédique*, November 1768, pp. 19–37 and December 1768, pp. 29–41. The bibliographical details of the translation are: Thomas Reid, *Recherches sur l'entendement humain d'après les principes du sens commun* (Amsterdam, 1768). The *Bibliotheque des sciences et des beaux arts* reviewed it in vol. 28 (1767), July, August, September, part I, article I, pp. 1–26, and it was reviewed by the *Journal Encyclopédique*, 1764, pp. 29–37. For the entire problem of the transmission of British literature to Germany *via* France, see Blassneck, *Frankreich als Vermittler englisch-deutscher Einflüsse im 17. und 18. Jahrhundert.*

5. *Neue Zeitungen von gelehrten Sachen*, 14 June 1764, pp. 377–78, 377.

Anzeigen appeared on 6 March 1769. It concerned the first volume of Oswald's *Appeal*. The reviewer begins his discussion by noting that the work constitutes

a curious phenomenon in this enlightened age, since it shows a writer who accuses philosophers and theologians of not knowing common sense [*Menschenverstand*] and of having argued themselves out of all the sciences by means of logical deductions.

But, he continues, though the work has several shortcomings (not exhibiting the strictest order, not adhering to logical connection, as well as giving murky refutations of its enemies and failing to develop its own position sufficiently),

we have through careful reading found this work to be important. It is important for putting a halt to the dangerous mania for demonstration [*Demonstriersucht*]; for deciding the dispute about innate ideas; for judging the system of the modern British philosophers which dissolves all moral obligation into feelings, and for showing the folly of the sceptics and infidels in the proper light. For all these reasons we consider a complete extract of this work to be very instructive and entertaining.[6]

He then goes on to praise the author for showing what common sense consists of, what weight and reputation it has in the sciences, and how much damage has been done by going beyond its judgment. Towards the end of his discussion, after having tried to show how important the contributions of the author of the *Appeal* are, he again criticizes the style of the work, but hastens also to reaffirm the validity of Oswald's basic principles:

However, at times, the author appears to us to go too far in his crusade for the reputation of common sense, as when he declares, for instance, that all arguments against infidels and the proofs of God's existence as put forward by Derham, Ray or others in similar form, are superfluous. But it is not possible to judge his aim until the second volume which, as he promises on p. 380, will show the application of his principles to religion. The present work contains only *the general principles*, which, with their proper limitations and after subtraction, *are indeed true*.[7]

6. *Göttingische Anzeigen*, 1769 number 28 (6 March): 265–275, 265f.
7. Ibid., p. 274 (emphasis mine).

The second volume of the *Appeal*, which appeared in 1772 and delivered the promised application of the principles of common sense to religion, was also reviewed in the *Göttingische Anzeigen*. It is called an "important book," whose "great aim" is "healing people of the mania for demonstration and disputation by drawing their attention to the homely [*häuslich*] principle of truth and virtue."[8] But the reviewer seems to be somewhat disillusioned, and he is much more critical than in the review of the first volume. His "expectation has not been completely fulfilled." Though he still finds that "the unknown author writes in a very lively and interesting manner" and has many good things to say about particular aspects of the book, he concludes the review on a rather sour note:

There are things which rightfully could be criticized in this work. Is it not really only a dispute about words when the author rejects all proofs of basic principles? The proper representation of basic principles, which he calls for, is just what others call proof. Thus Clark, Derham, Ray and others have done in their proofs of the existence of God really nothing else than to make basic principles ostensible [*sinnlich gemacht*]. Or they have represented them in a proper fashion. At times the author also expresses himself very vaguely, so that we could accuse him of impeding the spirit of investigation.[9]

Yet, the positive response to the the first volume is not wholly lacking:

the great merits of having represented the basic truths of religion in a manner as enlightening as sympathetic, and of having shown the absurdities of the sceptics to be quite disconcerting, cannot be denied to the author. His work is a strong remedy for both the mania of demonstration and the mania of doubt.[10]

Given this on the whole favourable review of the original *Appeal* in one of the most important philosophical journals of Germany, it is no surprise that a translation of the entire work appeared soon thereafter. In fact, the translator notes in his Preface to the translation that it was the favourable reaction to this work in England as well as in Germany that induced him to translate it, and this even though, as he assures his

---

8. *Göttingische Anzeigen*, 1773, number 35 (22 March): 289–99 and number 44 (12 April): 370f., 289.
   9. Ibid., pp. 289, 371.
   10. Ibid., p. 371.

readers, the work "is in fact directed against a kind of enemy of religion that does not yet exist in Germany."[11]

In spite of the fact that the original of the *Appeal* was reviewed extensively in the *Göttingische Anzeigen*, its translation was also discussed in great detail. Although the reviewer of the translation confesses that he thinks of the book in very much the same way as had the reviewer of the original, his judgment is somewhat different (or it has changed in the meantime).[12] The assessment is much more critical. Now the *Appeal* is found not to be an adequate remedy for exaggerated rationalism and scepticism, and the review is very critical of most of the details, even though it still exhibits a certain sympathy for Oswald's basic approach:

The author has a great and meritorious aim, and his main thought is correct. But he does not develop it with the complete clarity and distinctness that would make it convincing and reliably applicable. There are basic truths, or immediately evident propositions; our understanding has the capability of knowing them in the same way that it is forced to accept the conclusion of a thorough and evident proof; we should not be tempted to try to prove these basic truths, but should be content to see whether somebody has enough common sense [*Menschenverstand*] to grasp them. All this is correct. But the questions: What, in fact, are basic truths? Which propositions come close to the basic truths in that they are conclusions, but conclusions of such immediacy that they can just as little be forced upon us as basic truths as they can be proved geometrically by means of principles not closely related? And, how can objections against these two species of truths be answered by an explanation of the kind and degree of approval which is demanded, or by any other means? All these important questions are neither in general nor in application treated by the author with thoroughness. Instead, he has engaged in the uncertain determination of the difference between the cognitive faculties of animals and humans, and has succumbed too much to the impulse of passion and ridicule.[13]

Thus the work which was first hailed as a strong antidote to extreme rationalism and scepticism, which, though blemished by minor stylistic deficiencies, was regarded as a promising advance in philosophical thought, is now seen more soberly. It does not deliver what it promises.

11. Jakob Oswald, *Appelation an den gemeinen Menschenverstand zum Vortheil der Religion*, 2 vols., tr. F. E. Wilmsen (Leipzig, 1774) pp. vii–viii.

12. *Göttingische Anzeigen*, 1773, number 97 (13 August): 834–38; see especially p. 834. It is likely that Feder is the reviewer. For the reasons see note 16 in chapter IV below.

13. Ibid., p. 834.

The zeal and the constant use of ridicule, which were first seen as mere stylistic shortcomings, are now judged much more severely and considered to stand in the way of proper philosophical examination. This reviewer emphasizes that all propositions which are not basic truths in the strictest sense of the word can be proved or justified. "Simply to invoke common sense in these cases, and to decry the enemy's disagreement as evil and nonsensical, or to ridicule him without refutation is, though suitable for dim-witted zealots and enthusiasts, not thorough, and it can even be detrimental to the truth."[14]

In the review of the second part of the translation the tone becomes still more critical:

This language does not reflect the proper disposition for the investigation of truth, nor even the way to argue in order to convince and win over those who are in error. Children may be frightened off by means of such scoldings, but not men.—If the author had less fire of imagination and more penetration, if he had more calmly and precisely investigated the philosophical systems which he wanted to hurl away in this way, he would in many cases have gone to work differently and would have been more useful.[15]

Concurrent with this reception of Oswald's *Appeal* was that of Beattie's *Essay*. In fact, of all the works by the Scottish common-sense philosophers none was more quickly taken note of and assimilated in Germany than this work. It appeared in 1770, and it was reviewed in January 1771 by the *Göttingische Anzeigen*.[16] Like Oswald's *Appeal*, Beattie's *Essay* was not received uncritically. The reviewer of the *Göttingische Anzeigen*—again most likely Feder—though far from hostile, found a number of shortcomings in this work as well.

Attempting to put Beattie into the proper perspective, the review begins with a reference to the earlier attempts at refuting scepticism published by Reid and Oswald. Beattie is understood as agreeing with his predecessors on all essential points, though

he is different from the others in that he attacks the matter more polemically and at the same time at its basis, and in its whole extension. But he assaults Hume in such a way that he does not only talk to him without the moderation

14. Ibid., p. 837.
15. *Göttingische Anzeigen*, number 8 (19 January): 60–61, 61.
16. *Göttingische Anzeigen*, 1771, number 12 (28 January): 91–96.

customary to the others. He also tries to prove by means of a full register of examples how dangerous the doctrines and how shallow the proofs contained in Hume's book are.[17]

The course of the argument in the Essay is charted as follows:

In order to be able to determine which arguments deserve to be accepted and which to be rejected, he [Beattie] shows first that in all kinds of cognitions and science the arguments depend upon basic principles which cannot be proved themselves and which we are forced to accept instinctively (through the essential laws of thought, or at least through the nature of our understanding). For this purpose he runs through the different kinds of cognition [*Erkennt-nisarten*] and proves his proposition especially with regard to mathematics, physics, the proofs of the existence of objects, the qualities of our most inner nature, the belief in testimony, etc. From all this he draws the conclusion that all arguments, however evident and methodological in appearance, are nonsensi-cal and unfounded, when they contradict such immediate sensations and principles which the instinct forces upon us . . . and there is supposed to be a special faculty, different from rational thought, which enables us to compre-hend and hold on to these principles, namely the *sensus communis* (we do not dare to use here the common German expressions "*gemeiner Verstand*," "*gesunde Vernunft*" for the "common sense" of the original).[18]

The reviewer finds the differentiation between common sense and reason as the faculty of inference "still a little hasty," but believes that Beattie's conception that "truth is for us what we are forced to believe and falsity what we are forced to reject, can be brought to a correct principle," and considers Beattie's enterprise important.[19] Moreover, the author is praised for his good intentions, his great knowledge of antiquity and his excellent style of writing. "One also finds *correct and exact thetic and anti-thetic remarks* [in the work]," but in a project such as Beattie's

great penetration is necessary in order to see the strength of an objection which may at times be hidden and to notice all the difficulties, so that they may be resolved at their base, or, where this is impossible, to save the contested opinion through a more exact examination. Moreover, it is necessary not to reject the premisses for the sake of a consequence, when the mistake is really to be found

17. Ibid., p. 92.
18. Ibid., pp. 92f.
19. Ibid., p. 95.

in the consequence. We have to develop and form our reasons in such a way that they do not only have an influence upon somebody who has already accepted our system, but meet the [full] strength of the enemy. We have not always found all these virtues in our author. For this reason a Hume would still have an easy game with him, as, for instance, when he wants to maintain against Hume that the principle of causality has another basis than our experience.[20]

He also objects to Beattie (and others) for accepting too many principles as immediately evident, arguing that it would be better and more thorough to accept as few first principles as possible. Nor does he like Beattie's mockery of metaphysicians. Nevertheless, he concludes that even though Beattie may not be capable of winning over an enemy to his side and to show the usefulness of truth, he "is a good fighter" and expects much from a treatment of moral truths, promised by Beattie.[21]

A more critical stance towards Reid, Oswald and Beattie appears to have been reinforced by the reception of critical discussions of their works in England. For example, Joseph Priestley's *An Examination of Dr. Reid's Inquiry into the Human Mind, Dr. Beattie's Essay on the Nature and Immutability of Truth and Dr. Oswald's Appeal to Common Sense*, which appeared in 1775, was immediately reviewed in the *Göttingische Anzeigen*. The reviewer (who says it was he who reviewed Beattie's *Essay* in 1771 and the German translation of Oswald's *Appeal* in 1774, and hence is likely Feder)[22] takes this occasion to note as "strange" that "the English philosophers have kept so quiet, while first Reid in a fine and witty manner, then Beattie with strong eloquence and with a noble heart shining through, and at last Oswald with insulting fervour, *have attacked the basic principles* not only of Locke's, but *of all philosophy*."[23] The *"new dialectic"* of Reid, Oswald and Beattie would deserve a thorough examination, and as such an examination he welcomes Priestley's work:

The author's principles are in most points identical with those of this reviewer. Though he has answered all objections of *these new dialecticians* against the

---

20. Ibid., p. 94 (emphasis mine).
21. Ibid., p. 96.
22. *Göttingische Anzeigen*, 1775, number 92 (17 August): 777–83. This review also makes explicit reference to the anonymous critique of Beattie in the *Monthly Review* of July 1773.
23. *Göttingische Anzeigen*, 1775, p. 777 (emphasis mine).

Lockian psychology and has uncovered the shallow, insufficient, incoherent, and dangerous elements in their philosophy, he could have been more moderate in the estimation of their aims and in the interpretation of their main thoughts, as well as more restrained in the consequences and softer in his expression.[24]

But the reviewer shows himself to be much closer to Reid and Beattie than Priestley. He defends, for instance, a great deal of Reid's argument against idealism and does not agree with Priestley that Beattie's conception of truth leads to relativism.[25]

II

The popular philosophers of Berlin, the so-called "neo-Wolffians," were more critical of the Scottish attempt to supply philosophy with a foundation in common sense. Whereas the Göttingers and some of the sensationists agreed with the general approach and the aims of the Scots, and were only discontented with some of the details of the Scottish theory, the philosophers connected with the *Allgemeine deutsche Bibliothek* appeared to be unable to accept the very aims and the approach of the Scots, finding only certain details worthy of further development. This is shown by the review of the works by Oswald and Beattie in the *Allgemeine deutsche Bibliothek*.

When this journal published reviews of both Oswald's *Appeal* and Beattie's *Essay* in 1776, the reviewers made this the occasion for a fundamental critique of all common-sense philosophy.[26] The review of Oswald's book is introduced by a rhetorical question which sets the tone for the entire critique:

What is it, if not a kind of despair that causes several new defenders of religion in Great Britain, people like Reid, Brattie [*sic*], and the author of the work here reviewed, to leave all philosophy behind, and to take refuge in common sense [*schlechter [sic] Menschenverstand*] in the fight against Hume and other enemies of religion.[27]

24. Ibid., p. 778 (emphasis mine).
25. The entire dispute about idealism is characterized as being a merely verbal one. Reid and Berkeley were in full agreement. Therefore, Priestley could have accepted much of Reid's position with regard to our belief in external objects.
26. See *Allgemeine deutsche Bibliothek*, vol. 28, i (1776): 157–59 and Supplement to vols. 13–24 in three vols., vol. i (1776): 497–503.
27. *Allgemeine deutsche Bibliothek*, vol. 28, i (1776): 157.

Oswald should have fought his enemies with the same weapons as they had used: philosophical arguments. He and his friends should not have turned against philosophy by appealing to common sense.[28] To give the latter the function of the highest judge in all matters philosophical is not only anti-metaphysical, but also non-philosophical. The philosophers of common sense have really a mistaken view of their most fundamental principle. Common sense is not a constant and basic faculty of human beings and, as such, independent of philosophy. On the contrary, common sense is dependent upon philosophy. It has developed to its present state together with philosophy.[29] And this explains why it is not the same for all nations and all times in the history of humanity. If only for this reason, the "anti-metaphysicians" or common-sense philosophers deceive themselves when they appeal to common sense in order to censor philosophy.

Philosophy, that is rational investigation, is the last judge of common sense; and common sense without reason is nothing more than superstition. Therefore, Reid, Oswald and Beattie must be considered as enemies of philosophy. The reviewer admits that more needs to be said, but he has not enough space:

To save the honour of philosophy . . . would require a treatise and not a review such as this. We can allow only so much space to a foreign book in the *German Bibliothek*, and this holds even more so for a book of such slight importance, a book which is hardly worthy of the toil of such a skilled translator as Mr. Wilsen (for Oswald is undoubtedly the most lightly armed of the three fighters for common sense).[30]

The German translation of Beattie's *Essay* is treated no more positively. Like Oswald, Beattie is understood as abandoning reason altogether and as taking refuge in common sense. His animosity to the over-reliance upon reason in metaphysics is taken to be enmity against reason itself. In particular, he is scolded for not having defined his "conception of truth so exactly and so correctly that there could at least be no ambiguity in this regard." Because of this failure, it is argued, Beattie's entire system is pervaded by obscurity. To say that truth is what our constitution determines us to believe, and falsity what our

28. Ibid.
29. Ibid., p. 158.
30. Ibid., p. 159.

constitution determines us to reject, is not a sufficient criterion for this concept, and it invites ambiguity and confusion.[31]

While the reviewer is willing to accept Beattie's unusual distinction between immediately certain or intuitive truths and truths which require proof, between truths of common sense and proofs of rational argument, he cautions his readers that "so important and essential a difference as the author claims, is not established thereby."[32] In other words, the distinction does not suffice to differentiate between common sense on the one hand and reason on the other. We need an objective criterion, not a merely subjective or psychological one. First of all, the basic principles are really limited to only two: the law of contradiction and the principle of sufficient reason. All other propositions are, says the reviewer, capable of proof. We usually accept many other propositions without asking for proof; a superior mind is capable of seeing intuitively, as it were, the truth of a greater number of propositions than a dim-wit sees; and different cultures hold different principles as intuitively certain.[33] Considerations such as these are sufficient to show the reviewer how vague and uncertain the distinction of Beattie really is, and how it allows him to increase the number of first principles beyond all limits.

While this reviewer believes that even his short account makes clear "how shallow and unsatisfactory his [Beattie's] theory is," he nevertheless believes it to be worth his while to investigate the arguments by means of which Beattie supports his theory of common sense. But all his criticisms of these arguments are again based upon his view that Beattie is an enemy of reason. According to his understanding of the doctrine of "common sense," the Scotsman is not allowed to rely on reason at all. Beattie is seen as demeaning the understanding, and as inhibiting the progress of science by making the understanding the servant of common sense and by thus placing the latter beyond all criticism.[34]

In any case, he argues, the radical distinction between common sense and the understanding is as false as it is dangerous. The two principles cannot be separated in the way in which he sees Beattie separating them. Common sense and the understanding are one and the same

31. *Allgemeine deutsche Bibliothek*, Supplement to vols. 13–24, vol. i, p. 497. This is clearly not just directed at the Scots, but constitutes also a criticism of Germans like Feder and Lossius.

32. Ibid.

33. Ibid., pp. 498–503.

34. Ibid., p. 502.

power. We only call it by different names in accordance with the different functions which this power fulfils. The truths of common sense are the truths of the understanding which have been established long ago and have become almost instinctual by their constant use in daily life. If Beattie's distinction were to be understood in this way, it would be correct. But,

if it were correct to say that common sense is the highest judge of truth, it would also have to be correct that we can measure the degree of warmth or cold in the air better by natural feeling than by means of a carefully constructed thermometer.

In conclusion, he finds:

This may be enough to show the weakness of this enemy of speculative philosophy. If space and time allowed it, I would also show him to the reader as one of the most unlucky and silly makers of consequences [*Consequenzmacher*]. For he fights against the theories which he does not like especially by means of spiteful conclusions. Most of all he attacks Berkeley's doctrine of the non-existence of matter and the theory of the necessary determination of human actions. He succeeds best against Hume who, in his book about human nature, has driven scepticism to such heights and entangled himself in his own web so thoroughly that it does not require outstanding discernment to convict him by means of his own words as well as by the consequences of them.[35]

But these severe criticisms of Oswald and Beattie in the *Allgemeine deutsche Bibliothek* do not mean that all the philosophers close to the Berlin enlightenment rejected their views outright. I have noted that Sulzer's early criticisms of Hume's scepticism, though aiming at a *metaphysical* refutation, were to some extent similar to those of the Scots.[36] And Friedrich Gabriel Resewitz, an early friend of Mendelssohn, Nicolai, and Lessing and a collaborator in the project of the *Literaturbriefe*, refers approvingly to the German translation of Beattie's *Essay* in his treatise on pedagogy, *Erziehung des Bürgers zum Gebrauch des gesunden Verstandes*, of 1773, observing among other things:

It is strange. Everybody thinks highly of common sense. Everybody appeals to it as a certain criterion of correctness. But we know it better by a kind of feeling than by investigation. Few have inquired what it might be; and those who have

35. Ibid., pp. 502f.
36. See Sulzer, *Vermischte philosophische Schriften*, vol. 2, pp. 66f. (in "Sulzer's Leben" by Blanckenburg).

done so, like Beattie in his *Essay*, recognize its value, but rely upon it as an inexplicable, or not fully explainable feeling, rather than trying to determine exactly what it is and what it is not, as they should do. It would indeed deserve the meditation of a philosophical mind.[37]

Resewitz is not satisfied with Beattie's discussion of common sense. But he grants that the Scotsman has at least tried to shed light on this neglected issue. And while he himself does not even try to give a more exact account of common sense because he thinks this would lead him too far away from his topic, the improvement of pedagogical practice, what he does offer as the rough outline of such a more exact account of common sense is deeply influenced by Beattie.[38]

Most of the Berliners appear to have been more impressed by Reid than by Oswald and Beattie. That they knew the contents of the *Inquiry* and assumed them to be well known is shown by the review of the German translation of Reid's *Inquiry* in the *Allgemeine deutsche Bibliothek* of 1783. It does not make any reference to the arguments or theories advanced by Reid, but restricts itself entirely to the evaluation of the quality of the translation. On comparison with the original, the reviewer find it very good and truthful to the English, though he notes a few minor mistakes.[39] Because the *Inquiry* was available in French (and, to some extent, also in English) philosophers could safely be assumed to know it.[40]

III

From the middle of the seventies onwards the Scottish trio, Reid, Oswald, and Beattie, had acquired notoriety in Germany as the enemies

---

37. Resewitz, *Erziehung*, p. 20; see also the review of this work in *Allgemeine deutsche Bibliothek*, vol. 22, i (1774): 325ff., especially 327.

38. He differentiates clearly between "common sense," on the one hand, and "healthy understanding," on the other. Common sense "is the embodiment of those principles which man has unconsciously collected from his intuition, his natural sensations, and the immediate judgments following them" (*Allgemeine deutsche Bibliothek*, p. 327) He characterizes common sense, very much like Beattie, as giving rise to "natural sensations" and "immediate judgments"; his account of healthy understanding is similar to the Wolffian account of *sensus communis*. But he could make a distinction similar to Reid's between common sense and common understanding. Compare with Eberhard's view.

39. Thomas Reid, *Untersuchung über den menschlichen Geist, nach den Grundsätzen des gemeinen Menschenverstandes* (Leipzig, 1782). Review: *Allgemeine deutsche Bibliothek* 52 (1783): 417.

40. See this chapter above.

of scepticism and idealism. Neither of these fashionable topics could be discussed without at least a passing reference to them. But not everyone agreed with their critique of scepticism and idealism, and not everyone was as well informed about Reid as about Oswald or Beattie. Thus Tiedemann rejected their theories as irrelevant and as being without any philosophical merit without any detailed knowledge of them, as is shown by the Introduction to the second volume of his *Untersuchungen über den Menschen*:

some regard the proofs of the Idealists as so superior that they have abandoned the way of argumentation altogether and have fought them only by appealing to the *consensus omnium*, using the new name "common sense" [*Menschen-Verstand*). In this way *Reid* and *Oswald* have, without being aware of it, conceded the victory to the Idealists. For, if the principles of the Idealists cannot be refuted by reasoning, an appeal to the general belief of the human species will not make them suspicious to the penetrating thinker.[41]

If common sense and reasoning are contradictory, we either have to agree to what reasoning shows to us, or we have to reject both the results of reasoning and the sentiments of common sense. But we can never rely upon common sense to overthrow the conclusion of a demonstrative proof.[42] For

the authority of common sense stands always upon very weak feet, and it cannot overturn the strength of irrefutable demonstrative proofs. . . . Nothing can supersede demonstrative and irrefutable proofs. We would fall into complete scepticism, if we were to take away the authority of these proofs.

Thus Tiedemann takes a strongly rationalistic position against any appeal to the opinion of the masses (or, at the very least, one that strongly resembles the stance taken by the reviewer in the *Allgemeine deutsche Bibliothek*). After having disposed of the Scots in this fashion, he goes on to boast that he has

believed it necessary to oppose the idealists not with common sense but with reasoning. One has already won much, if one can show to them that their proofs do not establish in any way what they are supposed to establish, and one

41. Tiedemann, *Untersuchungen*, vol. 2, p. iv.
42. This squarely contradicts what Zart maintains, namely, that Tiedemann "regards common sense and experience as the highest principles of knowledge, just like Irwing and Lossius" (*Einfluss*, p. 166). He also gives a wrong reference on pp. 167f. and seems to confuse Berkeley with Reid and Oswald.

has won completely if one opposes them then with still other and more powerful reasons. Both I have tried to do, and I flatter myself to have ended these disputes by these means.[43]

Given the general acquaintance of German philosophers with the works of the Scots, it cannot come as a surprise that Tiedemann was soon taken to task for his misinformed and boastful statements. In the *Erfurtische gelehrte Zeitung*, Tiedemann's reviewer confesses that he does "not know what to think with regard to these statements." He asks Tiedemann when the proofs of the idealists have actually come to be considered as irrefutable, not whether he is to believe that Tiedemann wishes to go so far as to claim that he was the first to oppose the idealists with reasoning. Perhaps, he goes on,

it was only supposed to hold of *Reid* and *Oswald*. But how can one corner an enemy better than by admitting so much of his view as can be done without endangering the truth, and then inferring the opposite conclusion from his principles, just as *Reid* has done it. And this did not happen completely without proofs . . . So much is true: not all non-idealists have had the aim of becoming involved in a bull-fight with the idealists. They have only listed principles with which idealism is not compatible. But this was not their main purpose. Who wants to accuse them of having conceded victory to the idealists because of this? Others did not think it worth their while to refute the idealists point by point, since their assertions are contrary to all sensation and all common sense, and they either made only mockery of them or said we have to start from a common point of departure if we want to reach agreement. This point of departure they regarded as the nature of our sensations and common sense. These two were thought to be the judge of these matters. But this, the author believes, is not the correct way.[44]

Tiedemann was so stung by this review that he found it necessary to give a rejoinder to it in the Appendix to the third volume of his *Untersuchungen*. There he argues that he had never claimed that he was the first who opposed the idealists with reasoning and arguments, and, furthermore, that he had not misrepresented the Scottish philosophy of common sense, since Oswald saw indeed "in common sense a criterion of truth which decided everything without reasoning, that he always opposed common sense to reasoning, and regarded its percep-

43. Tiedemann, *Untersuchungen*, vol. 2, pp. iv–v.
44. *Erfurtische gelehrte Zeitung*, 1778, vii (Thursday, 22 January): 57–62, 57f.

tions as intuitions which are not allowed to be further developed or proved."[45] To the charge that he had misrepresented Reid in particular, who had opposed the idealists with arguments, he answers: "in order to decide this completely I would have to have his book, but I do not have it."[46] With disingenuous generosity he concedes that Reid may have used arguments, but only to continue that, if he has, "then he has not been faithful to his basic principles."[47] For, "if one wants to refute scepticism and idealism with the weapons of common sense, one has to stop reasoning, or one does not say anything whatsoever."[48]

If Tiedemann's treatment of Reid was certain to cause some surprise, his actual reasoning against idealism is even stranger. Everything Tiedemann puts forth as "irrefutable proof" can already be found in some form or other in Beattie's *Essay*. But, while Beattie is clearly ironical, presenting his "arguments" to make fun of philosophers, Tiedemann seriously offers them as "powerful reasons."[49] Accordingly, the reviewer of the *Erfurtische gelehrte Zeitung* pointed out quite correctly that Tiedemann had, in fact, nothing new to offer and that his approach is just as much an appeal to common sense as that of the Scots.[50]

This episode makes clear, among other things, that Reid, Oswald and Beattie had both enemies and friends in Germany. Their arguments against scepticism and idealism did command some attention. But their effect upon the German views concerning idealism and scepticism in general and Berkeley and Hume in particular by no

45. Tiedemann, *Untersuchungen*, vol. 3, Anhang, p. 54.

46. It could perhaps be argued that Tiedemann is saying only that the *Inquiry* is not at his disposal at the moment. But would he not have said then that he does not remember what Reid said? In any cause, though it is more than likely that he heard of Reid in Göttingen, he cannot have studied him very carefully.

47. Ibid., p. 55.

48. Ibid. This reasoning is certainly strange. After admitting that he does not know Reid, he dares to accuse him of not being faithful to his basic principles. Moreover, even if Tiedemann's characterization of the structure of the appeal to common sense were correct ("common sense decides clearly that there is matter, therefore, you, the idealist, are out of your mind, when you maintain the contrary" ibid.), it is not clear why this should necessarily preclude any use of reasoning.

49. Compare, for instance, Beattie, *Essay*, pp. 284f., and 255 with Tiedemann, *Untersuchungen*, vol. 2, pp. 19–23, and 28–29. Both try to use food and wine as counter-examples against Berkeley.

50. *Erfurtische gelehrte Zeitung* pp. 59f. The reviewer argues that Tiedemann's arguments are also appeals to common sense and finds that "[i]n this way the dispute has long ago been resolved by Reid, Beattie, Search, and others."

means exhaust the Scottish influence. How the Scots were found relevant for German problems can perhaps best be seen by turning briefly to Garve and his discussion of the Scottish theory of perception.

Garve was one of the Germans who was greatly interested in Scottish philosophy from about 1770 until the very end of his life. Thus in his Inaugural Address in 1770 to the University of Leipzig, *Legendorum philosophorum veterum praecepta nonnulla et exemplum,* he called attention to Reid's critique of the theory of ideas and his common-sense approach to philosophy.[51] And his highly successful translation of Ferguson's *Institutes of Moral Philosophy* (1772) contained an extensive and sympathetic, though somewhat misleading note on Reid's theory of sensation.

Starting from a characterization of Berkeley, who, Garve thinks in agreement with Reid, has been led to deny the reality of bodies because of his acceptance of ideas as mediating mental entities, he points out that

Reid . . . admits Berkeley's premisses, but denies the conclusion . . . no sensation can really be similar to the quality of the body by which it has been occasioned. But he concludes from this: since none of the sensations are, in any special sense, pictures of the objects, they are all equally arbitrary signs of them. Nature has determined that we should have concepts of objects only through these signs, that we must think them whether we want to or not, and this despite the fact that our sensations do not resemble the qualities of bodies in the way in which a picture resembles its original—all this shows that bodies must exist. Otherwise we would not be able to give any reason whatsoever for this necessary and arbitrary representation of outer objects.

Garve also points out that Reid and his follower Ferguson re-affirm Locke's distinction between primary and secondary qualities as real:

In all sensations, Ferguson says, I ascribe certain qualities to bodies. These qualities are seen as the occasions of the sensations. This is shown by the common usage of our language, which ascribes warmth and colour to the body. But while there are some sensations with regard to which I only suppose what the quality would consist of, as for example with regard to warmth and colour, there are others which I do not only assume but conceptualize, such as figure and solidity.

51. Garve, *Legendorum philosophorum veterum. Praecepta nonnulla et exemplum* (1770). Reviewed in the *Göttingische Anzeigen* of 8 November 1771. Reprinted in Fülleborn's *Beyträge zur Geschichte der Philosophie.* The section on Reid is to be found on pp. 195f.

This matter, if pursued, would lead us too far astray, for there is indeed still some obscurity here which would warrant perhaps a more exact investigation of the senses and their instruments . . .[52]

Garve's discussion turned out to be quite influential for the further development of German thought. For it was essentially this "more exact investigation of the senses and their instruments" that was to preoccupy German philosophers during the next decade, and the works of Reid often provided not only the starting point, but also some valuable suggestions for the attempted solutions.[53]

52. Adam Ferguson, *Grundsätze der Moralphilosophie, übersetzt und mit einigen Anmerkungen versehen von Christian Garve* (Leipzig, 1772), pp. 320ff.

53. This is especially true for Tetens.

IV

The Scots in Göttingen

I

GIVEN the reception of the works by Scottish philosophers in the *Göttingische Anzeigen*, and given the close affiliation of the University of Göttingen, the "Georgia Augusta," with Britain, it is not surprising that the philosophers of Göttingen, Feder and Meiners, were closely acquainted with Scottish common-sense philosophy.[1] Meiners thought so highly of Beattie's *Essays* of 1776 that he edited a German translation of it in 1779.[2] His connections with the Scots must have been general knowledge at that time, for in his Introduction to it he says that Beattie does not need to be introduced to the German public, and "least of all" by him.[3]

Meiners is full of praise for the *Essays*, and he objects only to "the fierce polemical tone" of the *Essay on Truth*. While he "cannot agree to many of Beattie's principles," as developed in this philosophical polemic, he fully agrees to the results of Beattie's aesthetic inquiries. They are, he says "of all philosophical works on these topics the ones in

1. During the eighteenth century Hannover was actually part of the British Empire by "Personalunion." Accordingly, the university, founded in 1734 by a British ruler, had the closest links with Britain. By the 1770s it had become one of the most modern, most successful, and most respected institutions of higher learning in Germany. It was unique in Germany because of its Anglo-Saxon outlook, and it was of the greatest importance in the transmission of British thought to Germany. For an interesting account of the merits of the University of Göttingen see Gedicke's report to the Prussian ministry of education, which is available in English translation in *European Society in the Eighteenth Century*, ed. Forster and Forster, pp. 312–320.

2. Jakob Beattie, *Neue philosophische Versuche*, 2 vols. (Leipzig, 1779). The Vorrede makes clear that Meiners is not the actual translator.

3. Ibid., vol. 1, p. 7.

which I have found the greatest and most noticeable agreement with thoughts that I had thus far reason to call my own." And he observes: "if it did not sound conceited after these remarks . . . I would have no scruple to predict that every reader, even the most advanced thinker, will find new and important thoughts in every section."[4]

How important Beattie became to Meiners in aesthetic matters may be seen from his *Grundriss der Seelenlehre*, which appeared in 1786. Zart finds that Meiners relies on Beattie "in the representation of the laws of the association of ideas," that in his aesthetic theory he "appropriated Beattie's theory of instincts and followed Gerard's teachings only insofar as they are mediated by Beattie," and he sees him as consulting Beattie in his opposition to Berkeley and Hume as well as on "many other issues."[5] But this is, if anything, an understatement of Meiners's dependence on Beattie. One may go so far as to say that he consulted Beattie on every issue he raised—it is difficult to find any discussion in the *Grundriss* in which he does not refer directly or indirectly to Beattie. Section 3 of his sixth chapter, entitled "On Wit and Humour," for instance, reads as follows:

The ridiculous, the main object of wit or the comic does not happen without a certain incongruity [the last word is in English in the original]. But not every incongruity causes laughter or makes objects ridiculous (a). To be ridiculous, to become ridiculous, to be made ridiculous, are very different things. No object is so great that it cannot, by some parody or other, be made to appear ridiculous without really being so (b). Things can *become ridiculous* through incongruities of parts or qualities, or of the causes and effects between them (c), or with regard to space and time (d), or through incongruities resulting from relations of similarity or dissimilarity, identity or non-identity, dignity or baseness, greatness or smallness, and finally through diminishing and increasing (e).
(a) Beattie explains the ridiculous not quite correctly in my opinion. II, pp. 37, 38, 173.
(b) The opinion of Lord Shaftesbury is well known. See Home I, p. 484, Beattie at the passage already referred to, as well as pp. 69-71, 82-85, 99, 111, 112.
(c) Beattie I, c., pp. 54, 56, 124.
(d) Beattie I, pp. 58-61, 69-71, 83-85.[6]

4. Ibid., p. 9.
5. Zart, *Einfluss*, p. 153.
6. Christian Meiners, Grundriss der Seelenlehre (Lemgo, 1786), pp. 90f. Meiners mentions Beattie often. See pp. 49, 67, 73 (three times), 75 (four times), 77, 78, 79, 85, 86, 89 (twice), 92 (three times), 93 (twice), *etc., etc.* Lichtenberg spoke of Meiners's works as "paltry compilations."

Most other sections in this work exhibit the same dependence upon Beattie. Whether Meiners is dealing with memory, imagination, the distinction between reason and understanding, language, or truth and error, he always refers to the Scotsman and uses the latter's distinctions and arguments (even where he professes disagreement). It should perhaps also be pointed out that he does not use Beattie's doctrines and arguments in establishing new and interesting facts or theories. He simply repeats them with minor (and, quite often, pedantic) modifications.

Meiners also published a review of Beattie's *Dissertations Moral and Critical* in the *Göttingische Anzeigen* of October 1784. In it he notes that the style of "the excellent Scottish philosopher" is not as "concise and beautiful," and that the work does "not contain the wealth of new thoughts and observations, that one is used to from the *Essays*." The reason for this he sees in the fact that the *Dissertations* are only extracts, taken from Beattie's lectures. The review itself consists mainly of a summary of the contents of the work. The only further criticism he has to offer is that Beattie's explanations do not exhaust their subject matter.[7] It may therefore appear that Meiners could not make as much use of this work by the "excellent Scottish philosopher," and that he was a little disappointed for that reason.

Another Göttinger who appreciated Beattie just as much as Meiners was Lichtenberg.[8] He appears to have become more closely acquainted with Beattie's *Essay* during a visit to London in 1775, and then to have continued to study it upon returning to Göttingen in 1776. That he thought highly of Beattie and was, in fact, preoccupied with the latter's common-sense approach philosophy is shown by many of the aphorisms he wrote during this period.[9]

7. *Göttingische Anzeigen*, 1784, number 165 (14 October): 1649–54, 1649, 1654.

8. Commentators so far have almost completely neglected Lichtenberg's relations to Feder and Meiners. But they are important. Together, for instance, they founded a philosophical club. Even Mautner's comprehensive biography *Lichtenberg, Geschichte seines Geistes* manages to restrict references to Feder to four incidental remarks. For Lichtenberg's early, quite amicable relation with Feder and Meiners see Lichtenberg, *Schriften und Briefe*, vol. 4, pp. 281, 312, 313, 448, 733, as well as the aphorisms B 388, C 52 (I refer to the aphorisms according to this edition as well, though I use only the customary combination of letters and numbers).

9. See especially the following aphorisms in which Beattie is mentioned by name: Reisebemerkung 201, *Werke*, 2, p. 692; D 666, E 257, E 400, E 407, E 408, E 415, E 420, E 450; *Werke*, 3, p. 380; see also E 453 and E 338, E 377, E 380, E 460, E 513, F 56, F 202, F 204, F 205, F 233, F 245, F 323, F 441, F 448, H 142, J 251, J 439, L 401, which do not refer explicitly to Beattie, but which are clearly concerned with his view.

Commentators tend to discount Beattie's influence upon Lichtenberg as a short-lived "temporary disavowal of his own nature" without any lasting consequences. But there is reason to believe that the Scotsman was much more important to the German than that.[10] However that may be, it is significant that such an astute and sensible thinker as Lichtenberg, together with many of his contemporaries, felt that Beattie had something of importance to say:

Most that is good and useful can be done and said without leaving the diocese of Beattian philosophy; nay more than when we lose our way in exquisite subtleties. His philosophy is for human beings, the other for professors. Analysis of feeling.

To refute the sceptic is truly impossible. For, which argument in the whole world will convince the man who can believe absurdities? And, do all who want to be refuted deserve refutation? Not even the greatest rowdy fights with everyone who challenges him. These are the reasons why Beattian philosophy deserves esteem. It is not a completely new philosophy. It only starts higher. It is not the philosophy of the professor, but that of human beings.

And it is telling when he observes:

I do not want to determine whether the subtle metaphysical hair-splitters may be very good people, when the refutation of similar, but evil-minded, thinkers is needed. But I do know this much from my own limited experience: the most sensible people, the practical and powerful thinkers [*Starkdenker*] who always see the best without deception, the inventors of useful things, the trusted advisors who express themselves concisely and forcefully, all these people like the Beattian philosophy.[11]

Thus Lichtenberg, who, according to Herbert Schöffler, was brought "almost automatically to the gate of Kantian thought" by way of British philosophy, attests to the importance of Beattie in Göttingen (and, indirectly perhaps) for the developments of German thought that led up to Kant. Even if Lichtenberg's appreciation of Beattie did not last as long as that of Meiners or Feder—something that, at the very least, is debatable—his acceptance of certain tenets of Beattian philosophy was one stage on his way through British philosophy to Kant.[12]

10. See, for example, Grenzmann, *Johann Georg Lichtenberg*, and Mautner, *Lichtenberg*, pp. 244f., 208. This view is highly questionable, however.

11. E 411, E 418, E 403.

12. Schöffler, *Deutsches Geistesleben zwischen Reformation und Aufklärung*, p. 229; see also p. 228.

II

The most important philosophical influence of Scottish common-sense philosophers in Göttingen was on Feder. He knew the Scots well, as his many references to them throughout his works show.[13] Thus his important textbook *Logik und Metaphysik* of 1770 (2nd ed.) refers to Reid's *Inquiry* in the context of a discussion of truth and objective knowledge, noting that it is well worth reading. Indeed, its very last page has a reference to Oswald's *Appeal* that characterizes it as being opposed to "the barren and dangerous mania to demonstrate everything," and as falling perhaps into the other extreme, that is, "not rationally to investigate the connection of concepts and judgments, but to prefer to glean the truth from some sort of inner feeling or common sense."[14] Such remarks can be found in most of his works.[15]

How much Feder is aware of Reid and his followers, and how well he knows their works, can also be seen from one of his last reviews in the *Göttingische Anzeigen*—a review which, appropriately enough, concerns Reid's *Essays on the Intellectual Powers of Man*—Feder introduces the work as follows:

The author has been known for some time as the defender of the natural way of thinking against the exaggerated subtleties of speculative philosophy and the resultant wrong-headed [*verkehrte*] sceptical and dogmatic way of thinking. Indeed, he is known as the leader of the Scottish philosophers of this persuasion who have lately come into the fore. Moreover, his system is still entirely the same as that in his *Inquiry into the human mind* [*sic*]. Now he deals only more extensively with the higher faculties of cognition, whereas he was

13. Feder was clearly one of the most influential philosophers in Germany before the success of Kantian thought. His textbooks were used at many universities and went through numerous printings and editions. But after Kant's attack on the review of his first *Critique*, in which he had a hand in so far as he edited it, his reputation was irreparably damaged. See Feder, *Leben*, pp. 129ff. Feder's career is typical for that of philosophers of his generation. What happened to him suddenly was no more than what all the so-called "popular philosophers" went through sooner or later. Their reputation has not yet recovered from Kant's blow to it.

14. Feder, *Logik und Metaphysik nebst der philosophischen Geschichte im Grundrisse* (Göttingen, 1769, 2nd ed. 1770), pp. 256, 571f.; see also pp. 513f. I quote in accordance with the second edition.

15. See, for instance, Feder, *Institutionis logicae et metaphysicae* (Göttingen, 1781), pp. 12, 14, 28, 29, 79, 111, 258f., 320; *Leben*, p. 447; see also *Philosophische Bibliothek* 1 (1788): 219f.; 2 (1789): 83–118 (a review of Reid's *Essays on the Active Powers of the Human Mind*); and 4 (1791): 129–39.

more concerned with the external sense in the earlier work and showed the consequences of the resulting basic cognitions only in application and as they relate to the higher faculties of cognition.[16]

But Feder not only knew the Scots, he also appreciated them very much. In another review of the same work in the *Philosophische Bibliothek* he welcomes it as "the most important foreign product of speculative philosophy which has become known during the last years. It is the work of an old thinker, long famous in and out of England."[17] Confessing quite openly that Reid's philosophy has in many parts his highest approval, he never fails to call attention to the "great and meritorious aim" of the Scots. Nor does he make ever a secret of his belief that their "main thought is correct."[18]

His objections to the Scots appear to concern mainly their tone of criticism, and in particular their constant use of ridicule, irony and wit.[19] Thus he notes with satisfaction that the *Essays* of Reid are written in a cooler and much more detached style than his *Inquiry*. But he also objects to the Scots for wanting to declare too many doctrines to be basic truths, and does not like it that Reid, in a number of cases, relies too much upon his "favourite argument . . . from the universal characteristics of the languages to natural and basic cognitions." While Feder thinks that such inferences are actually correct in many cases, he also thinks that they must be used with greater care than Reid appears to do.[20]

16. *Göttingische Anzeigen*, 1787, number 63 (21 April): 626–30, pp. 626f. Since the reviews appeared anonymously, it cannot always be said with certainty whether Feder is the reviewer. But Feder says in his autobiography that he reviewed in the *Göttingische Anzeigen* from 1769 on. The reviews in the *Philosophische Bibliothek* have his *signum* "F," and he identifies himself in this journal as the author of the review in *Göttingische Anzeigen* of 21 April 1787. Further, the reviews of Beattie's *Essay* (28 January 1771) and of the German translation of Oswald's *Appeal* (13 August 1774 and 19 January 1775), found in the University of Göttingen's library copy of the *Göttingische Anzeigen*, contain notes in the margin (in an eighteenth-century hand) identifying Feder as their author. The reviewer of Priestley's *Examination* claims to be identical with the reviewer of Beattie's *Essay* and the German translation of Oswald's *Appeal*. He must therefore also be Feder. The *Göttingische Anzeigen* reviews of the original English edition of the *Appeal* do not, on the other hand, seem to be Feder's work.

17. *Philosophische Bibliothek* 1 (1788): 219.

18. *Göttingische Anzeigen*, 1774, number 97 (13 August): 835; and 1787, number 63 (21 April): 628.

19. See the previous chapter.

20. *Göttingische Anzeigen*, 1787, pp. 626, 628.

III

There are parallels between the Scots and Feder in his first works as well as in his last ones. He relies on Reid's principle of veracity in his discussion of the trustworthiness of human testimony.[21] He appropriates Reid's appeal to ordinary language and its distinctions and rules as relevant for metaphysics.[22] His understanding of scepticism and idealism is clearly coloured by Reid's account.[23] He accepts Reid's theory that our sensations and the objects do not stand in a pictorial relation and, just as Reid does, he accepts the validity of the distinction between primary and secondary qualities.[24]

But Feder never became a follower of the Scots in the sense of accepting all or even most of Reid's theory of knowledge. In fact, it is not even clear that he understood Reid's view in all its subtlety. Being really interested only in Reid's pronouncements on first truths, Feder neglects his analysis of perception (even though, as we have seen in Chapter I, Reid's first truths cannot be understood in isolation from his account of perception). As Zart points out, Feder in his early years "was not greatly interested in the investigation of problems of logic and the theory of knowledge and only later was he concerned to mediate between Locke and Wolff as well as between Reid and Hume."[25] Consequently, his appreciation of the details of Reid's theory appears to have developed slowly, even though there are references to Oswald and Reid in the earliest editions of his textbook on logic and metaphysics.

This has as much to do with the development of his own thought as it does with that of German philosophy in general. For the two aspects in

21. See especially Feder, *Logik und Metaphysik* (2nd ed., 1770), pp. 253ff.

22. Ibid., p. 231: "Since *instinct* is so opposed to the doubts concerning the existence of external objects, some people have considered it best to regard the idealists as madmen and not to honour them with a refutation . . . But what if the entire dispute is merely a verbal one?" See also *Göttingische Anzeigen*, 1775, p. 779: "The reviewer still believes that this peculiar dispute cannot be resolved in any other way than by showing how it is based solely upon words, and that the disputants are fully at one in the matter. Basically, this appears to have been Berkeley's opinion as well. However, one must have thought a great deal about our concepts of existence in order to find this treatment thorough." See also below.

23. See Feder, *Logik und Metaphysik*, pp. 227ff., especially p. 231 (quoted in note 19 above), where he seems to allude to the Scots. He refers to Reid by name several pages later.

24. See the following, especially the passages quoted from *Logik und Metaphysik*.

25. Zart, *Einfluss*, p. 129.

Reid that appeared most important to him were also the two aspects that turned out to be most significant for the German philosophical discussion during the last third of the eighteenth century. These were the problem of idealism and the problem of the justification of the basic principles of human knowlege.

Because Feder does not entirely agree with the Scots' account of knowledge, it is impossible for him to accept all of their solution to these two problems. Whereas the Scots think that, though all knowledge begins with sensation, it need not be derived entirely from sensation, he believes that external and internal sensation are the only original sources of knowledge. Reason can only work with the materials supplied by these senses and has therefore only a limited function. The function of reason or "higher cognition" is "to find the concepts which sensation does not give to us immediately, though their basis already lies in sensation." Therefore "the sensations always have to remain authoritative in particular cases in so far as we can neither demonstrate their existence away, nor can overturn our accepted rules by reason. For the general propositions have to be based upon the agreement of particular sensations." To illustrate the relation between these two basic faculties Feder uses an allegory:

Sensation is like a sailor who always keeps close to the coast, reason like a sailor who crosses the ocean. If there is more danger in the latter, there is also more hope of gain. But the *basic laws of sensation* must be to reason what the compass is to the sailor.[26]

Thus for Feder sensation not only provides the materials for all rational thought, it also remains the guide of reason in the formation of general conceptions. Even the principles of truth, justice, and beauty are not so much principles of reason as principles of sensation. We feel what is true, what is just, and what is beautiful. We know it immediately and not through discursive thought. Our human understanding is essentially tied to sensation and to think as a human being means for Feder to think in accordance with our sensations and feelings and the laws which govern them. Reason has to stay within the bounds of sense, and "if reason opposes the natural sensation, it works against itself and is no longer *healthy* reason."[27] All this shows how the Scottish concep-

26. Feder, *Logik und Metaphysik*, pp. 242, 247.
27. Ibid. Compare with Lichtenberg E 415, E 420, E 450: "We should follow our feeling . . . insofar I recommend Beattian philosophy." See also E 456.

tion of a common *sense* with certain basic laws became of importance to Feder, and informed his response to idealism.

The main enemies of common sense and all sound philosophy, in Feder's view, are idealism and scepticism. Their refutation is one of the most important goals of his philosophy. In fact, it would not be entirely inappropriate to call his philosophy "anti-idealism."[28] But in his earliest works it is not quite clear whether he actually knows any idealistic philosopher first hand. For instance, in the second edition of his textbook on logic and metaphysics (1770) he does not yet mention Berkeley, whom he later regards as the idealist *par excellence*, but simply refers to "the idealist." It could very well be that he knows of the position of this "idealist" only through secondary sources, that is, mainly through Oswald and Reid.[29]

In any case, though he finds it necessary to argue against this position of the sceptical idealist, he also believes that "the dispute with the sceptic is usually made more difficult than it has to be, since philosophers want to prove too much and do not allow the sceptics to be correct where they are correct." The real problem must be seen as follows:

Nobody seems to have gone so far as to deny his own existence and the existence of the sensations of which he is aware. The existence of the qualities which we notice in the sensations cannot be denied either. That we feel some things with pleasure, others with repulsion, others as external, cannot be doubted. But all this means in general terms only that *we sense what we sense actually as we sense it, or: whatever appears appears.* But whether what appears is real, whether there really are objects external to us, and if there are, whether they are of the kind they appear to us to be, and finally whether there is truth and foundation for science in this appearance in and for itself, about this one can dispute.[30]

Yet Feder believes he is in possession of an effective weapon against these doubts. More exactly, he employs a strategy very like Reid's, arguing that the idealists have fallen victim to a confusion of language.

But the actual arguments advanced by Feder are not at all the same.

28. Tiedemann, a student of Feder and Meiners, is actually characterized as "anti-idealist" by his biographer. What holds of Tiedemann to some extent also holds of Feder.

29. But compare his later view as expressed in his reviews. See note 22 above.

30. Feder, *Logik und Metaphysik*, pp. 228f.

Answering the idealist, he says:

As far as I can see, you have the same representations of objects as I have. You see them as though they were external to yourself. This is proved by your behaviour with regard to them. You know very well the difference between a merely occasional or temporary appearance which is refuted by the much more constant appearance and by countless other representations, and the many things which constantly appear in the same way in innumerable instances and innumerable persons, as long as they are in an orderly frame of mind. These latter appearances are in accordance with the nature and end of human beings. This constant appearance in the orderly and most perfect state of human nature as well as in true sensation I call, with the rest of humanity "being." And this you call, together with a few others, incorrect. But if it does not cause any discomfort to call "being" what appears to all humans in this way ... why do you not want to speak as all other people speak, and why do you want to cause confusion in our whole system of concepts and thoughts by banishing one word?[31]

When compared to Reid's analysis of the matter, Feder's sounds naive and ill informed. Though the last appeal to the idealist puts him in very much the same league as Oswald and Beattie, his preceding analysis shows that he has very little in common with them. While they rejected any form of mediating entity, such as "idea" or "appearance," Feder relies on these.[32] His entire argument amounts to claiming that "constant appearance in sensation" means "to be." But this does not seem to be very different from Berkeley's claim that "to be" is "to be perceived." Whereas Berkeley, arguing against materialism, said that to be is to be perceived, Feder, arguing against what he takes to be idealism, says that to be perceived (in a certain way) is to be (at least for us and our limited minds). This reversal does not add anything new. Nevertheless, his strictures appear to have been generally accepted as realism, while Berkeley's position was commonly rejected as idealism, probably because the Germans did not know the writings of the "idealist" Berkeley very well.

After having established the reality of "external" objects in this way, Feder goes on to show that the qualities of objects are real in the same sense. It is quite clear to him that we cannot perceive things as they are in themselves, "for we sense only a modification of ourselves, even

31. Ibid., pp. 231f.
32. See especially Beattie, *Essay*, pp. 283–85.

though we usually say that we sense an object."[33] But this only means that "the true qualities of objects, which cause our sensations, are not revealed through sensation, and that through sensation we only know what an object is for our organs [of sensation]."[34] Since appearance is the only possible reality for us, we must also be allowed to attribute those qualities which constantly recur to the objects themselves.

In his review of Beattie's *Essay* of 1771, Feder comments also on Reid's rejection of the theory of ideas. Here it is clear that Reid is too radical for his tastes: the theory of ideas "could very well be correct, even though we can easily go wrong in its interpretation and employment." And in his review of Priestley's *Examination* he claims that the differences between Reid and Berkeley can be resolved by "showing how this dispute depends entirely upon words, and that the disputants are completely at one in the matter, which basically appears to have been Berkeley's opinion as well."[35]

Thus Feder does not accept Reid's argument that the theory of ideas necessarily leads to idealism and scepticism. He thinks it a mere historical accident that Berkeley and Hume have followed Descartes and Locke. The "theory of ideas" is very difficult to understand and employ, but it can be made to work—and one of the things Feder sets out to do is just to interpret and employ the theory correctly.

Hence, when Feder claims in his *Über den Raum und die Caussalität* that he never "was an anti-idealist of the usual sort" and that he always opposed the "supposed *demonstrations* of the reality of the world of objects," and therefore agrees "*in substance* with Kant on *most* points regarding idealism," he is not being disingenuous. His realism is not so

33. Feder, *Logik und Metaphysik*, p. 233.

34. Ibid., p. 234. Compare this with Lossius.

35. *Göttingische Anzeigen*, 1771, p. 91, 1775, p. 779; see also 1787, pp. 627f.(in the context of a review of Reid): Reid's "main attack is still directed at the principle that the ideas are the immediate object of all perceptions of the soul. This he regards as the basic error of philosophers like Hume, Berkeley, Locke, Malebranche, Descartes. (Here is still more verbal dispute than the author seems to notice, and his investigation is not varied enough, especially with regard to the several kinds of pathological illusion). Indeed, 'idea' is not the fitting expression for the most inner modifications from which the perceptions of the soul originate. To say that all objects of sense perception are ideas is to sacrifice the fact, to deny consciousness, to confuse language, and all this for a hypothesis. But if these modifications, which originate from sensations and sensible perceptions, remembrances and judgments of all kinds, depend to a much greater extent upon these ideas, they have less of an immediate basis than the author wants to maintain."

radically different from Kant's empirical realism/transcendental idealism as is usually thought. In fact, the only criticism he has to make is
that Kant has removed himself too far and "without need" from the
common way of talking about this matter.[36]

By contrast, in his conception of healthy reason or common sense
which forms the basis for his theory of truth, Feder is very close to the
Scottish conception of common sense. Throughout all of his philosophical works he emphasizes that he is convinced of the importance of
the Scottish theory that common sense consists of certain basic
principles or first truths. Thus in 1771, in his review of Beattie's *Essay*,
he argues: "the conception of truth, that truth for us is what we have to
believe and falsity what we are forced to reject, can be reduced to a
correct principle."[37] In 1774, in his review of the German translation of
Oswald's *Appeal*, he finds "there are basic truths, immediately evident
propositions; our mind has the ability to know them and is therefore
forced to accept them. . . ." We should not attempt to prove them
because they are intuitively certain; "all this is correct."[38] And in 1788,
in his review of Reid's *Essays on the Intellectual Powers*, he claims that the
chapter on basic truths is the most interesting one as well as the one
from which the characteristic outlook of Reid's philosophy mainly
derives.[39]

But this basic agreement of Feder with the Scots does not mean that
he uncritically accepts their entire account of common sense and truth.
He advances several fundamental criticisms, thus modifying the
Scottish view considerably.

First of all, Feder rejects Beattie's claim that common sense constitutes a special human faculty, a kind of intuition, different from our
rational faculty. The "differentiation between the *sensus communis* and
the faculty of inference is somewhat too hastily made," he finds.[40]
Common sense, according to Feder, is rather a certain part or aspect of
our understanding. Secondly, he thinks the Scots have failed to

36. Feder, *Raum und Caussalität*, p. 65.
37. *Göttingische Anzeigen*, 1771, p. 95; see also pp. 91f. Feder finds, however, that
Beattie's formulation of this principle remains ambiguous. Meiners, by the way, rejects
basic principles in general, and Beattie's special form of them in particular. See his
Grundriss der Seelenlehre, p. 182. Zart, *Einfluss*, p. 134, ascribes mistakenly Meiners's point
of view to Feder.
38. *Göttingische Anzeigen*, 1774, p. 834.
39. *Philosophische Bibliothek* 1 (1788): 43.
40. *Göttingische Anzeigen*, 1771, p. 93. Compare with Zart, *Einfluss*, p. 131.

determine the nature and the extent of the first truths carefully enough. Therefore they have, among other things, been led to assume too many first truths. Thus they include immediate inferences from basic truths among basic truths. But these immmediate inferences can be doubted. In fact,

all propositions which are not basic truths in the strictest sense can be doubted in a certain manner and for some time without [creating] nonsense; they can be proved or justified by giving reasons (either apagogic or apodictic, a priori or a posteriori ones).[41]

Basic truths in the strictest sense, by contrast, are not capable of proof. They are of such a kind that "our understanding must accept them without any reasoning whatsoever." Therefore,

such propositions can only be those which indicate what lies immediately in inner and outer sensation, and which indicate this only as an appearance [*Schein*]. It seems to me that there are such and such things; I am aware that the whole is equal to all its parts. About such propositions we cannot dispute. Moreover, nobody who has understood the meanings of the words in these propositions has ever doubted them seriously.

But to say, for instance, that what appears to us in sensation really does exist means already to draw a conclusion. "It is an inferred truth, a judgment which has its real logical reason in the mediating thought that the mediating expression 'externally existing visible objects' should not and cannot mean anything other than just this conscious and enduring appearance of the natural sensations." Even the principle of the constancy of nature is an inference, or a judgment presupposing reasoning:

The proposition that the same conjunction of objects, qualities and changes which we have observed thus far will hold always and everywhere, a proposition upon which most of our inferred knowledge about reality is based, is in itself in no way a first principle in the strictest sense. To some extent it has its basis in the natural association of ideas. And this is the only basis Hume assigns to this proposition. In doing so he has caused not only much commotion, but has also occasioned all the lively activities of the preachers of common sense and the fear of the proposition that all our knowledge is based

41. *Göttingische Anzeigen*, 1774, p. 837; see also *Philosophische Bibliothek* 1 (1788): 54.

upon particular perceptions [*Gewahrnehmungen*] of sensation. But this proposition is also based upon imitation. It has its logically sufficient reason, on the one hand, in the fact that we cannot regard that which has never happened as a certain possibility and, on the other hand (and most importantly) in the experience that the causal proposition is never, or, at least, very rarely deceptive, and that we are much better off in accepting it than we would be in accepting any other proposition.[42]

For Feder "all our general propositions concerning nature, and especially the law of causality, are nothing but extended experience."[43] But this extending of particular experiences into general propositions does, of course, presuppose certain principles which allow us to differentiate between valid and invalid extensions.

These "basic principles of the human understanding" are "the generally accepted law of contradiction and the principle of sufficient reason."[44] They are, in fact, the only two immediate principles of common sense Feder is willing to admit. As he had earlier remarked in his review of Beattie's *Essay*:

to accept only a few propositions as immediate principles, as *principia formalia veritatis*, namely those which everybody accepts as such, and to prove with their help all the others (at least whenever this is requested), is in final analysis better than declaring very many propositions as immediately evident, as our author does, together with most patrons of common sense. In any case, exacting investigators of the soul know how rare are the really immediate and pure judgments of sensation [*Empfindungsurteile*].[45]

The differences between Feder and Reid arise mainly from two circumstances. First of all, Feder was influenced by Wolff and firmly convinced of the validity of the laws of contradiction and sufficient reason. Even though he rejects the method of trying to deduce all human knowledge from these two first truths (as the earlier rationalists had done) he still believes that everything can be explained by means of these two principles and the materials given in sensation. Because he feels so confident in this he can reject Reid's principles of common sense as too numerous.

Secondly, Feder rejected the Scottish critique of the theory of ideas

42. *Göttingische Anzeigen*, 1774, pp. 835ff.
43. Feder, *Raum und Caussalität*, p. 166.
44. Ibid., p. 167.
45. *Göttingische Anzeigen*, 1771, p. 95.

and attempted instead to revise it in such a way that the critique no longer applied. In this he is also rather close to Hume, whose moderate scepticism is not too distant from Feder's. Thus Feder is not much worried by the essentially Humean view that our belief in causal relations is based on repeated observations of succesions of ideas.

But it is doubtful whether he saw the full force of Reid's critique because he did not seem to understand that, if this critique is correct, the theory of ideas cannot be saved by means of minor terminological changes. Though he claimed that much thinking was necessary to see that the ideal theory involved a fundamental confusion of language, it is not clear that he himself gave enough thought to this matter. Instead, he more or less followed Locke, going on as though Reid had not said much of value in his critique of the way of ideas, and in doing so even thought he was more thorough than the Scots. Since not all principles of common sense are basic principles or first truths in the strictest sense, and since only two of them are constitutive of the human mind, Feder did not equate the appeal to common sense with an appeal to irreducible truths that are not in need of any justification.

For this reason he could hold that his appeal to common sense does not block the further investigation into the origin and scope of human knowledge. For him, to say that a judgment is a judgment of common sense only means that it is more basic than most others and is therefore accepted by everyone.

It was in this way that the *justification of common sense* became a problem for Feder. While the Scots could not have thought of anything more preposterous than a *justification* of common sense, to him—and most other German philosophers—such a justification appeared a natural and necessary enterprise. In the details of this justification he is greatly dependent upon Locke and Wolff, and hence has little original to offer. But it is most significant that he recognized the importance of the problem of basic truths and their relationship to, and role in, knowledge.

What is also significant is that Feder's conception and formulation of this problem were highly dependent on Reid, Oswald, and Beattie, and that these philosophers also provided him with hints for his attempted solution. But because he was not able to free himself from the views and theories of his predecessors, he did not get very far in the development of an original system.[46]

46. His philosophy remained in a very real sense a "critique of books and systems" (Kant, Axii).

None of this should suggest that Feder was simply a shallow and indifferent mediator of British influences in Germany. He was a responsible thinker who tried his best to develop a consistent synthesis of German rationalism and British empiricism. His intentions were not very different from those of Kant in his pre-critical period, and his problem can be usefully compared to what the latter called Hume's problem.

That Feder found the Scottish theory of common sense as basic principles of knowledge important for his synthesis, and thus considered it relevant for the goals of German philosophy at this time, is certainly of great significance for the understanding of the further development of German thought during the eighteenth century. For, whatever else may be said of Feder, he brought the problem of first principles of knowledge as principles of common sense into the focus of philosophy. He may not have been entirely clear about these principles himself, but he was clear enough for other philosophers to follow. He saw the importance of these principles, and by showing with Reid and Beattie that they are essentially connected with sensation, he argued that pure reason could not be considered as an absolute and infallible criterion of truth. Though he appeared to want to criticize philosophy on the basis of common sense, he usually simply used common sense as a regulative device, as is shown by his two rules, according to which we should govern all our thought: (1) be cautious and do not accept opinions which contain a contradiction, and (2) examine the basis of your judgments. Take care that they are not based upon fleeting appearances, but upon natural representations. The maxim "Be guided by the *firmly founded* and unchanging parts of your inner and outer perception," he says, "can therefore be regarded as the basic rule that contains everything needed for the correct use of the human understanding or common sense."[47] And it was certainly this *regulative* principle that guided Feder in his criticisms of philosophical systems. Thus, though he recognized very clearly that Reid "attacked the basic principles not only of Locke's, but of all philosophy," he himself wanted to continue to philosophize in a more moderate, but still very traditional way.[48]

47. Feder, *Raum und Caussalität*, pp. 266–68; see also Feder *Leben*, p. 249.
48. *Göttingische Anzeigen*, 1775, p. 777.

V

Scottish Common Sense and German Sensationism

I

THE GERMAN PHILOSOPHER who went farthest in the acceptance of physiological explanations of the workings of the human mind was Lossius. He is considered as the most radical materialist philosopher of the German enlightenment, and his most significant work, *Die physischen Ursachen des Wahren* of 1774, is often taken as the example of a materialistic philosophy in eighteenth-century Germany.[1] It is said that in this work the last step is taken in the direction of replacing the key disciplines of logic, ethics, and theology with anthropology and psychology. Because Lossius appears, for example, to explain contradictions as "conflicts of nerves," his work is considered to be something of an oddity, or as an unwitting *reductio ad absurdum* of crude materialism.[2] But the work has also been acknowledged by Ernst Cassirer as significant in its own right, and warrants a closer examination, if only for the important role it played in the philosophical discussions of its time.[3]

---

1. See Beck, *Early German Philosophy*, p. 332n. See also Cassirer, *Enlightenment*, pp. 116f.

2. See, for instance, Beck, *Early German Philosophy*, p. 332n.; and Cassirer, *Das Erkenntnisproblem*, vol. 2, pp. 448–56.

3. See Buhle, *Geschichte*, vol. 4, pp. 565f. and von Eberstein, *Versuch einer Geschichte*, vol. 1, pp. 328–38. See also the review of *Physische Ursachen* in *Göttingische Anzeigen*, 1775, number 62 (25 May): 525f. and Tetens, *Philosophische Versuche*, pp. 520, 530–33. In comparison with his first work, all his other publications are of lesser importance. His second major work, *Unterricht der gesunden Vernunft*, 2 vols. (Gotha, 1776–77), is actually

Even though Lossius professes to follow strictly the method of observation, even though he developed a clear-cut theory and is far removed from being an indifferentist, he also adhered to the eclectic and popular approach to philosophy.[4] He depended upon others to supply him not only with his issues but also with his theories. His originality consists therefore not so much in the creation of a completely new theory, but rather in a new, and perhaps unexpected or surprising, combination of known theories. By far the most important contributors to his thought are Bonnet and Beattie.[5] Their works, together with Garve's German translation of Ferguson's *Institutes of Moral Philosophy*, are the ones that are most frequently quoted, and his philosophical system can be characterized as the attempt at a synthesis of the common-sense approach with a materialistic account of human nature. He seems to want to supply Beattie's theory of truth with a foundation in the physiological organization of man. More particularly, he is trying to show the physiological basis of Beattie's "instinct" by appealing to the theories of Hartley, Priestley, Condillac, and Bonnet.

He hopes to establish by means of his materialistic reduction the manner in which "our conception of *reality* is *rooted in the categories of our understanding without having to vanish into complete subjectivity.*"[6] In this way he also hopes to be able to develop a theory of truth which would answer the sceptic once and for all. Cassirer believes that in this attempt of Lossius a "novel conception" is revealed, which, though "still completely embedded in unclear and dogmatic presuppositions," became centrally important for the German enlightenment (and, in

---

only a compendium for the use of his students in connection with his lectures. But it appears to have been successful as a book, even though its character, and need of explication, are very evident. Thus he says in his discussion of the distinction between primary and secondary qualities: "Of what Locke, Berkeley, Reid, Ferguson and Garve have said . . . we will talk in the lectures" (*Unterricht*, vol. 1, p. 245). The reviewer of this work in the *Gottingische Anzeigen*, 1777 (7 August): 747–51, notes that Lossius is in it much more moderate in his use of physiological explanations than in the earlier one.

4. The method of observation is "the only one possible in these matters" (*Physische Ursachen*, Preface). Compare also with Meiners, *Revision*, p. 53.

5. Beattie is quoted or mentioned by name on pp. 3, 7, 15, 27, 59, 145, 230, 236, 238; Reid is referred to on pp. 3, 7, 55, 95. See also *Unterricht*, vol. 1, pp. 245, 33f.; vol. 2, p. 159.

6. Cassirer, *Erkenntnisproblem*, vol. 2, p. 451 (emphasis mine).

fact, for the theory of knowledge in general) when better formulated by Tetens.[7]

Lossius's synthesis of the common-sense approach and materialism attempts to keep two levels of explanation as independent of each other as possible. There is, first of all, the attempt to give a psychologically or phenomenologically correct description of the human mind, its concepts and its principles, and an attempt to unify this into a consistent theory of truth. Secondly, there is an attempt to explain the features established by description, where *to explain* means *to reduce to human physiology*. Beattie's *Essay* is especially important for the descriptive level of his theory. In fact, Lossius depends to such an extent on Beattie that one might be tempted to speak of unqualified acceptance and simple repetition.

The very Introduction of the *Physische Ursachen* bears witness of the fundamental importance of the Scots for Lossius. Since he develops his theory of truth as a defense against sceptical arguments, he begins with a short historical account of the opposition between sceptics and and dogmatists. While the dogmatical and sceptical philosophers are usually seen to be so radically opposed to each other that no fruitful discussion could have taken place, Lossius finds that this is wrong. Actually, the *arguments* of the dogmatists and the sceptics are not all that different; only the *conclusions* differ radically. Skeptics and dogmatists have always learned more from each other than they cared to admit. As Carneades confessed that he could not have developed his theory without Chrysippus, so, Lossius believes, one might say in more recent times that

perhaps *Beattie* and *Hume* stand in the opposite relation to each other as Carneades and the Stoic Chrysippus; and *Reid* would perhaps not be the one he is, if *Berkeley* had not existed. *Beattie* opposes instinct to Humean doubt, and *Reid assumes Berkeley's* principles for doubting the reality of bodies, and he proves the opposite argument. But all this does not satisfy someone like *Garve*. This excellent philosopher still sees darkness where they see light.[8]

The discussions of the sceptics and the dogmatists show not only that a simple affirmation or negation of absolutely certain criteria is a fruitless exercise, but they also can supply us with hints for the solution

7. Ibid.
8. Lossius, *Physische Ursachen*, p. 3.

of the problem of truth. Lossius believes he has learned enough to see that there is a middle way in the doctrine of truth, a way "which shows itself as soon as we differentiate between the reality of objects, their representations, and the way in which representations of things originate within ourselves."[9] This distinction allows us to see that we should not be concerned with the reality of external objects when dealing with truth. This so called "metaphysical truth" is in reality no truth, but a necessary presupposition of all talk of truth.[10] As such, it clearly cannot be investigated by us. All that is left for us to examine is truth attainable by human beings, that is, truth dependent upon the presupposition of the existence of things in themselves. But such an investigation must be concerned mainly with our representations of objects, with their mode of origination, and with their relation to our judgments and concepts.

Instead of identifying truth in perception with the reality of external objects, we should realize, Lossius argues, that truth is the relation, or, perhaps better, is a property of the relation between ourselves and these external objects. All truth attainable for human beings must be relative; and it must be relative in two respects: (1) it must be of things which are related to us and (2) it must be truth in accordance with our (human) mental organization, i.e. we cannot know truth absolutely but only truth as it is for us.[11] These two ways in which truth is relative are closely connected for him. They are aspects of one and the same problem. But he argues for them separately; and the discussion of both aspects shows a pronounced dependence upon the arguments and theories of Reid, Beattie, and Ferguson.

To bring home the second point, Lossius compares human beings to complicated machines, such as clocks. Just as clocks work in accordance with certain fixed laws dependent upon their mode of construction, so human beings have to perform their actions in accordance with laws governing their physical and mental organization. The only difference between men and machines consists in the fact that men can know certain things about their internal constitution, while we do not usually

9. Ibid., p. 6.

10. This should not be taken to mean that the existence of external objects is doubted in any way by Lossius. He thinks, on the contrary, "the existence of objects alone has absolute certainty" (*Physische Ursachen*, p. 234).

11. Ibid., pp. 6f. Compare with Meiners, *Revision*, p. 242, Lichtenberg, Aphorisms C 236 and L 253, and the passages of Feder quoted in the previous chapter. Lossius knows, of course, of the connection between Feder and Beattie.

assume this of machines. But even here the difference is far from being absolute. For, "as soon as we admit that man is a finite being, we also have to admit that we demand something impossible when we ask him for an exact analysis of his inner constitution. Only for the creator of human nature are we what the machine is for the artisan." It depends only upon God "how far human beings can go in spiritual perfection, in the knowledge of truth and what is truth for them. And this is how I understand *Beattie* when he says: the truth does not depend upon man, but upon the creator of nature."[12] In fact, this second aspect of Lossius's claim that truth is only truth in relation to our mental organization is nothing but a variation of Beattie's claim that truth is that "which the constitution of my nature determines me to believe and falsity that which the constitution of my nature determines me to disbelieve."[13] Lossius himself underscores this when he draws attention to his belief that "Beattie is correct," and that he is, as he himself admits, basically expanding on what he understands Beattie to say.[14]

In order to support his view that, essentially, truth is only possible through a relation between ourselves and objects, Lossius offers a sort of ordinary language argument. He maintains that it would be nonsensical to speak of truth in abstraction from human beings and objects. In a world without human beings and without objects the notion of truth could not arise. Truth without humans and objects "does not constitute a concept at all." Objects in complete isolation from humans would be whatever they are, but they would be neither true nor false. In the same way, for a mind without any body and any relation to other objects no other truth than perhaps that of its own existence would arise.[15] Truth and knowledge require both a subject and an object, and when we talk of truth, we are not concerned with objects in themselves, but with the relation of objects to ourselves.

The appeal to ordinary language is reminiscent of Reid. And Lossius appears to be just as dependent upon Reid here as he was in the discussion of the first aspect. If there were any doubts, they would be dispelled by the following passage, in which he finds that

12. Ibid., p. 15; see also pp. 27, 59, 85f., 145, 228–32, 238, and 255.
13. Beattie, *Essay*, p. 30.
14. Lossius, *Physische Ursachen*, p. 59; see also p. 27.
15. Ibid., pp. 16f. But even this is doubtful to him. For it is not clear whether a mind "could be the object of its own observation without being connected to a body. For we have no reason to suppose that the mind could think or be capable of securing materials for observation without a body" (p. 17).

it is not necessary to note that each organ notifies us of the being of bodies which are essentially different from our own body. If the objects which cause our sensations were not really existing externally to us, we could not understand how these sensations could arise as effects within us, as *Reid* has maintained.[16]

Lossius's next step is to determine the relationship between the knowing subject and the known object in greater detail. The mind or "the substance which thinks in ourselves" cannot experience things directly or immediately. It can only do so by means of its organs of perception, the nerves and the brain. Thus, "with regard to its cognitions the soul can be no more than what the body allows it to be."[17] This brings us back to the second aspect of truth. Even though truth is possible only because of a relation between subject and object, it is really only the subject that is open for examination. For we cannot be certain whether things are actually as we perceive them.

Whether or not the objects really are as we think they are does not matter, but only whether we are capable of thinking of them in a way different from that in which we actually do think of them. It would have been possible for the creator of nature . . . to fit the human eye in such a way that a space delineated by three lines appeared circular. We would be just as proud of the certainty in our cognition then as we are now. For, who is qualified to say whether the objects do not also possess other qualities than those we can perceive now. . . . The proposition "these objects are contradictory" implies therefore only what they are for our organs. Otherwise, they may, in their nature, really be this way or not. Nothing depends on this here. *Reid* has proved the former some time ago.[18]

Since Reid has proved to Lossius's satisfaction that "our ideas are not to be regarded as copies or pictures of the external objects," the dispute about the nature of things in themselves is an idle one for Lossius.[19] We have to concentrate upon the nature of our representations and concepts.

In the further characterization of these representations and concepts Lossius shows even greater dependence upon Beattie. He argues that our representations allow us to know one thing about the external

16. Ibid., p. 95.
17. Ibid., p. 18.
18. Ibid., pp. 54f.
19. Ibid., p. 72. Compare also Zart, *Einfluss*, p. 158.

objects, namely that they exist. Of this we can be just as sure as of our own existence. Using the very arguments and examples employed by Beattie, he seeks to establish that this knowledge of the existence of objects is "a basic fact, which has to precede all investigations. Without it we could not explain the origin and development of thought. Our nature forces us, if we listen attentively, to accept the real being of matter and the world of objects without further investigation." And where Beattie had argued that the idealist who attempted "to get out of the way of a coach and six horses at full speed . . . acts just as inconsistently with his belief, as if he ran away from the picture of an angry man, even while he believed it to be a picture," Lossius finds that "anyone who would want to regard the material world as a bundle of ideas and thus give only ideal existence to the world, deserves as little a refutation as the person who sees a horse racing towards himself and believes it is only an idea."[20] Ridicule is the only response such doubts really deserve. Accordingly, Lossius very much likes "the mockery with which *Beattie* treats *Berkeley* to show the ridiculousness of his whim," and in order to underscore this point he goes on and cites *two full pages* of Beattie's mockery of Berkeley.[21] We cannot but believe in the existence of external objects and must reject any argument that supports the contrary.

The same holds also for our belief in the existence of our self. We must reject Hume's arguments against the self, Lossius argues. But it is far from clear whether he knows Hume's *Treatise* at all. Again he is dependent upon Beattie. Though he does not indicate that he is doing so, he *quotes* Beattie's version of Hume's argument against the existence of a substantial self and he "refutes" Hume with almost the same words Beattie had used.[22] In this dependence upon the nature of our

---

20. Beattie, *Essay*, p. 289; Lossius, *Physische Ursachen*, p. 147.

21. Lossius, *Physische Ursachen*, pp. 230–32. The passage quoted by Lossius is from Beattie's *Essay*, pp. 284f. (German translation pp. 218–20).

22. Given that pp. 228–30 are nothing but a "medley" of quotes from Beattie's *Essay*, and that pp. 230–32 are straight quotation from the same work, there are four consecutive pages of Beattie in Lossius's *Physische Ursachen*. How dependent he is upon the Scotsman may also be seen from pp. 145f., where he observes: "*Beattie* believes we can find the sources of *Hume's* scepticism in *Descartes*. This could be true, but not in the sense in which Beattie believes." One would now expect Lossius to go on and criticize Beattie, and he does give the impression of doing this, when he says: "But if *Descartes* and *Malebranche* had had more respect for the philosophers of ancient times, many of his [*sic*] doctrines would have been supported by better reasons, if the ancients had not been completely abandoned. Surely this has done more harm than his principle of the

constitution, the beliefs in the existence of the self and of the external objects constitute models for all other recognition of true and false. Our acceptance of truth is always accompanied by "a certain necessity which the rules of truth force upon us so that we cannot but reject something through which they would be overturned. This is how I understand the *instinct* which *Beattie* requires for truth."[23]

But for once Lossius is not quite satisfied with Beattie's characterization of truth: "Whether truth consists in instinct itself is another question. For the belief in or approval of a certain matter is already an effect or consequence of the preceding principles of truth. Therefore we have to go further." In "going further" he finds another Scottish philosopher very helpful, namely Ferguson, who attempts to develop the rules or principles of truth from the history of the human mind.[24] We know from experience that certain sensations occur always in the presence of certain objects. From this we conclude that there is a certain relation between these changes and the objects: a relation of cause and effect. Lossius calls this the "material connection," and he believes it "suggests" (*überführen*) not only the existence of the sensation itself and that of the object, but also a special principle of truth, namely, the "material or metaphysical principle of truth." His principle is that it is impossible that one and the same sensation should not occur, if the same object, under the same circumstances, acts upon our organs. This contrasts with his second, or "formal or logical principle of truth," which is that whenever we notice a certain change in our organs of sensation, a certain thought arises; in fact, always the identical thought with an identical change in an organ. These two principles are the foundation for our feelings of necessary approval with regard to truth and necessary rejection with regard to falsehood. They are the basis for what Beattie calls instinct.

In connecting this psychological or phenomenological account of the workings of the human mind in sensation with its material or physiological *Unterbau*, Lossius finds Beattie useful again. He adopts

----

necessity of doubting everything . . ." Compare with Beattie, *Essay*, p. 233: "If *Descartes* and his disciple *Malebranche* had studied the ancients more and indulged their own imagination less, they would have made a better figure in philosophy." Thus even where Lossius seems to criticize Beattie, he is simply repeating what the latter has already said.

23. Lossius, *Physische Ursachen*, p. 27. Compare Lichtenberg, Aphorisms E 377, E 380, L 956; but see also E 460.

24. Lossius, *Physische Ursachen*, pp. 28, 27n.

the latter's characterization of truth as something sensed or intuited; but he gives this feeling the further quality of being pleasant, when approving something as true, and being painful, when rejecting something as false.[25]

In answering the question of how these feelings of pleasure and pain arise in the human soul, he brings in all of his theories about "systems of fibres," "nerve juices," and "life spirit," and tries to show how these explain the workings of our mind. But he never makes up his mind which of these physiological accounts is the best. Whether his explanations are plausible or not need not be decided here, for after this "materialistic interlude" Lossius turns again to psychological description and maintains:

If all these causes which we have required for truth are present, it is impossible that their effect should fail to appear. Accordingly, there is a certain necessity with which we have accepted something as true when we see it as such, even if this necessity does not rule out error. We cannot but give in to the evidence, as the excellent *Feder* puts it. And thus *Beattie* is correct when he calls truth that which the character of my nature determines me to believe, and falsehood that which the character of my nature determines me to reject.[26]

It is clear, then, that the fact that Lossius argues in favour of a more thorough account or explanation of the facts concerning the human mind, by reducing them to physiology, should not obscure the fact that, for him, as for Beattie, it is in the final analysis God who determines what is true or false.

However, while Beattie is content to explain truth merely in terms of our *nature* and its *organization*, of *instinct* and *common sense*, Lossius believes there is gain in reducing these terms to *fibre systems* and *nerve juices*. But it is far from clear how this makes our concept of reality as "rooted in the categories of our understanding" any the less "chimerical" or "subjective" than Beattie's account. All Lossius has done is to add an intermediate step between our principles and our creator. Thus, it is perhaps no surprise that he returns to Beattie's way of talking after he is through with his materialistic reduction. Beattie wanted to show in his *Essay* that,

except we believe many things without proof, we never can believe any thing at all; for that all sound reason must ultimately rest on the principles of common

25. Ibid., p. 271.
26. Ibid., p. 59.

sense, that is, on principles intuitively certain, or intuitively probable; and consequently that common sense is the ultimate judge of truth to which reason must continually act in subordination. To common sense, therefore, all truth must be conformable; this is its fixed and invariable standard.[27]

And Lossius is similarly convinced that

the truth of a demonstration or argument cannot be judged by itself. There have to be certain principles which existed prior to demonstration. But, if we do not want a regress *ad infinitum,* we have to stop with such principles as are based upon the basic facts of human nature and are principles or basic laws of thought. These presuppositions are of such a kind that we cannot explain and comprehend the progress of thought without them. These basic principles cannot be demonstrated in any way. They are by their very nature not capable of demonstration. For I cannot postulate anything prior to them, and therefore they carry their own evidence.[28]

Even if Lossius is different from Beattie in believing that these principles precede common sense and do not amount to common sense itself, his theory, like Beattie's, also issues finally in a theory of common sense.

II

The main conclusion of Lossius's theory, namely that truth is neither absolute nor objective, but only subjective, is in radical contradiction to the rationalistic account of truth as found in the works of Wolff and his followers. For Lossius truth is not essentially different from beauty. Both are subjective and relative, both depend upon our feeling or sensation and the laws which govern it, and neither one has any foundations in any kind of ontological structure of the universe itself.[29] If only for this reason, his theory had to appear sceptical to his contemporaries. In fact, Lossius himself admits at the very beginning of the *Physische Ursachen* that he found himself bothered by the fact that "the uncertainty of human cognition appeared to be an immediate

27. Beattie, *Essay,* p. 42; see also p. 51.
28. Lossius, *Physische Ursachen,* pp. 85f.
29. For Lossius thought has become "a truthful feeling, since we cannot think that we think, but have to feel it" (*Physische Ursachen.,* p. 61); see also p. 76: "Apart from sensation we cannot demand another criterion of truth. Sensation is the last criterion, and we have to stop here, if we want to realize our ideas." Lossius is close to Riedel and Feder in this regard.

conclusion of the principles accepted by me.″[30] But, he tells us, when he investigated this point further, he became convinced that there are many things with regard to which all human beings finally must agree. And this, he says, is how the treatise on common sense, or Part II of his work, came into being.

It is notable that Lossius considered this the most important part of his book and that it is, if anything, still more dependent upon Beattie than the first part. Thus, just like Beattie, he rejects a formal definition of common sense and proposes as the only possible alternative a nominal definition through an enumeration of the objects and characteristics of common sense. Again, just like Beattie, he begins his discussion with a consideration of the different senses of "common sense": *sensus communis*, public sense, *koinonoemosyne*, *koinai doxai*, etc. The only exception is that he also deals with the German *gesunde Vernunft* and its cognates. But he decides still in favour of Beattie's usage of this basic term:

Finally common sense is also to be differentiated from reasoning, and this is the meaning of the word which *Beattie* accepts. He understands by this term that faculty of the soul which recognizes truth and produces belief [*Glauben*] not through a chain of arguments, but by means of immediate, instinctual and irresistible impressions. This faculty is neither founded upon education nor habit, but upon nature. It does not depend upon our will, but judges according to a certain determined law as soon as an object which falls into its realm shows itself. As such, it is quite properly called sense, and since it operates, if not upon all men, then upon the majority of them, it is also called common sense.[31]

Further, this common sense is for Lossius "the touchstone of truth in so far as it can be known by men. It is what the test of an arithmetical example is in arithmetic, or it does the same service."[32]

Lossius next proposes to undertake a broad investigation of the proper field and the function of common sense. And this becomes for him the question as to how common sense can become the "*standpoint*" of truth for human beings—a question that he thinks divides itself

30. Ibid., p. 8.

31. Ibid., p. 238. This, again, is taken *word for word* from the German translation of Beattie's *Essay* (p. 34, original, p. 41). Nor, again, does Lossius identify the passage as a quotation. The preceding two pages are also no more than a summary of Beattie's long discussion of the different meanings of "common sense."

32. Lossius, *Physische Ursachen*, p. 238.

naturally into the following three questions: "(1) How do doubts with regard to the senses dissolve through common sense? (2) What influence does common sense exert upon reasoning? And, finally, (3) How is it possible not to give in to probability and moral certainty?"[33]

The first question addresses the problem of the reliability of the senses. If we do not know anything of the objects themselves, but only the effects they have upon us, we must ask how we can be certain of the reliability of our knowledge. Lossius points out that we really have no reason to doubt our experience. Examples of sense deception, such as a bent stick in the water, or the apparent size of the moon, are only apparently in contradiction to our ordinary experience. If we consider the medium through which we perceive them, or the distance, we must conclude that they have to look different from normal cases. Since all the qualities of objects are dependent upon their relation to us, the qualities must change, when the relations of the objects to us change. The question that arises now is "How can we reach certainty, or: How can common sense become the point of union between the appearance [*Schein*] of the senses and the truth of objects which we feel?"[34] Lossius tries to solve this problem by appealing to general consent. However, it is an appeal with a difference. For he does not simply argue that it consists in the factual agreement of human beings, but rather that it must be found in the *necessary* agreement of all human beings. We cannot but come together in our sensations of objects, since we are all organized in the same way. We must feel pain when we come into contact with fire, and we have to believe in the existence of external objects when we sense them.

Secondly, common sense does not merely assure us of the reliability of the senses; it is also "the judge of all products of the understanding."[35] It is concerned with all natural or philosophical truths. Among these there are a number that need no proof whatever, as for instance, that one half of a horse will follow the other, even when we spur it only on one side; that the sun will rise tomorrow as it did yesterday; that

33. Ibid., p. 260. Lossius uses "standpoint" for "standard" in the same way as the German translation of Beattie's *Essay*. His phrase "common sense as the standpoint of truth for men" is identical to the heading of Chapter II of the *Essay*.

34. Lossius, *Physische Ursachen*, p. 263.

35. Ibid., p. 250. Compare this with Beattie, *Essay*, p. 51: ". . . for all that is sound reasoning must ultimately rest on principles of common sense, that is, principles intuitively certain, or intuitively probable; and consequently, that *common sense is the ultimate judge of truth, to which reason must continually act in subordination*" (emphasis mine).

2 + 2 = 4; that God is God; that I possess a body which belongs to nobody else; etc. But even those propositions which are in need of proof "do not fall completely outside of the realm of common sense." For why do we ask for proof, if not for the reason that the truth of a proposition should be made evident, and this is nothing but the demand to change a mediate truth into an immediate truth, or to enable common sense to comprehend a proposition which it could not comprehend before. As soon as the proof has been understood, "the same happens in the soul that also happens when it apprehends an immediate truth."[36]

But common sense is also responsible for the basic premises of all inference, namely the law of contradiction and the principle of sufficient reason. As the basic principles of all human thought, they cannot be proved but have to be intuited by common sense. All other propositions of "artificial reasoning" can, in principle, be reduced to the most basic propositions, although any comprehensive attempt to do so would be, Lossius says, ridiculous.

Therefore, even derivative truths belong to the realm of common sense, partly because of the evidence of the proof through which they are derived from their premises. From all this it becomes clear that the approval that common sense gives has to be regarded as the test of the truth of a proposition.[37]

Just as with regard to the senses and the products of thought, so with regard to morality: it is common sense that makes agreement between human beings possible. But Lossius has little to say about this topic, which lies somewhat outside of his basic concern. He notes only that most nations praise and reject the same actions and believe that certain circumstances require certain actions, and he asks: "What is this belief, if not nature or common sense? And this means that we cannot give further reasons that the observation of certain duties is just. All we can say is that reason teaches us thus and not otherwise."[38]

Thus common sense is for Lossius not only the foundation of human knowledge, but also of human conduct. Moreover, it is even the foundation for our hope for a future life and our belief in the immortality of the soul. While those philosophers who want to include

36. Lossius, *Physische Ursachen*, pp. 242f.
37. Ibid., pp. 245f.
38. Ibid., p. 274.

even mysterious or revealed truths in common sense go too far, according to him, since revealed truths are not "products of the understanding," common sense is all we need in order to see the moral certainty of the two above-mentioned propositions. In any case, in moral matters common sense is a much better guide than pure reason. For "common sense thinks these concepts of morality in accordance with the senses and by means of examples, almost in the same way as the poet." Therefore it is much more effective in influencing the behaviour of the common man who would only be confused by the abstract reasoning of the philosopher of pure reason. If common sense and literary taste unite they can truly bring progress to any nation on earth—or so Lossius optimistically believes.[39]

III

In the preceding section it has been shown that Lossius has taken his theory of truth and common sense directly from Scottish sources and modified them only slightly. There is not only a striking similarity between the theory of Beattie, Ferguson and Reid, on the one hand, and that of Lossius, on the other—a similarity which often extends to the terminology, phraseology, and form of argument—but also Lossius's own admissions of having used the Scottish theory at crucial point in his argument. It almost appears as though the German translation of Beattie's *Essay* always lay open upon the table while Lossius was writing his *Physische Ursachen des Wahren*. Insofar as it is possible to prove the dependence of one philosopher upon another, it has been shown that Lossius depends for the establishment of his laws of thought upon the Scots.

For this reason Cassirer's assertion that a "novel conception" shows itself in Lossius's conviction that the "concept of being can only be thought in accordance with the laws of thought," while at the same time holding on to "objectivity," or, better perhaps, "intersubjectivity," must be taken *cum grano salis*. It was perhaps novel when the Scots first proclaimed it but it was certainly no longer a novelty when the *Physische Ursachen* appeared in 1774 in Germany. It was not even a novelty in Germany. Feder and Meiners had already developed a sort of "instinct theory of truth" on the lines of the thought of Reid, Oswald and Beattie. Garve as well had drawn attention to the importance of Reid

39. Ibid., pp. 276, 249–54.

and Ferguson in this regard in 1772. Lossius only expands their views and applies them more radically.[40]

Taken as a characterization of the general outlook of German

40. But Lossius was by no means the only one. Materialism and common sense seems to have appealed to a great number of philosophers (not to speak of physicians and literary figures). One of the most important materialists who was also influenced by the Scots was Platner. He appears to have known Reid, Oswald, and Beattie very well. In any case, there are references to their works throughout his writings (see, for instance, *Philosophische Aphorismen*, vol. 1 [2nd ed., 1784], pp. 66, 250, 262, 273, 280, 301, 364; and [3rd ed., 1793], pp. 99, 142, 225, 433; see also Ernst Platner, *Gespräch über den Atheismus* [1781], p. 262). Moreover, he differentiates clearly between Reid on the one hand and Oswald and Beattie on the other, and whereas he usually mentions Reid favourably, he often mentions Oswald and Beattie only in order to dismiss them. The latter two are not to be taken seriously as enemies of Hume's scepticism because their arguments amount to little more than "mere declamation" and "preaching." But Reid's *Inquiry*, he notes, can be read "with great profit also with regard to skepticism" (Platner, *Philosophische Aphorismen*, vol. 1 [2nd ed., 1784], p. 262; see also pp. 250 and 280). That scepticism is the logical outcome of the "system of ideas" is more or less accepted by him. Though he argues in his later works that scepticism is irrefutable and that therefore Reid could not have achieved anything against Hume either, Platner still appreciates Reid and thinks that "he alone distinguishes himself." But he distinguishes himself "more through other perfections of his work than through very striking reasons against Hume" (ibid., [3rd ed., 1793], p. 368). These "other perfections" of Reid consist for Platner in the theory of sensation. And especially his own tests concerning the acquisition of space in blind persons appear to have been influenced by Reid. It is in the context of discussions of perceptual problems that explicit references to Reid can still be found in the latest edition of the first volume of his *Aphorismen*. Thus he refers to the *Inquiry* "vol. 1, chapter 3, sections 3ff" in his remarks about sensory illusion in vol. 1, p. 66 [2nd ed.], p. 99 [3rd. ed.]), and he finds him still "very instructive" with regard to the "nature of the sensory representations of space apart from sight" (vol. 1, p. 301 [2nd ed.], p. 433 [3rd ed.]). Compare Zart, *Einfluss*, p. 202, who seems to overstate Reid's influence on Platner in this regard, however. Accordingly, he considered this Scotsman together with Locke, Leibniz, Wolff, Hume, and Tetens as one of the most important analysts of the human mind before Kant (Platner, *Aphorismen*, vol. 1, [3rd ed.], 1793, pp. 334f). This estimation of Reid by a philosopher of the reputation of Platner is most significant. For an account of the importance see Wreschner, *Ernst Platner*, pp. 9f. Kant quotes Platner approvingly in his *Prolegomena* and draws attention to his acuteness (*Prolegomena*, ed. Beck, p. 97n.). Karl Leonhard Reinhold, one of the most influential early followers of Kant, calls Platner, together with Eberhard, Tiedemann, Reimarus, Feder, Meiners, and Selle, "the most renowned philosophers of our nation" (*Versuch einer neuen Theorie des menschlichen Vorstellungsvermögens* [Prag and Jena, 1789], p. 155; see also p. 310).

But even Beattie assumes a greater importance in Platner's later works. Thus he observes that the discussion of determinism found in the *Essay* is basically very similar to Kant's discussion of freedom (see *Aphorismen*, vol. 1 [2nd ed.], p. 332n. Compare also Cassirer, *Enlightenment*, pp. 116f). Beattie may not be a very good philosopher, but exactly for that reason the philosophical weaknesses of a certain approach to moral philosophy show more clearly in his work than in that of a thinker of greater acuteness.

philosophy around 1775, Cassirer's claim is quite correct. Several German philosophers had concluded at this time that what we call truth does not so much have to do with the way in which the universe as a whole is structured, but is, rather, dependent upon the constitution of ourselves:

> Here is . . . a new thought still completely embedded in unclear and dogmatic presuppositions. We can determine the concept only in accordance with the laws of thought; but the laws of thought are, in final analysis, nothing but an arbitrary choice of the creator of nature, that is, they are founded upon a *metaphysical* basis. Could this inner ambiguity be removed, could this view that our concept of reality is rooted in the categories of our understanding be held, without making this concept chimerical and letting it evaporate into the mere "subjective?" It is again the achievement of *Tetens* to have asked this question in a concise way.[41]

Of course, as will be seen, in formulating the question in the way in which he did, Tetens had great help from Reid, Beattie, and Lossius.

If Lossius accomplished anything, he showed how difficult it was to *justify* our beliefs in the reality of the objective world. Reid, Oswald, and Beattie were not greatly interested in justification, but Lossius, like most other Germans, was convinced of its necessity. For how else could idealism and scepticism be refuted? Yet Lossius's materialistic *Unterbau* for the "instinct theory of truth" was not acceptable to most Germans, for it only seemed to push the problem one step further back.[42]

However, Lossius's theory still reveals an interesting twist in the approach to the justification of our notions of truth and falsity. In order to explain certain "appearances" he found it necessary "to go somewhat further back and search for the basic principles which have to be presupposed in order that we may call something true or false."[43] One might indeed be tempted to call this approach a transcendental deduction. But it is clear that Lossius, though believing that he was undertaking such a "deduction," is not primarily concerned with a Kant-like *justification* of these laws, but with their *reduction* or *analysis* into processes within systems of fibres, or a certain phlogiston, or a nerve juice, or even a life spirit.[44]

---

41. Cassirer, *Erkenntnisproblem*, vol. 2, p. 451.
42. See this chapter above.
43. Lossius, *Physische Ursachen*, p. 20.
44. Ibid., p. 10. There he calls attention to Lambert's observation that Locke had done an anatomy of concepts, while Leibniz had engaged in their analysis.

In summary, Lossius's theory really offers nothing radically new compared with the "instinct theory of truth" as it can be found in Feder, Meiners, Lichtenberg, and several other German thinkers of this period. But it very clearly shows again the tendencies present in German thought in the seventies of the eighteenth century. Lossius clearly did not feel inclined in any way to reject the theory of ideas. In fact, his materialistic account was only possible because he accepts phenomenalism. But, like the Scots, he emphasized basic principles, even if, like most of his contemporaries, he wanted to go farther than the Scots. He was not satisfied with description, but wanted in some sense to account for these basic principles. Where Feder felt a psychological account of the origin of these principles in sensation and thought would do, Lossius attempted a physiological reduction. Both seem to realize in the end that they had not succeeded, and both fell back upon common sense. Lossius reassured himself as follows:

> But could this doctrine not be dangerous, if regarded from a different point of view? Could it perhaps not even be possible to draw from it conclusions dangerous for morals? Could the difference between virtue and vice and the morality of our free actions, be abolished through it? I do not think so in the least. *The protection of instinct and common sense is my guarantor for this. This is the middle way between the all too strict dogmatism and the squinting scepticism.*[45]

Thus in actual fact Lossius, like Feder before him, *used* common sense as a *regulative principle*, while pretending to analyse it.

45. Ibid., pp. 144f.; see also p. 8: "The uncertainty of all human cognition seemed to be an immediate consequence of the principles assumed by me. But the investigation of this doubt showed to me where all human beings have come together in all their relative knowledge of truth. This is how the treatise on common sense originated."

VI

Scottish Common Sense and German Metaphysics

I

HOW WELL KNOWN Reid must have been in Berlin can be seen when we consider that Moses Mendelssohn had read the *Inquiry* in French before 1770, and had become interested enough to want to read and possess the original. For in 1770 he asked his friend and publisher Friedrich Nicolai to secure the book for him in English.[1] He must have been impressed, for in a letter of 24 July, 1774, he outlines a basic reading course in philosophy for a young man, includes the *Inquiry* as the critique of sensationism, and recommends that Condillac be read in conjunction with Reid.[2]

The way in which Reid's *Inquiry* is pitted against Condillac's *Sur l'origine de connaissances humaines* shows clearly that Mendelssohn believed Reid had powerful arguments against sensationism of the type that supported a materialistic interpretation of human nature. This is corroborated by the essay "Die Bildsäule," which appeared in 1784, that is, almost ten years later than the above-mentioned letter. In this "psychological-allegorical dream" Mendelssohn refers, as Fritz Pinkuss says, "with special appreciation" to Reid and Beattie.[3] They "and the other friends of common sense, who have gone to war against the Bishop [Berkeley] are not fooled by these false subtleties and do not trust any speculation that is opposed to common sense."[4] Further,

---

1. See Mendelssohn, *Neuerschlossene Briefe Moses Mendelssohns an Friedrich Nicolai*, pp. 32f.
2. See Mendelssohn, *Gesammelte Schriften*, vol. 3.1, pp. 305f.
3. Pinkuss, "Moses Mendelssohns Verhaltnis zur englischen Philosophie," p. 453.
4. Mendelssohn, *Schriften*, ed. M. Brasch, vol. 2, p. 242 (subsequently referred to as "Mendelssohn, *Schriften*").

Mendelssohn takes one of the most characteristic doctrines of the Scots to be the maxim that "philosophy must not confuse again what common sense has separated and differentiated."[5]

Similarly, Mendelssohn's friend and follower, Johann August Eberhard, can also be shown to have known Reid's *Inquiry*. His *Allgemeine Theorie des Denkens und Empfindens*, which won the prize of the Berlin Academy for 1776, not only alludes to Reid's position, but expressly refers to the *Inquiry*.[6] According to Wundt, this work "most distinctly exhibits the most remarkable connection of Lockean and Leibnizian thoughts with aesthetic elements." And while he is perhaps exaggerating when he goes on to say that "no other book than this work by Eberhard can give us such clear insight into the state of the doctrine of sensation at the time," it is also clear that Eberhard's *Theorie* is important for understanding the epistemological goals of the late German enlightenment.[7] The significance of the fact that Reid is found important in this successful book should not be underestimated.

In his Introductory Lecture at the University of Halle, published as *Von dem Begriff der Philosophie und ihren Theilen*, Berlin, 1778, Eberhard also shows a certain dependence upon Reid. For he objects in very much the same way as did Reid (and Beattie after him) to the usage of "idea" as referring to all mental contents. He himself wants to apply the term only to the concepts of the understanding, and believes himself to be asking for a return to the usage which Plato makes of this concept.[8]

Accordingly, it cannot be denied that even the most conservative German philosophers of the late eighteenth century found the Scottish theories useful to some extent. There are, in any case, numerous

5. Ibid.

6. Eberhard, *Allgemeine Theorie des Denkens und Empfindens* (Berlin 1776), pp. 187f. (edition of 1786, pp. 186f.). Von Eberstein, *Versuch einer Geschichte*, 1, p. 421 finds that this work "appears to have brought the Leibniz-Wolffian psychology to its highest perfection." Another philosopher who found Reid useful, Hermann Samuel Reimarus, is also closely connected with Mendelssohn, Lessing, Nicolai, and Eberhard. See also Zart, *Einfluss*, p. 100, and Wundt, *Aufklärung*, p. 287. That Karl Phillip Moritz, a translator of one of Beattie's works, was closely connected with Mendelssohn is perhaps also of interest.

7. Sommer, *Grundzüge einer Geschichte*, p. 232.

8. Eberhard, *Von dem Begriff der Philosophie und ihren Theilen* (Berlin, 1778), p. 15. Compare especially with Reid, *Inquiry*, pp. 256ff. and Beattie, *Essay*, p. 155. See also Kant, *Critique of Pure Reason*, A312/B368–A321/B377, as well as Eberhard's *Philosophisches Magazin* 1 (1788–89): 16f. and 49.

references and allusions to them throughout their works.[9] But much more important than the many particular effects of the Scots' thought upon that of these Germans is the German metaphysicans' general *Auseinandersetzung* with Scottish common sense. The more formalistic and "thorough" rationalism of the Germans required them either to reject, or, in some ways, come to terms with the informal and intentionally "shallow" approach of the Scottish common-sense philosophers. And in this regard Eberhard and Mendelssohn differed most significantly.

II

Eberhard was concerned with the development of a general theory that would account for both thought and sensation, as is shown by the very title of his important *Allgemeine Theorie des Denkens und Empfindens*. Since the earlier Wolffians had mainly been interested in man's rational nature, while the British philosophers had concentrated upon sensation, it is not surprising that with regard to thought Eberhard relies mostly upon the Germans, and turns his attention to the British only when dealing with sensation. But it is clearly the latter aspect of his theory that is most interesting and important to him and his contemporaries. For he agreed with most of them that the Wolffian account of the rational nature of man was essentially correct, though somewhat one-sided because of its failure to account for our sensitive side and its connection with rationality.

More particularly, Eberhard sees "most recent speculative philosophy" as best characterized "by its discoveries in the theory of sensation." The older philosophers had completely neglected these sensations and had looked upon "the lower faculties of the soul with proud disdain." The two events which occasioned this change with regard to the theory of sensation are identified by Eberhard as Leibniz's discovery that the Newtonian characterization of secondary qualities also applied to the primary qualities, which "advanced psychology a great deal beyond Locke;" and, secondly, "the observa-

9. See, for instance, Eberhard, *Allgemeine Theorie*, pp.187–88n; *Vermischte Schriften* (Halle, 1784), Preface, and p. 161; *Neue vermischte Schriften* (1788), p. 100; *Handbuch der Ästhetik für gebildete Leser aller Stände*, 4 vols. (1807–20), vol. 2, p. 469 (Campbell), *Philosophisches Magazin* 4 (1792): 101f. For Hutcheson see especially *Sittenlehre der Vernunft* (Berlin, 1781), pp. 46–50, 132f.. For the Scottish influence upon Eberhard in general compare Zart, *Einfluss*, pp. 119–127, especially 121f.

tions about moral sensations" by Shaftesbury, Hutcheson, and their British followers.[10] Eberhard wants to account for these discoveries and observations from a somewhat Wolffian perspective.

He believes, however, that the British theories, particularly Hutcheson's theory about internal sense and Reid's theory about external sense, are not well enough grounded. Philosophy has to go farther. Hutcheson and Lord Kames "have stopped half-way in their explanation of the appearances of internal sense, just as Reid has stopped half-way with regard to the external senses in the *Inquiry on human mind on the principles of common sense* [sic]."[11]

But it is significant that Eberhard, one of the most conservative Wolffians of his generation, can go at least "half-way" with Hutcheson and Reid. They not only supply him with a starting point, but also guide him for quite a while on his way to a unified account of thought and sensation. Thus Eberhard sees the distinction between sensation (*Empfindung*) and cognition (*Erkenntnis*) in very much the same way as Reid sees the difference between sensation and perception. Both Eberhard and Reid believe that sensation is non-referential, that is, suggests no object apart from itself, while perception or, as Eberhard says, cognition, *necessarily* has an object.

However, while Reid does not want to give an account of why perception is necessarily perception of an object, Eberhard wants to do just this by construing perception as an act of thought or reasoning. Reid simply points out that our constitution forces us to believe in objects as being necessarily connected with perception, and that *this does not involve reasoning*. But Eberhard identifies the state of cognition with that of reasoning:

In thinking, the soul regards the object with which it is concerned as external to itself, whereas in the use of the faculty of sensation it believes that it has to do with its own state. The psychological deception is unavoidable, given the nature of these states. When I see the objects themselves distinctly, and when I differentiate their parts well from one another in the state of thought, I have to extend this distinctness also to myself as the thinking subject. I must differentiate myself, as that which thinks, from the objects, as what is thought. This is enough. When I think these two things as being different: myself, the subject, and the objects of thought, which concern me, the soul represents the objects as being external to myself.[12]

10. Eberhard, *Allgemeine Theorie*, pp. 5, 7, 9.
11. Ibid., pp. 187f.
12. Ibid., p. 45.

There are thus definite systematical and terminological similarities between Eberhard and Reid. Both distinguish between two different mental states and characterize them in fairly much the same way. Moreover, they even use the same terminology. Both use "belief" in order to describe the difference of perception from sensation, and both characterize this belief as unavoidable.[13] But there are also fundamental differences, all of which are the result of Eberhard's basic rationalistic stance. He thinks it is necessary to go beyond Reid's descriptive account, and to give an explanation by means of thought. In attempting to explain he uses the terminology of Leibniz and Wolff. That this involves the acceptance of what Reid called the theory of ideas or the ideal system does not bother him.

Like most other Germans, Eberhard cannot accept Reid's critique of the ideal system. He rejects the theory of immediate perception, and argues that we can only *think* objects; and this is the reason why he talks of "psychological deception" in the difference between sensation and perception. However, this difference cannot obliterate the great similarity between Reid's and Eberhard's account of the distinction.

By allowing thought to play a fundamental role in the perception of objects, Eberhard has created a problem for himself, a problem that may be considered as one of the most fundamental in his *Allgemeine Theorie*, namely, "how things which appear so different as *thought* and *sensation* can still consist of one and the same material, and how this common material had to be differently modified in order that two so different appearances could arise."[14] The Scots, according to Eberhard, had no such problem because they wanted to explain everything by sensation. But he finds that this lends to "the faculty of sensation an importance which it does not deserve according to its nature." When the Scots use a certain feeling of truth and of good, or a sense of truth and a moral sense to explain all of our knowledge, they are turning away from true philosophy, for "it is the duty of philosophy to banish this feeling from science itself and to show to it its true function."[15] This is so because an "inexplicable feeling of truth" is neither a secure guide in our investigations nor a possible means of communicating our convictions to others.[16]

---

13. Ibid., pp. 44ff.
14. Ibid., pp. 34f. Compare Kant, *Critique of Pure Reason*.
15. Eberhard, *Allgemeine Theorie*, pp. 184f. This appears to be also directed against such philosophers as Feder and Meiners.
16. Eberhard argues that common sense and moral sense have not hindered the

It can easily be shown, according to Eberhard, that in many cases the understanding necessarily contradicts common sense, and that it is correct in doing so. The understanding can comprehend, for instance, that the asymptote of a hyperbola can never meet the latter, while this appears to be contradictory to common sense. Therefore, the true is not what is felt to be true, but what is *understood* to be true. True is what can be comprehended, false is what cannot be comprehended, and, "if we want to explain this comprehensibility, we will have to show that we cannot assure ourselves of this in any other way than by step by step reduction to undeniable basic principles."[17]

For Eberhard, it is thought that lies at the basis of both our rational faculty and that of sensation. Hence common sense and moral sense must also be explained as forms of thought. Like the early Mendelssohn, from whom he is likely borrowing, he believes that these two principles are really not senses at all. They only function like senses.[18] Actually, they are "depositories" of truths of reason, and they can therefore be rationally explained. The true function of feeling is

not to be the source of truth, but to be a depository of all clear judgments which are kept in the soul by consideration or conscious abstraction, so that they may express themselves in all cases with a rapidity that is characteristic of sensation. That there is a moral sense in the latter meaning cannot be doubted. It is differentiated from conscience through the circumstance that it (1) feels morality in general, and (2) also in the actions of others. But conscience is concerned only with the judgment of one's own actions. Therefore we may say that the former acts only as a lawgiver and the latter only as a judge. In this way we avoid both errors [*Auswege*], namely, on the one hand, an overly exaggerated estimation of the moral sense, according to which it becomes a first principle that is independent of reason, a highest judge of all moral matters, and, on the other hand, an equally exaggerated contempt which denies the usefulness of a moral sense. It is useful to show the closest sources of approval and choice to people. It is also possible to stop with these observations, as long as one does not declare the inner senses hereby observed to be independent sources, as Hutcheson, Home [Kames] and others do.[19]

The same considerations also apply, of course, to common sense. It is

---

adoption of the most immoral practices in otherwise highly devoloped societies. It is not clear why he does not consider these examples just as telling against reason.

17. Ibid., p. 187.
18. For Mendelssohn see this chapter below.
19. Ibid., pp. 185f. See also Eberhard's *Sittenlehre der Vernunft*.

not an original sense either, but has to be traced back to more ultimate principles on which it depends.

It is important to note, however, that Eberhard does *not object* to common sense and moral sense as such. His objection is only to the use Hutcheson, Reid, Kames, and others have made of these senses as absolute tribunals of truth, good, and reality. For him, they derive their validity from the understanding and have to be checked by it. However great the evidence of common sense may be,

it is a mistake to rely solely upon it. Plato summarizes what I have dealt with here . . . as follows: wisdom, science and opinion are three kinds of perfection of our faculty of cognition. Wisdom is the immediate intuition of eternal truths themselves. Science is the certain knowledge which we obtain through meditation and education. Opinion, however, is the approximate estimate which arises suddenly, and which usually informs the business of men concerned with the administration of the republic. Since opinion acts with the greatest rapidity and presses towards the greatest decisions, Plato believes that one must ascribe a divine origin to it. We cannot fail to recognize that what Plato calls opinion is identical with the quick, strong, but uncertain effects of the understanding [*Verstandesinstinkt*] and feeling of truth [*Wahrheitsgefühl*], which we have just described. Plato characterizes it correctly, when he assigns to it a role in everyday life, but regards science alone as capable of certain cognition.[20]

This evaluation of common sense and its principles surely would have struck the Scots as unfair. They did not think that it consisted of such a variety of components, and they would not have accepted its identification with opinion in Plato. Common sense for them was characterized as the source of the first principles of human thought, an "immediate intuition" or even "revelation" of "eternal truth," and thus much more similar to what Plato (at least in accordance with Eberhard's interpretation) called wisdom.[21]

Consequently, Eberhard's criticism does not really meet the Scots. But it does meet the half-hearted adaptations of their theory by such people as Resewitz, Feder, and Lossius, who attempted a synthesis of Wolffian and Lockian principles with those of the Scots, and who believed they were more thorough than the Scots.[22] That he could not

20. Eberhard, *Allgemeine Theorie*, pp. 192f.

21. See especially Beattie, *Essay*, p. 42. Reid and Beattie even speak of "revelation" and "inspiration" in this context.

22. And in any case it may be his compatriots that he wanted to criticize.

clearly differentiate these echoes from the authentic voice of the Scots themselves shows perhaps how little Eberhard was capable of appreciating the more subtle aspects of the Scots' theory, though it may perhaps also go towards showing how thoroughly Scottish common sense was assimilated by the Germans.

It appears, however, that Eberhard later came to see the true character of the Scottish theory more clearly and to appreciate it to a greater extent. In any case, the incorrectness of his characterization of the Scots is to some extent rectified in "Clairsens und Tiefheim oder vom gemeinem Menschenverstande" in his *Vermischte Schriften* of 1784. In this work he differentiates between what he calls "healthy human understanding" and "common human understanding," meaning by the former

the undeniable truths which are contained in the *basic principles* of human cognition and in *immediate* experiences . . . those are the first truths from which I have to start all investigations, and to which all investigations have to return. To go beyond them is impossible, since they are in and of themselves undeniable, and since there can be no other truths which would be more evident . . . Doubts which one might bring forward against such truths of healthy human understanding should not confuse me, since it is impossible to advance genuine doubt against undeniable truths; though it may be useful for the sciences to show the baselessness of even such doubts.[23]

Thus Eberhard's "healthy human understanding" is identical in meaning with "common sense" as defined by Reid and Beattie.

By "common human understanding" Eberhard understands

that degree of understanding which most people are capable of. It comprises therefore only those cognitions which do not require a higher degree of training through education and meditation. The experiential knowledge of common sense can therefore only be that which can be obtained from common experience, that is, without a higher degree of attention, without deeper investigation, without artificial instruments, and without preparation. Everything that comes to us only through artificial experiments and careful investigation is unattainable for the genuine common human understanding and must be excluded from its realm.[24]

It is not difficult to recognize in this "common human understanding"

23. Eberhard, *Vermischte Schriften*, p. 145.
24. Ibid., p. 149.

Reid's "common understanding," that is, "the more obvious conclusions drawn from our perceptions by reason . . . by which men conduct themselves in the common affairs of life and by which they are distinguished from idiots."[25]

At this point, the only important difference between the German and the Scot consists in the fact that Eberhard accepts fewer basic principles than does Reid. He mentions only such propositions as "Every quantity is equal to itself" and "What is, is."[26] Further, he wants to draw a sharp dividing line between science on the one hand and common sense on the other, while Reid sees continuity between the common understanding and science. For the latter science consists only of "the more remote conclusions drawn from our perceptions by reason."[27] And it is indeed difficult to see how Eberhard is going to maintain the sharp distinction between the two. What is to count as an instrument for the acquisition of knowledge? Certainly, a microscope or a telescope will count as such. But what about eye-glasses? The differential calculus may count as a theory, but what about simple arithmetic?

In any case, in spite of this difference, Eberhard's distinction is clearly identical with that of Reid. It is therefore somewhat surprising when he suggests that it is his own invention and criticizes the Scots for not having made it, saying that "the Scottish philosophers *Beattie, Reid, and Oswald* have caused much confusion in this matter by overlooking this distinction."[28] For through their neglect "they have opened the door to *Schwärmerei*, on the one hand, while, on the other hand, facilitating a certain scepticism by assigning to judgments we accept only on the basis of some obscure feelings, the very same status as to proper axioms." Eberhard finds that "this feeling is so different in different persons that it cannot possibly serve as a reliable criterion and touchstone of truth."[29]

But it is not clear that he has done anything different from the Scots. He also fails to give clear criteria for the distinction between genuinely first truths and those of the common human understanding. Yet this is most important for the aim of his dialogue. For he wants to reject the appeal to common human understanding as a principle of orientation

25. Reid, *Works*, vol. 1, pp. 185f. (*Inquiry*, ed. Duggan, pp. 212f.).

26. He rejects "truths" concerning the nature of God as first principles, for instance. (*Vermischte Schriften*, pp. 145f. This appears to be directed against Oswald.

27. Reid, *Works*, vol. 1, p. 185 (*Inquiry*, ed. Duggan, p. 213).

28. Eberhard, *Vermischte Schriften* Preface.

29. Ibid.

in philosophy, while keeping the appeal to the healthy human understanding.[30] But, just as he fails to make sense of the distinction between science and common human understanding, he ultimately fails to make a clear distinction between these two faculties.

However, it is very clear *why* he wants to make these two distinctions. If there were no clear distinction between science, common human understanding, and healthy human understanding the same maxims would apply to all of them just as Reid had claimed when he identified Newton's *regulae philosophandi* with the maxims of common sense.[31] But Eberhard, talking through Tiefheim, the philosopher at home in the depths of knowledge, finds these rules too restrictive. He answers Clairsens, who wants to restrict knowledge:

In this way you will greatly limit the dimensions of the map of philosophy, nay, even of knowledge in general . . . Consider in how many respects science would have to be held back, if it was restricted only to the truths of the common human understanding.

Because Eberhard has so narrowly defined the common human understanding and differentiated it so sharply from science, he can argue:

The realm of the understanding is far too narrow to enable a nation which wants to be worthy of being called "enlightened" not to go beyond it. But if you allow the philosopher to go beyond the limits of the common human understanding in the field of experience, why do you want to prohibit this in the field of reason?

Eberhard believes that

the investigation *must transgress completely into the field of the insensible ideas*, if it is to be brought to its final completion; just as much in order to convince us of the reality of the objects of the senses as of the simplicity of substances in whose changes are founded all appearances which we perceive in the body. How can I even hope to obtain in such investigations the same evidence as in truths of the common human understanding?

For this reason Tiefheim (or Eberhard) really has no choice, unless he

30. But at times he seems to want to reject even this appeal.
31. Reid, *Works*, vol. 1, p. 97 (*Inquiry*, ed. Duggan, p. 4).

is willing to give up the kind of speculation German philosophers traditionally have engaged in—and he says as much:

I know that some people who still call themselves philosophers have taken this position [that we have to be satisfied with the "quick feeling of truth of the healthy human understanding"]. Whether they have done so for reasons of convenience or because of desperation, I do not want to decide. . . . *I cannot take this position for the following reasons: (1) Common sense [Gemeinsinn]* often needs to be rectified by science, unless they mean common sense as consisting only of genuine first truths. Common sense says the earth is standing still, science says: it is moving; and people believe the latter. *Next*: several questions asked by nature and reason are not answered at all by this very same common sense. How do the representations of the qualities and changes of bodies come into the soul? The Cartesian philosophy says: the soul itself supplies them, or, instead, God supplies them at the occasion of the impressions which the sense organs receive from the bodies. The philosophers of common sense in England [*sic*] *Reid, Beattie, and Oswald* say: they impress themselves in the soul as the seal in the wax. If you make objections to this answer, they stop you and request you to cease the inquiry.[32]

Eberhard does not want to stop short his inquiry, but wants to push it "completely into the field of non-sensible ideas." Because he does not want to be restricted and held back by common sense he rejects it.

Thus he considers common sense and rational thought to be, in the final analysis, quite different. Philosophy has absolute priority over common sense, since it is not only more certain, but also covers a wider field. Philosophy is a science, that is, it is rational. Common sense is unscientific and lives by approximations. He is willing, though, to accommodate his results to common sense and hopes that, as the majority of people become more and more used to the difficult enterprise of metaphysics, they will also accept the results of philosophy. But Eberhard's hopes were as unfounded as his metaphysics. The majority of people came to reject the claims of pure reason. And another philosopher, namely Immanuel Kant, was more successful than the Scots in arguing that the common human understanding does indeed define the limits of all speculation.

Even speculative philosophers of Eberhard's persuasion came to doubt the absolute priority of speculation over common sense, finding it more and more necessary to appeal to common sense in order to

---

32. Eberhard, *Vermischte Schriften* pp. 148f., 150, 160f.

orient their speculations. Mendelssohn is a clear example of this. In consequence, Eberhard's "Clairsens and Tiefheim" seems, in this context, like a rearguard action fought by speculative philosophy against the common-sense critics of pure reason. Eberhard here shows himself to be just as much of a reactionary as he later did in his fight against Kant's critical philosophy.

III

Moses Mendelssohn is one of the most important philosophers of the German enlightenment. Lewis White Beck has aptly described him as "the epitome of popular philosophy at its best . . . To understand Mendelssohn is to know the final will and testament of popular philosophy."[33] This lends special significance to any influence of the Scots upon Mendelssohn's general philosophical outlook—and this both in historical and systematical respects.

That there is a Scottish influence upon Mendelssohn is most clearly shown by his latest works and especially his *Morgenstunden*, a work that belongs in the context of the philosophical discussion of the seventies, even though it was written well after the appearance of Kant's *Critique of Pure Reason*.[34] Mendelssohn claims himself that a nervous disability had made it impossible for him to analyse and think through the works of "Lambert, Tetens, Platner, and even those of the all-crushing Kant." He claims to know them only through reviews and from reports of his friends, and he says that in 1785 philosophy for him "still stands at the point at which it stood in approximately 1775."[35]

There are many similarities and parallels between Mendelssohn's arguments in his last two works and those advanced by the Scots —similarities and parallels that almost certainly are the result of direct or indirect influence. Like Reid (and Eberhard), Mendelssohn makes a phenomenological distinction between the thought, the object which is thought, and the subject which thinks within every act of thought. He follows Reid in using this distinction to establish our belief in the existence of objects. Just like Reid, Mendelssohn speaks of "immediate sensation" and its evidence; and just like Reid and his Scottish and

33. Beck, *Early German Philosophy*, pp. 323f.
34. See Keyserling, *Moses Mendelssohn*, pp. 406–9; Pinkuss, "Verhältnis," pp. 449–90. See also Zart, *Einfluss*, pp. 111–119 and Altmann, *Moses Mendelssohn*, pp. 285, 659–61.
35. Mendelssohn, *Schriften*, vol. 1, p. 299.

German followers, he relies upon appeals to ordinary language, believing that many philosophical paradoxes are the result of a misuse of language.[36] He even agrees with Reid and the others that certain questions are unanswerable, and criticizes "the methods and results of philosophical speculation with almost the same words as the Scottish school."[37]

But all this should not mislead us into thinking that Mendelssohn is simply copying the Scots. Although he avails himself of the Scottish arguments against sensationism, he himself does not want to go as far as rejecting representationalism altogether. He remains an adherent of the theory of ideas and seems to feel that, with certain appropriate modifications, it can be made to work.[38] Moreover, despite his criticisms of speculative philosophy, Mendelssohn himself still continues to be a speculative philosopher. He is far from wanting to give up all the rights of pure reason.

This is also shown by the most important and most discussed new principle introduced in the *Morgenstunden,* namely, the requirement that metaphysics should orient itself through common sense. In regard to this principle, Mendelssohn is most dependent upon the Scots, and his appeal to ordinary language and the rejection of certain questions as illegitimate is, to some extent, a consequence of the acceptance of common sense as a guide. Here Mendelssohn comes closest to simply following Reid and to breaking with Wolff. But even here he is not really defecting to Scottish common sense, but is attempting to use common sense to reinforce his speculative intentions.

Wolff and his early followers allowed that common sense or natural logic were already in the possession of some of the truths to be discovered by speculation or pure reason, but they clearly favoured the judgment of pure reason (very much in the same way as does Eberhard).[39] Whenever there was a difference of contradiction between ordinary language or common sense and pure reason or scientific philosophy, the decision of the latter was thought to be

36. For this and the claim that certain questions cannot be answered he was taken to task by Kant. See Kant, *Werke,* ed. Weischedel, vol. 3, pp. 288–90.

37. Pinkuss, "Verhältnis," p. 452.

38. See, for instance, Mendelssohn, *Schriften,* vol. 1, p. 337. There he claims that some concepts must be accepted as *Darstellungen* and not just as *Vorstellungen.* This discussion of necessary or natural belief is clearly influenced by Reid. See also Mendelssohn, *Werke,* vol. 1, pp. 278f., for instance.

39. See this chapter above.

binding. For Mendelssohn this has changed. Speculation is no longer to be trusted. It is suspect and needs to be constantly checked, if it is not to lead us to absurdities. The criterion for these controls of pure reason is the agreement of speculation and common sense:

Whenever reason lags so far behind common sense or even strays from it and is in danger of losing its way, the philosopher will not trust his reason and he will not contradict common sense. Instead, he will silence reason whenever he does not succeed in leading it back to the beaten path and to catch up with common sense.

This is why Mendelssohn espouses the regulative principle of orientation in thought:

As soon as my speculations lead me too far away from the highway of common sense, I stand still and try to orientate myself. I look back to the point from which we have departed and I try to compare my two guides. Experience has taught me that in most cases the right is on the side of common sense and that reason has to favour speculation decisively if I should leave common sense and follow speculation. Nay, in order to show me that the steadfastness of common sense is only ignorant stubborness, reason has to show to me how common sense could possibly have strayed away from the truth and could come on the wrong way.[40]

Thus even a decision against common sense is possible, though highly unlikely. In fact, Mendelssohn goes so far as to say that, whenever he finds a contradiction in speculation and has thoroughly considered the arguments for both sides, he allows common sense to make the final decision: "under these conditions I recognize *common sense* as the *highest tribunal of truth*. And its judgment seldom fails under these circumstances."[41]

In this way, under the influence of the Scots, common sense has become of the highest importance for Mendelssohn, as important as it had been for the Scots.[42] But, unlike the Scots, Mendelssohn does not

---

40. Mendelssohn, *Schriften*, vol. 1, pp. 370ff.

41. Mendelssohn, Letter to Winkopp, 24 March, 1780, *Gesammelte Schriften*, vol. 5 (1844), p. 565.

42. It is difficult to say in what way Mendelssohn's theory is different from Reid's. Pinkuss, "Verhältnis," pp. 453–55, argues that the relation between reason and common sense is different. The Scots oppose common sense to reason, while Mendelssohn claims that they are identical; and that he uses common sense as a regulative principle, while the

take common sense to be absolute or infallible, as some have maintained.[43] Both common sense and reason "can lose their way, both can stumble and fall." Yet, and in this the importance and usefulness of common sense consists, "if this happens, it is at times harder for reason to get up again." Neither reason nor common sense has any kind of priority. For both are in the final analysis expressions of one and the same basic faculty. "Common sense and reason are basically one and the same." They "flow from the same source."[44]

In this theory of the ultimate identity of reason and common sense Mendelssohn is very close to Eberhard (and most of his German contemporaries). But, unlike Eberhard and most others, he has drawn the final conclusion from this position. If common sense and reason are expressions of one and the same faculty, then they also stand on one and the same level, and it is not clear how one could have absolute priority over the other. The same principles must apply to both, and speculative reason must have the same limits as common sense and submit to the same criteria. Pure Reason can be criticized on the principles of common sense, just as common sense can be criticized on the principles of pure reason. In fact, this latter enterprise is most important in philosophy. We must try to show how any "particular assertion of common sense . . . can be converted into rational cognition."[45] Accordingly, "the only task" Mendelssohn assigns to his "speculations is to correct the assertions of common sense and to convert them as far as possible into rational knowledge."[46]

Scots see in it the "necessary presupposition of all knowledge." But these differences are not as fundamental as Pinkuss believes. First of all, Reid himself more or less identifies reason and common sense in his later *Essays*. (See Reid, *Works*, vol. 1, p. 425 and also Grave, *The Scottish Philosophy of Common Sense*, p. 115.) He gives two functions to reason: one intuitive, the other deductive, and argues that common sense is a different name for the intuitive function. Secondly, Reid (and Beattie) certainly understood common sense *also* as a regulative principle. In fact, it has been argued that this is the primary understanding of "common sense" for Reid. (See Taylor's review of Grave's *The Scottish Philosophy of Common Sense* in *Philosophical Review*, July 1961.) Thirdly, Mendelssohn also speaks of first principles, or axiomata, which are necessary for all knowledge. (See Mendelssohn, *Schriften*, vol. 1, pp. 320, 334f., 364f., for instance.) Therefore, the difference, if there is one, is only one of emphasis.

43. See, for instance, Uebele, *Johann Nicolaus Tetens*, p. 147.

44. Mendelssohn, *Schriften*, vol. 1, pp. 325, 341. Compare this with Eberhard's view as represented above. It is also interesting to note that Feder criticizes Beattie's claim that common sense is a special faculty.

45. Mendelssohn, *Schriften*, vol. 1, p. 337.

46. Ibid., p. 477.

This is, of course, a far cry from the theory advocated by the more traditional followers of Wolff. Mendelssohn's pronouncements have the ring of resignation. Whereas Eberhard still wants to uphold the right of speculation to go beyond the field of experience and common sense, Mendelssohn accepts these limits, and is not even sure, it seems, whether all the claims of common sense can be rationally understood or justified. There is certainly some irony in all this: Wolff and his earliest followers considered common sense as a preliminary and rather imperfect expression of the truths of reason. Rational and scientific examination was thought to be absolutely necessary in order to make these truths secure. The later Wolffians, like the young Mendelssohn and Eberhard, for instance, still gave absolute preference to reason and tried to understand common sense *in analogia rationis*. But the "final will and testament" of the German enlightenment shows a complete reversal, and amounts to an attempt to institute common sense as the highest tribunal of truth in matters metaphysical. Mendelssohn openly admits what was the actual practice of most philosophers of the period. For Feder, Lossius, and most others also relied upon common sense as their means of orientation, and as a highly important criterion of philosophical truth.

VII

Scottish Common Sense and Tetens's Analysis of Thought in Perception

I

JOHANN NICOLAUS TETENS is perhaps the German philosopher most influenced by the Scots. Tetens always starts his own discussion at the point where the Scots left off, and his own considerations are greatly influenced by the Scottish analysis of the problem of perception. Dissatisfied with the state of German speculative philosophy as he found it, he turns to observational psychology for his method and to common sense for the subject matter of his philosophy. Thus he declares that the method he has used "is the method of observation; the one which Locke and our psychologists have employed in their empirical psychology," and that "the cognitions of common sense are the field which must be worked in philosophy."[1] According to him, traditional German metaphysics has not sufficiently been aware that

there is a *theory of reason* which is independent of all systems of metaphysics. The concepts and principles of the understanding are used without having

---

1. Tetens, *Philosophische Versuche*, pp. iii/iv; *Speculativische Philosophie*, p. 13 (all quotations are given in accordance with the reprint of the Kant-Gesellschaft). Tetens refers to the Scots by name in *Speculativische Philosophie*, pp. 10. 11, 12, 70; *Philosophische Versuche*, pp. 55, 298, 329, 331, 332, 333, 335, 365, 367; 372n., 382, 392, 412, 441, 461, 478, 496, 503, 512. 515, 517, 518, 530, 567n., 571, 572, 631. To Berkeley he refers by comparison only on pp. 391, 392, 394. 400. 467, 480, 485, 489, 515, 516. 571, 591. Given these many references to, and acknowledgments of, the Scots, his dependence upon them could not go completely unnoticed. See, for instance, Sommer, *Grundzüge*, pp. 256f.; Dessoir, *Geschichte*, p. 54; Zart, *Einfluss*, pp. 170, 172n., 1777; Uebele, *Tetens*, pp. 72f., 93, 142; and Schlegtendahl, *Johann Nicolaus Tetens Erkenntnistheorie in Beziehung auf Kant*, pp. 46f. But the exact nature and extent of the Scottish influence upon Tetens has never been discussed.

been exactly determined, distinctly analysed, or having been brought into a system. There are no preceding general speculations about substance, space and time, etc. . . . *Reid, Hume, Beattie, Oswald* as well as several German philosophers have removed all doubts about this through the examples they have brought forward. Indeed, it would not have needed as much declamation for this purpose as especially *Beattie* and *Oswald* have employed.[2]

The true function of speculative philosophy cannot be to suspend or fight this common-sense theory of reason, but only "to secure and clarify it." The task of metaphysics must be the analysis of common sense, or perhaps better, the clarification of the "metaphysics of common sense." Speculative philosophy is the "friend" of common sense, and it has "descended from" common sense.[3]

Granted, Tetens does not think that the Scots have satisfactorily resolved the problems they took up.

For this it would have been required to investigate the nature of human cognition up to its first beginnings, and even more to explicate the procedure of the power of thought in the attainment of knowledge more exactly and more carefully than *Reid* or *Beattie* or *Oswald*, in spite of their otherwise superior perspecuity, appear to have done.[4]

But they have made a beginning. And, according to Tetens, Reid especially has "made many beautiful observations which belong here."[5]

Given his estimation of the Scots, it should be clear that Tetens found them useful. Indeed it is easy to show that he was influenced by them, and that this influence was of fundamental importance for the development of his own views. There are essentially four different, though closely related, contexts that show this: (1) his analysis of perception, (2) his genetic account of the origin of our notions of objective reference, (3) his theory of common sense, and (4) his treatment of the laws of thought as being objectively necessary. Since Tetens's most important contribution to the philosophical discussion of the time is to be found exactly in these four areas, the Scottish influence is of special importance—and this not only for the under-

2. Tetens, *Speculativische Philosophie*, p. 10; see also pp. 3–9, and 12, as well as *Philosophische Versuche*, pp. 558–77.

3. Tetens, *Speculativische Philosophie*, p. 12.

4. Ibid.

5. Tetens, *Philosophische Versuche*, p. 372n. Compare with Eberhard.

standing of Tetens himself, but also for the development of German philosophy in general. Tetens's theory represents an important step between Feder and Lossius, on the one hand, and Kant, on the other. It is his philosophy that makes clearer than any other Kant's connections with his contemporaries.

II

Much like all the other Germans discussed so far, Tetens is unable to follow the Scots in rejecting the "theory of ideas." He does not accept Reid's arguments that this theory leads necessarily to idealism and scepticism. In fact, the "principle" that "all external objects are only judged in accordance with their representations within ourselves" expresses for him one of the most fundamental presuppositions of all philosophy.[6] And though he admits that some philosophers have been led by this principle towards idealism and egoism, he does not think that this is an inherent fault of the theory of ideas.

What *Reid* calls the ideal philosophy, or the principle that all judgments about objects originate only from impressions or representations of objects is surely innocent in this regard . . . the British philosopher should not have denied this principle in accordance with his usual insight.[7]

Though Tetens notes several times that the theory of ideas "is completely innocent" with regard to idealism, he does not offer any arguments against Reid and Beattie—either because he is too convinced of the correctness of the theory of ideas, or because he does not know any. In fact, some of his claims sound very much as though he finds it necessary to reassure himself, and to persuade himself that the theory of ideas and idealism have nothing in common. Could it be that he is haunted by the idea that *all* of philosophy must lead to idealism?

However that may be, unlike many of the other German philosophers, Tetens had not only read the works of the Scots carefully, he also took their critique more seriously. He clearly thought that their criticisms point towards real weaknesses in the theory of ideas and thus towards the need for modifications. Thus he tries to revise this theory in such a way that certain aspects of the Scottish critique no longer apply.

6. Ibid., p. 367; see also p. 392.
7. Ibid., p. 372. Compare with Feder.

Because there is no way in which we could determine whether or not sensations and their objects are similar—it being impossible for us to be acquainted with the objects apart from our sensations—he accepts Reid's criticism that sensations and the sensed objects cannot be said to be similar in any way, nor to stand in a pictorial relation to each other.[8] Furthermore, he also agrees with the Scots that the mind is both passive and active in perception, and that the earlier empiricists are wrong in ascribing complete passivity to the mind in this regard. Like Reid, he differentiates not only between the act of perception, its subject, and its object, but also different aspects within the act of perception itself, namely, a sensible and a judgmental component.[9] And for this reason he comes to the conclusion that ideas cannot be simple or atomic mental contents that would enable us to explain all other mental contents and actions.

Tetens holds that there are three different kinds of mental contents: *Empfindungen* or sensations, *Vorstellungen* or representations, and *Ideen* (*Gedanken*) or ideas. Though it has to be kept in mind that these sensations, representations, and ideas are for him mental states or even mental objects—whereas Reid does not admit such "things"—his understanding of "sensations" is significantly influenced by Reid's use of the term. Like Reid, he declines to explain sensation itself;[10] like Reid, he believes that we can sense only what is present, and contrasts sensation in this way to memory and imagination;[11] and like Reid, he differentiates between ideas and sensations, arguing that ideas have objects whereas sensations do not. At times, Tetens even uses the word "perception" instead of his usual "*Idee*." Further, when he finds it

8. Tetens, *Speculativische Philosophie*, pp. 4f. That he is very much aware of Reid in this context becomes especially clear from *Philosophische Versuche*, p. 333: "*Reid* says that this sensation of hardness has nothing in common with the hardness in the body, and this is certainly true. It is something subjective in the soul, while the hardness of the body is something objective in the object."

9. For a more thorough discussion of this aspect of Reid, see chapter I above. For Tetens's view see below.

10. Reid, *Inquiry*, chapter II, section 3: "They are all simple and original and therefore inexplicable acts of the mind." Tetens, *Philosophische Versuche*, p. 165: "What is feeling or sensation? I admit at once that I am incapable of explaining it. It is a simple expression of the soul, which I do not know how to analyze into simpler ones."

11. Ibid., p. 165. On the next page he even seems to be arguing specifically against Reid's view that there are no mental representations involved in memory.

necessary to talk about Reid in this context, he makes clear that his "*Idee*" corresponds to the latter's "perception."[12]

But if the correspondence between "sensation" or "*Empfindung*" and "perception" and "*Idee*" is beyond doubt, it is also clear that Tetens's "*Vorstellung*" or "representation" does not correspond to anything to be found in Reid's work. Tetens considers these representations to be some sort of mediating link between sensations and ideas. Sensations do not disappear without a trace, but they leave certain lasting effects, consequences or marks. And these "marks are a kind of picture [*Zeichnungen*] which the soul retains of its changes and can recover at will whenever it wants to use them."[13] Like Hume's ideas, Tetens's representations are "copies" of our sense impressions. They do not necessarily have to resemble those previous states, but they usually do; and they are differentiated from their originals only "by a lesser degree of vivacity."[14]

However, the similarities that may exist between representations and sensations are not what is important to Tetens. It is their correspondence or analogy with each other, which is "the general analogy between effects and causes," that is most interesting. The representation *refers* to a sensation because it has been caused by that sensation. And "this *reference of representations to other preceding modifications is their essential characteristic.*"[15] Yet this analogical or referential characteristic does not allow us to say anything about the sensations in particular. The analogy between sensations and representations

is only an *analogy* of the *identity in the relations of the qualities*, not a similarity of the absolute qualities themselves. It is not the complete similarity of the lamb and the mother sheep, but the similarity between a statue of stone or metal and the body of the animal or the human being which it represents.[16]

Since the sensations of which the representations are marks have been caused either by previous states of ourselves or by external objects, we may not only say that the sensations immediately correspond or refer

12. Ibid., p. 162: "... ideas, or as *Reid* says, perceptions ..." p. 333: "*Reid* says ... the *perception* or the *idea* ..."
13. Ibid., p. 16; see also p. 13.
14. Ibid., pp. 19f.
15. Ibid., pp. 20, 17.
16. Ibid., p. 20.

to the external objects which have caused them, but also that the representations correspond or refer to these objects by the mediation of the sensations—even if it is not clear how we come to relate particular sensations to particular objects.

It is not difficult to see that Tetens develops here a variant of Hume's theory of impressions and ideas (though he does so by means of the Wolffian conception of representation). He is thus trying to improve the very theory Reid and Beattie were arguing against. Tetens is very much aware of this, and he explicitly rejects Beattie's arguments against Hume's distinction between impressions and ideas: "*Beattie's* objections to this true principle of *Humean* scepticism should not mislead us. They are based upon a misunderstanding, as so many views of this author." Tetens is also quite aware that "according to *Reid's* philosophy there is no similarity between the impressions of sense and the representations," or, as he should have said, the perceptions.[17] But he is undeterred and develops this part of his theory in conscious opposition to Reid as well:

Reid says that the sensation of hardness is not in any way similar to the hardness in the body, and that is certainly true . . . But he adds to this that the sensation has also nothing in common with the *perception* or *idea* of hardness, which represents the objective quality to us, as in a picture. I answer to this that the feeling is indeed different from the idea. But does this mean that the feeling is not the material for the idea?[18]

For Tetens the sensation is the material for the idea. The idea is a representation, that is, the "trace" of a sensation that has been made more distinct. But everything that is contained in the idea must, he thinks, already have been contained in the representation, and therefore also in the sensation, even if in an obscure form.[19]

However, here as elsewhere, Tetens does not simply reject Reid without learning from him. For the account he gives of the relationship between sensation, representation, and idea is influenced by Reid and goes far beyond anything said by Hume. Just as Reid had argued that our sensations are natural signs of objects, so Tetens argues that representations are natural signs of sensations. The account so far given

17. Ibid., pp. 55n, 412.
18. Ibid., p. 333.
19. Ibid., pp. 93ff.; especially p. 94; see also pp. 327–36.

does not exhaust the complete *significative nature of representations*. Representations are not simply and conveniently used by us as signs and pictures of things because they have an analogy with them. They also have a characteristic which reminds us automatically, as it were, that they are signs of other things. This characteristic refers us to other things as objects, which are different from their representations, and it allows us to see these objects *through the representations and in them*. The reason for our natural inclination to believe that we are not dealing with pictures and representations of things, but with . . . things themselves, consists in this characteristic given here.[20]

Tetens uses not only the very same terminology as Reid and Beattie, and speaks of "natural inclination" and "natural sign" in order to characterize the significative or referential character of representations. He also gives a similar account of the origin of their signicative character.[21] As had Reid, who argued that all our sensations are necessarily accompanied by a belief in the present existence of their object, so does Tetens hold that each of our sensations contains the "occasion" for the judgments that they are sensations of objects. But whereas Reid declined to give an answer to the question, "why sensation should compel our belief of the present existence in a thing," since he believed that "no philosopher can give a shadow of a reason, but such is the nature of these operations. . . . Because they are all simple and original and therefore inexplicable acts of the mind," Tetens believes he can go on to a more fundamental level.[22] For him sensations are simple and original, but representations and ideas are not. Representations consist of marks of sensations and certain rudimentary judgments that are connected with them. This is connected with what Reid had argued in his *Inquiry*: sensations are connected with certain natural judgments or beliefs. When we smell a rose, for example, the belief in the existence of the rose is inevitably suggested to us. Tetens can be seen to agree to this, and to argue that these "judgments, which are already connected with the sensations, have been drawn together with the sensation into their reproduction," that

20. Ibid., p. 21; see also Tetens, *Speculativische Philosophie*, p. 3, where he speaks of a "natural inclination to identify ideas and objects" because of which common sense believes that we are "dealing immediately with objects and not with impressions and representations." He is very much aware of Reid's theory of suggestion and natural signs. as his *Philosophische Versuche*, pp. 329–36, 365–69, 372, and 503 show. He also employs the language metaphor and speaks of ideas as written words (see pp. 363ff. and 432).

21. Ibid., pp. 77 and 83. On p. 77 he refers obliquely to Reid and Beattie.

22. Reid, *Works*, vol. 1. pp. 105f. (*Inquiry*, ed. Duggan, p. 25).

is, representation. Though these judgments have their "occasion" in sensation, they are for Tetens "effects of reflection, or of the faculty of thought, or of that of judgment, or whatever one may wish to call it."[23]

Under the influence of Reid, Tetens has come to the conclusion that thought is much more closely connected to sensation than the traditional empiricist doctrine had allowed. Thought does not simply consist in the comparison of ideas, but must already play a role in our acquisition of ideas, representations, and sensations. So Reid has shown him how to connect a more Leibnizian emphasis upon reason with an uncompromising empiricism. But Tetens is not so clear on the role thought has to play in *sensation*. While he is confident about its role in representation, he is uncertain about its connection with sensation. Thus, whereas he says at times that there are judgments already "connected with the sensations," at other times he expresses doubt:

If we conclude in analogy with those cases which can be observed with some degree of distinctness, we must say that the activity of thought does not connect *immediately* with the *sensations* about which we think, but with its representations.

Reid is of the opinion that some of our first judgments must precede the *simple apprehension* of objects, that is, precede the ideas of subject and predicate. He was led to this, without doubt, because of the rapidity with which the actions of thought follow the actions of sensation in several cases, so that they merge into one noticeable activity of the soul.

It is difficult to observe the real limits, to say where the preceding *sensation* and *representation* ends and where *thought* begins.

Tetens is more certain about the role which thought plays in the formation of ideas:

Representations become ideas and thoughts. By themselves they are neither ideas nor thoughts. The picture of the moon is only the material for an idea of the moon. The representation still lacks form: the *idea* contains apart from the *representation* also consciousness, a perception and differentiation. An idea presupposes comparison and judgments, if we are to consider it as the idea of a certain object. These latter are the effects of *feeling* and *thought*, which can be separated at least in theory, though in nature they are intimately connected with the idea.[24]

23. Tetens, *Philosophische Versuche*, p. 75. Compare with Eberhard. Tetens is clearer because he is closer to Reid.

24. Ibid., pp. 461–526; see also pp. 337–43, 365, 413. This problem is highly relevant for the discussion of Kant's Transcendental Deduction.

An idea is first and foremost "a *representation with consciousness*, a picture that has been made into the sign of an object."[25]

Tetens has modified the traditional theory of ideas to a significant extent. He has realized that ideas cannot be uncomplicated and unstructured basic elements of all knowledge, which explain everything without needing explanation themselves. The particularistic interpretation of ideas is rejected by him; the real task has become the attempt to exhibit the role which thought processes *necessarily* play in the acquisition of knowledge.

Tetens realizes the complex nature of the perceptual process. He transforms the mental objects mediating between the perceiving subject and the perceived objects into signs with a structure, a structure which leads us to take them as signs of external objects. But the basic problem of the theory of ideas remains: how can we be sure of the objective validity of our knowledge? How can we say that we know *objects*, if we are never directly acquainted with them? Tetens is clearly aware of this question. In fact, the attempt to answer it is one of his most central concerns.[26]

III

Tetens may be said to attack the problem of objective knowledge in two steps: the first is concerned with showing how our notions of objectivity arise, while the second deals with our reasons for accepting our sensations, representations, and ideas as signs of objects. The first step, which will be dealt with in this section, is not in any way concerned with the legitimacy of our claims to objective knowledge, but merely with a description of the genesis of our conception of objectivity.[27]

Tetens begins his discussion with the problem as presented by Reid and Beattie; and he makes no secret of this, losing no time in telling us that the Scottish theory—which, according to him, claims that our judgments about the objective reference of our acts of perception are immediate results of instinct—is the point of departure for his own discussion. Accordingly, he entitles the first section of his essay on this problem "Whether the Knowledge of the Existence of External Objects

25. Ibid., p. 94. Most Germans of this time taught, under the influence of Leibniz, that we are *not* aware of representations *qua* representations, and that we need apperception to accomplish this.

26. Ibid., pp. 369f. and 363.

27. Ibid., p. 393.

Can be Regarded as Instinctual Judgments of the Power of Thought."
Further, he says that the Scottish answer is satisfactory up to a point,
and that he is willing to go along with it, so far as it goes. His criticism is
that it does not go far enough:

The thought that we represent other objects to ourselves is so immediately
woven into our ordinary ideas of sensation that we are hardly aware of any
preceding act of reflection. Therefore we cannot blame *Reid, Home, Reimarus*
and others too much, when they considered the thought of objectivity and
subjectivity as the effect of instinct. In a certain sense they have not said
anything false. The expressions of the power of thought are all the expressions
of one basic faculty which finally can be analysed into certain general and
naturally necessary kinds of action. These can only be observed to exist, and we
are not allowed to derive them from other, farther removed principles. But on
the other hand, it is a mistake to appeal immediately to instinct with regard to
any particular effect.[28]

Thus, even though there are "innumerable cases in which we believe
that we are immediately concerned with the sensed objects," we would
"cease the investigation all too prematurely" if we were to rely too much
upon instinct. To do so is almost the same as the old convenient appeal
to occult qualities.[29]

There are general instinct-like laws of judgment, or at least, there are things we
have to assume as such because they are basic laws for us, according to which
our faculty of thought must think objects as identical and different. There can
be several of these laws which we cannot reduce to one general principle. But
the question is now: To what extent are our judgments about the *objectivity* of
representations . . . or about the internal and external reality of represented
objects, effects of the power of thought which can be understood on the basis of
other general and necessary laws of this faculty; and to what extent do they
require their own basic laws, with which they are in accord?[30]

However, Tetens's own answer is, in the light of his great promises,
rather disappointing. For, in the end, his view is very like that of the

---

28. Ibid., p. 365; see also pp. 372ff. The long note here shows that Leibniz, Locke,
and Reid are most important for Tetens in this context. But he also refers to Ferguson's
Institutes in the German translation of Garve.

29. Tetens, *Philosophische Versuche*, p. 366; see also p. 372n.: "*Reid* . . . and his followers
consider these judgments about the objective reality of things as instinctual effects of the
understanding, of which no other reason can be given. But he supplies many nice
observations which belong here." See also p. 412.

30. Ibid., pp. 366f.

Scots. After some debate as to how we come to differentiate between two different classes or "heaps" (*Haufen*) of sensations, that is, those of inner and those of outer sense, he concludes with the help of Lord Kames, to whom he refers approvingly several times, that our judgments about the objectivity of our representations are indeed natural judgments.[31]

It is natural, necessary, and in accordance with the laws of the faculty of thought, when I think: *my body is a really existing object, and it is not my self. The tree, which I see and feel, is a really existing object for itself*, and [it is] neither my soul nor my body. This conclusion is against *Hume* and *Berkeley*. But I shall not use it any further.[32]

In the end, then, the only difference between Reid and Tetens seems to be the latter's insistence that the judgments concerning the reality of objects are judgments of thought. In some sense this difference is minimal, as Tetens himself admits. But it does foreshadow the way in which Kant will attack the problem of objectivity.[33]

Tetens may appear somewhat ungrateful when he on several occasions points out that the Scots have really not answered Hume, have not been thorough enough, and "have opposed *Hume* and *Berkeley* with common sense in an indeterminate way."[34] Common sense does not need philosophy: it will always be victorious over people like Hume and Berkeley. But more seriously: Reid and Beattie "have

31. Ibid., p. 395 (reference to Lord Kames *Versuch über die Grundsätze der Moralität*, 3rd essay); p. 396: "The phenomenon is really just as Mr. *Home* has observed it. The question is only from what cause its character is determined."

32. Ibid., p. 400. His discussion of the self shows that he knew of Hume's bundle theory of the self.

33. Ibid., p. 365: "*Reid, Home, Reimarus*, and others . . . have in a certain respect said nothing false;" p. 441: "I would therefore, together with *Reid*, say without hesitation that it [the judgment connected with sensation] is the effect of an instinct."

34. Ibid., p. 392; see also p. 331. Talking about the differences between ideas and representations he finds: "Mr. *Reid* and his followers have entangled themselves in these difficulties, and in order to get out of them again they have accepted the opinion that no other reason or explanation of the origin of the first ideas can be given . . . than that they are essentially different sensations . . . and are only effects of instinct. About them we can only ask *of what kind* are they, but not how they *originate*. There is no doubt that they are effects of the instinct, which means, effects which originate from the nature of thought. *Locke* and the other philosophers, who are contradicted by them, have not denied this. But they have affirmed that the kind of action of the natural faculty and its laws can be analyzed and reduced to general rules." See also pp. 333ff. and *Speculativische Philosophie*, p. 12.

included among the principles of common sense, old prejudices that have long been discarded by true philosophy. Thus, together with the principle of scepticism, they have denied 'the principle that all external objects are only judged in accordance with their representations within ourselves.'" Moreover, "they overthrew the tribunal of analytic and deductive reason, so that one might say that common sense should come to the aid of the sceptics and idealists in defending certain propositions against Reid and Beattie."[35]

But Tetens himself does not give a satisfactory explanation of the role of thought in sensation either. He has not made clear how thought connects with sensation; and he has not shown why it guarantees objectivity or justifies our belief in the existence of external objects. But then, this is not all he has to say on this matter, since he also addresses himself to it in his discussion of the objective laws of thought.[36]

IV

In his discussion of common sense, Tetens, like most of his German contemporaries, takes as his point of departure his view of the essential component of the Scottish conception of common sense: "its opposition to discursive reasoning."[37] He agrees that this characterization is essentially correct. His only objection is that the Scots themselves did not adhere strictly enough to this position. Oswald and Beattie, especially, have ascribed things to common sense that cannot possibly be part of it, *qua* sense. They include among its principles propositions "which are incomprehensible without a very highly developed understanding, or one that is sharpened by deliberation, reflection and knowledge."[38] If the distinction between common sense and reason is to be plausible, we cannot give the name "common sense" to all conscious thought, that is, to distinct concepts, inferences, and general theories, as to the presuppositions of all thought.[39]

35. Tetens, *Philosophische Versuche*, p. 292. All this sounds very much like Kant's later pronouncements on common sense.

36. See section V of this chapter below.

37. Ibid., p. 507f. "This is how *Reid, Beattie,* and *Oswald* understood the term, though their explanations of it are otherwise indeterminate."

38. Ibid., p. 508; see also 512: "What *Oswald* has passed off as cognitions of common sense truly does not belonq to it." He thinks especially of his theological convictions.

39. Ibid., pp. 508, 559; *Speculativische Philosophie*, pp. 5–10.

Whether or not this characterization of the Scottish conception of common sense is correct, it must be immediately noted that, if these remarks suggest Tetens himself makes a sharp distinction between common sense and reason, they are misleading. The two are for him, as they were for Eberhard, Mendelssohn, and (at least the later) Reid, different expressions of the same basic faculty, namely, the faculty of thought.[40] "*Common sense* is nothing other than the the *faculty of thought* in so far as it judges about objects by being immediately related to them." If discursive thought, or reason, is conscious, then common sense is a sort of unconscious thought. It involves certain "unnoticed transitions from one judgment to another, transitions which are, when more carefully considered, indeed confused and contracted deductions and inferences."[41] Since both are expressions of the same basic faculty, since both function in accordance with identical principles and in very much the same way, they are not different in kind, but only in degree. In fact, their only difference for Tetens consists in our not being aware of the functions of common sense.[42] Because we are not aware of the thought processes presupposed by common-sense knowledge, it *appears* that it is immediate, and it is for this reason that we describe common sense as a sense. The Scottish characterization is therefore quite correct for Tetens. But here, too, he believes we must go farther and be more thorough: we must try to make conscious the unconscious reasoning of common sense.[43]

Because common sense is no distinct faculty of the human mind, and because there is thus no clear demarcation between it and reason, Tetens does not find it fruitful to define "common sense" primarily by reference to its place in the geography of the human mind. Instead, he defines it by reference to the body of knowledge to which it gives rise. "Common sense" and "reason" in his work refer therefore not so much to subjective mental faculties as to certain classes of judgments. The judgments attributed to "common sense" are further subdivided into three subclasses, common sense proper, cultivated human under-

40. Tetens, *Philosophische Versuche*, pp. 572ff. Common sense and reason have their own spheres and need each other. They can never really contradict, but both can fail, and both can correct each other (p. 565).

41. Ibid., pp. 510, 509. Examples of such reasoning are given by him in the first sections of his *Speculativische Philosophie*.

42. Tetens, *Philosophische Versuche*, pp. 508ff.; *Speculativische Philosophie*. pp. 6ff.

43. For this reason he also finds it difficult at times to differentiate between sensation and thought.

standing, and learned human understanding.[44] The latter two are higher developments of common sense proper. But he does not make much of this distinction and usually talks exclusively about common sense proper. The subdivisions only show again how for Tetens common sense and reason shade off into each other.

That degree of the human understanding "which all *healthy* and *fully intact* human beings, endowed with the ordinary senses, have obtained when they are fully grown and judge about things and qualities . . . is the common sense. Its cognitions amount to the *universal human opinions*, to the *sensus communis hominem*." "Common sense" refers to that stage which "*all* human beings usually reach through the internal organization of their nature and the influence of external factors."[45] These descriptions show that Tetens understands "common sense" in a wider sense than Reid. His "common sense" comprises also what Reid called the "common understanding."[46]

This has certain consequences for the function which Tetens assigns to common sense. He can say on the one hand that we have given "a great authority" to common sense and this "not without reason," and note on the other hand that it cannot be an absolute tribunal of truth.[47] Common sense makes agreement between human beings possible, and it suffices for the most complicated matters of daily life. Neither the hunter, nor the sailor, needs more knowledge than it can give. Even scientific disputes can be solved at this level, and moral philosophy does not have to go beyond common sense either. For all normal concerns we need no more complicated concepts that those of common sense.[48] But the fact that all human beings agree on something, the fact that a certain proposition is sanctified by common sense, does *not* show that it is true.[49]

First of all, though all the judgments of common sense appear to be *necessary* judgments, they are only *subjectively* necessary, that is, they are necessary for us. Secondly, they are not all necessary in the same way. If only for this reason, the mere acknowledgment of the necessity of

44. Tetens, *Philosophische Versuche*, pp. 511–14.

45. Ibid., p. 511.

46. See Reid, *Works*, vol. 1, pp. 185f. (*Inquiry*, ed. Duggan, pp. 212f.). See also Norton, "Thomas Reid's *Curâ Primâ* on Common Sense."

47. Tetens, *Philosophische Versuche*, pp. 511f.

48. Ibid., pp. 508–14; *Speculativische Philosophie*, pp. 6–11.

49. Tetens, *Philosophische Versuche*, pp. 507f. He could very well be echoing Hume in this regard. See also my "Hume's Antinomies."

common-sense judgments is not enough for philosophical purposes. We must inquire into the sources of their necessity. Reid, Oswald, and Beattie have neglected to do this. They have ceased their inquiries too early:

It would have been the real task of the British philosophers who made it their business to justify the principles of common sense against *Hume* and *Berkeley*, to have become involved in the particulars of this problem. They should have shown with regard to every kind of *common sense cognition* how much of it *necessarily* has to be accepted as true *through the nature of the understanding* and how much depends upon the association of ideas.[50]

What the Scots have neglected to do, Tetens sets out to accomplish. But in his discussion of the different kinds of necessity to be found in common sense, he is again depending upon the Scottish theory of common sense.

In accordance with the basis upon which necessity is founded, Tetens differentiates the following subjectively necessary ways of thinking: (1) Subjectively necessary forms of judgment. These are founded upon

the nature of the faculty of thought. We know at least some of these general laws of nature to which the understanding *qua* understanding is just as much subject as light is subject to the laws of refraction.[51]

Among these are the laws of contradiction, of the excluded middle, etc.[52]

(2) There are necessary judgments "in which the *necessity of thought* depends upon the *ideas* and their qualities, or upon the *material* of the judgment." Among these Tetens counts what he calls "particularly necessary judgments," that is, laws of geometry, such claims as

50. Ibid., p. 515; see also p. 517: after having explained what he thinks is necessary for the refutation of scepticism, he goes on: "However, if one goes to work as did *Reid*, *Beattie* and *Oswald* and assumes as an absolute principle that when common sense thinks of a certain matter in such and such a way this is a secure criterion of truth, and when even reason's right to vote in matters of truth, prejudice and error is taken away, how can the skeptic ever be convinced? Is it too much to say that this approach is contradictory to common sense?"

51. Tetens, *Philosophische Versuche*, p. 500.

52. He says he does not know whether all these laws can be reduced to the law of contradiction, as the Wolffians hold.

"nothing can exist without a cause," and "a multitude of such propositions which *Reid* and *Beattie* have called suggestions of reason."[53] The first kind of necessary truth is above all scepticism, representing formally necessary principles of all thought. The second kind may be doubted, though it cannot be disproved either. "The subjective necessity of the latter kind is also a *physical* necessity, and the circumstances and presuppositions upon which their necessity depends cannot be separated from the understanding."[54]

There is also a third kind of necessity for Tetens, a necessity which is accidental. These are (3) judgments which are subjectively necessary because of habit. "Mr. *Hume* and several others after him have mistaken this necessity for the first kind of *natural necessity*, or rather, they have recognized it as the only kind of necessity."[55]

Given this distinction between different kinds of subjective necessity, Tetens can run through the catalogue of principles of common sense mentioned by Reid ("the judgment about the existence of a real world, about the causal connections of objects within the world; the distinction of the present sensations from the past in memory and the future in anticipation, our belief in foreign witness") and find that "the one is an association of ideas and a generalization of particular judgments, the other, however, a natural law of thought; and in a certain sense the faculty of thought is always determined by a combination of the two in these cognitions. And this makes the approval and the conviction

53. Ibid., p. 503; see also pp. 495f.: "There are still more of such *relational thoughts* which do not result from the comparison of two related ideas, but from the *idea of one of them* . . . Mr. *Reid* has called this latter class of judgments, *judgments of suggestion* [*Suggestionsurtheile*], judgments from a *natural propulsion*, or from inspiration." See also pp. 478f.: "There is one subjective necessity in geometrical demonstrations, another one in general kinds of thought. The latter may be called *propositions of suggestion*. They are also to be found in judgments of sensation and in the belief with which we accept testimony by others. Mr. *Beattie* has endeavoured to show the nature of this necessity. But he does not appear to have reached its foundation and origin. For in order to do this it is not sufficient here and there to note the *kind of subjective necessity* in the thoughts. Though the *objective necessity* is judged in accordance with this subjective necessity, we also must show the *basis of this necessity* in the understanding, or at least the universal law of thought which determines the naturally necessary ways in which thoughts and judgments function. This entire fertile field has been left by Mr. *Beattie* and his predecessors as obscure as it was before. I cannot make up for everything. But I shall try to put greater emphasis upon some of the more elevated places which afford an outlook upon the most important areas."

54. Ibid., p. 504.
55. Ibid.

necessary." Thus, he goes on, "we may take the word common sense in whatever sense we want, it is obvious from the nature of common sense that the kinds of *subjective necessity* differentiated above will be found among its effects."[56] For this reason we have to examine common-sense principles; we are not to accept them as absolutely true without inquiry. Since common sense, like reason, depends upon the principles of thought, and since philosophical investigation is essentially a rational enterprise, an analysis of common-sense principles necessarily leads to an examination of the principles of all thought for Tetens. The analysis of *subjectively* necessary principles of common sense leads in this way to the analysis of the *objectively necessary* laws of thought. Only through such an analysis can we differentiate mere prejudice and habitual judgments from genuine principles of common sense. This is something which, according to Tetens, the Scots never realized.[57]

v

Up to this point Tetens has always relied on the Scots to supply him with the starting point of his discussion, to guide him in the course of his own investigation, and even to give him hints for his attempt at a solution of his problems. Now he appears to have reached a point at which they can no longer help him.

But this is not actually so. Whatever grand claims he makes about the investigation of the role of objective laws of thought in knowledge and his supposed advance beyond the Scots, even here he not only starts from a position greatly determined by them, but also concludes with a theory that is not very different from theirs.

For he starts from Lossius. And Lossius's theory that truth consists essentially in subjective necessity is, as shown earlier, nothing but a modification of Beattie's (and Feder's) theory of truth. Thus, when Tetens starts with a critical discussion of Lossius, he is not far removed from the state of the problem as determined by the Scots. Furthermore, his conclusion, that "necessary laws of *thought* lead common sense towards the existence of external objects, as the causes of its external sensations," is nothing that would have shocked Reid.[58] But in

56. Ibid., pp. 514f.
57. But for them the natural judgments, even though connected with sensation, are already objective.
58. Tetens, *Philosophische Versuche*, p. 548 (emphasis mine).

reaching this conclusion, Tetens makes a number of interesting moves that may have shown Kant his way towards the Transcendental Deduction.

The question concerning objective truth arises for Tetens as follows:

> We know from observation the *subjective* necessity which forces us to think in accordance with the general laws of the understanding. We feel that we cannot think square circles . . . upon this subjective necessity we base the *objective* necessity: the impossibility of thinking differently is ascribed to the objects external to the understanding. Our ideas are no longer ideas within us. They are things external to us. The qualities and relations we perceive in the ideas are represented to us as qualities and relations of the objects themselves. They belong to the objects even apart from our thought, and they would have to be recognized by any other thinking being. This is a consequence of instinct. It is an effect of common sense. The old metaphysics has noted something correct in this approach and has accepted as its axiom that truth is something *objective*.[59]

Lossius had seriously questioned this metaphysical conception of truth, and he had argued that truth was just as subjective and without foundation in the ontological structure of the universe as beauty.[60] But Tetens believes: "this is the fiercest attack which scepticism could make upon reason."[61]

In order to answer the question posed by Lossius's *Physische Ursachen* it is necessary for Tetens to determine first "what really counts with regard to truth, and what the belief that objects are really as they are represented amounts to. Then we have to consider the way in which we reach this judgment and the reasons which lead us to it."[62] First of all, it is clear that when we define truth as the correspondence of thought and objects we cannot mean anything other than analogy by "correspondence." Ideas have the same relations to one another as the objects to which they correspond. Comparing objects with ideas is really nothing more than comparing representations. Thus the question amounts to asking whether we have any reason, or whether there is any law which forces us to consider the relations of the ideas as relations of the objects themselves. The problem is whether or not "the relations which we perceive in our ideas are merely *subjective relations*, that is,

59. Ibid., p. 519.
60. See chapter V above.
61. Tetens, *Philosophische Versuche*, p. 520.
62. Ibid.

relations depending on the nature of the kind of perceptions we have. The point of the matter is not to be found in this question."[63]

The second matter in need of clarification is the meaning of the claim that our knowledge is objective. What does it mean to say that the objects really have the characteristics we ascribe to them? Since we do not perceive the objects directly and immediately (as Reid had argued but Tetens rejected), but only by means of sensations, representations, and ideas, this claim cannot be taken literally either. What we have to mean, according to Tetens, is that the objects do not just appear to me in a certain way, under certain circumstances and at a certain time, but that they necessarily have to appear in this way to everyone and at all times.[64]

After these qualifications, the "true sense" of Lossius's problem emerges:

Thoughts consist in the relations which we perceive in our impressions . . . If the relations which we note in our impressions are simply dependent upon this kind of impression, their entire analogy is merely subjective, and the incompatability of, for instance, square and round in one figure, is only an incompatability for us. But if these relations are independent of the nature of impressions, and the same as every other thinking being must see in his impressions, then the impossibility of a square circle is an *absolute* and *objective impossibility*.[65]

We cannot go further, Tetens believes, with this question. He has resolved the problem of the objectivity of our cognitions into that of their intersubjectivity, and by doing so he has shifted the problem from sensation to thought. For Tetens, as for most of his German contemporaries, intersubjectivity is possible only through thought. Against the objection that there might be other beings with different laws of thought, Tetens argues that to pose this impossibility is to abandon the aim of his inquiry and to frame a new one. Furthermore, we cannot think an understanding that can think square circles. Therefore, even if there were such a thing, it would not be an understanding. This, for Tetens, shows that the question is irrelevant.[66]

The problem concerning the objectivity of knowledge is now reformulated as follows:

63. Ibid., p. 523.
64. Ibid., pp. 523–25. This is not unlike Feder's "constant appearance."
65. Ibid., pp. 525f. Compare also with Feder.
66. Ibid., pp. 526f.

If we replace the words *objective* and *subjective* with the words unchanging subjective and changing subjective, then we do not have to take into account the faculties of thought of other beings, of which we have no concepts . . . For this is the same as when we ask what depends upon the special organization of our organs or our constitution and what is necessarily and always so, and remains so as long as our self remains a thinking being, even if the bodily organs of thought are changed.[67]

After these reformulations, Tetens's answer to the question concerning the objectivity of knowledge, or, as it reads now, "whether the laws of thought are only subjective laws of our faculty of thought or whether they are laws of any faculty of thought whatsoever," has become surprisingly simple. Since we cannot think any other faculty of thought than our own—for if there were such a faculty of thought with other laws, it could not be called "thought" in the same way as our faculty—the truths of reason "are objective truths, and the fact that they are objective truths is just as certain as the fact that they are truths in the first place. We cannot doubt or deny the former, just as we cannot doubt or deny the latter."[68]

More difficult is the question whether our knowledge based upon the sensations is objective, or whether it is "at most a steady subjective illusion."[69] Tetens agrees with most of his contemporaries that a great part of our knowledge through the senses is indeed such a subjective appearance, but he wants to show that there are also cases in which we can be sure about the objectivity of our representations. And in those cases our belief in objective reality is "so necessary that it is impossible for us to think the contrary." Though I can make mistakes and erroneously ascribe characteristics of my representations to the objects themselves, there are also cases "which I cannot doubt without exaggerating scepticism very much."[70]

But is this a satisfactory answer, given Tetens's own pronouncements on the matter? That we "are often assured" or "strongly believe" that objects are really there and are what they seem to be has never been in doubt. What has been in doubt is whether we are ultimately justified in holding these beliefs, or whether they are illusory. The Scots thought

67. Ibid., pp. 527f.
68. Ibid.. p. 533.
69. Ibid., p. 534. It seems Tetens is here alluding to Feder. In any case, his tactics of "reformulation" remind one somewhat of Feder.
70. Ibid., pp. 540f.

that these beliefs belong among the basic principles of thought, and that, as such, they neither needed to be nor could be justified. Tetens rejected that approach as too simple and as unphilosophical. Yet, after much discussion he adopts a theory that is not appreciably different from that of the Scots. Like Reid, Oswald, and Beattie, he assumes that our sensations are much more reliable than the sceptic supposes. But, whereas the Scots had claimed that this reliability of sensation was granted *immediately* by certain basic principles or beliefs, Tetens, who believes that these basic principles are principles of thought, and who, furthermore does not think that thought can be immediately related to sensation, should have given an account how knowledge becomes reliable through the influence of thought. But he does not succeed in explicating "the procedure of the power of thought in the attainment of knowledge more exactly and more carefully than either *Reid*, or *Beattie* or *Oswald*" had done.[71] Reid's theory of suggestion and natural belief serves not only as his starting point, but also remains his model from beginning to end.

Accordingly, Tetens's conclusion is very much the same as that of the Scots (as well as Feder and Lossius):

Necessary laws of thought lead common sense towards the existence of external objects as the causes of external sensations. Just such laws bring forth the judgments about impressions. But the same laws lead common sense to the thought that the relations of the impressions are, under certain conditions, also the relations of objects.[72]

Apart from the fact that Tetens's account is formulated in a terminology compatible with what Reid called the "ideal system," there is little substantial difference from Reid and the other Scots. Tetens does *not* show "more exactly" how the laws of thought enable us to know in the first place. He says that the belief in the existence of objects originates by means of a natural law of thought, but Reid had already said that a natural law requires us to "regard our impressions as corresponding signs of objects." Moreover, Tetens himself uses the term "school of nature," a term also used by Reid, in order to explain how we come to consider our representations as signs of real objects.[73]

Even if Tetens has not succeeded in going beyond Reid, he has

71. See notes 4 and 53 of this chapter.
72. Tetens, *Philosophische Versuche*, p. 548.
73. Ibid.

made, under the influence of Reid, an interesting move: by reformu-
lating the question concerning the objective validity of knowledge in
close connection with his conception of laws of thought, and then
trying to answer this question by linking these laws with perception, he
has started the discussion of an important issue. It remained for Kant
to give a more satisfactory answer. But if this is so, then Kant's
"execution of Hume's problem in its widest extent" owes, at the very
least indirectly, a great deal to Reid.[74]

74. When Kant, in the *Prolegomena* (ed. Beck. p. 7), finds that "to satisfy the conditions
of the problem, the opponents of the great thinker [Hume] should have penetrated very
deeply into the nature of reason, so far as it is concerned with pure thinking—a task
which did not suit them," he seems to be influenced by Tetens.

VIII

Scottish Common Sense and the German Counter-Enlightenment

I

THERE can be no doubt that Johann Georg Hamann, Johann Gottfried Herder and Friedrich Heinrich Jacobi were thoroughly familiar with the Scots. Thus Hamann referred to the French translation of Reid's *Inquiry* as early as 1772;[1] and because he actually possessed this work, it is very likely that he acquired it in Königsberg shortly after its publication in 1768.[2] That he also knew of Beattie as early as 1772 and must have studied his *Essay* rather carefully soon after it appeared in German is clear from his correspondence with Herder. This means that he was one of the people who knew Reid from the very beginning of his influence in Germany (and this, even though he lived in far off Königsberg).

Herder came to know Beattie's work no later than 1772, as is shown by his letter to Hamann, dated 1 August 1772.[3] But the evidence with regard to his knowledge of Reid is not so clear. Robert T. Clark, for instance, claims that "the Scottish philosopher Reid, whose system would undoubtedly have appealed to Herder, was probably not read by him until our author's last year, when Reid's criticism of Berkeley is mentioned in the *Adrastea*."[4] Several circumstances speak against the correctness of Clark's view, however. First of all, there is internal

---

1. See notes 21 and 22 below.
2. The fact that this version of Reid's *Inquiry* was available in Königsberg will be important to remember in the chapter on Kant.
3. See note 39 of this chapter below.
4. Clark, *Herder, His Life and Thought*, p. 204.

evidence in the text to which Clark refers, a note to Berkeley's *Theory of Vision*. Probably because the work itself was not easily available in Germany, Herder refers the reader to Reid's account of Berkeley's theory: "See Thomas Reid's *judgment* of it in his *Untersuchungen über den menschlichen Verstand* in which he utilizes the work very much himself."[5] The reference is to the German translation which appeared in 1782. But Herder has the title wrong in two places. He refers to it as "*Untersuchungen,*" not "*Untersuchung,*" and as being about the "*menschliche Verstand*" and not about the "*menschliche Geist*" as it reads in German. This points to an earlier reading of the work, I believe. Herder may be quoting from memory.

Secondly, it is indeed more than likely that Herder, who was very much interested in psychology and always aware of its latest developments, would have read the *Inquiry* by 1782 at the latest, when it became easily obtainable in German. Since he had reviewed Beattie's work himself, and must have known about his connection with Reid, there was an added incentive to study Reid as early as 1772.

Thirdly, Reid was, as we will see, of great importance to Hamann; and Herder was not only thoroughly familiar with Hamann's thought, but also deeply influenced by it. And Hamann's *Philologische Einfälle und Zweifel* of 1772, an unpublished critique of Herder's views on language, refers to Reid at a crucial phase in the argument. Herder understandably had a burning interest in this work, made every effort to obtain a copy of it, and successfully got hold of the original manuscript.[6] As soon as he read the manuscript he had another motive to consult Reid's *Inquiry*. Depending on when this was, he could easily have obtained the French translation.

Haym characterizes Herder's review of Beattie as his attempt at making peace with Hamann after their falling out over their differences on the origin of language. If Herder knew already in 1772 that Hamann considered Reid to be a witness against Herder's views on language, then the choice of a book by Beattie, who was seen as a follower of Reid, would have made some sense. By praising the views of Reid's follower he may be seen to have reaffirmed his agreement with Hamann.

But be all this as it may, Herder must, at the very least, have known Reid by name and reputation, if only because of the references to him that can be found in many of the important philosophical works with

5. Herder, *Werke*, ed. Suphan, vol. 24, p. 404 (*Adrastea*).
6. Haym, *Herder nach seinem Leben und Werken*, vol. 1, p. 530. and Hamann, *Sämtliche Werke*, ed. Nadler, vol. 3, pp. 423f.

which he was acquainted. Furthermore, Beattie's *Essay* makes reference to him, and Hamann called Herder's attention to the *Essays on the Intellectual Powers of Man* in 1786.[7]

Although Herder does not mention Reid until the *Metakritik* and the *Adrastea* even in contexts where one may reasonably expect him to have done so, this does not prove that he did not read him. References to others were not given as freely in eighteenth-century Germany as is customary today.[8] Thus Kant, who, as we know, wrote his first *Critique* with a book by Tetens open on his desk, nowhere in that work refers to the latter. On the other hand, though it is very likely that Herder knew Reid early, this cannot be proved. Therefore it is better to concentrate on Beattie's influence upon him, which, in any case, is significant all by itself.

With regard to Jacobi matters are, if anything, still more complicated. Though it is beyond doubt that Jacobi's thought is highly dependent upon that of Reid, it is not clear when and how Jacobi learned of him. His references to Reid, especially in the light of the Scotsman's pervasive influence upon him, are rather sparse.[9] One may even get the feeling that Jacobi is trying to downplay, or even hide, his Scottish indebtedness. But, whether or not these feelings are justified, there is enough evidence to show that Jacobi found Reid important for the development of his own epistemological theory.[10]

Given Herder's and Hamann's connections with the Scots, Jacobi

7. See note 38 of this chapter below.

8. See, for instance, number LXXVII of the *Frankfurter gelehrte Anzeigen*, in Herder, *Werke*, ed. Suphan, vol. 5, p. 452: "The spirit of British philosophy appears to have made its way beyond Hadrian's wall and has collected a small group of its kind in the Scottish Highlands. Ferguson, Robertson, Gerard, Beattie and Millar are far more important than the dull Search, and because they have chosen their field in unison, as it were, their philosophy becomes still more valuable. For it is mostly philosophy of the shapes and changes of human kind in agreement with history and experience."

9. For an exhaustive discussion of all the references see Baum, *Vernunft und Erkenntnis*. Though I have learned a great deal from Baum, I disagree with his general interpretation of Jacobi. I do not believe that Reid's influence alone can show that Jacobi was *not* an irrationalist precursor of modern *Lebensphilosophie*. The examples of Herder and Hamann clearly show that a Reidian influence can coexist with such a view.

10. This has been convincingly shown by Baum. But he has been criticized by Hammacher (in a review in *Zeitschrift für philosophische Forschung* 24 [1970]: 625–33), Düsing (in a review in *Philosophische Rundschau* 18 [1971]: 105–16), Höhn (in a review in *Kant-Studien* 62 [1971]: 113–20), Lauth (in a review in *Archiv für Geschichte der Philosophie* 54 [1972]: 97–103) and Karl Hommann, *F. H. Jacobis Philosophie der Freiheit* (München, 1972), pp. 251–53. Though some of the criticisms advanced are justified, none of them disprove the importance of Reid for Jacobi.

must have become aware of their theory rather early. Further, he was a close friend of the German translator of Beattie's Essay, Heinrich Wilhelm von Gerstenberg, as well as of Feder, who counted Jacobi among "his oldest friends among the philosophical writers of Germany."[11] Thus it is reasonable to suppose that, as an alert participant in the philosophical life in the seventies of the eighteenth century, Jacobi had come across the works of the Scots rather early as well.

In any case, from 1785 onwards Reid assumed a very special importance for Jacobi. It is most likely that he read (or reread) Reid's *Inquiry* around 1785. And it is certain that he acquired his *Essays on the Intellectual Powers of Man* in 1786. That he was impressed by Reid's thought becomes apparent from two different sources. One is a distant echo of his reading of Reid, communicated by Jacobi himself in a letter to J. Neeb in 1814:

Together with the praise I also owe you a few critical remarks; most notably about Thomas Reid, whose *Essays on the Intellectual Powers of Man* which appeared in 1786 [*sic*], you certainly cannot have read. For, if you had read this work, you could never have ranked him as low as Oswald and Beattie. And you could not have said that with all his weapons he had not even touched Hume, this giant among thinkers. Kant, who made similar remark in the *Prolegomena* ... could not have read the *Essays*, this masterwork of the matured thinker, either. For the *Prolegomena* appeared earlier.[12]

The second testimony is from Wilhelm von Humboldt's journal of his journey through Germany in 1788. Jacobi had said to Humboldt:

We do not perceive, as is usually maintained, merely the picture of external objects. We perceive these objects themselves .. . . This perception occurs, as Reid has said quite correctly, *by a sort of revelation* [English in the original]. Because of this we do not demonstrate that there are objects external to us, but believe it. This belief is no acceptance in accordance with probable reasons. It has a greater and more imperturbable certainty than a demonstration can ever supply.[13]

Yet in the dialogue *David Hume* Jacobi never refers directly to Reid, but

11. For Gerstenberg see Wagner, *Heinrich Wilhelm von Gerstenberg und der Sturm und Drang*, vol. 1, pp. 169f. For Feder see Feder, *Leben*, p. 213.

12. Jacobi, *F. H. Jacobis auserlesener Briefwechsel*, ed. Roth, vol. 2, p. 445.

13. Wilhelm von Humboldt, "Tagebuch der Reise nach dem Reich 1788," in his *Gesammelte Schriften*, ed. Leitzmann. vol. 14, p. 58.

only to a review of the *Essays* in the *Allgemeine Literatur-Zeitung*. It is in a later edition of his *Woldemar*, a novel that gives expression to his *Weltanschauung* of Storm and Stress, that he mentions the Scottish philosopher and hints at his importance.[14] But it is clear that Jacobi kept himself well informed about Scottish common-sense philosophy in general, and that he knew, for instance, Dugald Stewart's *Account of the Life and Writings of Thomas Reid.*[15]

II

Not only did these Germans know the Scots well; they clearly also appreciated them very much, and may even be shown to have had a special affinity for them. The works of the Scots played a most important role in their arguments with each other as well as in those against their opponents.

How central the Scottish influence is for the understanding of the counter-enlightenment becomes clear from the role which Reid's *Inquiry* and Beattie's *Essay* assumed in the relationship of Hamann and Herder. In 1772 Herder had published a treatise entitled *On the Origin of Language*. In it he claimed that human beings, unlike animals, are not governed by instinct, and argued that language could have arisen only because of this absence of instinct in humans. Against Condillac and others, who had tried to explain the origin of language by giving an account of how mankind had learned to associate signs and objects, Herder objected that "this account presupposes the really important step as already taken." That is to say, it takes for granted "that some things can stand for others, that there can be such a thing as a sign." He believed instead:

14. Jacobi, *Werke*, ed. Roth and Köppen, vol. 2, p. 170. Jacobi introduces a young man named Carl Sidney who is described as having studied philosophy in Edinburgh and as being a follower of Ferguson. It is particularly pointed out that Reid was Ferguson's most important teacher. Sidney himself values Reid so highly that Woldemar is astounded. In order to explain his high estimation of Reid, Sidney says: "I am certain that you will remember my judgment with approval at some time in the future, namely, when the deeply pondered last work of this thinker about the human understanding and the will, a masterwork, will reach you. He will perhaps hold it back for a few years in order to bring it closer to perfection." (The action of the novel is supposed to take place long before the appearance of Reid's last two works. But it is strange that Jacobi fails to mention the *Inquiry* which presumably appeared before the action is supposed to take place.)

15. Jacobi. *Werke*, vol. 2, p. 54.

Man, placed in the state of reflection which is peculiar to him, i.e. when his reflection has for the first time full freedom of action, did invent language. For what is reflection? What is language?

This reflection is characteristically peculiar to man and essential to his species; and so is language and the invention of language.

Invention of language is therefore as natural to man as it is to him that he is man.[16]

Reflection or *Besonnenheit* is the expression of man's freedom, or the absence of instinct characterized positively.[17]

Hamann disagreed strongly with Herder, especially for his use of "invention" with regard to language. He agreed that human beings are essentially free, and that we need the concept of freedom in order to be able to make moral judgments. Because we are absolutely free "neither *instinct* nor *sensus communis* determine the human being; neither *natural* nor *institutional* law determine the sovereign."[18] But man's absolute freedom does not preclude his being naturally predisposed to certain things rather than others. Even if one believes that *sensus communis* and instinct do not rule man absolutely, one need not deny them any rule whatsoever. Man is very similar to animals in his organization and has therefore also natural faculties. This means that he has also instincts. But man's instincts are different from those of other animals in that they are modifiable. While it prescribes a certain limited sphere to animals, the "*point of view* of man extends to the *universal* and loses itself in *infinity*, as it were."[19]

This description of instinct and *sensus communis* allows Hamann to introduce Reid as a witness against Herder—a witness who shows that, though we have to learn language, we no more invent it than we invent walking. For Reid, language belongs to those "powers of which nature has only planted the seeds in our minds, but has left the rearing of them to human culture," and the theory of natural and acquired language together with that of natural and acquired perception plays an important role for understanding human nature. In fact, in his *Inquiry*, Chapter VI, sections 20 and 24, entitled "Of Perception in General" and "Of the Analogy Between Perception and the Credit we give to

16. Herder, *Essay on the Origin of Language*, tr. Gode, in *On the Origin of Language: Rousseau and Herder*, tr. Moran and Gode, p. 115.

17. Ibid., pp. 103–15.

18. Hamann, *Werke*, ed. Nadler, vol. 3, p. 38.

19. Ibid., p. 39. This is roughly also Hume's point of view.

Human Testimony," Reid develops a surprising parallel between perception and language, an analogy at which he hints throughout his work. He finds that "there is a much greater similitude than is commonly imagined, between the testimony given by our two senses, and the testimony of men given by language." Indeed, he says somewhat later, "so great is the analogy between these two, and the analogy between the principles of the mind, which are subservient to the one, and those which are subservient to the other, without further apology we shall consider them together."[20]

Hamann appears to agree fully with all of this. Language is both natural and has to be learned:

Man *learns* to use and master all his limbs and senses, he *must* and *wants to* learn equally much. Therefore the *origin of language* is as natural and human as is the the origin of any other of our actions, faculties and skills. However, though every apprentice *contributes* to his education according to his inclinations, his faculties and the opportunities he has to learn: *learning*, in the proper sense, is just as little invention as it is mere remembering.[21]

Employing Reid's very terminology, Hamann characterizes the origin of language as a "twofold education of sensual revelation and human testimony."[22] Like Reid, who maintains that without natural language we could not possibly attain artificial language, and that natural language, original perception, and their respective principles, are the presuppositions for all thought, he argues that "invention and reason already presuppose a language and allow as little of being taught without language, as arithmetic allows of being thought without numbers."[23]

Reid is also important for Hamann in his "description" of the relationship between the understanding and the senses. And this has certain consequences for Hamann's understanding of language as well. Using a comparison that sounds very Hamannian indeed, he finds that the relationship between the senses and the understanding is "probably" very similar to the relation between the stomach and those

20. Reid, *Works*, vol. 1, pp. 184, 194f. (*Inouiry*, ed. Duggan, p. 210, pp. 234f).
21. Hamann, *Werke*, ed. Nadler, vol. 3, p. 41.
22. Ibid., pp. 39f.
23. Reid, *Works*, vol. 1, pp. 196f., 117f. (*Inquiry*, ed. Duggan, p. 238; see also p. 55); compare Hamann, *Werke*, ed. Nadler, vol. 3, p. 21. Compare also *Werke*, ed. Nadler, vol. 3, p. 31.

"vessels which secrete the finer and higher juices of the blood, without whose circulation and influence the stomach itself could not fulfill its functions."[24] But however much this sounds like Hamann, it may very well have been lifted out of Reid's *Inquiry*. For in arguing against certain physiological accounts of what happens in sensation, Reid asks ironically:

Is it not as philosophical, and more intelligible, to conceive, that as the stomach receives its food, so the soul receives her images by a kind of deglutation? I might add, that we need only continue this peristaltic motion of the nervous tubes from the *sensorium* to the extremities of the nerves that serve the muscles, in order to account for muscular motion.—Thus nature will be consonant to herself; and as sensation will be the conveyance of the ideal aliment of the mind, so muscular motion will be the expulsion of the recrimentitious part of it. For who can deny, that the images of things conveyed by sensation, may after due concoction, become fit to be thrown off by muscular motion? I only give these hints to be ingenious, hoping that in time this hypothesis may be brought up into a system as philosophical, as that of animal spirits, or the vibration of the fibres.[25]

Hamann obviously liked this kind of satire; and being a voracious, though self-conscious, eater himself, who often used analogies between foods and philosophical matters, he must have enjoyed this ironical comparison; especially so because Herder (against whom all this is directed) had a predilection for materialistic accounts. I suggest, then, that the entire passage following Hamann's analogy should be seen against the background of Reid's account of natural and artificial language. This becomes clear when one sees that Hamann goes on to say:

Nothing is in our *understanding* without having been in the senses first: just as there is nothing in our body that has not gone first through our own stomach or that of our parents. The *stamina* and *menstrua* of our *reason* are therefore in the most authentic sense *revelations* and *traditions*, which we receive as our possessions, transform into our juices and powers and become thus able to fulfil our destiny to partially *reveal* and partially *transmit* the *critical* and *archontic* dignity of a political animal . . . even if it was also assumed that man came into the world as an *empty* skin: just this deficiency would enable him to gain more enjoyment of nature through *experiences* and of the community of his own kind through *traditions*. Our reason at least originates from this twofold

24. Hamann, *Werke*, ed. Nadler, vol. 3, pp. 39f.
25. Reid, *Works*, 1, pp. 181f. (*Inquiry*, ed. Duggan, p. 199).

education of sensual *revelations* and human *testimonies*, which are communicated through similar *means*, namely signs, as well as in accordance with similar laws.*

*See *Recherches sur l'entendement humain d'après les Principes du sens commun par Thomas Reid.* Ouvrage traduit de l'anglois a Amsterdam, 1768.[26]

The similarity of all this to Reid's account of the parallelism of language and sensation is striking. Hamann not only uses the very same words, that is, "revelation," "sign," and "tradition," but he also puts forward very much the same views. But it would perhaps be too much to say that Hamann and Reid held the same theory of perception and belief, for Hamann never really develops a full-fledged theory. Since he is not a very systematic thinker in any case, he offers little more than suggestions for further thought. But in these suggestions Reid's contribution cannot be overlooked.[27]

Also very similar to Reid are the conclusions for philosophy in general that Hamann draws from his account of language. Metaphysics, he finds, has

its school and court language; both are suspicious to me, and I am neither capable of understanding them nor of using them myself. Therefore I almost assume that our entire philosophy consists more of language than of reason. The misunderstandings of innumerable words, the *prosopopoieas* of arbitrary abstractions, *the antitheses tes pseudonymou gnoseos*, nay, even the most common figures of speech of the *sensus communis* have created a whole world of questions, which have been brought up with just as little reason as they have been answered. We still have to do with a *grammar* of reason, of writing and of their common elements.[28]

26. Hamann, *Werke*, ed. Nadler, vol. 3, pp. 39f.

27. This similarity extends even to the details of Hamann's and Reid's accounts. Thus they agree on the "expressive nature" of natural language. And given their fundamental agreement it is perhaps not surprising that James G. O'Flaherty's attempt at a systematic reconstruction of Hamann's theory of language should present a view that is significantly similar to Reid's. The very headings of O'Flaherty's study show this similarity: "The Primacy of Natural Language," "Natural Language as a Clue to the Nature of Reality," and "Hamann's Tendency to Draw Inferences from Natural Language to Reality." O'Flaherty is not aware of Reid and nowhere in the book refers to him, but his argument for considering Hamann's theory of language as his most important contribution to philosophy is unwittingly also an argument for the importance of Reid. (See his *Unity and Language*.)

28. Hamann to Jacobi, 1 December 1784, Hamann, *Briefwechsel*, ed. Ziesemer and Henkel, vol. 4, p. 272.

That these criticisms of the misuse of language by philosophers are not without connection to Reid's influence may be seen again from the *Philologische Einfälle und Zweifel*. Immediately after his reference to Reid's *Inquiry*, Hamann criticizes philosophers for always having given "the bill of divorce to truth by differentiating what nature has joined together and by perversely" joining together what nature has set apart.[29] Against this background we have to see also Hamann's remarks in the *Metakritik*. Kant has artificially separated reason from language and common sense. Since for Hamann rational thought is impossible without language, and since language depends for him upon "natural language," "sensual revelation," and "human testimony," the "purifications" or "purisms" of critical thought do not, in fact, aid a better understanding of reason, but rather destroy it altogether.[30]

The Scottish influence upon Hamann is perhaps most visible in his analysis of the history of modern philosophy and the role of idealism and scepticism in it. For both Hamann and the Scots, modern philosophy is a gradual development towards idealism. Erwin Metzke evaluates the Scottish influence as follows:

Hamann characterizes Hume as standing in an idealistic tradition . . . Hamann, however, is thoroughly concerned with reality, with being itself. He wants a historical and physical realism . . . Hamann rejects Hume exactly for attempting to give a theory and justification of his belief . . . Therefore, the rejection of the idealistic conception of causality by Hume . . . From here Hamann's great interest in Reid is understandable as well.[31]

29. Hamann, *Werke*, ed. Nadler, vol. 3, p. 40.

30. Ibid., p. 284. Similar pronouncements can be found all through Hamann's works. Thus he draws attention to the fact that philosophers "deceive and are deceived" by the "confusion of language" (p. 31). "Without word, no creation—nor world; here is the source of creation and government. What is sought in eastern cisterns lies in the *sensu communi* of linguistic usage, and this key transforms our best and most desolate philosophers into the most senseless mystics, and the most simple Galileans and fishermen into the most profound searchers and harbingers of God's wisdom" (Hamann, *Briefwechsel*, vol. 5, p. 272). But "all languages in general are based upon one language, namely nature, whose master and creator is a spirit which is everywhere and nowhere . . ."—"What God has joined together, no philosophy can separate, just as philosophy cannot join what God has separated. Adultery and sodomy are sins against nature and reason. They are the elements of the original sin of philosophy, and the dead works of darkness, done with the organs of our internal and external life, of our physical being (=nature) and of our metaphysical being (=reason)" (Hamann, *Briefwechsel*, vol. 5, p. 95).

31. Metzke, *Hamanns Stellung in der Philosophie des 18. Jahrhunderts*, p. 76 and 76n. See also Unger, *Hamann und die Aufklärung*, p. 185. Unger finds that Hamann appreciates

But perhaps more has to be said. It is not just that Hamann's opinions coincide with Reid's, and that, as a realist, he found Reid important. I believe that through Reid and Beattie he learned much about the connections between realism and idealism in philosophy, and that he took over the *Scottish* view of the history of philosophy. Thus, when he wrote to Herder in 1781 that he has just "finished the third part of Malebranche's *Recherches* as a source of Humean philosophy, as well as Berkeley, whose first part [he has] read through, *together* with Beattie's two volumes [probably the *Essays*]," he shows that he allowed Beattie to colour his view of Berkeley and Hume and their position in the history of philosophy.[32]

Also interesting in this context is Hamann's so-called "theory of faith." For it reveals the same close relationship to Scottish views. But, though there is almost certainly some effect of the Scots to be found in this doctrine, the exact nature and extent of this influence is difficult to determine. It is true that Hamann's early pronouncements on faith (made in connection with Hume) "can hardly be taken as a systematic presentation of 'the doctrine of faith'"; that in the *Socratic Memorabilia* he "preaches more than he conceptually develops"; and that only in connection with his later statements on this subject—all made after he knew Reid and Beattie—certain faint outlines of such a theory emerge.[33] Accordingly, he may have been influenced by the Scots and their belief that the "original and natural judgments are . . . the inspiration of the Almighty, no less than our notions of simple apprehensions."[34] But because even his latest thoughts are far from

---

Reid "obviously as a counter-weight to Hume's scepticism." This is perhaps too vague to be helpful. Unger's earlier *Hamanns Sprachtheorie im Zusammenhang seines Denkens*, which also refers to the Scots (p. 99n.), is just as general: "Mainly because of the opposition to Hume he values the philosopher Thomas Reid." More recently, Hamann's relation to Hume, especially as it concerns the former's "doctrine of faith," has received some critical attention. See Merlan. "From Hume to Hamann," his "Hamann et les *Dialogues* de Hume," his "Kant, Hamann-Jacobi and Schelling on Hume," Swain, "Hamann and the Philosophy of David Hume." See also Alexander, *Johann Georg Hamann. Philosophy and Faith*, O'Flaherty, *Johann Georg Hamann*, and especially Beck's Introduction to his edition of the first edition of Jacobi's *David Hume über den Glauben oder Idalismus und Realismus* of 1787. It appears to me that the consideration of Reid's influence on Hamann will make necessary certain modification of the standard interpretation of the Hume-Hamann relation. But it is not possible to provide these here.

32. Hamann, *Briefwechsel*, vol. 4, pp. 316f. (emphasis mine).

33. Swain, "Hamann and the Philosophy of David Hume," p. 345; and Metzke, *Hamanns Stellung*, p. 72.

34. Reid, *Inquiry*, ed. Duggan, p. 268 (Reid, *Works*, 1, p. 209).

developing a consistent theory, it is very difficult to establish the exact role the Scottish influence played in his thought.[35]

What is clear is that Hamann thought very highly of Reid, and that when late in his life he heard of Reid's *Essays on the Intellectual Powers of Man* through a review in the April 1786 issue of the *Allgemeine Literatur-Zeitung* of Jena, he wrote to Jacobi:

Reid, whose *Inquiry into the Human Mind* I possess in French, has published *Essays on the Intellectual Powers of Man*. They excite all my attention and I wish and hope soon to read at least a review of the book in the *Monthly Review*.[36]

In the following months he keeps reminding Jacobi of this work. Because he plans to visit Jacobi soon, he asks him to buy the book so that he has "something to read for such an unfortunate occasion when he can neither speak nor think." And in a later letter he reminds Jacobi again of his wish to read Reid: ". . . one meal I hope to enjoy at your place: Reid's *Essays* . . . Such a work you must possess. In this regard I still allow myself a little curiosity, though I do not expect even here a clarification of the question what man is . . ."[37] After having been told by Jacobi that the *Essays* are waiting for him, Hamann tells even Herder about how he is "looking forward to a fine meal at Pempelfort [Jacobi's residence], namely to Reid's *Essays* which lie ready for him there."[38] So, no matter how many definite influences of Reid upon Hamann can be established, it is obvious that the latter had the highest respect for this Scotsman and expected much from his *Essays*. It is, therefore, reasonable to suppose that he had learned still more from the *Inquiry* than I have suggested here.

35. See Hamann, *Werke*, ed. Nadler, vol. 3, pp. 39–40; but see also *Johann Georg Hamann, der Magus im Norden, Leben und Schriften*, ed. Gildemeister, vol. 5, pp. 21f.), vol. 5, p. 517: "I do not know what Hume means by faith, nor what we both understand by it, and the more we talked or wrote about it, the less we would be able to catch this quicksilver" (Hamann to Jacobi, 30 April 1787).

36. Hamann, *Briefwechsel*, vol. 6, p. 230. The letter is dated 5 January 1786, but the review appeared only in the April issue of the *Allgemeine Literatur-Zeitung* of the same year. It is therefore likely that Hamann first found out about the *Intellectual Powers* through a short notice of the October 1785 issue of the *Critical Review* that was published in the *Allgemeine Literatur-Zeitung* of 8 December 1785, p. 268. The *Monthly Review* published a review of Reid's work only in September and October 1786. (See also *Allgemeine Literatur-Zeitung* January 1787, p. 179.)

37. See the following letters: 18 June 1786 (Hamann, *Briefwechsel*, vol. 6, p. 421); 10 June (Hamann, *Werke*, ed. Gildemeister, vol. 5, p. 552); and 27 April 1787 (ibid., p. 508).

38. Hamann to Herder, 2 July 1787, Hamann, *Schriften*, ed. Roth and Wiener, vol. 7, p. 360.

III

If Hamann had the greatest appreciation for Reid, Herder very much likes Beattie, the author of the *Essay*. On 1 August 1772 he writes to his friend in Königsberg that he had received books by Ferguson, Millar, and Beattie, and that "Beattie is undoubtedly the greatest of these three: even though the good man has said less in an entire book than you have said on one page about Socrates's faith and ignorance."[39]

Perhaps this can be taken to mean that what Herder likes in Beattie is the latter's affinity to Hamann. How much he liked Beattie's philosophy and how he understood it becomes even clearer in his review of the German translation of the *Essay* for the *Frankfurter gelehrte Anzeigen* of 1772. In it he exuberantly praises the Scot as a fighter for *the* truth:

Finally, again, a man who has philosophized about man as a whole, and with man as a whole in mind. Head and heart and artery of life in him do not yet appear to be so immeasurably far removed from one another as in most metaphysicians. *Beattie* is a friend of, a fighter, a zealot for the truth, but not for that colourful, iridescent kind of truth which a few rays of sunlight paint upon the dark, cloudy, and watery brain of *so-called* philosophers. Such truth shines on fumes and dissolves with them. Our author is one of those *robust [baumstarken]* people with whom healthy reason [*gesunde Vernunft*] is everything, and with which even the "understanding' [*Verstand*] cannot so much as compare itself (for we Germans; and that should have been noticed by the translator! call common sense in this opposition to the understanding rather *Vernunft*). He thus boldly attacks the hair-splitters, quibblers, metaphysicians, idealists, sceptics, and whatever else I should call them. And he shows or wants to show that all their sophistries are only shadows on the wall, which, however beautiful, cannot displace anything of substance, having no substance themselves.[40]

Herder goes on to praise Beattie emphatically for his anti-metaphysical stance, greeting his book as extremely relevant in "our times, which certainly are more characterized by quibbling than by common sense, and more by hair-splitting [*vernünfteln*] than by reason [*Vernunft*]." All lovers of philosophy are advised by Herder to read the first part, "Of the Standard of Truth," and especially also the third part which deals with the "imperfections of school logic," the "present degeneracy of moral science," and the "consequences of moral scepticism." They constitute a "strong sermon against such shadow

39. Herder to Hamann, 1 August 1772, Hamann, *Briefwechsel*, vol. 3, p. 13.
40. *Frankfurter gelehrte Anzeigen*, 1772, pp. 666f.

play and hair splitting—a sermon which, on the whole, nobody can deny to be true, valuable and important." He also endorses Beattie's characterization of common sense as an immediate sense of truth and falsity, far superior to all the logic taught at schools and universities.

Beattie's most valuable insight, Herder says, is that "man does not exist for metaphysical speculation, and when he begins to separate reason from healthy understanding [*gesunder Verstand*], speculation from feeling and experience—then Daedalos and Ikaros have left the secure ground of mother earth. And whereto can man lose his way with his waxen *pennis homini non datis*, whereto can he fall?"[41] Thus Herder praises Beattie not only for his negative stand on metaphysics, but also for his positive view on the nature of man. He sees Beattie as advocating a holistic view of man in very much the same way as Hamann and he himself do.

Common sense, as analysed by the Scotsman, is, Herder writes, this "healthy sense of truth," these "simple and strong nerves and drives of humanity," this "divine organ," and is most important for the Storm and Stress view of man as well. Its intuitive character, accessible to everyone without artificial means and false education, can serve to emphasize "natural man." This explains the great approval with which he quotes Beattie's claim that "every kind of knowledge can be reduced to first and simple principles and that all evidence becomes finally intuitive, and that common sense is the true [*eigentliche*] standpoint [standard] of man."[42]

The review is designed to show Beattie as a witness to the legitimacy of the aspirations of Storm and Stress. He is styled a "man of genius" after the taste of the movement. The rudeness and apparent simple-mindedness, the dogged determination to fight for *the* truth, all these things which are most severely criticized in Beattie by other philosophers, are what appeal most to Herder in this review. And, just like Beattie's *Essay*, the review itself appears to be intended as a "strong and wholesome sermon" for strong minds, different from the wishy-washy talk usually offered by mere "thinkers." It is this basic agreement in the *Weltanschauung* of Beattie and Herder that determines much of the tone of the review.

But the conclusion of the first instalment of the review already allows a glimpse at what Herder will take to be the shortcomings of the *Essay*:

41. Ibid.
42. Ibid., p. 668.

Here, apprentice, you are led a very straight and simple path. You leave here to the right the swamp full of factitious false lights, and to the left you leave that ruin of demonstrations in the mathematical manner, where you always would have to crawl *idem per idem* up and down, and you walk straight away—but whereto now? The author says toward the truth. But what this truth would look like, and what it would really be, our author himself may not know. Otherwise he probably would not want to force us fervently to it, but lead us gently towards it, and show it to us softly and quietly. However, he does not do this. But then again, which mortal has done it? That he forces us upon the correct path and praises it to us from afar is good at this time. Let a few start out and walk: perhaps they will find the land of gold. And he even says that we have it all around us, if we only open our eyes.[43]

The second part of the review deals with the second part of Beattie's *Essay*. It is much more negative. Beginning by saying that he is not really satisfied with this part of the work and its attempt to characterize and refute Berkeley's idealism and Hume's scepticism, Herder goes on to point out that Beattie has refuted neither.

There are, according to Herder, three considerations which show that Beattie's very purpose in the latter part of the *Essay* is self-defeating: (i) all declamation is useless against cool sophists such as Hume; they are not heated by warm oratory; (ii) it is wrong to judge any system by its consequences; people do not always act in accordance with their theoretical convictions, and therefore the practical consequences of a theory can be ascertained only with difficulty; moreover, even the best theories can be applied to evil ends; (iii) "Hume is indeed a bad reasoner in metaphysical matters, but the idealist Berkeley has been treated unfairly. I regard his system, just like the systems of Spinoza, Fenelon, Leibniz and Descartes, as *fiction*." Herder even asks which philosophical system was ever more than fiction or poetry; and he claims that "Berkeley's poetry is great, discerning, and well written throughout. As poetry, it is also difficult, I believe, indeed, *impossible* to refute with other arguments of *poetic reason*. Beattie certainly did not refute Berkeley."[44]

Herder concludes his discussion by evincing genuine regret that the author of the *Essay* has "humiliated the *splendour of his truth* to *apish shapes* and then goes on to quote a key passage of Hamann's *Socratic*

43. Ibid., p. 669.
44. Ibid., p. 675.

Memorabilia as saying "with a few subtle strokes perhaps more than the entire book" by Beattie.[45]

This review is important not only for Herder, but also for our understanding of his relation to Hamann and for the evaluation of Beattie's contribution to the movement of Storm and Stress in general. It certainly was noticed and considered to be important. Goethe referred to it as "pure gold," for instance. And Hamann must have been aware of it as well, since it was Herder's attempt at a reconciliation. Hamann had used Reid to accentuate the differences between himself and Herder. The latter now uses a review of Beattie to emphasize their fundamental agreement. The Scottish common-sense philosophers figured centrally in the thought of both.

When, in 1774, the first volume of an anonymous philosophical novel, *Lebensgeschichte Tobias Knauts des Weisen, sonst der Stammler genannt*, appeared, Hamann and his friends in Königsberg read it, liked it, and speculated on Herder as its author. Hamann thought that Herder's "predilection for Beattie and the physiology of Unzer shimmer[ed] through in the *Knaut*."[46] This episode further supports the importance of Scottish writers for the self-understanding of these Germans.

How important Beattie was for Herder in this early period of Storm

---

45. Ibid., p. 676. Herder quotes the following passage: "our own existence and the existence of things outside of us must be believed and cannot be determined in any other way . . . What one believes does not, therefore, have to be proved, and a proposition can be most incontrovertibly proven without being believed. There are proofs of truths which are of as little value as the application, which can be made of the truths themselves; indeed one can believe the proof of a proposition without giving approval to the proposition itself. The reasons of a Hume may be ever so cogent, and the refutation of them only assumptions and doubting; thus faith gains and loses equally with the cleverest pettifogger and the most honourable attorney. Faith is not the work of reason, and therefore cannot succumb to its attack, because faith arises just as little from reason as tasting and seeing do . . ." The translation is taken from O'Flaherty's *Hamann's Socratic Memorabilia, A Translation and Commentary*, pp. 167–69. I have substituted "feeling" for O'Flaherty's "sensibility" as a translation of Hamann's "*Empfindung.*"

46. Hamann, *Briefwechsel*, vol. 3, p. 75. One day earlier Hamann had written: "For heaven's sake, do please tell me, do you have any part in the *Knaut*? So many inner characteristics, but no external one of your damned, twisted [*rot-deutsch*] style. I could swear to it in my heart, but I haven't had the heart to say it with my mouth." Herder was not the author of the work, and he answers on 27 May 1774 (ibid., p. 92): "I have not fabricated the *Knaut*, and I do not know how, having read one page, you could have suspected me of having done it. As far as I came, the gold-nuggets swam in the water." For the image of "gold" see above.

and Stress may also be seen from his *Provinzialblätter an Prediger*. This work, designed as a series of letters, is meant to defend Protestant ministers against the accusations of Hume. At the same time, it also represents Herder's rejection of the theology of the enlightenment. And Beattie is invoked as a witness against both Hume and enlightenment theology.

Herder singles out the well-known Berlin cleric Johann Joachim Spalding for a special attack.[47] Such philosophical theologians as the latter are completely incapable of refuting Hume. In fact, "the casuistics of these new Sunday-theologians" are no help at all, for religion must be defended not by words, but by deeds. Spalding is a weakling who waters down Christianity in order to make it more acceptable, and he must be opposed to robust men such as Martin Luther. "Where," Herder asks, "is a strongman, a second simpleminded and uneducated Luther, a Luther of head, and heart, and breast, and writing?" It appears to be Beattie whom he regards, at least for a time, as coming closest to this idol. For, as one fragment to the *Provincialblätter* shows, he planned to write a "dialogue between Spalding, Beattie and Hume" on "whether there still is a church and a common interest of the priests."[48]

That he not only regarded Beattie as a witness to his basic *Weltanschauung* during this period but also found some of the details of his philosophical theory useful, becomes clear in his *Älteste Urkunde des Menschengeschlechts* of 1774. In this "*monstrum horrendum*" of a book (Hamann), Herder further develops his theory of feeling as the basis of all more refined understanding. "Dark" feelings and beliefs are seen to lie at the basis of all knowledge. The comparison of the soul with sight and knowledge with light is disqualified by him as a mere play with words—a play with words, however, that has had serious consequences for philosophy. For this "mere play is responsible for the fact that the most important doctrines of humanity, the philosophy of *intuition*, of *evidence*, of *sign*, and of *experience* are still so deep in night and doubt."[49]

The beginnings of such a philosophy of intuition, evidence, sign, and experience he sees in Lambert's *Phänomenologie*, in Mendelssohn's essay on evidence, and in Beattie's *Essay*.[50] Here, again, the central

47. Haym. *Herder*, vol. 1, p. 605.
48. Herder, *Werke*, ed. Suphan, vol. 7, p. 175.
49. Ibid.
50. Ibid., vol. 6, p. 270.

importance of Beattie for Herder is underlined. In fact, he is mentioned as the equal of two of the leading German philosophers of the time. Moreover, Beattie is found relevant for one of the most important issues that had concerned Herder in his treatise *On the Origin of Language*: how can there be such a thing as a sign in the first place?

To be sure, like Hamann's obscure suggestions, Herder's musings about the nature of sign, evidence, and experience do not allow us to determine more exactly the Scottish influences. But perhaps such an exact determination is not of primary importance when one is dealing with such seminal thinkers as Hamann and Herder. For they were important not so much because they developed clearly thought-out theories, but rather because they made suggestions that proved to be fruitful and far-reaching in the works of others. How seminal many of their suggestions were often becomes evident only in the works of thinkers who came after them. One of these thinkers was Friedrich Heinrich Jacobi.

IV

I have already mentioned how Reid's account of the development of the ideal theory influenced Hamann's analysis of the history of modern philosophy. Jacobi, who further developed this theory, was affected by the Scottish theories as well.

"Nihilism" became a fashionable term in the nineteenth century. It was—and still is—used to express the experience of the triviality, meaninglessness, and emptiness of modern life. For Jacobi, who has been credited with having been the first to use the term with a definite meaning, nihilism constitutes the necessary result of all philosophy.[51] This is because philosophy aims at the rational justification of matters that cannot be justified, but must be accepted on faith or feeling. Being necessarily disappointed in its search for "foundations," philosophy leads to the rejection of all that makes life meaningful.

But, even if Jacobi is the first to have used the term "nihilism" for this view, the view itself hardly originates with him. As Baum points out quite correctly:

51. See Süss, "Der Nihilismus bei F. H. Jacobi," in *Der Nihilismus als Phänomen der Geistesgeschichte*, ed. Arndt, pp. 65–78, p. 65.

in essence [*der Sache nach*] Jacobi's aim to reveal the development of thought towards nihilism as the tendency of the history of Western thought is already fully contained in the views of Thomas Reid. Given his intimate knowledge of the works of Reid, there need not be any doubt that Jacobi has received the most important suggestions for this theory from Reid.[52]

Jacobi's scattered remarks on nihilism—whether they actually deserve to be called a theory need not be debated here—do indeed bear a striking resemblance to the view of the history of philosophy as developed by Reid, and as also held by Beattie and Hamann.[53] All these thinkers see in philosophy a basic tendency to move farther and farther away from the natural beliefs revealed in sensation or feeling, and to rely more and more upon rational thought. They believe that in this way an ever greater part of reality is denied, until universal scepticism, that is, the denial of the self and external objects is reached. The Scots, Hamann, Jacobi, and to some extent Herder also, all believe that the existence of our self and of objects must be grasped intuitively, while to philosophy it is a "scandal" that we cannot rationally prove the existence of external objects.

The basic mistake, or, as Hamann would say, the "original sin," of philosophy is that philosophers do not begin with objective knowledge, but with subjective states, and that they try to prove the existence of objects from these subjective states. In this way philosophers will never establish the existence of real objects—or so these Scots and Germans believe. All that philosophers will be able to do is prove the existence of some "ideal" objects. For the understanding in isolation from the senses is, in fact, cut off from all objective knowledge, since the objects themselves appear only in sensation. When the philosophical understanding finally becomes aware of this, it, according to Jacobi, discovers necessarily

that what philosophy has hitherto generally called *nature* and its general laws are nothing other than the human mind itself with its thoroughly subjective representations, concepts and connections of thought. Nature, thus far *believed*

52. Baum, *Vernunft*, p. 43.
53. Reid's account is to be found in his *Inquiry*, especially chapter I, sections 3–7, and chapter VII; see also *Essays on the Intellectual Powers of Man*, Essay II. For Beattie's very similar views, see his *Essay*, chapter II, section 1. Baum mentions only Reid in this context.

to be objective . . . vanishes for the philosophical understanding into nothing when it is severed from external sensation. In the presence of the faculty of cognition everything, the knowing and the known, dissolves into a superficial imagining of imaginations, that is, into something which, objectively, is nothing. There remains only a strange intellectual realm of strange intellectual dreams without sense [*Deutung*] and reference [*Bedeutung*].[54]

In trying to grasp reality by means of rational thought, philosophy finds nothing (or even "nothingness"), a mere appearance. By transforming the objective reality known in sensation into mere representation, reality vanishes altogether. The end of all philosophy is nihilism. Neither I nor anything else exists.[55]

Like Reid, who sees universal idealism, or the theory in which there is "neither matter nor mind in the universe; nothing but impressions and ideas," as the outcome of Western thought, Jacobi argues that nihilism is the outcome of philosophy. But whereas Reid claims only that idealism is the *factual* outcome of Western thought, Jacobi appears to believe that nihilism is the *necessary* or inevitable consequence of *all* philosophy.[56] For Reid idealism is necessary only if we accept certain premisses: those connected with the view that there are mediating entities between the self and its objects. Philosophy itself may not be at fault. "We ought not despair of a better," he finds, and his philosophy is indeed the attempt to furnish such a better alternative. Jacobi is much more pessimistic. But he does agree to everything the Scot has to say on the history of philosophy:

ever since Aristotle an increasing tendency has asserted itself in philosophical schools, namely, to quite generally subjugate immediate cognition to mediate cognition: the *faculty of perception*, originally basic to everything, to the faculty of reflection, dependent upon abstraction; the original to the copy; the meaning to the word; reason to the understanding. This went even so far as to allow the complete submersion and disappearance of the former in the latter.[57]

54. Jacobi, *Werke*, vol. 3, p. 372; see also p. 210, and vol. 2, pp. 19, 105, 216, as well as Baum, *Vernunft*, p. 35. For Jacobi's *David Hume* (*Werke*, vol. 2, pp. 1–310), see also Beck's edition of the first edition of this work.

55. Reid, *Works*, vol. 1, p. 293 (*Essays on the Intellectual Powers of Man*, ed. Brody, p. 199).

56. See Baum, *Vernunft*, p. 35: For Jacobi "nihilism is the result, the last aim of all thought." He refers to Jacobi, *Werke*, vol. 3, p. 317f. It is not entirely clear to me whether the difference between Reid and Jacobi is as great as Baum suggests.

57. Jacobi, *Werke*, vol. 2, pp. 11f. Baum notes that Jacobi differs from Reid in letting the ideal system begin only with Aristotle and not with Plato, criticizing Jacobi as being

Further, Jacobi also agrees with Reid on the ultimate nature of the mistaken view, that is, the acceptance of the "theory of ideas."[58] That "idealism" and "egoism," the terms used by Reid to signify what Jacobi later calls "nihilism," were indeed also used by Jacobi in his early works is shown clearly by Baum. But it can be added that even in his later works Jacobi often uses the phrase "nihilism or idealism," and that in his famous letter to Fichte he himself states that he uses "nihilism as an abusive term for idealism."[59]

Baum, however, does not see any connection between Reid and Jacobi with regard to the term "nihilism" itself, but shows that the term was used in German before, even if in a different sense.[60] Nevertheless, Jacobi's debt to the Scots does not appear unlikely even with regard to this term, if one considers Beattie's characterization of the final state of philosophy:

So that we are now arrived at the height of human wisdom, that intellectual eminence, from whence there is a full prospect of all that we can reasonably believe to exist, and of all that can possibly become the object of our knowledge. Alas, what has become of the magnificence of external nature, and the wonders of intellectual energy. . . . All around, above and beneath, is one vast inanity, or rather an enormous chaos, empressed with darkness universally and eternally impenetrable. Body and spirit are *utterly annihilated*; and there remains nothing (for we must again descend into the jargon of metaphysics) but a vast collection, bundle, mass, or heap, of unperceived perceptions.[61]

In fact, terms such as "annihilation" occur several times in Beattie's *Essay*. The German translation uses "*vernichtet*," but it could well be that Jacobi read or reread Beattie in the original. In any case, Jacobi resembles in his philosophical style Beattie more than Reid, and even the evocation of despair found in Beattie is similar to some of Jacobi's

---

less consistent in this regard. But Reid, at times, also makes an exception for Plato. See, for instance, Reid, *Works*, vol. 1, pp. 203f. (*Inquiry*, ed. Duggan, pp. 256f.).

58. See Jacobi, *Werke*, vol. 2, pp. 36ff. (*David Hume*, ed. Beck, Appendix, pp. 36ff.), for instance.

59. Jacobi, *Werke*, vol. 3, p. 44.

60. Baum, *Vernunft*, pp. 44f. Baum has discovered the term in a handbook on medieval philosophy, edited by Johann Andreas Cramer, which appeared in 1786. Another writer who used the term was J. H. Obereit. See Homann, *Jacobis Philosophie der Freiheit*, p. 152n. for exact details and further references.

61. Beattie, *Essay*, pp. 267f. *et passim*. Even Reid speaks at times of "annihilation," though with less emphasis.

outpourings. But whereas Beattie saw the epitomy of scepticism and idealism in Hume, Jacobi found it in Kant and his followers.[62]

V

In Reid's thought the critique of the history of Western philosophy was intimately connected with an alternative account of perception. Instead of the ideal system, Reid proposed a realism—a realism that does away with mediating "mental entities" between the perceiving subject and the perceived object. The same also holds for Jacobi. His view of the history of philosophy is also founded in his theory of perception, which is Reidian as well.

One reason that Jacobi thought Reid's theory of perception so useful is to be found in his dispute with Mendelssohn. In 1785 Jacobi had published his private correspondence with Mendelssohn under the title *Über die Lehre des Spinoza in Briefen an Herrn Moses Mendelssohn.* In this work Jacobi had not only tried to show that Lessing was really Spinozist (and, according to public opinion, therefore an atheist), but had also tried to discredit Mendelssohn. But his attempt backfired. Instead of exposing the Berlin enlightenment philosophers as clandestine atheists, Jacobi found himself accused of being a religious fanatic and an enemy of rational thought; and this not without reason, for Jacobi had argued in his letters that sensation and revelation—belief in perceptual contexts and faith in religious contexts—were of the same kind. Using the language of Pauline-Lutheran theology, he had claimed that we are "all born into faith and have to remain in faith." Playing on the ambiguity of the German "Glaube," he suggested religious significance even in mere perceptual contexts.[63]

Jacobi's *David Hume über den Glauben oder Idealismus und Realismus* is essentially the attempt to show that the accusations levelled against him were completely unfounded. He argues that the terms "faith" and "revelation" are commonly used in epistemic contexts and that this has nothing to do with religion. Like Hamann and Herder before him, he finds Hume and his Scottish critics very helpful in trying to show this, for he argues that they had already used "faith" and "revelation" in his

---

62. Hamann suggests that Jacobi is "more useful in exclamation than in rational inferences" (Hamann to Jacobi, Jacobi, *Werke*, vol. 4, part 3, p. 384). Much in Jacobi's style reminds one of Beattie, though he does not share the latter's elegance and clarity. For Jacobi's actual critique of Kant along Reidian lines see Chapter IX below.

63. See, for instance, Jacobi, *Werke*, vol. 4, part 1, pp. 210f.

sense.[64] Thus Hume's "*Essays*" are characterized as "a book *in defence* of faith," and many long passages of the *Enquiry Concerning Human Understanding* are quoted in order to show that Jacobi had used the term in Hume's sense.[65] But, even though he refers several times to Hume in this regard, it appears to be Reid's theory of natural belief that is his most important source.

That Hume rather than Reid is emphasized has to do with the fact that the latter is also suspected of being an "enemy of reason," whereas Hume is commonly regarded as an "*enemy of religion.*"[66] Hume is, accordingly, the better witness in this context. This does not mean that Hume is an authority for him. That his own theory of faith is in the end quite different from that of Hume is made clear by Jacobi.[67] For, although he argues that the phrase "revelation of sensation," which corresponds to "faith," is common in English, French, German and several other languages, he admits that Hume could never have said that the "objects reveal themselves through the senses":

64. Jacobi's relationship to Hume is almost the same as that of Hamann. Neither one simply "follows" Hume as is often asserted.

65. Jacobi, *Werke*, vol. 2, pp. 152f., 156ff. (*David Hume*, ed. Beck, pp. 33f., 38–48; the quotations are given in both English and German).

66. This is a merely tactical move, and a questionable one at that. In any case, Hamann accused Jacobi of dishonesty in this regard. To Jacobi's claim that Mendelssohn has "burdened" him without reason with "Christian convictions" which were neither Christian nor his (Jacobi, *Werke*, vol. 2, p. 144; *David Hume*, ed. Beck, pp. 23f.), Hamann objects: "How can you accuse Mendelssohn . . . of having burdened you with Christian conviction . . . and that without *the slightest cause*? To be born into faith, is that Humean or philosophical or . . . ?" (Hamann, *Werke*, ed. Gildemeister, vol. 5, p. 506). In a closely related matter Hamann calls Jacobi a "liar" outright. See also Knoll's excellent discussion of this letter in *Johann Georg Hamann und Friedrich Heinrich Jacobi*, pp. 43–56.

The letter of Hamann to Jacobi of 27 April 1787 is also reprinted in Jacobi's *Werke*, vol. 4, part 3, pp. 346–52. It is interesting for the kinds of things that are deleted. None of the references to Reid are retained. They are: "Are these not assertions of human authority, when you are more concerned about *Hume, Reid* and *Spinoza* than about the matter itself, and when you *justify* and *extenuate* your justification by means of their doctrines . . .?" The letter of 13 January 1786, also containing a reference to Reid, is completely suppressed in that edition, and the letters of 8 June 1786 and April 1787 are edited in such a way that the references to Reid do not appear. Roth says in his Preface that he "would not have dared to publish certain passages . . . without Jacobi's expressed consent" (p. v), and professes to have included only material that "concerns Jacobi and his works" (p. iv). Does Reid's influence not concern Jacobi and his work? Why have references to him been, for the most part, removed?

67. Ibid., vol. 2, pp. 149f (*David Hume*, ed. Beck, pp. 29f.). Jacobi—the *I* in the dialogue—ironically claims that he has something better to offer than arguments, namely *authority*. This authority is Hume. But he draws attention to the similarity of his

This idiom cannot occur in *Hume* with the same emphasis I have placed upon it because he always leaves undecided, among other things, whether we really perceive *external* objects, or whether we perceive objects merely *as though* they were external to ourselves. For this reason he also says ... "realities, or what is taken for such." According to his entire way of thinking, he had to be, in speculative thought, more inclined to sceptical idealism than to realism.[68]

Only the "decided realist" will use the expression in the way in which he, Jacobi, has used "revelation." Reid was such a decided realist, and he did use "revelation" in the sense in which Jacobi used it in this dialogue. But Jacobi does not bother to point that out.

That Reid is the source for his doctrine of faith and revelation becomes clear also from the following:

By what other name shall such a decided realist call the means by which the certainty of the independent existence of external objects, apart from representations, comes to him? He has nothing upon which he could base his judgment, nothing but the thing itself, nothing but the *factum* that the objects are really in front of him. Can he use a more fitting word for this than revelation? Is not here truly the *root* of this word, the *source of its usage*? ... That this revelation deserves to be called truly wonderful follows automatically ... for we have no other proof of the existence of such an object than the existence of this object. Therefore we must find it simply incomprehensible that we can become aware of such an existence.[69]

Of even more interest for Jacobi's relation to Reid is the next step in his exposition. Believing that it has indeed been established that our awareness of the existence of external objects is "a truly wonderful revelation," the interlocutor muses: "but at least it is not an immediate revelation, or is it?"[70] The question of *immediate* perception clearly

---

approach to that of Descartes, who dedicated his work to the philosophers of the Sorbonne because they were an authority and because truth itself counted for so little, saying, "[t]hat the Sorbonne was no authority for Descartes himself does not need any reminder." Why do we need a reminder that Hume was no authority for Jacobi (and Hamann)? Compare also Jacobi, *Werke*, vol. 2, p. 164 and *David Hume*, ed. Beck, p. 49. In the first edition Jacobi says "*Hume* or some other famous man of just as good [*gutem*] a name;" in the second edition this reads "*Hume* or some other famous man of just as authoritative [*geltendem*] a name."

68. Ibid., p. 165 (pp. 50f.). The appeal to ordinary language reminds one of Reid.

69. Ibid., pp. 165f. (p. 51). The passage from which this quotation is taken is quite different in the first edition.

70. Ibid., p. 167 (p. 53). Incidentally, the notion of "immediacy" plays no significant part in Jacobi's letters to Mendelssohn.

comes from Reid; and Jacobi follows Reid by trying to show that the revelation is "immediate with regard to ourselves. For we do not know what *really* mediates it. But to deny it for this reason, or to reject this factum as contradictory to reason itself, as the idealist does, this is not in accordance with the true philosophical spirit."[71] If we try to explain this basic fact by an account of its origin in certain operations of the understanding, as most philosophers actually try to do, if, in other words, we attempt to show that our knowledge of the existence of objects is mediated by the understanding, we will "necessarily fall into the trap of the idealist."[72] In reality,

I experience in one and the same indivisible moment that I exist and that objects external to myself exist; and in this moment my soul is as passive with regard to the object as it is passive with regard to itself. No representation, no inference mediates this twofold revelation. Nothing in the soul steps between the reality external to the soul and the reality within the soul. Representations are not yet existing; they originate only afterwards in reflection, as shadows of things which were present.[73]

For Reid and Jacobi, "sensible revelation" or "inspiration" and "natural belief" or "faith" are indeed only two different sides of one and the same problem. The reality which reveals itself in external sensation does not need any other witness, since it is itself the strongest witness of all reality.[74]

All this sounds very much like Reid; and Baum is quite correct when he finds that the latter's philosophy can "frankly be declared as the main source of Jacobi's theory of knowledge."[75] Anyone who knows the works of Reid and his Scottish followers will find little new in Jacobi's epistemology. For it is thoroughly dependent upon Reid not only in its broad outlines but also in many of its details.[76] Jacobi's doctrine of

71. Ibid., p. 168 (pp. 53f.).

72. Ibid., p. 173 (p. 59).

73. Ibid., p. 175 (p. 64, the "in reflection" is added only in the second edition); compare this with the accounts given by Eberhard and Tetens.

74. Ibid., pp. 19, 59, 107, 178, *152ff.* (Appendix, pp. 19, 59, 107, and pp. 67, *33ff.*).

75. Baum, *Vernunft*, pp. 74 and 92.

76. Jacobi agrees with Reid that, just like sensationism, rationalism also involves a theory of ideas and thus leads to scepticism and idealism (see Jacobi, *Werke*, vol. 2, p. 29; Appendix, p. 29). In the same way as Reid, he calls the idealism of Descartes, Malebranche, and Berkeley an "imperfect and half idealism," and contrasts this half idealism with the higher idealism of Hume, who denies not only the material world but also the self.

immediate cognition and natural faith is almost identical to Reid's theory. It is only less consistent and rigorous because Jacobi allows himself to speak of "representations" in some sense.[77]

Late in his life Jacobi boasted that he was "a realist as nobody else had ever been before . . . and there is no reasonable middle system between total idealism and total realism."[78] He even went so far as to claim that the "third [thing] between the knowing subject and the object to be known, which has been assumed ever since Locke, was thoroughly removed by myself first, as far as I know."[79] But Berkeley and Reid had done so long before Jacobi—and he should have known it. In fact, it is evident that he did know it in 1788, when he told Wilhelm von Humboldt that "we do not perceive, as is usually maintained, merely the picture of external objects. We perceive the objects themselves . . . as *Reid* said quite correctly, by a *sort of revelation*."[80] Jacobi's views on the removal of the third thing between subject and object are taken from the works of Reid. In many respects Jacobi's and Beattie's relationships to Reid are similar, and if Tetens deserves perhaps to be called the "German Reid," Jacobi should have the honour to be called the "German Beattie." But because he does not admit his debt to Reid as openly as did the original Beattie, much of what is originally Reid's came to pass as Jacobi's "*geistiges Eigentum.*" Since, in Germany, he overshadowed Reid so completely, the effects of this are felt even today.

77. See Jacobi, *Werke*, vol. 2, pp. 230ff., for instance.
78. Jacobi to Jean Paul, 16 March 1800, in *Werke*, vol. 1, p. 239.
79. Jacobi to Bouterwek, 1 January 1804, in *Friedrich Heinrich Jacobis Briefe an Friedrich Bouterwek*, ed. Meyer, p. 64 (quoted after Baum, *Vernunft*, p. 70).
80. See footnote 13 of this chapter.

IX

"Reid, Oswald, and Beattie" and Kant

I

MOST philosophical scholars do not think it likely that Kant knew Reid. Further, those who admit the possibility are not convinced that Reid (and Beattie) could have contributed anything of significance to Kant's critical philosophy. For this reason, I will try to show in some detail that (1) Kant must have known the Scots much better than has been thought so far, and (2) he could have found their views relevant. At the very least, they were important for his original conception of Hume's problem. But very likely they also had an influence on his proposed solution—and not just a negative influence.

1. Kant was in basic agreement with his contemporaries.[1] Therefore, it is reasonable to suppose that he could have found their thought helpful in many respects, even if in the end his view differed very much from theirs. Furthermore, it is also reasonable to expect that Kant would find helpful the same sources as did his contemporaries. Since they considered the Scots important enough to discuss them in their works, we may ask: Why should Kant, who had, according to his own admissions, learned much from Hutcheson, the progenitor of Scottish common-sense philosophy, and from Hume, the object of their

1. See Chapter II above. Kant's critical problem was at the beginning almost indistinguishable from the problem faced by Feder, Meiners, Tetens, and Eberhard at about the same time. All these philosophers were concerned with a "revision of metaphysics, and more particularly with the differentiation of the sensible from the intellectual" in the field of theoretical and moral philosophy, for from such a "universal theory of thought and sensation" an answer regarding the status of metaphysics was expected.

criticism, be an exception in this regard? Why should he have been less interested in their works than the philosophers in Göttingen and Berlin?

There is, it appears to me, no reason at all. On the contrary: (i) It is more than just likely that, from the *early seventies*, Kant knew the names "Reid, Oswald and Beattie" and had a fairly good idea of what they stood for. Each of the major German philosophical journals had reviewed some of the works by the Scottish common-sense philosophers (and by doing so, they had drawn attention to the others). Kant almost certainly read at least a few of these reviews. In fact, some of Kant's later criticisms sound very similar to those offered in the reviews. On these grounds one could say that Feder's review of Beattie's *Essay* in the *Göttingische Anzeigen* (1771) must have been read by Kant. Herder's review of the German translation of Beattie's *Essay* in the *Frankfurter gelehrte Anzeigen* (1772) could hardly have escaped him either, for not only did Kant himself closely follow the work of his former student, but Hamann (for whom this review had a special significance) also had every reason for calling Kant's attention to it.[2] The reviews of Oswald's *Appeal* in its German translation in the *Göttingische Anzeigen* (1774-5) and of Beattie and Oswald in the *Allgemeine deutsche Bibliothek* (1776) can also be assumed to have been read by Kant. (ii) There are the references to the Scots in the works of Garve, Feder, Eberhard, Lossius, Platner, Tiedemann, and (most important) Tetens, any or all of which might have been noticed by Kant. (iii) Hamann and Krauss, with whom Kant is known to have discussed Hume, certainly also must have mentioned Reid, Oswald, and Beattie, for their outlook was similar to that of the Scots—and Kant even "honoured" them with the same title: "misologist."[3] But there were also the English merchant Green and the Scotsman Hay with his partner Motherby. Kant often dined with them, and Hamann reports that philosophy was discussed on occasions.[4] (iv) Kant himself

---

2. Kant knew Herder very well, and the review did constitute something of a reconciliation between Hamann and Herder. See Haym, *Herder*, vol. 1, p. 533.

3. See Kant, *Correspondence*, ed. Zweig, p. 93, for instance.

4. See, for instance, Hamann's report concerning the discussion of Hume's *Dialogues* in Königsberg (Hamann, *Briefwechsel*, vol. 4, pp. 205ff.) or Hamann's frequent messages to Jacobi concerning Kant's position in the so-called *Pantheismusstreit*. Hamann, by the way, called himself ironically a "misologist." For an extended discussion of Hamann's relationship to Kant see Heinrich Weber, *Hamann und Kant* (München, 1904). For the significance of Hamann's library see Immendorfer *Johann Georg Hamann und seine Bücherei*.

took some pride in his supposed Scottish ancestry, and seems to have had a predilection for things Scottish. This in itself might have been enough to awaken his interest in Reid, Oswald, and Beattie. But however that may be, (v) Reid's *Inquiry* was available in Königsberg in French (in the library of Hamann), and the German translation of Beattie's *Essay* could be found in the library of the University of Königsberg.[5]

To sum up, both the state of general philosophical discussion in Germany in the 1770s and the personal surroundings of Kant in Königsberg are virtually certain to have called Kant's attention to the works of the Scots. Could he have resisted studying them in more detail, or is there any reason that would have made him want to resist such a study? I do not think so. On the contrary, there is every reason to suspect that Kant read the Scots. He was, after all, a voracious reader with a good memory. He read, according to Hamann, "*everything current (alles Neue)*" and he wrote, according to Mendelssohn, for "those few adepts who are up on the latest things, and who are able to guess what lies undisclosed behind the published hints."[6] Why should it be assumed, therefore, that Kant needed the published hints of his contemporaries to become aware of the works of the Scots? Is it not much more likely that Kant learned of the Scots at about the same time as other German philosophers, who were up on the latest things, learned of them? Mendelssohn, Garve and Feder, who surely belong in this category, knew of Reid before 1770.[7] Hamann, who owned the 1768 French translation of Reid's *Inquiry*, referred to it as early as 1772.

5. For the availability of the German translation of Beattie's *Essay* in Königsberg, see Janitsch. *Kants Urteile über Berkeley*, p. 36n. Janitsch reports that he has seen a copy of Beattie's *Essay* in German translation from the University library of Königsberg, which somehow found its way into the "Library of Strassburg." I do not know whether the work is still in Strassburg. Nor do I know what supported Janitsch's guess that this "was perhaps the exemplar that Kant himself used," but I believe that it is unlikely that this guess is correct. For Kant worked until 1772 in the Schlossbibliothek in Königsberg. Probably early in the nineteenth century the Schlossbibliothek and the library of the University of Königsberg were joined (see Schubert, *Immanuel Kants Biographie*). Accordingly, I would suppose that the "doublettes" of some books were sold or given away to other libraries. Beattie's *Essay* could easily have been such a doublette. Why was the copy of the University of Königsberg, and not that of the Schlossbibliothek, given away? Perhaps because the latter was more valuable. Why? Could it be that Kant himself catalogued it, or that there were in it marginal notes by Kant? We probably will never know.

6. See Hamann to Jacobi, 20 November 1785, Jacobi, *Werke*, vol. 5, part iii, p. 114 and Mendelssohn to Kant, December 1770, Kant, *Correspondence*, ed. Zweig, p. 68.

7. See the appropriate chapters above.

The work must, therefore, have been available in Königsberg before that time.[8] It cannot be ruled out, then, that Kant, who could read French, read Reid's *Inquiry* soon after the French translation appeared.

Yet the evidence for Kant's reading of the Scots is still stronger. In his *Prolegomena*, he indicates very clearly that he has studied their works. For how else can he say that "it is positively painful to see how utterly . . . Reid, Oswald, Beattie, and lastly Priestley, missed the point of the problem?"[9] Thus Kant knew them well it seems—well enough to offer a criticism that is both germane and accurate. Moreover, he characterized the reading experience as one that stood out. It was not just one of many because it did *not* leave him *indifferent*; it was *positively painful*, and, as such, presumably also one that concerned him greatly. The received interpretation of these statements not only takes no account of this, but actually depends upon viewing Kant as a careless writer, who passes off common prejudices without having examined the original works themselves.

Given this experience, one should expect other traces of the Scottish influence upon him. And there are other expressed references and many thinly veiled allusions to the Scots—none of which have as yet received the attention they deserve. The earliest such reference of Kant can be found in the *Vorlesungen über Philosophische Enzyklopädie*. In the section entitled "Metaphysics" Kant points out that metaphysics needs critique. We can do without criticism in mathematics, since there we have propositions upon which we can rely.

But in metaphysics the critique of pure reason is most essential. A more recent Englishman has written an *Appeal to Common Sense*. He maintains that everything is already contained in common sense. But this is false. Suppose I say, everything that happens has a cause, then if I examine this sentence, and consider its origins, the proponent can scream very much, and say that everybody can understand it just like that, but I can still ask where the proposition originates. For, in this case all intuition which I have in mathe-

8. Between 1766 and 1769 Kant lived in the house of Kanter, the bookdealer. The French translation of Reid's *Inquiry* appeared in 1768. That it was available in Königsberg is proven by Hamann's possession of it. (Hamann, by the way, had very close connections with Kanter.) According to Vorländer, *Kants Leben*, p. 58, "professors and other writers often met there [in Kanter's house]. On each mail day, when the newly published books were laid out at 11 o'clock . . . [o]ne conversed, disputed, and wrote letters in Kanter's office, as if one were at home." Kant could have learned in this way of Reid's *Inquiry* almost immediately after the appearance of its French translation.

9. Kant, *Prolegomena*, ed. Beck, p. 6.

matics . . . is absent. He could say that everything I have ever found has had a cause, but I cannot say this universally. I have here a proposition that is not borrowed from the object itself. For, in my concept nothing can be found other than that something comes to be that did not exist before.

I say: Everything that originates must originate from something that also originates: therefore it must also follow that there is no first beginning. But it is also clear that in a series of subordinated cognitions there must be a beginning. These two propositions are equally clear. But they still contradict each other. The middle is this: I myself say that these propositions are not as clear as 2 + 2 = 4. On the contrary, we must investigate here. Therefore, I say the investigation concerning the origin of the actions of reason is the business of metaphysics. I will say, therefore, that all actions are only valid under the conditions of sensibility, and if this reason, restricted by sensibility, puts us into circumstances to think completely *a priori* and apart from experience, then our knowledge is universal. It is a very special procedure of the understanding to think by itself, completely separated from experience.[10]

In the *Prolegomena* Kant is still more critical. He is not simply content to point out that the Scottish approach is wrong, but goes on to attack it sharply. The context is again that of the causal principle. "Hume has demonstrated irrefutably that it was perfectly impossible for reason to think *a priori* and by means of concepts such a combination . . . For it implies necessity." And, though Hume drew false conclusions from this important discovery, claiming that the concept of causality was fictitious (and metaphysics impossible), his discovery should have led philosophers to rethink the foundations of metaphysics. But this did not happen—mainly because of the Scots who

so misconstrued his valuable suggestion that everything remained in its old condition, as if nothing had happened. The question was not whether the concept of cause was right, useful and even indispensable for our knowledge of nature, for this Hume had never doubted; but whether the concept could be thought by reason *a priori*, and consequently whether it possessed an inner truth, independent of all experience, implying a perhaps more extended use not restricted merely to objects of experience. This was Hume's problem. It was solely a question concerning the *origin*, not concerning the *indispensable* need of using the concept.[11]

10. Kant, *Vorlesungen über Enzyklopädie und Logik*, ed. Lehmann, pp. 59f. The text (based on notes by a student) contains grammatical inconsistencies which I have corrected here.

11. Kant: *Prolegomena*, ed. Beck, pp. 6f.

Singling out Beattie, Kant goes on to attack the Scottish appeal to common sense as a "subterfuge" and an "appeal to the opinion of the multitude, of whose applause the philosopher is ashamed." Moreover, "Hume might fairly have laid as much claim to common sense as Beattie and, in addition, to a critical reason (such as the latter did not possess)."[12]

Throughout the *Prolegomena* further objections to common sense as a tribunal of truth can be found.[13] And there are passages in other works which show that Kant knew Scottish common-sense philosophy rather well.[14] Thus, in the "Postulates of Empirical Thought" of the *Critique of Pure Reason*, he calls attention to the fact that his use or "postulate" differs greatly from that of the Scots. For he interprets the word

not in the sense in which some recent philosophical writers, wresting it from its proper mathematical significance, have given to it, namely that to postulate should mean to treat a proposition as immediately certain, without justification or proof. For if, in dealing with synthetic propositions, we are to recognize them as possessing unconditioned validity, independently of deduction, on the evidence merely of their own claims, then no matter how evident they may be, all critique of understanding is given up. And since there is no lack of audacious pretensions, and these are supported by common belief (though that is no credential of their truth), the understanding lies open to every fancy, and is in no position to withhold approval of those assertions which, though illegitimate, yet press upon us, in the same confident tone, their claims to be accepted as actual axioms. Whenever, therefore, an *a priori* determination is synthetically added to the concept of a thing, it is indispensable that, if not a proof, at least a deduction of the legitimacy of such assertions should be supplied.[15]

There cannot be much doubt that the Scots figure prominently among "the recent philosophical writers" Kant has in mind here and that Beattie in particular is one of the most important among these.[16]

Kant objects to these writers largely because their reliance upon

12. Ibid., p. 7.
13. Ibid., pp. 24f., 61, 83, 118f., 120.
14. Ibid., pp. 26, 36, 84n. and 119.
15. A232f.=B285f. Compare Kant, *Prolegomena*, ed. Beck, p. 119.
16. The phrase "some recent philosophical writers" reminds one of the other phrase "a more recent Englishman has written" (see note 12 above). It was Beattie who used "axiom" in perhaps the most conspicuous way for the principles of common sense. But see also Oswald, *Appeal*, pp. 260f., 357. 360, for instance.

intuitively certain principles or axioms cuts off all critical investigation of knowledge-claims: for, if we accept such axioms in empirical thought, then, no matter how evident the axioms may be, "all critique of understanding is given up." And that means for him, all attempts to raise metaphysics to the level of a science are also given up. This sounds very much like Tetens's criticism of the Scots. But Kant has more to say. On the Scottish account only *naturalism* is possible.

The *naturalist* of pure reason adopts as his principle that through common reason, without science, that is, through what he calls sound reason, he is able, in regard to the most sublime questions which form the problem of metaphysics, to achieve more than is possible through speculation. Thus he is virtually asserting that we can determine the size and distance of the moon with greater certainty by the naked eye than by mathematical devices. This is mere misology, reduced to principles.[17]

For Kant, such naturalism is an evasion of the issue. Metaphysics is not just concerned with the analysis or description of the origin of our concepts and judgments; it is also concerned with the justification of some of these concepts and judgments in knowledge-claims. Only because philosophers have found it impossible to succeed in metaphysics by means of strict proofs have they resorted "boldly to appeal to the common sense of mankind—an expedient which is always a sign that the cause of reason is in desperate straits—rather than to attempt new dogmatic proofs."[18]

Common-sense philosophy, or naturalism, and philosophy are seen by Kant as being radically opposed with regard to the proper method of metaphysics. The common-sense naturalist has given up the attempt to raise metaphysics to the level of a science. Therefore he cannot be considered as a serious contender, and he has nothing to offer to the critical Kant. Though he may be the "defender of the good cause," his defence is very weak. Probably alluding to Reid, Oswald, or Beattie, Kant finds that "ridicule and boasting form his whole armoury, and these can be laughed at, as mere child's play."[19]

Thus, Kant's attacks upon common sense in general and the Scots in particular show not only that he is opposed to them but also that he

17. Kant, A855=B883; see also Kant, *Prolegomena*, ed. Beck, p. 61.
18. Kant, A783f.=B811f.
19. Kant, A743=B771; this seems to be a foreshadowing of his accusation that the Scots are "impudent" (Kant, *Prolegomena*, ed. Beck, p. 61).

knows them well.[20] He is aware of their fundamental opposition to Hume and mentions them in special connection with the causal principle. He has some definite idea of the nature of their appeal to common sense and seems to be acutely conscious of their having insisted that the principles of common sense are axioms of all thought. And no matter how negatively he responds to Reid, Oswald, and Beattie in his published writings, there should no longer be any doubt that he knew their works. In fact, Kant's intense polemic against them suggests that there is more to his relationship with the Scots than his published writings suggest at first sight.

2. But, it may be asked, what could Kant possibly have learned from the Scots? Perhaps more than has been thought until now. As has frequently been noted, there were basically two answers to Hume's scepticism in the eighteenth century, a Scottish and a German one. The Scottish answer was given by Reid and his followers, the German answer was that of Kant himself. There is much that separates these two answers. But—and this is not completely unknown either—there are great similarities as well. Thus Dugald Stewart argued that everything in Kant's work can already be found in British thought, going so far as to suggest that Kant may even have plagiarized Reid, Oswald, and Beattie.[21] Franz Brentano is another philosopher who believed that the differences between Kant and Reid are negligible. Indeed, he found that both could be criticized for adopting the same basic epistemological stance.[22]

If we assume that Stewart and Brentano—as well as a number of other philosophers—are not completely wrong, then, given that the Scottish answer precedes that of Kant by fifteen years, *and* given that Kant had some *knowledge* of the Scottish theory, it is only reasonable to suppose that the similarities between Kant and Reid are, indeed, the result of influence and not simply explicable as accidental historical parallels.

In any case, an investigation of the way in which the Scottish answer

---

20. This influence seems to have had consequences even with regard to certain details of Kant's position. Compare, for instance. the summary of his perceptual vocabulary—and especially the rejection of "idea" in its common broad usage—in A319f.=B376f. with Beattie's *Essay*, p. 155. But see also Reid, *Inquiry*, ed. Duggan, p. 257ff. (Reid, *Works*, vol. 1, pp. 204f.)

21. See Segerstedt, *The Problem of Knowledge*, pp. 37f.

22. Brentano, *Versuch über die Erkenntnis*, pp. 5–11, for instance. See also "Was an Reid zu loben," pp. 1–17.

to Hume presented itself to Kant is very necessary, if Lewis White Beck's characterization of the "strategic question" faced by Kant is correct:

How could he maintain scepticism in metaphysics—to which he was pushed by his study of Hume and his own discovery of the antinomies . . . without falling victim to eudaemonism in ethics and to a jejune appeal to common sense in the conduct of life and the development of science? How could he oppose Hume without falling in with Reid, Beattie and Oswald, who he thought were very uninspiring company? Could he give up supernatural metaphysics without making metaphysics out of naturalism?[23]

These are fundamentally correct questions. Furthermore, when Beck finds that what makes Kant's "answer to Hume possible—the rules of relating representations to each other introduce a synthetic element *a priori* into our empirical knowledge—also makes an answer to Leibniz possible: there is a perceptual or intuitional element in all *a priori* knowledge that is not emptily logical," one cannot help but notice the similarity between the answers of Kant and Reid.[24] Both, to speak generally, base their theories of empirical knowledge on a synthetic *a priori* element. Could it not be that Kant's "synthetic element *a priori*," or "the perceptual or intuitional element in" *a priori* knowledge is in fact inspired by Reid, and that the latter was more suggestive than is commonly supposed? Could it not be that the German answer to Hume is not only a development of the principles of Hume, but also of those of Reid?

Windelband suggested as much long ago when he said that the Scottish theory of common sense and original judgment is most relevant for the discussion of Kant's synthetic *a priori* judgments, and that Kant "begins at the point at which the Scots had stopped."[25] That this is true historically as well as systematically must now be shown.

23. Beck, "Kant's Strategy," in his *Essays on Kant and Hume*, pp. 3–19, 6.
24. Ibid., p. 16.
25. Windelband, *Geschichte der neueren Philosophie*, vol. 2, p. 54; see also his *Lehrbuch der Geschichte der Philosophie*, ed. Heimsoeth, p. 461n. Zart, *Einfluss*, p. 255f. disagrees. He argues that the similarity between Kant and Reid does not prove any influence. Since there are also similarities between Kant and Stewart, Kant could also be thought to be dependent upon the latter. But, as Zart observes, Stewart wrote ten years later than Kant. This argument of Zart's is singularly bad, as Stewart is also fundamentally dependent upon Reid. If both Kant and Stewart rely on Reid, the similarity is to be expected. Therefore Zart's claim that an "intimate relationship between Scottish and Kantian doctrines can hardly be observed" (p. 225) must be received with the greatest caution.

II

If we can assume that Kant read the French translation of Reid's *Inquiry* in 1768 or 1769—as it is quite reasonable to do—then it will seem entirely possible that his views on the epistemological status of our conceptions of space and time, on the one hand, and those of possibility, existence, necessity, substance, cause, etc., on the other, are influenced by Reid's theory of natural suggestion.

One of Reid's central claims was that extension, figure, motion, and space were not abstracted from sensation. In fact, he proposed the derivation of these concepts as an *experimentum crucis* "by which the ideal system must stand or fall."[26] For him, these conceptions, together with those of existence, cause, and others, are natural suggestions, that is, effects of instinct or of natural laws implanted in our mind.

Kant comes to very similar conclusions in his *Inaugural Dissertation* of 1770, that is, two years after the appearance of the *Inquiry* in French. What makes this agreement of Kant and Reid very conspicuous is that in 1768 Kant had held that space is objectively real and independent of the human mind. Between 1768 and 1770 something or someone changed his mind, so that he could say in the *Inaugural Dissertation* that space and time have been obtained

not by abstraction from the sensing of objects indeed . . . but from the very action of the mind, an action of co-ordinating the mind's sensa according to perpetual laws, and each of the concepts is like an immutable diagram and so is to be cognised intuitively. For sensations excite this act of the mind but do not. influence the intuition. Nor is there anything else here born with us except the law of the mind according to which it joins its own sensa together in a fixed manner as a result of the presence of an object.[27]

Reid and Kant are alike in thinking that an empirical derivation of the concept of space would necessarily undermine all certainty of knowledge and lead to idealism and scepticism. Furthermore, when Kant speaks of the importance of the "action" of the mind, of "immutable laws" which govern this action, of "intuition," and of "exciting," he sounds very much like Reid. What he says could be a

26. Reid, *Works*, vol. 1, pp. 128f. (*Inquiry*, ed. Duggan, p. 80).
27. Kant, *Selected Pre-critical Writings and Correspondence with Beck*, tr. and ed. Kerferd and Walford, p. 74; see also pp. 69 and 72.

further development of Reid's theory of natural suggestion.[28] The same also holds of Kant's account of intellectual concepts. They are for him "concepts abstracted out of the laws planted in the mind (by attending to its actions on the occasion of experience)" and they "never enter sensual representations as parts and so could not be abstracted from it in any way at all."[29]

Even Kant's basic systematic outlook in the *Inaugural Dissertation* greatly resembles that of Reid. For here Kant is what he later would have described as a transcendental realist. He thinks that the intellectual concepts, suggested to us at the occasion of sensation, allow us to think the objects as they really are. Both Reid and the Kant of 1770 base their realism upon certain "laws implanted in the mind," upon laws of which we become aware in sensation, but which form no part of sensation. The similarity is striking.

However, the similarity alone is not sufficient to establish an influence of Reid upon Kant, although one can say that Kant's contemporaries also noticed these same parallels. Tetens, for instance, although he believed that Kant was the first to say that space is the action of *co-ordinating* objects, characterizes Kant's conception of space as "a certain instinctual means of ordering co-existing objects," and draws attention to the affinities between the Kantian and the Scottish views by virtue of a lengthy prior critique of Reid's tendency to say that "this or that is the immediate work of instinct."[30]

While a Scottish influence as early as 1769 is *possible* only, such an influence is virtually certain after 1772. In this year Kant almost certainly read Beattie's *Essay* in German translation; and from this time on he most likely followed closely the further development of Scottish common-sense philosophy in Germany. The references in the *Enzyklo-*

28. I do not want to suggest that Kant's theory is actually such a development of Reid's suggestions. The evidence is rather slim. But the similarities are obvious. They are also observed by Charles Sanders Peirce. See the *Collected Papers of Charles Sanders Peirce*, ed. C. Hartshorne and P. Weiss, 8 vols., vol. 5, pp. 39, 53; vol. 6, p. 73. Peirce traces these similarities to the doctrine of immediate perception which he regards as shared by Berkeley, Reid and Kant. These similarities, quite independently of the question of influence, would deserve a more extensive treatment.

29. Kant, *Pre-Critical Writings*. p. 59; see also p. 58.

30. Tetens, *Philosophische Versuche*, p. 350 and pp. 331–33. For Tetens's view of Kant's theory in the *Dissertation* see also *Speculativische Philosophie*, pp. 21, 35, 40. The systematic parallels between Kant and Reid need to be discussed more thoroughly than is possible here.

pädievorlesung and the allusions in the *Critique of Pure Reason*, like the attack in the *Prolegomena*, attest to this.[31]

But what specifically did Kant learn from Beattie in 1772? The claim that he relied upon him for his information about Berkeley's "idealism" and Hume's *Treatise* constitutes almost a dogma of Kant-scholarship.[32] And there is reason to suppose that Kant did find Beattie helpful in this regard. Like most of his German contemporaries, he seems to have relied to a great extent upon the Scots for information concerning Berkeley's views.[33]

However, the theory that Kant relied upon Beattie's *Essay* as a sort of source book for Hume's early philosophy is not so plausible. While Berkeley's works were generally unavailable in German translation and were not very well known by Kant and his contemporaries, Hume's *Enquiries* were very well known, and even the *Treatise* had acquired some sort of notoriety.[34] Two of Kant's closest acquaintances in Königsberg had intimate knowledge of this work. Hamann owned a copy of the English original of it, and he reported to Jacobi on two occasions that Krauss, who had got to know the work through him, knew the *Treatise* "almost by heart."[35] Krauss and Kant not only frequently dined together, they also undertook long walks almost every day. That they did not often discuss philosophical questions is

31. It hardly needs pointing out that this chapter cannot be much more than a first step. A careful discussion of all the significant similarities and differences between Kant and the Scots would require another book.

32. To name only the most important sources, see Janitsch, *Kants Urteile über Berkeley*; Vaihinger, *Commentar*, vol. 1, pp. 342, 348; Stäbler *Berkeleys Auffassung*, pp. 46–67; Kemp Smith, *A Commentary to Kant's Critique of Pure Reason*, pp. xxviii/xxix, xxxin., Turbayne, "Kant's Refutation of Dogmatic Idealism"; Werkmeister, "Notes to an Interpretation of Berkeley"; Wolff, "Kant's Debt to Hume *via* Beattie"; Miller, "Kant and Berkeley: The Alternative Theories"; as I have shown above, there are other sources, such as Tetens and Lossius, for instance, from which Kant could also have gained information concerning the *Treatise*.

33. Berkeley was not very well known. See Stäbler and Janitsch. Even Tetens, who refers to the *Treatise*, does not seem to be well informed about Berkeley. Though the *Dialogues*, together with Collier's work, were translated by Tetens's teacher Eschenbach, his own work shows no influence by Berkeley.

34. Thus, though the *Treatise* was rare, it must not be assumed that it was unknown in Germany; nor even that it was unavailable.

35. Hamann to Jacobi, 22 April 1787, in Jacobi, *Werke*, vol. 4, part iii, pp. 339f.: "*Crispus* knows Hume by heart." Hamann to Jacobi, 27 April 1787, ibid.. pp. 348f. It is usually claimed that Hamann did not know the *Treatise* before 1781. But that is clearly false, given this translation. See Swain, "Hamann and the Philosophy of David Hume."

unthinkable, nor can one believe that Krauss never talked to Kant about the *Treatise*, a book so dear to him. Moreover, as I have shown elsewhere, Kant must have known the Conclusion of Book I of Hume's *Treatise*, translated by Hamann and published in the *Königsbergische gelehrte Zeitungen* of 1771. Indeed, it probably was his reading of this Conclusion that awoke him from his dogmatic slumber.[36]

Kant did not really need Beattie for factual information about Hume's early work, and his debt to Hume is not really a debt *"via* Beattie," as has been argued on the basis of Kant's confession in the *Prolegomena*. The question then remains: what, if anything, could Kant have learned from Beattie?

There are many things in the *Essay* that Kant must have liked. Thus the Introduction to its second part might have received his approval. Kant was working at the time on his treatise on *The Limits of Sensibility and Reason*, and thus Beattie's question as to how we differentiate genuine judgments of common sense from mere prejudices of education must have interested him, since it also raises the question concerning the relation between reason and sense:

Must every principle be admitted as true which we believe without being able to assign a reason? then where our security against prejudice and implicit faith? Or must every principle that seems intuitively certain, or intuitively probable, be reasoned upon, that we know whether it really be what it seems? then where is our security against the abuse so much insisted on, of subjecting common sense to the test of reasoning.—At what point must reason stop in its investigations, and the dictates of common sense be admitted as decisive and final?[37]

Beattie is thus very much aware of the problems confronting his account of knowledge (and, it appears to me, these questions show him in a better light than that in which he is usually seen). And if Kant can be supposed to have appreciated this passage, he must have liked what follows even more. For Beattie goes on to point out that

it is much to be regretted that this matter has been so little attended to: for a full and satisfactory discussion of it would do more real service to the philosophy of human nature, than all the systems of logic in the world; would at once exalt pneumatology to the dignity of science by settling it on a firm and unchange-

36. For a more thorough discussion see my "Kant's Conception of Hume's Problem."
37. Beattie, *Essay*, pp. 157f.

able foundation; and would go a great way to banish sophistry from science, and rid the world of scepticism. This is indeed the *grand desideratum* in logic; of no less importance to the moral sciences, than the discovery of the longitude to navigation.[38]

Beattie is not so vain or ignorant as to imagine that he can do, all by himself, what needs doing, but, he finds, "to have set an example may be of consequence." And perhaps it did have an influence on the critical philosophy of Kant. In any case, his pronouncements are similar to those of Beattie. The similarity extends even to the details. Both Kant and Beattie feel confident that they can "settle the boundaries," and they feel confident because "in some of the sciences [they have] been long settled with the utmost precision, and to universal satisfaction." And the sciences in which the boundaries have been settled are identified by both as "mathematics and natural philosophy."[39]

But if these passages, which show Beattie at his best, might have met Kant's approval, there are equally many which no doubt angered him. For Beattie's mockery of Hume's *Gründlichkeit* applied *a fortiori* to the type of metaphysics Kant was accustomed to as a German. Thus Beattie writes

A celebrated writer on human nature hath observed that "if truth be at all within the reach of human capacity, it is certain it must lie deep and abstruse" and a little afterwards he adds "that he would esteem it a strong presumption against the philosophy he is going to unfold, were it so very easy and obvious." I am so far from adopting this opinion, that I declare, in regard to the few things I have to say on human nature, that I should esteem it a very strong presumption against them, if they were not easy and obvious . . . [40]

Kant could not accept Beattie's tendency to ridicule thoroughness in metaphysics. When Beattie makes fun of Hume, saying "a witch going to sea in an eggshell or preparing to take a trip through the air on a

38. Ibid., p. 158; this is somewhat similar to what Hume says in the Conclusion of Book I of his *Treatise*. See also Beattie, *Essay*, pp. 141f.: "We sometimes repine at the narrow limits prescribed to human capacity. *Hitherto shalt thou come, and no further,* seems a hard prohibition, when applied to the operations of mind. But as, in the material world, it is to this prohibition man owes his security and existence; so, in the immaterial system, it is to this we owe our virtue and happiness."

39. Ibid., p. 160.

40. Ibid., p. 17.

broomstick is really a surprising phenomenon; but nothing to Mr. Hume, . . . 'launching out (as he well expresseth) into the immense depths of philosophy,'" we find an example of the "impudence" that Kant castigated in the *Prolegomena* and the first *Critique*.[41]

But, again, Kant's very criticism of the Scottish treatment of Hume reaffirms his dependence upon the Scots. When he observes, for instance, that Hume's "question was not whether the concept of cause was right, useful and even indispensable for our knowledge of nature" but "solely the question concerning the *origin*, not concerning the *indispensable* need of using the concept," he seems to be addressing himself to and playing with a specific passage in Oswald's *Appeal*, that is, a passage of a work that Kant had already singled out for criticism in his *Enzyklopädievorlesungen*. Oswald had found that

Mr. Hume's observations on the connection of ideas are just; and all he says on the particular connections he mentions, is worthy of attention; but not to the present purpose. The question is not, whether we actually believe the connection between cause and effect? for of that there can be no doubt; but, what reason we have to believe it? Through custom and habitual association of ideas, we fall into many absurd ways of thinking, and also of believing in contradiction to the plainest evidence . . . By resolving the belief of a truth so fundamental as is the connection between cause and effect, into habitual association of ideas, Mr. Hume hath given countenance to the dogmatism of the bigots . . .[42]

Kant's criticisms are, to some extent, justified. Oswald seems to ascribe to Hume the project of questioning the validity of the causal connection. Yet Oswald is very much aware of Hume's attempt to establish the origin of the casual principle, and he has clearly grasped that the question of origin has consequences for the application of the causal principle. Further, he agrees with Hume that the connection of cause and effect is not one of *reason*—the very point Kant so much emphasizes—feeling that "Hume did well in pointing out the prevailing absurdity of resolving our belief of primary truths into the force of reasoning: but he would have done better still if he had resolved it into

41. Ibid., p. 255; see also p. 167.
42. Oswald, *Appeal*, pp. 130f. I regret that I am not able to say anything about the further agreement of the German translation and Kant's criticism. I noticed the analogy only after the German translation was no longer accessible to me.

the authority of common sense."[43] Thus, when Kant implicitly criticizes Oswald for not having understood the difference between the origin and the application of the concept of causality he is not quite fair. Oswald does understand that difference. And, as Kant himself points out in other contexts, the question concerning the origin of a concept has important consequences for the use we can make of it. It is not *solely* a question concerning the source, but also a question concerning the validity of certain applications of the concept.[44]

Beattie is also aware of this, for he pronounces it as an axiom, clear, certain, and undeniable, that "whatever beginneth to exist, precedeth from some cause," and he claims:

I cannot bring myself to think, that the reverse of any geometrical axiom is more absurd than the reverse of this; and therefore I am as certain of the truth of this, as I can be of the truth of the other; and I cannot without contradicting myself, and doing violence to my nature, even attempt to believe otherwise.

For him, this principle

is one of the principles of common sense, which every rational mind does and must acknowledge to be true; . . . because the law of nature determines us to believe it without proof, and to look upon its contrary as perfectly absurd, and inconceivable.[45]

Thus Beattie, in fact, argues in much the same way as Oswald that the causal principle must be believed because it is a principle of common sense. Neither one of them simply claims that Hume is wrong because the causal principle is indispensable. They also argue that it is impossible to derive the principle from experience, that it is an *a priori* principle, presupposed by any experience. As a principle of common sense it has the characteristic of necessity.

But even if Kant had admitted this more clearly, he still would have objected to the way in which Reid, Oswald, and Beattie's theory had

43. Ibid., p. 133. One of the reasons why Oswald thought it necessary to resolve this principle into the authority of common sense, or, to establish it as the first principle of all knowledge, is surely his need for it in the attempt to prove God's existence.

44. But Oswald is not so naive as to believe that the existence of God could be *proved* by means of it. The belief in the existence of God is for him just as inexplicable as is our belief in the causal connection. See *Appeal*, pp. 106f.

45. Beattie, *Essay*, p. 111.

been "cheaply acquired" through simply declaring the causal principle to be a principle of common sense. For him the matter must be analysed much more deeply. When this analysis is completed it will be seen, according to Kant, that Beattie and Oswald try to make the causal principle do more than it can possibly do; they use it as a basis for conclusions beyond the limits of the senses and experience. The Transcendental Logic shows that none of the principles of the understanding, even if they are *a priori*, can be applied beyond sense experience.

By contrast, it is one of Beattie's expressed goals in the defence of the causal principle to rehabilitate its use in "the most important argument, that ever employed reason," namely, that argument "which from the works that are created, evinces the eternal power and godhead of the Creator."[46] And this Kant cannot accept; he is on the same side as Feder, who had already pointed out that "a *Hume* would still have a fair game with him [Beattie], . . . when he maintains against *Hume* that the principle 'everything that happens has a cause' has a wider field [*Grund*] than experience."[47] That is, both these Germans see that determining the field of valid application of the causal principle is *the* problem at issue in the Beattie-Hume dispute. But whereas Feder hopes for an answer along the lines of Beattie and Reid, an answer in which Hume no longer has a fair game, Kant takes Hume more seriously, trying to generalize the problem of causality and to determine its true consequences for all of metaphysics.

III

Kant describes the development of his own doctrine as follows:

I . . . first tried whether Hume's objection could not be put into a general form, and soon found that the concept of the connection of cause and effect was by no means the only concept by means of which the understanding thinks the connection of things *a priori*, but rather that metaphysics consists altogether of such concepts. I sought to ascertain their number, and when I had satisfactorily succeeded in this by starting from a single principle, I proceeded to the deduction of these concepts which I was now certain were not derived from experience, as Hume had attempted to derive them, but sprung from the pure understanding.[48]

46. Ibid.
47. *Göttingische Anzeigen*, 1771, number 12 (28 January): 94.
48. Kant, *Prolegomena*, ed. Beck, p. 8.

But, in a similar sense, this generalization of the problem of *a priori* principles can already be found in the works of the Scottish common-sense philosophers. In trying to prove that the causal principle is indeed an axiom, and that "it is on the same footing with other intuitive axioms; that is, we believe it, because the law of our nature renders it impossible for us to disbelieve it," Beattie makes a point of his discovery that *"Mr. Hume has not enumerated all the relations which, when discovered, give rise to certainty."*[49]

On this occasion, Beattie mentions only the principle of personal identity. But it is quite clear that he thinks this is only one among several principles of common sense. For his entire discussion is meant to prove that "except we believe many things without proof, we never can believe anything at all; for that all sound reasoning must ultimately rest on principles intuitively certain, or intuitively probable . . . this I shall prove by a fair induction of particulars."[50] Moreover, Reid, in the *Inquiry*, had already called attention to his belief that "a clear explication and enumeration of the principles of common sense, is one of the chief *desiderata* in logic."[51]

Thus it is not at all unreasonable to suppose that with regard to the generalization of Hume's problem Kant was helped along by suggestions of Reid and Beattie: Kant acknowledges that he has read their works, and the passages cited show very clearly that Reid and Beattie have already generalized Hume's problem. They argued that the connection of cause and effect is by no means the only concept by means of which *a priori* connections are suggested to us. Reid especially had "considered such of them as occurred in the examination of the five senses."[52] Could it be that Kant is acknowledging a debt by means

49. Beattie, *Essay*, p. 105 (emphasis mine).

50. Ibid., p. 51.

51. Reid, *Works*, vol. 1, p. 209 (*Inquiry*, ed. Duggan, p. 269). See also p. 99 (8): "This may truly be called an *analysis* of the human faculties; and till this is performed, it is in vain we expect any just *system* of the mind; that is, an enumeration of the original powers and laws of our constitution, and an explication from them of the various phenomena of human nature." See also Oswald, *Appeal*, pp. 85f.: "The anatomy of the human body hath been long a serious study . . . but the mind hath never yet come under the same careful inspection . . . its objects are not enumerated, its extent is not known, and its authority is little regarded; for which reason a standard of theologic, ethic and political truth, is to this hour a *desideratum* with the learned. On all these subjects we are become expert reasoners, but hardly know when or where to stop, or how to form a steady judgment."

52. Reid, *Works*, vol. 1, p. 209 (*Inquiry*, ed. Duggan, p. 269).

of his simile concerning the chisels and hammers of Scottish common sense and his own etcher's needle of critical reason? "Chisels and hammers may suffice a piece of of lumber, but for etching we require an etcher's needle."[53] This does suggest that Beattie was doing something similar to Kant's criticism, though in a very rough fashion.

In any case, in the Introduction to the first *Critique* Kant explicitly calls attention to his belief that "even common sense is never without certain *a priori* cognitions," and he calls special attention to the causal principle in this context.[54] It appears that in this belief he is closer to the Scots than he is to Hume.

To be sure, Kant's theory, and especially in the form in which it is expounded in the first *Critique* and the *Prolegomena*, is quite different from anything to be found in Reid, Oswald, or Beattie. Kant does not talk about "faith" and "belief" in first principles of "common sense." He speaks of "cognitions *a priori*" and "pure understanding." Where Reid confesses ignorance and invokes such terms as "suggestion" and "inspiration," Kant claims certitude and formulates the problem concerning "*a priori* determinations," which are "synthetically added to the concept of a thing." Reid and Beattie try to show, or are groping their way towards showing, that the principles of common sense are based on "laws of nature"; Kant tries to make clear that they "sprang from the pure understanding." Reid, Oswald, and Beattie unhesitatingly use the principles of common sense to "overstep all possible empirical employment"; Kant's major concern is with showing the essential limitation to experience of the principles of pure understanding. Reid and Beattie introduce their principles in a somewhat cavalier fashion; Kant wants to deduce his "starting from a single concept." In all this Kant was on his own. In this "most difficult task," the Scots could offer him no more assistance than the other metaphysicians.

What holds of the Kant of the late sixties also holds of Kant in the seventies. As Beck has said: "The most serious occupation of Kant in these years was the thinking of thoughts that no one had had thought before."[55] But this should not be taken to mean that the Scots could not have inspired Kant. For in 1772 they had a great deal to offer him.

53. Kant, *Prolegomena*, ed. Beck, p. 7.

54. B3 (I have substituted "common sense" for Kemp Smith's "common understanding"). There are also other passages in which Kant freely "appeals" to common sense; see, for instance, A184=B227.

55. Beck, *Early German Philosophy*, p. 457.

Both the positive influence of their generalization of Hume's problem and the negative influence of their "uncritical" extension of the validity of the principles of common sense beyond the limits of all possible experience provide starting points for Kant's critical development. And it seems likely that they had a greater significance than is commonly thought. Kant, like many other thinkers of that period, started off his critical inquiry where the Scots had stopped theirs. And, as Kant said himself, "if we start from a well-founded, but undeveloped, thought which another has bequeathed to us, we may well hope to advance further than the acute man to whom we owe the first spark of light."[56]

The similarity of the views of Kant and the Scots on the categories is greater than Kant's criticisms would have us think. Both insist, against Hume, that certain concepts are *a priori* and *necessary*. Both argue that these concepts cannot be explained by their origin in experience. While they may be suggested to us on the occasion of sense experiences, they cannot be reduced to them. The main differences between the Kantian and the Scottish account consists in Kant's attempt to be more specific and more thorough. Where Reid and Beattie plead ignorance, Kant thinks more can and must be said. His "Metaphysical" and "Transcendental Deductions" as well as the chapters on the "Schematism" and the "Principles" are the expression of this belief.

But these differences are more the result of an elaboration of certain common features of the two theories than they are fundamental differences between them. Whether the similarities are ultimately more significant than the differences I do not pretend to determine here. From a certain point of view the similarities are decisive, while from another the differences are much more interesting philosophically. Brentano is a very good example of one who emphasizes the similarities, while most Kantians take the contrary course. In this context not much depends upon deciding this issue. For even if it were argued that Kant had developed his own view in conscious opposition to that of the Scots, the historical and systematic connection would still have been established. Often the views of a philosophical opponent have a greater influence upon a philosopher than do those of philosophical allies. The Scots themselves, in their response to Hume, are a clear example of such influence.

56. Kant, *Prolegomena*, ed. Beck, p. 9.

IV

But if the Scots had an influence on Kant's conception of Hume's problem concerning the nature of the causal principle, then they may also be expected to have had an effect upon his doctrine of the antinomy of pure reason. For, as I have tried to show elsewhere, the antinomies and the causal principle are really different aspects of the *same* problem for Kant during the early seventies.[57] And it is especially the first antinomy—the world has a beginning/it has no beginning—that has close links with the causal principle.

The same close connection between the causal principle and arguments for a beginning (or the *creation*) of the world can be found in Beattie's *Essay*. Beattie believes that the causal principle is the "foundation" of the argument that God is the creator of the universe, and that in "so far as it resolves itself into this argument [it] is properly a demonstration, being a clear deduction from self-evident principle."[58] Consequently, he argues,

that many of the objects in nature have had a beginning, is obvious to our senses and memory, or confirmed by unquestionable testimony: these, therefore, according to the axiom we are here considering, must be believed to have proceeded from a cause adequate, at least to the effect produced, that the whole sensible universe has to us the appearance of an effect . . . cannot be denied: and that it had a beginning, and was not from eternity, is proved by every species of evidence the subject will admit . . . What is the universe, but a vast system of works and effects, some of them great and others small, some more, and some less considerable? . . . Each link of the great chain must be supported by something, but the whole chain may be supported by nothing . . . are not these assertions too absurd to deserve an answer?[59]

Thus Beattie more or less simply repeats the traditional claim that the world is an effect and therefore must have had a beginning and be caused by something.

But this is not all he has to say on this matter. Having argued for his own position, he also presents the contrary one, the thesis to his antithesis:

57. See my "Kant's Conception of Hume's Problem."
58. Beattie, *Essay*, p. 111.
59. Ibid., pp. 113–15.

The reader, if he happens to be acquainted with Mr. Hume's *Essay on a particular providence and a future state* will see, that these remarks are intended as an answer to a very strange argument advanced against the belief of Deity. "The universe," we are told, "is an object quite singular and unparalleled; no other object that has fallen under our observation bears any similarity to it; neither it nor its cause can be comprehended under any known species; and therefore we can form no rational conclusion at all concerning the cause of the universe . . ."[60]

Beattie then tries to reduce Hume's claim *ad absurdum* by showing that it involves a contradiction. Each thing in the universe

had a beginning . . . What thing in the universe exists uncaused? Nothing—Is this a rational conclusion? So it seems. It seems, then, that though it be rational to assign a cause to everything in the universe; yet to assign a cause to the universe is not rational![61]

In fairness to Beattie it must be said that he does not take the easy way out. He represents Hume's doctrine free from distortion and at its strongest; and because his final answer is not much more than a restatement of his original arguments, the clash of the two positions becomes just as apparent as the strength of the arguments against each position. All in all, Beattie's discussion of the causal principle in connection with the argument that the world has a beginning is particularly suited to call attention to the fact that both conclusions, *the world has a cause (and a beginning)* and *the world has no cause (and no beginning)*, are equally rational and can both be argued for rationally.

Kant says somewhat later in the *Enzyklopädievorlesungen* (in the very context of a reference to Oswald): "these propositions are equally clear, but they still contradict each other."[62] His solution to the problem is to show that the causal principle is applicable only in possible experience, that is, experience dependent upon our senses. It cannot be used to extend knowledge beyond the senses, as the Scots clearly wanted to do. He agrees with Beattie, "if the universe had a beginning, it must have had a cause . . . we necessarily assent to it, such is the law of our nature," but he also agrees with Hume (as represented by Beattie, perhaps): the world or the universe cannot be caused in the same way as particular

60. Ibid., p. 115.
61. Ibid., p. 117.
62. See the long quotation from the *Enzyklopädievorlesungen* given above.

objects in it, and thus it need not have a beginning. Here is only one example of the painful tension Kant might have experienced while reading Beattie's *Essay*.

The final version of Kant's first antinomy does not resemble the discussion of Beattie as much as does the version in the *Enzyklopädievorlesungen*. For, whereas the lectures make a clear connection between the temporal beginning and the causal principle, the final version represented in the *Critique of Pure Reason* refers only to time and space.[63] The causal principle is much more apparent in the third and fourth Antinomies. This does not mean, however, that there are no similarities. For instance, Kant argues *for* his thesis (the world is limited in time) by trying to disprove the antithesis that the world has no beginning.[64] In doing so he relies on the same implied claim as does Beattie, namely, that "up to every given moment an eternity has elapsed," making a move similar to that of Beattie, who observed in his *reductio ad absurdum* of the antithesis that "the Atheist will never be able to elude the force of this argument, till he can prove, that every thing in nature exists necessarily, independently, and *from eternity*."[65] No matter how different the final version of Kant's argument is from Beattie's account, it is clear that the latter's account of the application of the causal principle in "the most important argument that ever employed human reason" could also very well have been important when Kant first began to think about the problem that certain apparently unavoidable contradictions of reason posed for him.[66]

---

63. Thus in the version that is found in the first *Critique*, the first Antinomy looks indeed as though it originated directly from the problem of the *Dissertation* (mainly that of the reality of space and time). But if one looks at the way in which the first Antinomy represents itself in the *Enzyklopädievorlesungen*, it becomes clear that this is only the result of hard labour. For Kant seems to have confounded at first the problem of a beginning in time with that of the causal maxim. This confusion, if it is a confusion, is understandable, for Hume's question is "for what reason we pronounce it *necessary*, that every thing whose existence has a beginning, shou'd also have a cause" (Hume, *Treatise*, p. 78). The *Prolegomena* shows that it is "the extended use" of this principle, i.e. the use Oswald and Beattie want to make of it, that especially troubles Kant.

64. A427ff.=B455ff.; it is the only one of the Antinomies clearly developed in the *Enzyklopädievorlesungen*.

65. Beattie, *Essay*, p. 118 (emphasis mine).

66. Kant *Enzyklopädievorlesungen*, pp. 64f. In this context a restatement of the first Antinomy can be found as well: "In order to show the Antinomy we will try to prove that there is no first beginning. We want to argue synthetically (from above).

"I cannot know anything save through a reason/cause (*Grund*). Therefore I cannot

However, there is also reason to suppose that the discussion of liberty and necessity, Beattie's "second instance" showing "the danger of carrying any investigation beyond the dictates of common sense," had an influence upon Kant's discussion of the illegitimate extension of the principles of the human understanding "beyond the limits of experience." In fact, the third antinomy poses the same problem as Beattie's discussion of liberty and necessity. Furthermore, Kant's resolution of this issue is much the same as Beattie's. Both argue that the answer to the question concerning our liberty is not at all "*indifferent,*" and both argue that we have mainly a "*practical interest*" in arguing for our liberty. Finally, both regard the possibility of freedom as a "mystery," which cannot possibly be explained.[67]

This similarity between Beattie and Kant was not lost on other German philosophers. Platner, for instance, found it rather "strange" that Kant would be so close to the Scots in his discussion of freedom. For he felt that Reid and Beattie had some right to appeal to feeling in this context, but Kant did not, and should not have so appealed, given that he had so thoroughly discredited common sense and feeling in the first *Critique* and the *Prolegomena*. A contributor to the *Philosophische Bibliothek* also found it necessary to call attention to the fact that Hume, Reid, Kant, and Jacobi all agreed on the fact that, so far as practical reason is concerned, the appeal to "instinct" was unavoidable.[68]

In any case, Beattie's discussion of causality and freedom had a significant effect on German philosophers. Eberhard went so far as to suggest the dispute concerning freedom and necessity was between "*determinists* and *Beattians.*"[69] And Beattie's tendency to "*oppose metaphysics to metaphysics*" was also noted by Germans other than Kant. Feder, for instance, had already in 1775 called the Scots "*the new*

---

know the first in any other way than that it must have a reason/cause. The first must have begun to act as well, and then something must have preceded it, a change through which it was made to act.—This can also be applied to freedom in the transcendental sense and [we] can talk of it *pro et contra*. Moreover, there is a necessary being and there is none." This passage may serve to show again the intimate connection of the problem of the beginning of the world and that of causality for the early Kant.

67. Beattie, *Essay*, pp. 304, 328, 324ff. Kant, Ax, A462ff.=B490ff. (the entire section 3 of the "Antinomy"). But see especially A466ff.=B494ff. and Aviif. The entire discussion of the Antinomies relies greatly upon common sense concepts. Thus Kant talks a great deal of "common human reason," "inclinations of reason," etc.

68. For Platner see also Chapter V, as well as *Philosophische Bibliothek*, vol. 4 (1791): 112.

69. Eberhard, *Neue vermischte Schriften*, p. 100. According to this classification, Kant is a "Beattian."

dialecticians" and their thought "*the new dialectic,*" and, as early as 1771, had found many "correct and exact thetic and anti-thetic remarks" in Beattie's *Essay*.[70]

There are, then, good reasons to suppose that the Scots (and Beattie in particular) were of importance to Kant's first attempts to formulate the problem of the antinomies for himself. Windelband's suspicions that Kant may have started where the Scots left off may, accordingly, be true in more ways than one. Historically, at least, Kant's problem was of such a kind that the Scots may have been more important and more suggestive than hitherto has been thought.

v

But perhaps Scottish common sense is important for understanding not only the historical origins of Kant's thought but also the systematic ones. Perhaps common sense can serve also to make clearer what Kant's "metaphysical intentions" actually were.[71] And it could very well be helpful in discussing such "meta-critical" questions as, for example, "How is Critical Philosophy Possible?"—a question that, it is widely thought, Kant did not answer.[72]

Though it may appear to be strange and wrong-headed to try to show that common sense is of the greatest significance for a proper understanding of the systematic foundation of Kant's critical philosophy, this is exactly what I shall argue. It is true that Kant rejected common sense as a tool of philosophical justification in metaphysics. But, I shall contend, this does not mean that he rejected common sense altogether. On the contrary, Kant, like all enlightenment philosophers, consciously attempted to defend and justify common sense. His critical philosophy was not meant to supersede common sense, but to strengthen it.

To be sure, Kant had many negative things to say about common

70. Beattie's phrase occurs in the *Essay*, p. 107. But the whole of section 3 of part 3 of this work is concerned with the problem, and it could very well have reawakened Kant's interest in the problem of provable contradictory statements, which had given him "great light" in 1769. For Feder's remarks see *Göttingische Anzeigen*, 1775, number 92 (3 August): 778.

71. They may turn out to be entirely different from what the "metaphysical" school of Kant-interpretation, which heavily relies on them, has argued. See also the Appendix.

72. For a helpful discussion of this aspect, see Lewis White Beck, "Toward a Meta-Critique of Pure Reason," *Essays on Kant and Hume*, pp. 20–37.

sense and its use in metaphysics. But these remarks must be carefully considered. First, he had good reason to be annoyed with the philosophers who used common sense as the ultimate criterion of truth—and especially with those who were connected with the *Göttingische gelehrte Anzeigen*. For his first *Critique* was criticized for not indicating "the middle way between exaggerated scepticism and dogmatism, the correct middle road that leads, if not with full satisfaction, so at least with re-assurance to the most natural way of thinking."[73] The work was understood as revealing the dangers of metaphysics—acquainting the reader with "the considerable difficulties of speculative philosophy" and "presenting materials for the salutary consideration by the builders and defenders of metaphysical systems, who too proudly and boldly trust in their imagined pure reason." But it was rejected as a cure of the metaphysical disease. Kant felt that he had been treated like an imbecile, and he lashed out at those who had criticized him for not having given any solutions to the problems facing the philosophers of the time.

Though he did not know who wrote the review, he was reasonably sure that it was either Feder or Meiners or someone close to them. Because he knew that the Göttingers appreciated the Scots very much, and because, at this time, he felt contempt for the Göttingers, he did not attack them directly. Instead, he chose to criticize them indirectly by putting down their Scottish predecessors and models. Accordingly, the passage in the *Prolegomena* should be taken *cum grano salis*. What Kant says about the Scots may not be intended to criticize them so much as their German followers.

Second, some of Kant's closest acquaintances in Königsberg were clearly common-sense philosophers. Krauss, especially, whom he characterized as being affected by "naturalism" and "misology," appreciated the common-sense approach of the Scots. One of Krauss's favourite philosophers was Adam Smith. And what Hamann thought of Reid and Beattie has already been shown. So perhaps when Kant delivered his indictment of the appeal to common sense in metaphysics, he was reacting to his friends at home.

Third, these personal reasons were reinforced by more systematic considerations. For his critical philosophy was not rejected because it was thought to be too radical, revolutionary, or radically different from that of his contemporaries. It was, rather, seen in its essentials to be

73. Zugabe zu den *Göttingischen Anzeigen*, 1782, number 3 (19 January): 47.

very similar to the work of his contemporaries, while yet affecting certain sceptical and idealistic tendencies.[74]

Kant and his followers were greatly worried by this from the very beginning. Thus Kant himself attacked in the *Prolegomena* of 1783 those "scholarly men to whom the history of philosophy . . . is philosophy itself," and for whom nothing can be said which, in their opinion, has not been said before."[75] More particularly, he was worried because many

a naturalist of pure reason (by which I mean the man who believes that he can decide in matters of metaphysics without any science) may pretend that he, long ago, by the prophetic spirit of his sound sense, not only suspected but knew and apprehended what is here propounded with so much ado, or, if he likes, with prolix and pedantic pomp: "that with all our reason we can never reach beyond the field of experience."[76]

Likewise, Ludwig Heinrich Jakob, one of Kant's earliest followers, complained in 1786 that "nothing is less fair than the objection which is *often* made . . . in lectures, in private conversations, and at times in published writings: that the *Critique contains nothing new.*"[77]

Given this situation, it is not too surprising that Kant found it necessary to argue so vehemently against common-sense philosophers and their appeal to common sense. He had to show as convincingly as he could that his own critical philosophy was rather different from naturalism, and that it constituted a decisive improvement over previous theories, naturalism included. To do this, he emphasized the differences between himself and his Scottish and German contemporaries, aligning himself more with Hume's critical or sceptical philosophy.

But such a move was hardly a disinterested characterization of his affinities. Therefore, his arguments should not be taken as implying that he was altogether opposed to common sense. Nor should they be taken as an indication that at no time could Kant have learned anything from the Scots. Indeed, just as it is possible to make a case for a greater indebtedness of Kant to the Scots, it can also be shown that he himself

74. See the next chapter.
75. Kant, *Prolegomena*, ed. Beck, p. 10.
76. Ibid., p. 61.
77. Jakob, *Prüfung der Mendelssohnschen Morgenstunden*, p. x (emphasis mine).

thought much more highly of common sense than his negative strictures would lead one to believe.

First, during the earlier stages of his development, he thought just as highly of common sense as did most of his contemporaries. In fact, it appears that, at least for a time, he considered critique to be the business of common sense.[78]

Second, he still thought during the eighties that common sense is the source and the field of philosophy, that the fate of philosophy is intricately connected with common sense, and that philosophy cannot transcend common sense.[79] Thus he found that "metaphysics can never cease to be in demand—since the interest of common sense is so intimately interwoven with it . . ."[80] Moreover, the final agreement of common sense and critical philosophy "is the best confirmation of the correctness of the above assertions [that is, the outcome of the first *Critique*]. For we have thereby revealed to us, what could not at the start have been foreseen, namely, that in matters which concern all men without distinction nature is not guilty of any partial distribution of her gifts, and that in regard to the essential ends of human nature the highest philosophy cannot advance further than is possible under the guidance which nature has bestowed even on the most common sense."[81]

Third, this is even clearer in moral philosophy. For, as Kant points out in the *Foundations*:

without in the least teaching common reason anything new, we need only to draw its attention to its own principle, in the manner of Socrates, thus showing

---

78. See Kant. *Werke*, (*Akademie Ausgabe*), vol. 16, reflections 1567, 1568, 1573, 1574, 1575, 1577, 1578, 1579, 1585, 1586, 1589, 1591, 1595, 1602, 1612, 1614, 1619.

79. See Bxxxiv, for instance; see also A831=B859.

80. Kant, *Prolegomena*, ed. Beck. p. 5. It appears to me that one must even go so far as to say that metaphysics as "*Naturanlage*" is for Kant what the "metaphysics of common sense" is for Tetens. See Kant, *Prolegomena*, ed. Beck, pp. 75–98, and 116! See also Aviif., Bxxxif., and A528=B556, where the Antinomy is claimed to be based upon the assumption that the conditions and the conditioned are in space and time. "This is the assumption ordinarily made by the common human understanding [common sense], and *to it the conflict is exclusively due*" (emphasis mine).

81. Kant, A830=B858. W. H. Walsh has argued on the basis of such passages as this that Kant's criticism is meant to supply the common man with the weapons by means of which he can defend himself "against the attacks of sceptics or the sophisms of men of bad faith." See Walsh, *Kant's Criticism of Metaphysics*, p. 255.

that neither science nor philosophy is needed in order to know what one has to do in order to be honest and good, and even wise and virtuous.[82]

In the *Critique of Practical Reason* he goes even so far as to say that *"the justification of moral principles as principles of a pure reason could be made with sufficient certainty through merely appealing to the judgment of common sense."*[83]

Fourth, in the *Critique of Judgment* Kant argues that "the judgment of taste . . . depends on our presupposing the existence of a common sense" and that "only under the presupposition . . . of such a common sense, are we able to lay down a judgement of taste."[84] "We assume a common sense as the necessary condition of the universal communicability of our knowledge, which is presupposed in every logic and every principle of knowledge that is not one of scepticism."[85]

Thus, on the one hand, Kant seems to reject common sense as useless to the "science of metaphysics" and its foundation. But, on the other hand, he also acknowledges that common sense is of fundamental importance to his critical enterprise, going so far as to characterize it as a "critical faculty" and as the vehicle for emancipation from prejudice or the faculty of enlightenment.[86]

Is this not a contradiction or an inconsistency on Kant's part? Some philosophers have thought so. Platner, as we have already seen, found this circumstance rather strange. More recently, Helmut Holzhey, in his important *Kants Erfahrungsbegriff*, has observed: "Kant's position with regard to the philosophical role of common sense . . . is ambivalent and, in any case, not decidedly negative."[87] Paul Guyer, focusing on the role of common sense in the third *Critique*, wonders what exactly Kant is asking it to do in his work. He sees him suggesting that common sense as "the necessary condition of the universal communicability of our knowledge" is a constitutive principle, while at the same time asking whether it is only a regulative principle.[88] In the former case, common

82. Kant, *Foundations*, tr. Beck, p. 20.
83. Kant, *Critique of Practical Reason*, tr. Beck, p. 95 (emphasis mine).
84. Kant. *Critique of Judgment*, tr. Meredith, p. 83.
85. Ibid., p. 84.
86. Ibid, pp. 150–54; see also his essays on history as well as his essay on "orientation in thinking."
87. Holzhey, *Kants Erfahrungsbegriff*, p. 301.
88. The exact role of common sense in the third *Critique* does not seem to be clear to most commentators of this work. Guyer is no exception. In his *Kant and the Claims of*

sense would be important for his entire critical enterprise, while in the latter it would not necessarily be so important. Does that mean that Kant himself was confused about common sense, and that he wavered between rejecting it and giving it a role of some importance to play? Does Collingwood's observation fully explain Kant's views on common sense, that is, that "an intense polemic against a certain theory is a certain sign that the doctrine in question *figures largely* in a writer's environment and *even has a strong attraction for himself?*" Was Kant powerfully attracted to common-sense philosophy, while being prevented from following his inclinations by other systematically and historically determined commitments?

I believe more can and must be said. At the very least, it is possible to show that at one, even if perhaps rather superficial, level Kant was not at all confused, and that he knew exactly where "common sense" fitted in his critical philosophy. Though this does not mean that he was altogether clear about common sense, it does show that his view of common sense is more highly developed than previous accounts suggest.

The level at which Kant was clear was that of his "faculty psychology." Common sense is completely integrated in his system of the faculties. But because, like most of his German contemporaries, and especially Mendelssohn, he does not make as radical a distinction between common sense and reason as did the Scots, it is easy to overlook the importance of common sense. Common sense and reason are expressions of one and the same faculty of *thought*.[89] Accordingly they can be ultimately reduced to identical principles, and as reason is meant to clarify itself and its functions, so it is meant to clarify common

---

Taste, he spends many pages on a discussion of common sense, and whether it is a constitutive or a regulative principle, according to Kant. But he concludes on a rather sceptical note (see, for instance, p. 324). Though he believes Kant wanted "common sense" to be a constitutive principle, he does not think he has established it as such a one. See also Crawford, *Kant's Aesthetic Theory*. Crawford puts greater emphasis upon the "ideal" character of common sense, but he also calls it "the objective principle of the faculty of judgment" (see pp. 125–33). I believe Kant could not possibly have considered common sense, or the *sensus communis aestheticus* to be "constitutive" or "objective" (and the following sketch should give some indication why). But it is impossible to argue this in detail here.

89. This can be seen from his many reflections on common sense as well as from his interpretation of Mendelssohn in his essay on "orientation in thinking."

sense and its functions.[90] Therefore, to oppose reason and common sense in any simple way—although commentators often do so—is most misleading.

Further, just as Kant differentiates between speculative reason (and understanding), practical reason, and judgment, so he also differentiates between corresponding forms of common sense: common human understanding (or "*sensus communis logicus*"), common or ordinary (human) reason, which might also be called *sensus (communis) moralis*, and common sense (or "*sensus communis aestheticus*").[91] And the relationships between these different forms of thought with their corresponding forms of common sense differ in subtle ways.

Gilles Deleuze, in his *Kant's Critical Philosophy: The Doctrine of the Faculties*, which contains the most interesting and most positive account of Kant's theory of common sense thus far produced, is very much aware of this. Because he believes that "the doctrine of the faculties forms the real network which constitutes the transcendental method," the faculty of common sense in its various forms assumes the greatest importance.[92] For him, each of the three *Critiques* investigates a definite kind of "interest of reason" (i.e. a speculative one, a practical one, and an aesthetic one). These interests of reason are being defined by three different forms of common sense, and common sense is being defined as the accord of the faculties between themselves.[93] Accordingly, Deleuze thinks he can analyse common sense by showing how in "each Critique understanding, reason and imagination enter into various relationships under the chairmanship of one of these faculties."[94]

I do not think that Deleuze's model, though elegant, suggestive, and well worth exploring, is entirely correct. Matters are more complicated than Deleuze seems to realize. According to his analysis of the three forms of common sense as different "artificial faculties," Kant's analysis of the *sensus communis aestheticus* is to be taken as the model for understanding common sense in general. If all forms of common sense

90. This function of the critical enterprise is especially clear in moral philosophy. See *Foundations*, tr. Beck, pp. 90ff.

91. Kant *Critique of Judgment*, tr. Meredith, pp. 150–54. See also Kant, *Prolegomena*, ed. Beck, pp 7f., and his "What is Orientation in Thinking?"

92. Deleuze, *Kant's Critical Philosophy: The Doctrine of the Faculties*, tr. Tomlinson and Habberjam, p. 10.

93. Ibid., p. 21.

94. Ibid., p. 10.

expressed more or less equally valid interests of reason, there would be nothing wrong with this approach. We could start where Kant is clearest on the role of common sense, namely with the third *Critique*. However, Kant does not merely recognize three different, but equally important, interests of reason. He gives priority to one of these, namely the *practical* interest, and this has definite consequences for "common sense" in its two other senses. Deleuze distorts the Kantian doctrine by trying to show that it is really the last *Critique* that is most important because it "uncovers a deeper free and indeterminate accord of the faculties as the condition of the possibility of every determinate relationship."[95] I am not sure, either, whether Kant would agree with the description of all forms of common sense as resulting from an accord of the faculties. In any case, there is not much in Kant's text to support such an interpretation. Furthermore, on Deleuze's analysis it appears that common sense is for Kant the solution to the problem, whereas it is really the problem for him.

According to Kant, common sense is not well suited for the philosophical enterprise. Critical rationality is necessary precisely because it keeps

common sense in check and prevents it from speculating, or, if speculations are under discussion, restrains the desire to decide because it cannot satisfy itself concerning its own premises. . . . Thus common sense and speculative understanding are each serviceable, but each in its own way: the former in judgments which apply immediately to experience; the latter when we judge universally from mere concepts, as in metaphysics, where that which calls itself, in spite of the inappropriateness of the name, sound common sense, has no right to judge at all.[96]

So, unlike most of his contemporaries, Kant does not consider common sense to be more reliable than rational thought. On the contrary, it is less reliable because it is for him as speculative as rational thought, while being at the same time uncritical and dogmatic. In fact, for Kant it is common sense that actually gives rise to the antinomies. Accordingly, it would seem that critical reason has absolute priority over common sense. And that would mean that the traditional view of Kant's estimation of common sense is entirely correct.

95. Ibid., p. 68. However, I would like to point out that Deleuze's account deserves more attention than is possible here.
96. Kant *Prolegomena*, ed. Beck, pp. 7f; see also p. 25.

However, these passages—and others like them—concern only the
the relationship of common sense and theoretical or speculative reason
(or understanding). In practical and aesthetic contexts matters are
quite different. And the relationship between critical thinking and its
corresponding forms of common sense in moral and aesthetic contexts
is not analogous to that of speculative contexts.

To repeat, then: in *theoretical* or *speculative* contexts critical reason
has priority. But, and this is important to note, the same does not hold
with regard to aesthetics and ethics. Here reason has no clear priority
over common sense. Matters are more complicated. And these
complications carry over to theoretical contexts, if only because
practical reason is supposed to have priority over theoretical reason
with regard to the essential ends of humanity.

In aesthetic contexts common sense seems to play the most important role.[97] Kant goes so far as to identify the *sensus communis aestheticus*
with "taste, as a faculty of aesthetic judgement."[98] And if taste and
common sense are the same faculty by different names, it makes no
sense to speak of a priority of judgment or taste over common sense.

How important common sense in this meaning is for Kant can be
seen from his attempt to show that any particular aesthetic judgment
depends upon or presupposes common sense. We must *assume* a
common sense in order to be able to make aesthetic judgments:

The judgement of taste . . . depends on our presupposing the existence of a
common sense . . . Only under the presupposition, I repeat, of such a common
sense are we able to lay down a judgement of taste.[99]

Moreover,

we assume a common sense as the necessary condition of the universal
communicability of our knowledge which is presupposed in every logic and
every principle of knowledge that is not one of scepticism.[100]

Kant does not mean by all this that this common sense which, "as a
matter of fact [is] presupposed by us; as is shown by our presuming to
lay down judgements of taste" does "in fact exist as a constitutive

97. See Kant, *Critique of Judgment*, tr. Meredith, pp. 85, 150f.
98. Ibid., p. 85; see also 83.
99. Ibid., p. 83.
100. Ibid., p. 84.

principle of the possibility of experience."[101] On the contrary, as "nothing is postulated in the judgement of taste but . . . a *universal voice* . . . The judgement of taste itself does not *postulate* the agreement of everyone . . . it only *imputes* this agreement to everyone . . . The universal voice is, therefore, only an idea."[102]

The idea of an "universal voice" that Kant speaks of in this passage seems to be identical with what he calls later "the idea of common sense." And what he uses in the deduction of the judgment of taste is therefore *not* the principle of a common sense itself, but only the principle of an *idea* of common sense. And that strongly suggests that common sense or taste is "formed for us as a regulative principle by a still higher principle of reason, that for higher ends first seeks to beget in us a common sense," or that it is "only the idea of one [an artificial faculty] so that a judgement of taste, with its demand for universal assent, is but a requirement for generating such a con*sensus.*"[103] When we call taste common *sense* we must accordingly be "prepared to use the word 'sense' of an effect that mere reflection has upon the mind."[104] Thus, although Kant identifies the faculty of taste with common sense, this does not mean that common sense has an independent role to play. The priority of reason is still intact. For common sense, or taste, is an effect, an artificial faculty. And what creates it is a "principle of reason."

The "still higher principle of reason, that for higher ends first seeks to beget in us a common sense," is probably practical for Kant. At least, this is suggested by his conclusion of the discussion of judgments of taste, or the claim that taste or common sense is,

in the ultimate analysis, a critical faculty that judges of the rendering of moral ideas in terms of sense (through the interrelation of a certain analogy in both), and it is this rendering also, and the increased sensibility which these ideas evoke (termed moral sense), that are the origin of that pleasure which taste declares valid for mankind in general, and not merely for the private feeling of each individual. This makes clear that the true propaedeutic for laying the

---

101. Ibid., p. 85. Kant is asking this as a question. And he follows it up with: "These are questions which we are as yet neither willing nor in a position to investigate." But he later seems to answer it in the way I suggest.

102. Ibid., p. 56. The universal voice is said to be "resting upon grounds the investigation of which is here postponed."

103. Ibid., p. 85. This is also asked as a question here.

104. Ibid., p. 153.

foundations of taste is the development of moral ideas and the culture of moral feeling. For only when sensibility is brought into harmony with moral feeling can genuine taste assume a definite unchangeable form.[105]

This suggests at the very least that common sense as taste is intimately connected with practical reason and can ultimately be understood only in relation to it.[106]

But in practical contexts the relationship between reason and common sense (as common [human] reason) is also quite different from their relationship in theoretical or speculative contexts. Thus the categorical imperative is attained "*within* the moral knowledge of common human reason." It is established by the critique of practical reason "*without in the least teaching common human reason* anything *new*." Therefore, "the *justification* of moral principles as principles of a pure reason could be made with sufficient certainty through merely appealing to common sense."[107] Given that the relationship between reason and common sense in practical contexts presents itself for Kant in this way, we can hardly speak of the priority of reason over common sense here. Kant says that

here we cannot but admire the great advantage which the practical faculty has over the theoretical in ordinary human understanding [or, as I would translate: common sense]. In the theoretical, if ordinary reason ventures to go beyond the laws of experience and perceptions of the senses, it falls into sheer inconceivabilities and self-contradictions, or at least into a chaos of uncertainty, obscurity and instability. In the practical, on the other hand, the power of judgment first shows itself to advantage when common understanding excludes all sensuous incentives from practical laws . . . But the most remarkable thing about ordinary reason in its practical employment is that it may have as much hope as the philosopher of hitting the mark. In fact, it is *almost more certain* to do so than the philosopher.[108]

In practical contexts Kant stops just short of giving priority to common

---

105. Ibid., p. 227.

106. This short sketch of the role of common sense in aesthetics and ethics is by no means intended to be exhaustive. A full discussion—which seems to me very much needed—is impossible here.

107. Kant, *Foundations*, tr. Beck, p. 20 (emphasis mine); Kant, *Critique of Practical Reason*, tr. Beck, p. 95 (emphasis mine).

108. Kant, *Foundations*, tr. Beck, pp. 20f (emphasis mine).

sense. But, though he does not do the latter, it is clear that here reason does not have priority either.

Thus what is true in theoretical contexts is *not* true in practical ones: reason does not have priority over common sense. Both stand on a more or less equal footing. Though critical reason may be helpful, it cannot overrule common human reason. If we add to this what Kant says about the priority of practical over theoretical reason in the second *Critique*, it is clear that for Kant common sense must be much more important than has been generally assumed.[109] Even theoretical reason cannot have absolute priority over common sense. It must be careful not to rule out too much of what it cannot comprehend *qua* theoretical reason.

But none of this has to mean that Kant was ambivalent about the role of common sense. Unlike most of his contemporaries, who were somewhat confused about the actual role of common sense in philosophy—thinking that philosophy was somehow the clarification or justification of common sense, while at the very same time applying common sense in their attempted philosophical justifications—he never mixes up these two roles.

Kant makes a clear distinction. He rejects common sense as a criterion or tool of philosophical inquiry—be it in theoretical, practical, or aesthetic contexts. And all his polemic against common sense concerns *such use* of it. But he just as clearly *accepts* common sense as the field of philosophical inquiry. Because metaphysics and common sense are for him inextricably intertwined, the latter is relevant for him even in speculative philosophy, though it is perhaps more apparent in practical and aesthetic contexts.

Like most of his contemporaries, Kant also believes that common sense and reason are ultimately reducible to the same principles. His view is very close to that of Mendelssohn on this. But very unlike most of his contemporaries, Kant takes the apparent conflict between common sense and speculative or, for him, "scientific reason" much more seriously. For, he thinks, given the identity of the principles of reason and common sense, this conflict should not occur. But since, in fact, it exists, it must allow of explanation. To most of the Germans there appeared to be two alternatives: either common sense and reason do not have identical principles after all, or one (or both) can go wrong

109. Kant, *Critique of Practical Reason*, tr. Beck, p. 124–26: "On the Primacy of the Pure Practical Reason in its Association with Speculative Reason."

at times. The majority of Kant's contemporaries opted for the second alternative. But no matter which alternative they accepted, philosophy became a questionable enterprise. It became necessary to orient oneself in thinking, and indifferentism seemed to be inevitable.

Kant himself came to realize slowly and painfully that there was a third possibility: if common sense is reducible to the principles of all thought, and if both reason and thought rely on identical principles, then the conflict between the two could very well point to a basic problem with regard to pure rational thought.[110] Because common sense and reason contradict each other, the critical investigation of both is necessary; and this is why "the tribunal of the *critique of pure reason*" is instituted by Kant. It will, he is quite certain, "assure reason to its lawful claims, and dismiss all groundless pretensions, not by despotic decrees, but in accordance with its own eternal and unalterable laws."[111]

To the very same end the Scots had instituted the tribunal of common sense. In accordance with its "eternal and unalterable laws" all "groundless pretensions of rational thought" were to be rejected. For Kant, however, common sense acts by means of "despotic decrees;" and the validity of these decrees, however much Kant substantially agreed with them, is in need of justification. This justification, for him, can only consist in showing how they issue forth from the very nature of rational thought itself. The inquiry into the human mind on the principles of common sense needs to be pushed farther; there has to be also an inquiry into common sense on the principles of pure reason.

In any case, the level of common sense appeared to Kant to be a singularly bad point at which to cease philosophical inquiries, philosophy being first and foremost a critical enterprise, and common sense seeming to him essentially uncritical and dogmatic. Reason or rational thought, on the other hand, could be expected to be critical even of itself and its own claims. It therefore seemed to him much better suited "to undertake anew the most difficult of all its tasks, namely that of self-knowledge."[112]

It is thus quite understandable that Kant criticized the Scots for not

110. How long it took Kant to see that this is a conflict within reason itself is shown very well by Hinske's "Kant's Begriff der Antinomie." See also my "Dating Kant's 'Vorlesungen über Philosophische Enzyklopadie.'"
111. Kant, Axif.
112. Kant, Axi.

having pursued their inquiries as far as they could have. Following Hume, he may say that "to satisfy the conditions of the problem, the opponents of the great thinker should have penetrated very deeply into the nature of reason, so far as it is concerned with pure thinking."[113] So much is true: the Scots did not "satisfy the conditions of the [Humean] problem." But, and this is important to remember, they failed in this way not simply because it "did not suit them," as Kant alleges, but because they were convinced that it was *impossible in principle* to do so. They thought that human beings can never attain the kind of knowledge that an answer to "Hume's problem" requires, and hence that it must be solved by showing that, in accordance with the make-up of the human understanding, we cannot but accept such principles as that of causality.

According to the traditional view, Kant just as staunchly believed that Hume's problem *must* and (therefore?) *can* be solved: We must justify the principles which enable us to make knowledge claims. And everything that is considered most distinctive and most interesting in Kant is thought to be connected with this justification of knowledge claims in general.

But he does not ever appear to argue for the possibility and necessity of such justification. Much like the Scots—and especially like Beattie —he attempts to answer the questions "How is Pure Mathematics Possible?" and "How is Pure Science of Nature Possible?" He also conceives in analogy the questions "How is Metaphysics in General Possible?" and "How is Metaphysics Possible as a Science?"[114] But to answer the Scottish doubts concerning the possibility of an ultimate justification of the *a priori* principles of knowledge, he would also have to respond to the question "How is Critical Philosophy Possible?" For just this question the Scots had asked most seriously.

Does Kant give an answer to this further question? Current Kant scholarship, being very much aware of the problem, generally answers in the negative. In fact, some of the characterizations of Kant's final

113. Kant, *Prolegomena*, ed. Beck, p. 7. Compare this with Tetens's criticism of the Scots as quoted on p. 120 above.

114. This is how Kant formulates the problem in the *Prolegomena*. Professor Beck has, on several occasions, called attention to the fact that Kant's account, as given in that work, is in principle identical with the Scottish account. But there is even a similarity between the outline of the *Prolegomena* and Beattie's approach in the *Essay*. Like Kant, Beattie begins with the principles of mathematics and argues that philosophy must accept similar principles if it is to be convincing.

foundation for his critical philosophy sound peculiarly familiar to anyone acquainted with Reid and his followers. Thus Walsh thinks

what Kant does in the *Critique* is build on facts we all take as obvious in our non-philosophical moments, such facts as that we can make mathematical judgments, discriminate objective from subjective successions, make determinate statements about what is happening in ourselves, generally distinguish the real from the apparent. As thus stated, these are facts of a highly general kind; behind each of them lies a vast number of more particular facts. It is these which form the ultimate basis of Kant's philosophy.[115]

The Scots built on exactly the same kind of facts and argued *therefore* that philosophical justification was impossible. For them description had to replace deduction. If Kant was up to what the traditional interpretation has him doing, he would not only have begged Hume's but also Reid's question. Kant would take for granted that which Reid doubted; and he would demonstrate with *Gründlichkeit* that which Reid never thought of doubting.

To be sure, that is exactly what Hamann, Herder, and Jacobi thought—and these are the topics of their *Metakritiken*[116] But the question is whether this interpretation of Kant's enterprise is correct. Did Kant really want to answer Hume in such a radical way, did he want to supply the foundation for all of knowledge, or was he engaged in something more modest?[117]

Kant may perhaps even be criticized for not having paid enough attention to the "facts we all take as obvious in our non-philosophical moments." Reid had criticized philosophers for having seriously distorted the true character of sensations by describing them as some sort of mediating mental entities. The theory of ideas, he argued, necessarily leads to idealism and scepticism. If Kant is understood as a phenomenalist, he obviously must be interpreted as having accepted as one of the basic premises some version of the theory of ideas, or, more exactly, a theory of representation similar to that of Tetens.

There are passages that suggest he accepts mediating mental entities as one of his obvious facts, as for instance the following passage from the *Prolegomena*:

115. Walsh, *Criticism*, pp. 253f. See also Rescher, "The 'Special Constitution' of Man's Mind."

116. See the next chapter below. See also Sidgwick, "The Philosophy of Common Sense," p. 147.

117. See my "Kant's Transcendental Deduction."

long before Locke's time, but assuredly since him, it has been generally assumed and granted without detriment to the actual existence of external things that many of their predicates may be said to belong, not to the things in themselves, but to their appearances, and to have no proper existence outside of our representations. heat, colour and taste, for instance, are of this kind. Now if we go farther, and, for weighty reasons, rank as mere appearances the remaining qualities of the bodies also, which are called primary . . . no one in the least can adduce the reason of its being inadmissible.[118]

This shows that he does not think that Locke's theory, under a certain interpretation, has any detrimental consequences for philosophy. But it is no argument for Locke, nor, though probably directed against Reid, an argument against the latter. Does Kant beg this question of Reid as well?[119]

Again, this is what Hamann, Herder, Jacobi, and Aenesidemus Schulze thought. As we shall see, for them any rationalistic account of knowledge will fall into this trap. But, again, the question is whether things are as simple as all that. Kant's contemporaries generally rejected Reid's critique of the ideal theory, but they muddled the issue to such an extent that they persuaded themselves they were realists in very much the same sense as was Reid. Kant saw more clearly on this issue as well. In fact, this aspect of his thought may also be character-ized as a radicalization of tendencies already present in the thought of his contemporaries. He may be seen to have argued: if we accept the

118. Kant, *Prolegomena*, ed. Beck, pp. 36f. (He is speaking of Berkeley in this context. Could it be that he is relying on Reid here? Even if he did see the French translation, he must also have read the German one which appeared in 1782.) See also Kant, *Correspondence*, ed. Zweig, pp. 70–76, p. 71: "I asked myself: What is the ground of the relation of that in us which we call 'representation' to the object?" Kant thinks that this "constitutes the key to the whole secret of hitherto still obscure metaphysics." Reid, of course, would have agreed, but dismissed it as a pseudo-question. See also George, "Kant's Theory of Perception," and "Kant's Sensationism." I agree with most of what is said there, though my definition of sensationism is different. For George "the central thesis of sensationism" is that "there are non-intentional mental states in which no object, other than the state itself, is present, and that these are the foundation of all empirical knowledge." I would qualify the last phrase and say that for the sensationists these states are the only foundation of empirical knowledge. For this reason I would not classify Reid and Kant among the sensationists. But this is perhaps only a difference in labelling.

119. I do not want to claim that Reid's critique of Berkeley is essentially correct. But I do not understand why Kant, as well as most other German philosophers of the period, thought it unnecessary to respond to Reid's critique of the theory of ideas.

theory of representation, "transcendental idealism" is inevitable, and only "empirical realism" is possible.

It has frequently been argued in the past that the differences between Berkeley's immaterialism and Kant's critical philosophy are not as great as Kant wants to make us believe. Thus Feder felt that Kant's thought was basically similar to that of Berkeley. And more recently it has been argued that Kant more or less consciously appropriated the "insights" of the "eccentric Irishman" and that "Berkeley's point of view [is] secretly preserved by Kant."[120] What matters here is that Kant knew Reid's critique of Berkeley, and that it is therefore likely that his critical philosophy learned from Reid in this regard as well. Perhaps it can be shown that Kant's debt to Berkeley is a "debt *via* Reid."

That Kant has learned some things from the Scots should by now be clear. Windelband's observation "Kant begins at the very point at which the Scots had stopped" is well supported by historical and textual evidence. Accordingly, Scottish common sense is of central importance for an understanding of Kant's point of departure. And this has the most profound consequences for the interpretation of such notions as "justification," "naturalism," "idealism," "thing in itself," "rational faith," etc. The problems of justification and idealism, especially, show how relevant the systematic and historical connections of Scottish common sense and critical philosophy are for the understanding of Kant's problems. They are all, as Hamann might have said, "materials for a *Metakritik* of the critique of pure reason."[121] Therefore, should not Kant scholarship spend at least as much time and effort investigating Kant's "Scottish connection" as it is spending on the investigation of his "German background?"

120. Turbayne, "Kant's Refutation of Dogmatic Idealism," p. 224.

121. For further literature on this topic see Beck, "Toward a Meta-Critique of Pure Reason."

X

Scottish Common Sense and the Reception of Kant's Critical Philosophy

I

THE JUDGMENT that did the greatest harm to the reputation of Scottish common sense in Germany, as well as in most other countries, was clearly Kant's scathing attack upon Reid, Oswald and Beattie in the *Prolegomena* in 1783. Yet, among other things, this attack may also serve as evidence for the predominance of the Scottish approach in the German thought of the period. The *Prolegomena*, apart from being an introduction to the *Critique*, is also a sustained argument against the common-sense approach to philosophy. And Kant's attack on the Scots is more than just a passing remark upon some minor critics of Hume. The vehemence of the criticism alone suggests that he viewed common sense as a powerful philosophical force that had to be reckoned with, if his own philosophy was to succeed in Germany.

As previous chapters have shown, this adversary stance seems to be due more to accidental historical circumstances than to deep systematic incompatibilities between Kant's critical philosophy and Scottish common sense and its German adaptations.[1] Kant expected not only that he would be understood by the foremost philosophers of the time, but also that they would endorse his philosophy and help him spread it.[2]

---

1. See especially Chapters II and IX above.
2. He felt that they could accomplish what he himself could not, namely, give a popular expression to his thought. Given his belief that they were all up to very much the same thing, these expectations were not as preposterous as they may appear today. Some of Kant's contemporaries were still capable of recognizing themselves in Kant's critical philosophy. As will become apparent in this chapter, Feder, Platner, and Eberhard thought that Kant's critical enterprise was only an extension of the philosophy they themselves adhered to.

Further, it has been shown that Kant must not be understood as having ever rejected all the philosophical convictions of Reid and his followers. He is much more concerned with their method, which he clearly identifies with naturalism. He is very much aware that his positive doctrines are not all that different from those of the Scots and their German followers. He objects, rather, that they have been too "cheaply acquired."[3] His own work, like that of Tetens, must be understood as attempting to give a more secure foundation to the common-sense doctrine by penetrating "very deeply into the nature of reason, so far as it is concerned with pure thinking—a task which did not suit them [Reid, Oswald, and Beattie]."[4]

It is apparent that Kant's philosophy was successful against the Scottish approach and the German philosophers who followed it. Indeed, perhaps too successful; for Kant ended up discrediting not only their method but also some of the positive doctrines for which he stood. But the victory was neither immediate nor was it ever a complete one. Scottish common sense continued to play a significant role in German thought until the end of the eighteenth century.[5]

Though the fate of Scottish common sense was to be mainly the opposition to Kant's philosophy, there were also a number of philosophers who stressed the continuity of Kant's thought with that of the Scots—as, indeed, they stressed the continuity between Kant and themselves. Reid's *Inquiry* appeared in German in 1782. This was only *one* year after Kant's first *Critique*. Nevertheless, the translator is already aware of it. He notes that the *Inquiry* is an attempt to answer Hume's *Treatise*, a work "unknown" in Germany and "having for well known reasons become rare even in England." But, he says, since it also applies to Hume's *Enquiries*, which are known in Germany, Reid is still useful. For,

though there have been notes and additions by a famous German philosopher added to the German translation of the *Enquiries*, *Reid* still appears to have come closer to the source of the evil—if indeed there is evil in this matter—than any other enemy of Mr. Hume. I except the particular passages in which Mr. Kant (in the *Critique of Pure Reason*) contests with him.[6]

3. Kant, *Prolegomena*, ed. Beck, p. 61.
4. Ibid, p. 7.
5. It also continued to play a role in the empiricist undercurrent of German philosophy that leads right up to the present.
6. Thomas Reid, *Untersuchung über den menschlichen Geist, nach den Grundsätzen des gemeinen Menschenverstandes* (Leipzig, 1782), pp. iiif. The first review of the *Critique*

In fact,

Reid appears to know the location of the disease fairly exactly; perhaps he suffered himself a little from it. All the others chatter, sometimes stylishly, about the harm it causes and of its symptoms. Perhaps they can at times be of service to people who imagine themselves sick. But they do not make the body more healthy. They do not administer preventive medicine, and they do not bring order into the parts from which the sickness can originate. They are more useful to those who fear the disease, or those who dislike it, than to those who suffer from it. They are doctors without the knowledge of anatomy.[7]

Whether Beattie also belongs to this latter group the translator does not want to decide.

At least the work has been fairly well received among us; as far as I know, it has already been printed twice. But—*et habent sua fata libelli.*—And it does have such a truly alluring title! And the tone of Mr. Beattie is so preachingly philosophical! That is to say, not philosophically preaching, but just so that the book can be read even between sleeping and awakening. Moreover, the author carefully sprinkled his road with dainty flowers taken from old and new poets. What better thing could he have done to receive the general applause?—This much is certain to me, however, he would have left his essay unwritten if Reid had not written before him.[8]

Thus, whatever the judgment on Beattie's *Essay*, Reid's *Inquiry* deserves a thorough study on its own. Moreover, even if the Germans had known nothing of *Hume*, the *Inquiry* would still have value: "It is a healthy, beautiful and strong tree, a credit to the forest. The birds of the sky can find nourishment and shelter under it, and it fulfills all of its purposes, not just being planted in order to give a little shade in the heat of the sun."[9]

However, the translator seems to feel he must show that he does not agree with everything put forward by Reid in the *Inquiry*, and thus prove his impartiality. He approves of Reid's attempt to show that the representations of the soul are completely different from the qualities

---

appeared in the *Göttingische Anzeigen* in 1782 (number 3, 19 January, pp. 40–48). It is not much earlier than this Foreword, which, it appears to me, can serve to show that the clash between common-sense philosophers and Kant was not inevitable.

    7. Reid, *Untersuchung*, pp. iiif.
    8. Ibid., pp. ivf.
    9. Ibid., p. vi.

of the external objects, but he finds the rejection of the theory of ideas as a misuse of language very superficial. "For, in fact, we use language and figures of speech in accordance with appearances and not in accordance with nature and truth." Moreover, much could be said not only against the way in which Reid uses common sense against speculative philosophy, but also against his way of arguing against Berkeley and Hume in general: "But a Preface cannot be allowed to become a book."[10]

Among the particular passages of Reid's work, "which deserve perhaps a little rejoinder," the translator significantly chooses Reid's *geometria visibilium*, "which Mr. Reid opposes to the common geometry, and whose basic principles he presents in a manner that suggests he believes himself to have found a completely new idea. But considered carefully this geometry is nothing but perspective."[11]

D. Jenisch, the translator of George Campbell's *The Philosophy of Rhetoric* (1776), which appeared as *Die Philosophie der Rhetorik* in 1791, also referred positively to Kant and his *Critique* (to the great dissatisfaction of the reviewer of the translation in the *Allgemeine deutsche Bibliothek*). Jenisch tried to show in his notes that the faculty of pure reason is "in a way nothing other than common sense with its first and highest principles" and that the results of Kant's philosophy, namely his doctrines of morals and religion, "are not different from the irrefutable consequences of the principles of common sense, with which they also stand or fall."[12]

10. Ibid., pp. vif.
11. Ibid., p. viii.
12. George Campbell, *Die Philosophie der Rhetorik*, tr. Dr. D. Jenisch (Berlin, 1791), p. 167; see also p. 3: "Hurd, Beattie, Reid, Oswald and others have been translated and read with approval by some." For the relation of Kant and Campbell see pp. 166–69n., especially, p. 166: "I have here translated at least part of the long note of the English original in order to give my readers an idea of the dispute about common sense which is indeed important for philosophy and has been led by such important men as Priestley, Beattie, and Reid with great acuteness. If I may say so, our author is really on the right track, even though he could not be said to have exhausted the matter in all its depths. Because speculative philosophy has taken a turn through the newest philosophical revolution in philosophical literature among the Germans these matters can best be discussed here among us. For Kant's *Critique of Pure Reason*, which has turned the wheel of our speculative philosophy so entirely from the opposite side, is indeed nothing else than the explanation of our power of thought ..." The reviewer of the *Allgemeine deutsche Bibliothek* cxi (1792): 98–101 (signum: "Pk") finds that "Mr. Jenisch takes every occasion, whether appropriate or not, to sound the praise of Mr. Kant in the highest tones [*mit vollen Backen*]. If the reviewer knows this truly great man, he will not be pleased by praise

Another philosopher who stressed the continuity of Kant and common-sense philosophy, and who tried to mediate between the two, was Platner. He did not object to Kant as a "dangerous sceptic and idealist," but declared:

Honestly, I find it difficult to persuade myself that I am Kant's enemy, or that he disputes even one well-understood principle of the philosophy I adhere to. There is, I believe, only one philosophy and that is the true one. It begins its investigations from the principle that the certainty of human cognition can be shown only in relation to the faculty of cognition, and it withdraws at the end of its speculative course to the thought: experience, common sense (*) and morality—these are the best things in all the wisdom of this world. This true philosophy Kant wants, and this true philosophy I want. For those two main propositions are, if we are not entirely mistaken, the real aim of the critique of reason.
(*) However many bad things Kant appears to be saying of this common sense under the name of healthy understanding (he only rejects it as the judge in metaphysics), what he says in his theory of judgment on the one hand, and especially about doctrinal belief on the other hand, is a very distinct reference to the great rights of common sense in our secular way of thinking.[13]

Platner sees Kant's enterprise as a mere continuation of what has been "especially in more recent times a major objective in philosophy," namely "'the critique of the faculty of cognition.'" He fails to understand what he regards as Kant's exaggerated claims to originality with regard to this critical aproach. For Platner "the works of philosophers like Locke, Leibniz, Wolf, Hume, *Reid*, Tetens are full of investigations which aim at this."[14]

But Platner also uses this agreement of Scottish common sense and Kant's critical philosophy in order to criticize Kant, as for instance in the case of the doctine of freedom, where he finds that

it is not at all surprising that *Beattie* (*on Truth* II.3 in the *Essays*, pp.119ff.) and *Reid* (*Ess. on the intell. powers of man*, pp. 1589ff.[*sic*]) appeal to the feeling of

---

uttered in such a tone." I suspect that this translator of Campbell is identical with the Jenisch who was close to Hamann in Königsberg, and who went, according to Hamann, to Berlin as a "philologico-theologischer Glücksritter wozu er gute Aussichten hat" (Hamann, *Briefwechsel*, vol. 6, pp. 349; see also 373). This would further support my claim about the prevalence of the Scottish influence in the climate of opinion in Königsberg.
13. Platner, *Aphorismen*, 3rd ed., 1793, pp. vf.
14. Ibid., p. 334f. (emphasis mine).

freedom as a claim of common sense, when they attack determinism instead of refuting Hume. But it is strange indeed that the critical philosophy, which rejects the decisions of common sense in metaphysical disputes everywhere else, counts on this feeling in this case.[15]

A similar objection to Kant's theoretical philosophy is put forward by Eberhard, who wonders:

The critical philosophy assumes forms of thought, laws of the understanding, functions of the understanding. How does it prove the universality and necessity of these laws of the understanding and of reason, since it denies absolutely objective truth of cognition? From the fact that I have to think in accordance with them, it does not follow that everybody has to think in accordance with them. *With what right can critical philosophy reject the refutations of Humean scepticism according to Reid, Beattie and Oswald's method?* It is true, the principles of common sense are assumed by these Scottish philosophers as certain without proof and only on subjective grounds, but do the forms of thought and of pure intuition have another certainty, and can they be regarded as universally certain with more right?[16]

Moreover, it was also common to indentify Kant's philosophy more or less with the "idealism" and "scepticism" of Hume and Berkeley, and to oppose it with essentially the same reasons that had already been used by Reid, Oswald, and Beattie. Thus Meiners, who, as we have seen earlier, objected to "the fierce polemical tone" of Beattie's *Essay* in 1779, has much more understanding for the latter's approach now. In the Preface to his *Grundriss der Seelenlehre* of 1786, with express reference to Beattie, he says

Anyone who has had occasion to notice the impression which the Kantian

15. Ibid., p. 507.
16. Johann August Eberhard (ed.), *Philosophisches Magazin*, 4 vols. Halle, 1788–92, vol. 4 (1792): 101 (emphasis mine). Eberhard's overall strategy is, however, to claim that Kant has nothing new to offer to the philosophical world, and that his "critique of pure reason" is already contained in the Leibniz-Wolffian doctrine. This angered Kant very much. See Allison, *The Kant-Eberhard Controversy*. By the Leibniz-Wolffian doctrine he meant, of course, as much (and perhaps more) his own earlier thought than anything said by Leibniz. In 1787 Feder clearly believed he had all along been doing what Kant proposed (see Chapter II, note 37 above); and that Tetens did not think too highly of Kant's originality may be inferred from a remark by Feder as well (*Leben*, p. 108). Tetens's silence on Kant may perhaps be explained by his not wanting to get involved in a dispute. Feder also wanted nothing less than a fight with Kant. Eberhard, however, had no such scruples.

writings have made upon young people will really feel the truth of the remarks which Beattie made on the occasion of similar experiences: Nothing is more injurious to taste and good judgment that the subtleties of the older and newer metaphysicians, which favour verbal disputes and lead to nothing but doubt and obscurity. These musings exhaust the power of the spirit without reason, deaden the love of true learning, draw the attention away from the concerns of human life as well as from the works of art and nature which warm the heart and heighten the imagination. Finally, they unsettle the powers of the understanding, spoil good principles, and poison the source of human happiness.[17]

Feder is somewhat more subtle. In his *Über den Raum und die Caussalität*, which appeared one year after Meiners's *Grundriss*, he does not stoop to such mere *Konsequenzmacherei* as his younger colleague (and many other contemporaries) engaged in. But he does accuse Kant of confusion of language in very much the same way as Reid had accused Berkeley and Hume of such confusions. His discussion "Anti-Idealism in Accordance with the Simple and Solid Principles of Common Sense" is, in fact, an attempt to show that Kant neglects the fundamental distinction between a representation and its object. In this sense the discussion is essentially a repetition or restatement of Reid's arguments against Berkeley and Hume.[18]

Feder grants that "idealism certainly is not a doctrine that would cause murder and manslaughter"; it is merely a corruption of language. But as such a corruption it is the symptom of more fundamental mistakes in a philosophical system. Contradicting some of his earlier pronouncements, Feder argues that the claim that objects are nothing but representations within the human mind is "so contradictory to the nature of our understanding that the principles and basic concepts that lead to this doctrine must be rejected for this [very] reason."[19] This, of course, is essentially Reid's argument that the system of ideas is a hypothesis that is contradicted by actual facts of human nature, and that this is enough reason for rejecting it.

The remainder of Feder's critique of Kant also relies on Reid. Thus he argues that the common distinction between a representation and its object is fundamental for all our thinking, and that it should not be obliterated by philosophers, or declared to be mistaken. Moreover, the

17. Meiners, *Grundriss der Seelenlehre*. Preface.
18. Feder, *Raum und Caussalität*, pp. 65ff.
19. Ibid., p. 67.

fact that in sensation the object asserts itself as real marks the distinction between sensation on the one hand and imagination and memory on the other. This as well is a distinction well observed in ordinary language and accepted as obvious by everyone.[20]

While he identified in the earlier account "being" with "constant appearance," in *Über den Raum und die Caussalität*, he offers a very different view:

the term *reality, being*, means exactly, or at least first and foremost, what is the case in a sensation and not in a mere representation. Or someone should try to explain and develop the concept of reality without a relation to sensation. Neither does the soul have any other proof of its existence than this feeling. Through the difference of this feeling it knows itself as something real and different from its *representations* of other mental powers and states.[21]

A second distinction between representations and their objects that is denied by the idealist, but observed by common sense, is that objects are considered as *external* to the mind. So representations and objects are not considered as merely different mental contents. They also have a different status. Feder, like Reid, argues that there is really no reason to deny what our sensations and common sense testify to so vividly.

But the dispute with the idealist has brought to light also other characteristics of objects. While common sense and ordinary language are merely concerned with the reality and externality of objects, philosophers have also argued for the independence of these objects from us. However, this independence does not imply that the objects exist in the same way as we perceive them. We only know that they exist apart from us. We cannot, in principle, decide what these objects may be apart from their relations to the instruments of perception. Yet, that they must be thought to exist independently of us is also clear for Feder, if only because our sensations are different from imaginations. It is belief in the independent reality of objects that constitutes the difference between an idealist and a non-idealist philosopher.

All the major characteristics of Reid's critique of the idealistic position can be found in Feder's critique of Kant as well. Not only the distinction between perception and object of perception, its establishment through comparison with other acts of the mind, such as

---

20. This argument is clearly identical with the one that Reid advanced in his *Inquiry*, chapter II, section 3. (ed. Duggan, pp. 24–26), Reid, *Works*, vol. 1, pp. 105f.
21. Feder, *Raum und Caussalität*, pp. 69f.

imagination and memory, but also the emphasis upon our feeling for reality and his discussion of the difference between primary and secondary qualities are identical to Reid's account; even many of the details of his arguments can be traced to Reid. Thus Feder employs arguments from the perceptual experience of blind persons (and criticizes Kant severely for not having made a note of this issue in his discussion of space). Indeed, it is difficult to see any difference between Feder and Reid in their criticism of the idealistic position, if we consider *Über den Raum und die Caussalität* alone. Where there are any, however, we may be sure that they are the result of Feder's rejection of the claim that idealism has its origin in the theory of ideas. Even in his later work Feder is unwilling to follow the Scot in his rejection of "mediating mental entities," for one of his basic philosophical convictions is his sensationism.

Feder's desire to reduce everything as far as possible to sensation brought him ultimately into trouble. For it appears at times as if he wanted to reduce his two "basic principles of the human understanding," the law of contradiction and the principle of sufficient reason, to sensation, thus making them into empirical propositions. At least, this is how the Kantians interpreted him. And Johann Schulze, Kant's friend and follower in Königsberg, criticized Feder severely for this supposed circular argument in his *Prüfung der Critik der reinen Vernunft.*[22]

It is true, Feder does speak of a "deduction of our necessary concepts and judgments from feelings and perceptions," and he discusses the law of contradiction in this context. He traces it to experience and tries to explain how it could have arisen in experience.[23] But the question is whether this means that, for him, this law has its only source and

22. Johann Schulze, *Prüfung der Kantischen Critik der reinen Vernunft*, 2 vols. (Königsberg, 1789–92). Feder is accused of offering an argument involving a vicious circle. Feder attempts to answer this criticism in the *Göttingische Anzeigen*, 1789, number 21 and in his review of Schulze's work in the *Philosophische Bibliothek*, IV (1791): 201f. Zart also accepts the Kantian view and finds that Feder "does not want to base his system upon immediately evident truths in the sense of the Scottish school, since their characteristics are too uncertain" (*Einfluss*, p. 131). He sees him as following Locke and Hume "in tracing the law of contradiction to external sensation exactly as Locke does it," as explaining "the idea of causality in a Humean fashion. i.e. strictly empirically." But matters are not quite so simple. Feder is closer to Locke and Hume than Reid is. But he is also deeply influenced by Reid, and his theory is an attempt at a synthesis of Locke and Reid.

23. Feder, *Raum und Caussalität*, pp. 37ff.

foundation in experience. If it did, this would be a radical departure from his previous views as well as from Reid. Yet Feder never actually says that his two basic principles can be reduced to experience. Nor does his account actually need to be read as implying it.

Feder is opposed to innate ideas, and he treats Kant's theory of space as a version of the theory of innate ideas.[24] Because he thinks that the dispute about innate ideas is greatly hampered by misunderstandings, he first attempts to clarify his conception of them. If philosophers mean by "innate ideas" concepts contained in the mind prior to all experience, as he thinks Plato did, they are obviously wrong and have been disproved by Locke. But most philosophers do not hold such a view. They understand by "innate ideas" certain "*determinations*, faculties, powers or tendencies of the understanding which make it possible that at the occasion of certain modifications of the senses (impressions), certain perceptions, and at the occasion of certain sensual representations, certain concepts, arise."[25] If philosophers attempt to prove "innate ideas" in the latter sense, they are arguing for the obvious:

I admit gladly and believe it to be evident that there must be a predisposition or certain character of the human soul, without which it could never obtain a representation of space. Without the precondition of a *human* soul hardly anyone will believe *human* cognition possible

However, this holds not only for our representation of space, but also for all our other representations, such as impenetrability, motion, light and air, of colours and sounds and all of our sensations.[26]

In the same way it is, of course, also true of the law of contradiction and the principle of sufficient reason.

Thus Feder agrees with Kant that the human mind has an essential part in the formation of knowledge, and that it does impose some of its form upon the objects. He disagrees with Kant about the sources of the imposed form and necessity. Whereas he understands critical philosophy as declaring reason and its *a priori* concepts to be the only source of necessity and form, he sees this source in the senses. In order to counter Kant's claim that space must be an *a priori* form of representation, since, if it was not, geometry would depend upon perception

24. This is, of course, a mistake on Feder's part.
25. Ibid., p. 13.
26. Ibid., pp. 19f.

(*Wahrnehmung*) and thus be merely accidental, that is, not apodictically certain, Feder wants to show that necessity and apodictic certainty not only can, but must arise from sensation.

He asks: "Can I *know anything* without perceiving it? Therefore can there be *any* necessary knowledge and any general truth whatsoever for us, if all perceptions contain only accidental truth?"[27] This question brings him straight to the principle of induction and the problems Hume had with it: how can one isolated experience, or how can even repeated experiences of the same kind teach us anything about all of experience? How do necessary connections arise? Feder observes that

we *feel necessity* whenever we feel we cannot do something. This is often enough the case. For necessary is that of which the contradictory cannot exist. What we cannot change, we must leave as it is, and what we cannot leave as it is, we must change . . . In the particular case this is . . . only [the] necessity of the present state. It is *recognized as conditioned* as soon as we can change this state so that the necessity disappears. but if we can never and in no way change this state, if we cannot remove this necessity and cannot show how it could be removed, what should we the call this necessity? . . . an *absolute necessity*, at least for us . . . And if we were to find out that all people we know are under the same necessity, if we had not the least reason to suspect that it might perhaps be different in another human being or in any other being which feels, wills and thinks, would we still have to have any scruple to call this necessity . . . absolute and general?[28]

Necessity arises in sensation. But he does not want to claim on the basis of this argument that necessity is the *product* of particular sensations or experience. It is only the occasion, or the beginning of it. As Reid would have put it, this necessity is suggested in sensation.

In a reply to his critics Feder tries to make this clearer. Admitting that his account was not entirely clear and could have given rise to this interpetation, he also claims that he has not said anything wrong. With certain clarifications the original account still holds:

If I had answered the question in such a way that I had only described how several perceptions could reveal or teach the understanding a *reason* which necessarily determined it to create or accept a general judgment; if I had shown how this reason, in the case of the law of contradiction, is contained absolutely *a priori* in the nature of our understanding, even though the general concepts of

27. Ibid., p. 31.
28. Ibid., pp. 35ff. This is somewhat similar to Tetens's account of necessity.

being and non-being, of contradiction . . . are created little by little through several particular perceptions in us, and even though, if real knowledge of the object in intuition is to come about, they always must lead us back to the particular; if I had done all this . . . I still do not see where I erred and deserved reproof for my attempt to deduce the law of contradiction from sensation or particular perception. For, to say it again, I do not see how one can regard the sceptic as sufficiently refuted, if one has not shown that the basis of general and absolutely certain judgments can be found in the particular perceptions of the understanding.[29]

This goes to show that Feder is a not sensationist in the same sense as are Locke, Berkeley, Hume, and Condillac. He does not hold that an account of our general concepts and principles in sensation exclusively describes all the necessary conditions of their origin. Like Reid and Kant, he claims that all our knowledge begins with the sense experience, but it does not all originate from particular sensations. There are principles which govern our senses, and these principles are not the result of any particular perceptions. Every human being *qua* being human is endowed with them. They are a kind of natural sensation —conceptions which necessarily arise in sensation, but only at the occasion of particular sensations.

All this is very similar to Reid's account; and the fact is that Feder has accepted not only Reid's emphasis upon first principles as principles of common sense, but also his theory of how these first principles are suggested in sensation.[30] His later work is still more dependent upon the Scotsman's than was his earlier.

Be that as it may, Feder's claim that "what Kant calls the critique of pure reason has always been the only kind of metaphysics I could appreciate and the one I have tried to teach" also reflects his relation to Reid and his view of Kant's relation to Reid.[31] If Feder is right—and there really is no reason to doubt his word on this—then his reliance on Reid can perhaps suggest ways in which Reid *might* have been relevant for the early Kant.

That a reliance on Reid does not, for him, preclude an appreciation of moderate scepticism is shown by his report that as early as 1768

---

29. *Philosophische Bibliothek*, 4 (1791): 203. Compare also with Jacobi's criticism of Kant.

30. For Reid the first principles of common sense are also suggested in sensation and can therefore be traced back to it. But they are not the product of sensation.

31. Feder, *Raum und Caussalität*, pp. vii/viii.

I differentiated between two different kinds of common metaphysics, the *synthetic dogmatic* and the *analytic dogmatic*. After having declared my reservations with regard to both, I declared myself in favour of a third kind which I called *metaphysica indagatrix* (investigatory metaphysics), probably because I was afraid of the sensation which the name analytic-sceptical metaphysics would have caused.[32]

Like many of his contemporaries, Feder thought that Hume's more positive tenets could be supported by Reid's philosophy.

Others continued to view the Scots as the enemies of true metaphysics. Thus Eberhard found it necessary to include in his *Vermischte Schriften* of 1784 a dialogue entitled *Clairsens und Tiefheim oder von dem gemeinen Menschenverstande* in which he tried to delimit the function of common sense in philosophy and to secure the rights of speculative philosophy against its claims.[33] Apparently, still not aware of Kant's importance, he makes essentially the same objections to the Scots and common-sense philosophy in general that he will later make to Kant.

How important common sense and related concepts continued to be may also be seen from the so-called *Pantheismusstreit* between Mendelssohn and Jacobi. This philosophical dispute was something of a philosophical sensation in the eighties of the eighteenth century. Both parties can be seen to rely openly upon theories of common sense developed from Scottish sources. But while Mendelssohn emphasized the rationalistic aspects of the Scottish view, Jacobi was more interested in what has been called the empiricist component of Scottish common sense and advocated a fideism that came very close to outright irrationalism.[34] This paradox of similarity amidst opposition produced interesting responses. Thomas Wizenmann, a friend of Jacobi, maintained in his *Die Resultate der Jacobischen und Mendelssohnischen Philosophie von einem Freywilligen* (1786) that Mendelssohn's conception of "common sense" and Jacobi's principle of "faith" (*Glaube*) were in the final analysis identical; Kant, who stood much closer to Mendelssohn, found it necessary to point out the basic differences between Mendelssohn's overly confident rationalism and Jacobi's pessimistic anti-

32. Ibid.

33. Eberhard, *Vermischte Schriften*, pp. 135–76; see also Chapter III above.

34. Mendelssohn's publications of the last two years of his life, 1784–86, are just as dependent upon Reid as are Jacobi's. See the discussion of these two philosophers above. It is strange how two thinkers as different as these two could both rely on Reid.

intellectualism in his "What is Orientation in Thinking."[35] But neither Wizenmann nor Kant appears to have been able to free himself sufficiently from the "climate of opinion" of his time to see that the paradoxical similarity revealed in the opposition of Jacobi and Mendelssohn was much more fundamental and underlay the thought of the entire age.[36]

II

Although Scottish common sense still commanded considerable attention among German philosophers after 1783, the situation had changed. Scottish philosophy was no longer seen primarily as an antidote to Hume. It became instead a counterforce to Kant's critical philosophy. Thinkers of the most varying backgrounds held the Scots in high regard (often in higher regard than before the success of Kantian critical philosophy) because they provided a ready supply of weapons against Kant's supposed idealism and scepticism. This phenomenon can be observed in the course of the reception of Reid's *Essays on the Intellectual Powers of Man*, which appeared in 1785.

This work appears to have been reviewed first by the Kantian *Allgemeine Literatur-Zeitung* of Jena in April 1786. The reviewer notes at the very outset that Reid is already well-known in Germany through his *Inquiry*, and he characterizes the *Essays* as providing additional and improved weapons against scepticism. While noting that the basic principles of the work are already known through the earlier work of Reid, as well as that of Oswald and Beattie, he still thinks the Essays worth reading because it

is commended by a great variety of information, by clarity, precision and a very beautiful philosophical diction. He is a more thorough and calmer investigator than either of his two colleagues. What Hume said of them, namely that they are in philosophical war what the drummers and trumpeters are in political

35. See Kant, *Werke*, ed. Weischedel, vol. 3, pp. 267–83; and 286–91. Kant does not seem to see the fundamental similarity of Jacobi and Mendelssohn. He rejects Jacobi and accepts Mendelssohn (with qualifications). But the difference between the two is, in many respects, not much more than verbal. This was pointed out by Wizenmann (a follower of Jacobi).

36. However much the so-called "philosophers of faith" argue against reason, they are far more part of the epoch of the enlightenment than is usually acknowledged.

war, does not hold for him. Since the investigations upon which Reid concentrates are now also underway in Germany, we believe that it will not be disagreeable to our readers to hear such a good foreign writer as Reid about these matters.

The review then gives a short account of Reid's discussion of the ideal theory and characterizes his answer as follows:

He differentiates (Essay I, ch. I, p. 16) *conception* from *perception*. We would translate the former as *klare Vorstellung* [clear representation], for he defines it as a modification of the soul connected with consciousness, and would perhaps best render the latter as *Empfindung* [sensation]. Now his proof of the reality of the world of bodies is, of course, extremely easy. If the perception is a representation which has no inner object, but must have one in order to be different from other kinds of representations, it must have an outer object. But here all the difficulties from which the dualist wants to escape regrettably return through Reid's theory. How do the representations come into the soul from external objects? How does what was motion in the bodies become representation in the soul? What are conceptions which are not perceptions? And, most importantly, how can we think a change, a modification, which does not belong to some definite kind? It does not belong to the motions, since it is no modification of body, not to the thoughts, since these must have an immediate object. The soul must think something, and this something, which it thinks, is an idea. Thus the break which idealism has created between the spiritual and the material world does not appear to be healed in this way.[37]

Ill taken as some of the criticisms of the reviewer may appear, and however confusing his general characterization of Reid may be, the review does commend the work and certainly was designed to awaken interest in its contents.[38]

How differently the review affected such thinkers as Garve and Hamann may be seen from the following: Garve wrote on 1 May, 1786 to a friend whom he appears to have asked earlier to obtain a copy of the *Essays* for him: "Reid's *Essay on the Intellectual Powers* (or however the exact title may read) I no longer want to possess after having read the review. It contains well known, already too often said and repeated matters. In fact, not very much can be said about the human faculties in

37. *Allgemeine Literatur-Zeitung* 1786 (April): 181–83, 181f.
38. The reviewer seems to be annoyed by Reid's references to Wolff. He interprets this as the expression of a vain desire on Reid's part to appear knowledgeable about German philosophy. Reid does refer to Wolff's *Psychologia empirica*.

general terms."[39] But Hamann, on the other hand, wrote to Jacobi, apparently on the basis of the very same review, the work "excites all my attention." And, during the following months he did not cease to remind his friend to obtain a copy of the *Essays*, so that he could read it on his planned visit to him.[40]

The work was also favourably reviewed by Feder in the *Philosophische Bibliothek*.[41] And the first chapter of Essay VII, entitled "Of Taste in General," appeared in German translation in the *Neue Bibliothek der schönen Wissenschaften und der freyen Künste*, number 31 in 1786 under the title "Versuch über den Geschmack. Aus Dr. Reids neuesten Versuchen über die geistigen Kräfte des Menschen."[42] Thus, though Reid's late works were never translated into German in their entirety, their contents were known in Germany, through reviews and abstracts, even to those who could not read English. Moreover, since by this time the knowledge of English among the educated and philosophically interested was no longer a rarity, the fact that Reid's *Essays* were not translated does not mean that they were unknown or even little known in Germany. Indeed, the works of Schulze, Reinhold, Fries, and others show that quite the contrary is true.[43] Reid continued to be held in high esteem by philosophers of a more empiricistic persuasion and was never forgotten entirely.

Even Beattie continued to play a role. Though his reputation as a philosopher appears to have been damaged beyond repair, he was still highly regarded as a critic of the arts and literature, as can be seen from the reception of his *Dissertations Moral and Critical*. This work appeared in 1783 and was translated into German by K. Grosse in 1789, as *Moralische und kritische Abhandlungen*. The work appeared in three

39. Garve, *Briefe an Christian Weisse*, p. 248.

40. Hamann, *Briefwechsel*, vol. 6, p. 230.

41. *Göttingische Anzeigen*, 1787, number 63 (21 April): 626–30, pp. 627ff. *Philosophische Bibliothek*, 1 (1788): 43–62. See also vol. 2 (1789): 83–118, where Feder offers a very detailed account (35 pages) of Reid's *Essays on the Active Powers of Man*. But he only represents Reid without criticism, and he does not deal with the more general aspects of his theory, believing that they are too well known for a discussion to be interesting.

42. The very selection of the topic shows in what regard Reid could still be found important in Germany in 1786. Kant's *Critique of Judgment* appeared in 1790.

43. Schulze criticized Kant with the help of Reid's theory of perception. Reinhold clearly also moved closer to Reid in his later works, as has been shown by Baum in "K. L. Reinholds Elementarphilosophie." Fries, who in certain respects returns to Tetens's approach, regards Reid most highly. See especially Fries, *Tradition, Mysticismus und gesunde Logik, oder über die Geschichte der Philosophie*, pp. 404, 441–46.

volumes and the translator substituted a translation of Beattie's entire *Theory of Language* for the shorter essay on language contained in the original *Dissertations*.[44]

Perhaps no other work by Beattie received as much attention in Germany as this one. Not only did three lengthy excerpts from the work—on dreams, on language, and on the sublime—appear in translation in different periodicals, but also both the original and the German translation were reviewed in all the major journals.[45]

It was generally understood, and also admitted by the translator, that

44. Dr. Jakob Beattie, *Moralische und kritische Abhandlungen*, 3 vols., tr. Carl Grosse (Leipzig, 1789, 1790).

45. James Beattie, "Über das Erhabene," *Neue Bibliothek der schönen Wissenschaften und der freyen Künste* 30, i (1785): 5–52, ii (1785), pp. 195–228.

J.B., "Über das Träumen," *Magazin für die Naturgeschichte des Menschen*, Zittau and Leipzig, vol. 1, part i (1788): 25–70.

James Beattie, "Etwas über die Sprache (Auszug aus seiner *Theory of Language*)," *Magazin für die Naturgeschichte des Menschen*, vol. 3, part i (1790): 1–53.

Neue Bibliothek der schönen Wissenschaften und der freyen Künste 24 (1783): 182–84, 182: "Dr. Beattie, who has already gained a considerable reputation among critical writers, even though we would not count him among the first philosophical writers of his nation, reaffirms his merits through these essays."

Göttingische Anzeigen, 1784, number 165 (14 October): 1649–55.

Philosophische Bibliothek 3 (1790): 250.

Göttingische Anzeigen, 1789, number 143 (5 September): 1433f.

Ibid., 1791, number 12 (20 January): 120.

Allgemeine Literatur-Zeitung, 1789 (October): 6–8. The reviewer finds that Beattie has been long known and appreciated in Germany as a philosopher and poet."

Ibid., 1790 (October): 14.

Allgemeine deutsche Bibliothek xciv (1790): 467–70, 467f.: "As a speculative philosopher Beattie does not have the best reputation, but as an acute and tasteful writer, well acquainted with the spirit of classical literature, concerned with matters of taste and the philosophy of life, we have done justice to him. His remarks are usually subtle, at times new and surprising. When he begins to reason, however, we miss firm and certain principles as well as connection of concepts and plausibility of proofs."

Ibid., ci (1791): 136f.

The *Theory of Language* by Beattie was reviewed in the *Allgemeine Literatur-Zeitung* of 1788 (July): 286–88.

For Beattie's reputation see also the Preface by the translator of the *Dissertations*: "The universality with which the merits of my author are known makes the usual speech of a translator unnecessary . . . Anybody who seeks deep metaphysical speculation in this work will be very much amiss. Anybody who sees a deficiency in this may not be altogether wrong, given the present situation of philosophy. A plain, light, yet spirited course of ideas, acute use of ordinary experiences and not infrequent keen inferences from them, make this this book useful reading. The elegant diction, the calm and well-bred *colorit*, the elastic construction of the periods also make it pleasant reading."

it was not so much the work of a speculative philosopher as that of a literary critic. Nevertheless, as a literary critic, Beattie had something of interest to say for anyone attempting to understand literature philosophically.[46]

But after 1790 Kant's *Critique of Judgment* appears to have displaced most of the interest which the Germans still might have had in further works by Beattie. This development becomes very apparent in the reception of Beattie's *Elements of Moral Science*, whose first volume was translated into German by Karl Philipp Moritz (a close friend of Mendelssohn and Goethe) almost immediately after it appeared in English.[47]

In the Foreword the translator quite clearly wants to save Beattie's name as a philosopher by arguing that his aims are different from those of contemporary German philosophers. Beattie is not a speculative philosopher, but a moral philosopher. He investigates "metaphysical matters never farther than up to a certain point, namely up to the point from which they still can have a noticeable influence upon human conduct."[48]

But Moritz did not succeed. What he understood as self-limitation the reviewer of the *Allgemeine deutsche Bibliothek* interpreted as shallowness and inconsistency. His explanation was taken to be a mere excuse. For

the true philosopher never stops his investigation before he has found what really motivated him all along, namely an answer satisfactory to the demand of reason, or until he has found at least a reason which shows that what is sought lies beyond the limits of our faculty of knowledge. This book could have remained untranslated forever. For, what are we Germans to do with a hasty sketch in which the most significant discoveries and investigations with regard

46. How much Beattie was actually integrated into German aesthetic thought during this period can perhaps be seen from the French work, entitled *Recueil de pieces interessantes concernant les antiquites, les beaux-arts, les belles-lettres, la philosophie, traduites de different langues* (2 vols, Paris and The Hague, 1787). It consisted mainly of translations of German essays by such thinkers as Heyne, Lessing, and Klopstock. But it also contained two essays of Beattie: one on the difference between fables and romances, and the other on the sublime (both probably taken from the *Dissertations*). I have not seen the work itself, but only a review of it in the *Journal Encyclopédique*, July 1788, pp. 245–67.

47. James Beattie. *Grundlinien der Psychologie, natürlichen Theologie, Moralphilosophie und Logik*, vol. 1, tr. Karl Philipp Moritz (Berlin, 1790). Both the original and the translation appeared in 1790. Volume 2 never appeared in translation.

48. Beattie, *Grundlinien*, Preface.

to the important matters of human thought and our faculty of knowledge, being made in our fatherland today, are not even considered?[49]

Equally condemning was the review of the *Allgemeine Literatur-Zeitung* of Jena. It reviewed the *original* in 1792, obviously unaware of the fact that a German translation had already appeared in 1790 and been reviewed by the *Allgemeine deutsche Bibliothek* in 1791, for the reviewer argues:

it would be no gain for German philosophy, if one tried to transplant this book into German soil by means of translation. We would not as easily as did the people in his county excuse him for constantly dismissing the more difficult investigations, for declaiming and preaching more than explaining . . . In one word, the book will hardly be successful in Germany now.[50]

The reviewer has no trouble in classifying the kind of philosophy Beattie is advancing. It is *Popularphilosophie*. This term "sufficiently characterizes its merits, its indigenous deficiencies and errors, and, at the same time, the class of readers which will find satisfaction in this book."[51] It is quite clear that this "class of readers" to which the reviewer refers so condescendingly does not include anyone he would consider to be a true philosopher.

"*Popularphilosophie*" has become a term of abuse. Philosophical thought no longer consists in the clarification and development of the principles of common sense, as it did for Kant and his contemporaries. Kant's followers detach philosophical justification and common-sense beliefs from each other. The one no longer appears to have anything to do with the other.

Such philosophers as Tittel, a follower and commentator of Feder, "popular philosopher" *par excellence*, continued to consider Reid to be

---

49. *Allgemeine deutsche Bibliothek* civ (1791): 220–22, 221.

50. *Allgemeine Literatur-Zeitung*, 1792 (January): 63f., 64. The appearance of the original was already noted in the "*Intelligenzblatt*" of this journal of 20 November 1790. The *Philosophischer Anzeiger*, 1795, number 6, p. 48, referred its readers to the review of the second volume of this work by Beattie in the *Critical Review* of 1794: "Even though the English reviewer remarks that other writers have dealt with these matters in a more careful fashion, he still praises the book very much because of its content, its thoroughness and its beautiful and entertaining style. This part contains moral economy, politics and logic. The book is intended for academic lectures."

51. *Allgemeine Literatur-Zeitung*, 1792 (January): 64.

important. Indeed, Tittel thought him too difficult for the beginner in philosophy to understand.[52] But to the majority of intellectuals—and especially to the younger philosophers—referring to Reid (and Oswald and Beattie) appears to have become as suspect as the appeal to common sense.

III

However, this must not be taken to mean that the Scottish influence was over. It simply took on a different form. For some of the more profound critics of Kant continued to use the Scots to advance their Metacritique of the *Critique of Pure Reason*. The most important of these were the so-called philosophers of faith and their followers.

Hamann argued that Kant's position is essentially like that of Hume and Berkeley.

A great philosopher has maintained "that general and abstract ideas are nothing but particular ones, annexed to a certain term which gives them a more extensive signification at the occasion of individual things." *Hume* declares this assertion of the Eleatic, mystic and enthusiastic Bishop of Cloyne, *George Berkeley*, to be one of the *greatest* and *most valuable discoveries* which has been made in the republic of letters in our time.

First of all, it appears to me that the new scepticism is infinitely more indebted to the older idealism than this accidental, individual and occasional remark shows to us. Without *Berkeley*, *Hume* would hardly have become the *great philosopher* the *Kritik* declares him, out of similar gratitude, to be. But what concerns the *important discovery* itself: it lies open and revealed in the mere usage of language of the most common perception and observation of the *sensus communis*, and it does not need special penetration.[53]

Since Hamann had just been reading Beattie's *Essay* and Malebranche in order to find out about the sources of Berkeley's idealism, it is more than likely that his view on the prehistory of the first *Critique* (and

52. Gottlob August Tittel, *Erläuterungen der theoretischen und praktischen Philosophie nach Feders Ordnung*, 6 vols. (Frankfurt/Main, 1783–94), *Logik*, p. 421; see also *Metaphysik*, pp. 292f. and 297. On p. 297 Tittel refers also to Isaac de Pinto as a French follower of Reid. De Pinto's works were also translated into German. For de Pinto see Popkin, "Hume and Isaac de Pinto," especially p. 118.

53. Hamann, *Werke*, ed. Nadler, vol. 3, p. 283.

especially Berkeley's role in it) is also influenced by the Scots.[54] Extending the Scottish view of the Berkeley-Hume relation to one of Berkeley-Hume-Kant, Hamann indirectly accuses Kant of being an idealist as well as of being inconsistent in praising Hume so much while rejecting Berkeley so thoroughly. Without Berkeley, there would be no Hume; without Hume there would be no Kant. Therefore without Berkeley there would be no Kant.

Against this background, Hamann's cryptic judgment that Kant's *Critique of Pure Reason* contains too much "mysticism" also becomes, perhaps, a little clearer. For Reid had already described a certain "article of the sceptical creed" as "indeed so full of mystery, on whatever side we view it, that they who hold that creed, are very injuriously charged with incredulity: for to me it appears to require as much faith as that of St. Athanasius." Hamann may be taken as echoing this judgment while directing it at Kant, the "German Hume."

Hamann's ruminations and observations about Kant's "critical idealism" were further developed by Jacobi. And this development was as deeply influenced by Reid as were Hamann's original remarks. Thus the Scot's critique of Hume's philosophy concentrated upon the issue of the reality of external objects. Jacobi's critique of Kant concentrates on the same problem. For, Jacobi notes,

what we realists call real objects, or objects independent from our representations, the transcendental idealism regards only as internal beings. These internal beings *do not represent anything at all of the object that could be external to us, or to which the appearance could be related. They are completely devoid of all real objectivity and are merely subjective determinations of the soul.*

Moreover, according to Kant,

even the order and regularity in the appearances which we call *nature* we introduce ourselves, and we could not have found it, if we had not, or if the nature of our mind had not originally introduced it.

54. Reid, *Works*, vol. 1, p. 199 (*Inquiry*, ed. Duggan, p. 245). Hamann charges that the "*sensu communi* of linguistic usage" is the key that transforms philosophers into "senseless mystics." Reid says in the very context of the passage just quoted that "ideas, in the gradual declension of their vivacity, seem to imitate the inflection of verbs in grammar" and seems to think that this is one of the most mysterious "articles of the sceptical creed."

All this is proof enough for Jacobi to say that

the Kantian philosopher leaves the spirit of his system completely behind, when he says that the objects make *impressions* upon the senses, occasion sensations in this way, and *give rise to* representations. For according to the Kantian doctrine, the empirical object, which can only be an appearance, cannot be external to ourselves and thus be at the same time something other than a representation . . . The understanding *adds* the object to the appearance.[55]

But however much it is contrary to the Kantian view to say that objects make impressions upon our senses, it is impossible to understand how the Kantian view could even get started without this presupposition.

The very word "sensibility" is without meaning, if we do not understand a distinct and real medium between two realities, and if the conceptions of externality and connection, of active and passive, of causality and dependency are not already contained *as real and objective determinations* in it; and contained in it in such a way that the absolute universality and necessity of these conceptions as prior presuppositions is given at the very same time.[56]

In other words, one might say, Kant's categories of the understanding presuppose Reid's suggestions of sensation.

Similarly, as did Feder, Jacobi asks in effect why and how the understanding, rather than the senses, grants universality and necessity. Why are "laws of reason" more necessary than "laws of sensation"? Why are laws of thought "objective," while laws of sensation are only "subjective"? These questions can also be asked with regard to Eberhard, Mendelssohn, and Tetens, just as they can be asked with regard to Kant. All these philosophers criticized the Scots for having stopped short in their inquiry, for having been satisfied with merely subjective

---

55. Jacobi, *Werke*, vol. 2, pp. 299–304. The presupposition Jacobi is talking about is first and foremost sensibility and its laws (i.e. common sense) and not primarily the thing in itself. The latter is, of course relevant as a consequence, but it is *not* the presupposition. Our belief in the existence of such a thing in itself is only one among several principles of (common) sense. It should perhaps be pointed out that this interpretation differs considerably from the one usually given. It shows Jacobi to be still closer to Reid.

56. Jacobi, *Werke*, vol. 2, pp. 303f. Compare this with Feder's view.

necessity and not having traced this subjective necessity to the objective laws of thought.[57]

Jacobi criticizes the Kantian for this view. For him it is a mere prejudice. More particularly, he argues that the Kantian system itself presupposes such laws of sensation, and that the categories are faint copies or shadows of the basic principles of sensation. Without presupposing such principles of sensation we cannot enter the Kantian system, and with them we cannot remain within it.

The transcendental idealist cannot even attain the conception of an object that is "external to us in a transcendental sense."[58] For the conception of such an object is based upon the "truly wonderful revelation of sensation." Only the realist can attain the conception of such an object, since for him sensation is the passive state of being acted upon. But this feeling is only "one half of the entire state, a state which *cannot be thought merely in accordance with this one half.*"[59] It necessarily involves an object that has caused this state. External sensation necessarily suggests a really existent external object, and the laws which lead common sense towards these objects are not laws of thought but laws of sensation.

Herder follows Jacobi's lead. And if Feder accuses Kant of not having observed a fundamental distinction, Herder claims that Kant creates too many artificial distinctions. In his *Vernunft und Sprache. Eine Metakritik zur Kritik der reinen Vernunft* of 1799 he characterizes Kant's philosophy as a "splitting" (*zerspaltende*) one, as a "*philosophia schismatica.*" Wherever Kant looks, antinomies and splits arise; dichotomies are the work of critical philosophy.[60] Along essentially Reidian lines he argues further that Kant is only fulfilling the legacy of Hume, who

has seduced critical philosophy against her own will. In his sloppy way of philosophizing he assumed impressions and ideas and believed all knowledge to consist of them. For this and especially the unfortunate name of ideas he was accused by his countrymen more than he deserved. The critical philosophy follows Hume in this regard and reaches a goal Hume did not want to reach. Through an incidental remark to the effect that there are two sources of

57. Compare with Tetens.
58. Jacobi, *Werke*, vol. 2, p. 308.
59. Ibid., p. 309.
60. Herder, *Vernunft und Sprache. Eine Metakritik zur Kritik der reinen Vernunft*, 2 vols., 1799, vol. 2, p. 335.

human cognition, sensibility and understanding, whose common root is unkown, a dichotomy is created in human nature.[61]

Ironically alluding in the very introduction of his work to Kant's criticism of the Scots in the *Prolegomena*, he observes:

everything is whole only for the common sense; first the philosophical knife *a priori* has to do its work; then, if the thingless things on the one hand and the allthingful un-thing are about to appear to the critical idealist, we can judge from mere concepts alone.*

*Chisels and hammers may suffice to work a piece of wood, but for etching we require an etcher's needle. Thus common sense and speculative understanding are each serviceable, but each in its own way; the former in judgments which apply immediately to experience, the latter when we judge universally from concepts (*Prolegomena . . .*). And against whom is this said? Against Reid and Beattie. They are supposed to have used chisel and hammer. I hope that in the following *Metakritik* the etcher's needle has been applied as well and can be used even more acutely.[62]

All philosophers of faith argue that Kant's philosophy has removed itself too far from sensation and ordinary language. By trying to "purify" thought of the influence of the suggestions of sensation and the concepts of thought from the influence of ordinary language, critical philosophy becomes nihilism. There is no such thing as "pure reason." Reason is always "contaminated" by sensation and ordinary language. Thus any critique of reason must necessarily involve a critique of the preconditions of reason, namely a critique of sensation and ordinary language. Therefore, when T.M. Seebohm remarks in "Der systematische Ort der Herderschen *Metakritik*" that Herder develops essentially a *pre*-critical philosophy, he is quite correct, though he does not seem to notice that the *Metakritik* is not pre-critical in a historical sense alone. The frequency of references to philosophical works written before the appearance of Kant's *Critique* is no accident. Herder's *Metakritik* is most importantly pre-critical in a logical

61. Ibid., p. 331.
62. Ibid., pp. xiii/xiv. Seebohm. "Der systematische Ort der Herderschen *Metakritik*," p. 61, remarks that Herder "appeals in overbounding polemical frenzy to any arbitrary predecessor of the Kantian philosophy as a crown-witness against it." This is essentially correct. And it shows that Herder's references to the Scots in this work must be carefully considered.

or an epistemological sense.[63] For Herder, Hamann, and Jacobi want to exhibit the *pre*conditions and *pre*suppositions of critical philosophy, and this meant for them first and foremost an elucidation of the historical sources of Kant's thought.

In this task they found the works of the Scottish common-sense philosophers very helpful. Of special importance were the Scottish doctrines of natural language and natural sensation. The Scots had tried to show that all of our thought depends upon certain principles revealed in sensation and ordinary language, principles which, however humble they might appear, are absolutely basic to all other mental functions. These principles cannot be further justified, because they are presupposed in any justification. Thus justification is impossible in a fundamental sense. But the justification of our claims of knowledge is not only impossible, it is also unnecessary, if we realize that we have knowledge of the objects themselves and not knowledge of certain "mediating mental entities."

The philosophers of faith accepted all this. They rejected both the "ideal system" and justification. In fact, they pointed out that there seemed to be a certain necessary connection between these two basic philosophical convictions. Realism is incompatible with philosophical justification of knowledge claims as well as with the "ideal system." Common sense and ordinary language are opposed to both because common sense implies realism. Critical philosophy is deluded when it claims that it can offer logical justification for our knowledge claims. For, if it is true that metaphysics depends in the final analysis upon the constitution of the human mind, then it depends in the final analysis upon *facts* and not upon principles. And one of these facts is that human reason depends upon language. Moreover,

no deduction is required to prove the priority of *language* over the seven holy functions of logical propositions and inferences and their heraldry. Not only the entire faculty of thinking depends upon language ... but language is also the *centre of incongruity of reason with itself*.[64]

Thus Kant's antinomies are not antinomies of reason but antinomies of language. Philosophers are misled by language. Accordingly, a critique of language and its functions is of greater necessity than overly subtle

63. Seebohm, "Der systematische Ort," p. 61.
64. Hamann, *Werke*, ed. Nadler, vol. 3, p. 286 (*Metakritik*).

philosophical inquiries into the nature of pure reason. On this Reid, Oswald, Beattie, Hamann, Herder, and Jacobi agreed, and on this presupposition Hamann, Herder, and Jacobi founded the *Metakritik*.

The rejection of the Kantian "thing in itself" was only a part in this project. But it was the part which proved most influential. When Jacobi pointed out that Kant's acceptance of "things in themselves" was inconsistent, he meant to reduce Kant's transcendental idealism *ad absurdum*. But Fichte and especially Hegel saw this differently. Though they accepted Jacobi's criticism that the assumption of "things in themselves" was not in keeping with the spirit of Kantian philosophy, they themselves felt that this inconsistency was best removed by rejecting any attempt to develop an "empirical realism" and by embracing an "absolute idealism."

David Theodor Suabedissen offered an account of the philosophical alternatives which appeared to be the only possible ones for the German thinkers towards the end of the eighteenth century. In his *Resultate der philosophischen Forschungen über die Natur der menschlichen Erkenntnis von Plato bis Kant* (1805) Suabedissen argues that a universally accepted theory of knowledge is needed, but that it has not yet been found. "Dogmatists, criticists and idealists are still in opposition to one another and maintain . . . that they possess all principles of knowledge, while the sceptic disputes everything." But some advances have been made: (1) The problem (in so far as it allows of a solution at all) has been reduced to three points of view: either subjectivity and objectivity are both original and exist in isolation (dualism), or the subjective has to be derived from the objective (materialism), or the objective has to be derived from the subjective (idealism); (2) it seems that the first two approaches do not afford a solution; (3) therefore the problem must be solved by transcendental idealism or it cannot be solved at all. The last is maintained by the sceptic. And he concludes:

I hope that nobody will reject this result because the choice between idealism and scepticism, which is the only possible one resulting from the philosophical situation, is considered a dangerous choice. For idealism and philosophical scepticism will always be restricted to a small number of independent thinkers. Common sense is the most incurable dogmatist, and it should and will remain so. The sceptic is so much the friend of common sense that his entire doctrine consists in the claim that we cannot advance beyond the claims and facts of common sense. The idealist, however, will never dare the ridiculous enterprise of converting common sense because he aims at explaining it.

That he is aware of Reid and his Scottish and German followers is shown by his claim that Reid, Oswald, and Beattie's "new doctrine, which was opposed to Hume, necessarily had to spread Hume's way of thinking."[65]

But this remark is perhaps even more important for what it shows about the influence of "Reid, Oswald, and Beattie" in Germany. Hume might not have become as important for German philosophers as he ultimately did if his Scottish critics had not called attention to him. To understand his effects upon German thought one must also understand the influence of these common-sense philosophers, for "Hume's problem" was for German philosophers always also "Reid's problem." This is shown most clearly by the philosophers discussed in earlier chapters.

That the Scots remained important for German philosophy even after Kant should therefore come as no surprise. For Kant's relation to Hume was one of the most discussed topics in the early nineties of the eighteenth century. And Jacobi and Aenesidemus Schulze, the most important contributors to this debate, were as indebted to Reid as they were to Hume.

IV

However, there were other intellectual forces—forces that ultimately spelled the end of the Scottish influence in Germany. They found their expression in the writings of the so-called German idealists, Fichte, Schelling and Hegel and their epigoni, who found common-sense philosophers and what they stood for even more distasteful than had the earlier followers of Kant.

Thus Hegel's so-called "*Jenaer Schriften*" (1801-7) leave no doubt about his opinion of the role of common sense in philosophy: there is no role for common sense in philosophical speculation.

Speculation . . . understands common sense very well, but common sense does not understand the activity of speculation. Common sense cannot understand how that which is immediately certain for it, can for philosophy be at the very same time nothing at all.

___

65. Suabedissen, *Resultate*, pp. 439–44, and 200–203, 210. Compare this claim about the Scottish influence and its relation to Hume's philosophy with von Eberstein's *Versuch einer Geschichte*, vol. 1, pp. 358, 391f.; see also vol. 2, p. 113.

Not only can common sense not understand speculation, but common sense must hate, despise and persecute speculation . . .[66]

But philosophy is needed. For, though common sense suffices for the purposes of ordinary life and supplies us with "points of view which seem correct to us, points of view from which we begin and to which we return," we cannot absolutely rely upon them:

as soon as such truths of common sense are taken separately and in isolation, merely sensibly, as the form of knowledge, they appear to be queer and mere half-truths. Common sense can be confused by reflection.[67]

66. See Hegel, *Werke (Theorie Werkausgabe)*. vol. 2, pp. 31f. *(Differenzschrift)*; see also pp. 20–25, as well as 159f., 181f., 188–207, 219f., 240f., and 279, for instance. But Hegel appears to have thought more highly of Reid and his followers than of Hume. See, for instance, vol. 20, pp. 281–86. The very beginnining of this section is interesting: "Hume abolished [*aufheben*] the objectivity, the *Anundfürsichsein* of the determination of thought," Hegel says. "But among the Scots something else came forth. The opponents of Hume, at first, are Scottish philosophers. Another opponent must be seen in Kant in the context of German philosophy . . . what is opposed to Hume is the inner, independent source of truth for religious and moral matters. *This coincides with Kant. He opposes an internal source of truth to external perception.* But the internal source in Kant has an entirely different form from that of the Scots. Their internal, independent source is not thought or reason as such. The content which it derives from this internal source is concrete, and it also requires external material, experience, Those are concrete, popular principles, which are opposed both to the externality of the source of knowledge and to metaphysics as such . . ." (pp. 281f.). Somewhat later he adds regarding Reid. Oswald and Beattie: "In these Scottish philosophers a *third* turn has happened, namely, that *they also attempted to indicate the principle of knowledge in a certain fashion*. On the whole, they aim at the same principle as the Germans do. Especially a great number of Scottish philosophers have often made exquisite observations in the course of this investigation" (p. 283, emphasis mine). Hegel also wrote an essay called "On the Judgment of Common Sense about Objectivity and Subjectivity" which appears to be no longer extant. H. S. Harris suggests that it would be interesting to have it "because we might perhaps learn from it what Hegel made of the *Critique of Pure Reason*." It might be equally interesting for finding out what he thought of the Scots. See Harris. *Hegel's Development; Toward the Sunlight, 1770–1801*. It is perhaps interesting to note that the period of Hegel's development covered in Harris's book coincides almost exactly with the period covered in this work. When Scottish common sense was at the highest point of of its influence, Hegel was not yet ten years old, but his excerpts and notebooks show he knew well the works of Feder, Meiners, Eberhard, Garve, Mendelssohn, and many other philosophers of this period. It has been argued that, early in his life, during the dispute between Jacobi and Mendelssohn, he was on Mendelssohn's side. Later he clearly appreciated Jacobi more. See especially his *Vorlesungen über die Geschichte der Philosophie, Theorie Werkausgabe* vol. 2, pp. 159f., 181f., 188–207, 219f., 240f., 279, for instance.

67. Ibid., p. 31.

To remove the confusions and contradictions is the task of philosophy.[68] Accordingly, philosophical speculation cannot hope to gain anything from common sense. In fact, philosophical speculation cannot even hope to make itself understood to common sense. Therefore "popular philosophy" is a contradiction in terms:

Philosophy is essentially esoteric and as such is neither made for the mob nor is it capable of adaptation by the mob. It is only philosophy because it is exactly opposed to the understanding, and herewith even more to common sense, which is understood as the local and temporal limitation of a race. The world of philosophy is *an und für sich* a world turned upside down for common sense.[69]

Because philosophy is "exactly opposed" to common sense for Hegel, it is only natural that "large portions of his work can be read as a running polemic against common sense," as Hannah Arendt observes.[70] "True thought and scientific insight is only to be gained through the labour of the concept."[71] For Hegel

philosophy . . . does not consider the *inessential* determination, but only determination in so far as it is essential. The abstract or non-real is not its element and content, but the *real*, that which posits itself and lives within itself, the being in its concept. It is that process which creates and runs through its own moments; and the entire movement amounts to the positive and its truth. Therefore this includes just as much the negative, that which could be called false, if it were to be regarded as something from which one must abstract. But what disappears is to be considered itself as the essential . . . The appearance is this originating and passing away, which does not originate and pass away itself, but is in itself and amounts to the reality and movement of the life of truth. The true is thus the bacchanalian revel, in which no member is not drunken; and since every member dissolves as soon as it separates itself from the revel, the revel is just as much a state of transparent, unbroken quiet.[72]

Clearly, neither Scottish common sense nor critical philosophy could look particularly inviting from this point of view. The Scots' sobriety and self-limitation had to look all too ordinary. Hegel had to reject "the exoteric doctrine of Kantian philosophy that the *understanding is not*

---

68. Ibid., pp. 20f. So far, Hegel is not that different from Kant.
69. Ibid., p. 182.
70. Arendt, *The Life of the Mind*, vol. 1, p. 89; but see also Taylor, *Hegel*, p. 127.
71. Hegel, *Theorie Werkausgabe*, vol. 3 (*Phenomenology*), p. 65.
72. Ibid., p. 46.

allowed to transgress experience," if only because in this way "science and common sense worked into each other's hand in order to destroy metaphysics."[73] And, *a fortiori*, he had to reject the Scottish doctrine of Reid, Oswald, and Beattie. Since for him as well as for his friends and followers common sense and metaphysical speculation are incommensurable, to save "the speculative mysteries," the links between speculation and common sense, which Kant and his contemporaries had worked hard to establish and maintain, were finally severed by Hegel.[74]

In this way common sense became discredited not just as a philosophical tool, but also as the subject matter of philosophy. Never again were the works of Reid and Beattie published in German. The "*Schottische Schule*" ceased to be a living force in German philosophy and gradually came to be considered a philosophical oddity of no great consequence.[75] Moreover, even Reid's successors in Scotland began to find the "German answers" as expressed in Hegel's works more appealing than those of their forebears, as Hamilton's works amply testify. So it came about that "until a few years ago, the works of Thomas Reid were known only by specialists in the history of philosophy, and in so far as people did think at all about Reid and his school of common sense philosophy, it was generally thought that Kant had been right in dismissing them as naive thinkers. . . ."[76]

73. Ibid., vol. 5 (*Logic*, I), pp. 13f.
74. Ibid., p. 14.
75. This can already be observed in the earliest historical accounts of eighteenth-century German philosophy, as for instance in those of Buhle and von Eberstein. Most nineteenth-century historians mention the Scottish influence only with regard to Jacobi.
76. Brody, "Reid and Hamilton on Perception," p. 423.

Conclusion

IF ONE THING has become clear in the preceding discussion of the Scottish influence in Germany, it is that Scottish common-sense philosophy had a much greater impact upon German thought than has been previously assumed. Whatever may be objected to some of the more specific claims advanced in the preceding chapters, it is now apparent that Reid, Oswald, and Beattie were no less influential in Germany than in America, France, Belgium, or Italy, and that they played an important role in the development of German thought from after Leibniz and Wolff through Kant's critical philosophy and beyond. This is sufficiently shown by the sheer mass of references to "Reid, Oswald, and Beattie," as the enemies of idealism and scepticism.[1] Everyone seemed to know the Scots to some extent, and when, in the 1770s and 1780s, it became the philosophical fashion to oppose "empty philosophical speculation" to "sound common sense" the Scots began to influence German thought to a significant degree.

This shows itself in the very language spoken by philosophers and their public. For, as P. F. Ganz has shown, the German "*Gemeinsinn . . .* changes its meaning in the eighteenth century under the influence of the English 'common sense.'" While it was previously used as the German equivalent of the Latin "*sensus communis*" and meant often a "sixth sense," in the eighteenth century it becomes "semantically identical to the English 'common sense.'"[2]

---

1. See, for instance, Michael Hissmann's bibliographical account of the philosophical literature, *Anleitung zur Kenntnis der auserlesenen Literatur in allen Theilen der Philosophie* (Göttingen and Lemgo, 1778), sections 73, 75, and 96.

2. Ganz, *Der Einfluss des Englischen auf den deutschen Wortschatz*; see sections on "Gemeinsinn" and "common sense." I do not mean to suggest that this is entirely due to

It might be said that philosophical fashions or fads can fade away without any significant trace upon the important philosophical developments of the time. Against this I would like to argue that Scottish common sense was not without important consequences, and that it is, if only for this reason, important for the discussion of German thought. But perhaps more important, I would also like to suggest that the Scottish influence is also a story of "missed opportunities," and that because of this it throws an interesting new perspective upon the further developments of German thought and also of philosophy in general.

The discussion of the Scottish influence upon Feder-Meiners, Lossius, Eberhard-Mendelssohn, Tetens, Hamann-Herder-Jacobi and Kant has shown that the Scots had a significant role in altering the philosophical conditions in Germany. Their ideas prevented stagnation and gave new impulses to German thought—impulses that were just as important as those of Hume's supposed scepticism. In fact, the Germans used common sense not only to oppose Hume, but also to supplement, expand, and safeguard the more positive aspects of his thought. This is not as strange as it may sound, for Hume himself had already used common sense as a sort of safeguard in his first *Enquiry*. The German indifferentists in Göttingen and elsewhere realized that the critics of Hume were not as different from him as they suggested, and that the insistence upon first principles as principles of common sense was not altogether incompatible with Hume's theory.[3]

These same German philosophers also realized that the usage of Hume and his predecessors had made of "idea" was full of pitfalls for the philosopher, and that it too had to be modified. The German "theory of representation," which has its roots in Wolffian school philosophy, was significantly altered because of the Scottish "theory of ideas." This was especially evident in the thought of Tetens. Scottish common sense also showed to the Germans the connections between

---

Reid, Oswald and Beattie. Hume and Hutcheson, for instance, were clearly also important. For other British influences upon the German language that might be philosophically interesting see Walz, "English Influence on German Vocabulary of the 18th Century;" Erämtsae, *Englische Lehnpragungen in der deutschen Empfindsamkeit des 18. Jahrhunderts,* and his *Adam Smith als Mittler englisch-deutscher Spracheinflüsse.*

3. Hume himself connects his philosophy and common sense in the first *Enquiry.* See also Norman Kemp Smith's interpretation of Hume as advanced in his *The Philosophy of David Hume.* But Kemp Smith assimilates Hume's naturalism perhaps too much to the Scottish philosophy of common sense. For an incisive critique of his position see Norton, *David Hume.* See also my "Hume's Antinomies."

the thought of Descartes and Malebranche on the one hand, and Berkeley and Hume on the other. It made clearer to them that their own problems were not radically different from those of Hume. All in all, the Scots were very important mediators between German and British thought.[4]

Further, Reid, Oswald, and Beattie were also important in their own right. Some of the Germans actually realized that the Scottish theory gave an example of principles which, like the principles of Leibniz, were *a priori*, but which were not merely logical and empty as those of the latter. Thus they recognized that the Scottish theory of common sense allowed them to connect the Leibnizian emphasis on the *a priori* with a Lockean and Humean physiology of the mind. Under Reid's influence they came to see that perception is more than "confused thought," and that it does not consist of unstructured mental tokens which are referred by thought to external objects. Accordingly, Scottish common sense did prove helpful to the Germans in their development of a unified account of rational thought and sensation.

Given the general aim of the late German enlightenment—to develop an empirical rationalism or rational empiricism, and to attempt a synthesis of the empiricist and rationalist approach—the philosophical doctrines of Scottish common sense, especially as given by Reid, can be seen to be extremely relevant for German thought. Like Reid, the late German enlightenment viewed the traditional answers in philosophy as most questionable. They seemed to lead only to sceptical conclusions. But while the Germans still hoped to gain very much by a synthesis of (essentially Lockean) empiricism and (more or less Leibnizian) rationalism, Reid pointed out that there might be something fundamentally wrong with both. For him, the one as much as the other is based on a form of the theory of ideas; both involve the belief in certain mediating mental entities between the perceiving subject and the perceived object. And Reid argued that this belief in "ideas" leads necessarily (and almost automatically) to a denial of the existence of the external world, making objective knowledge illusory, or the very least, *problematic*. Because philosophers believed in the existence of mediating mental entities, the *justification* of objective knowledge, the central problem of the crisis of the German enlightenment, was inevitable. But Reid did more than point out this supposed implication of the theory of

4. This was also recognized by Goethe, who felt that this was one of the important achievements of the "worthy Scottish men."

ideas. He also offered an alternative to the traditional theories of rationalism and empiricism, an alternative that could accommodate radical empiricist tenets as well as rationalist ones: introspective or psychological analysis according to inductive principles is compatible with the acceptance of *a priori* principles, for instance; or the acknowledgment that all knowledge begins with sense impressions can go together with an emphasis upon the activity of the human mind.

Reid's theory also showed that the traditional view of perception as consisting of rather simple and unstructured "ideas" which mediate between ourselves and the objects is indefensible. He suggested that perception itself is much more complicated and highly structured. Neither the rationalists nor the empiricists had anything to say on this matter, believing that the senses and perceptions could provide us only with "simples," and that only thought or the comparison of ideas could give rise to complexity. Therefore, Reid's recognition of the structuredness of the perceptual act could serve as a very good starting point in the establishment of a theory which tries to take account of the sensible component in knowledge as well as of the rational principles required by it. His sharp differentiation between sensation and certain principles or notions suggested by it made clear that there could be certain things found *in* sensation or perception that were not really *of* sensation and perception, but supplied by the mind. Reid broke the continuum of sensation and thought that had thus far been accepted more or less unquestioningly by both the empiricists and the rationalists. But he tried to show at the same time that both are essentially related to each other, and that one cannot have the one without the other. This was most relevant for the problems facing the Germans after 1755.

Because the principles presupposed in all knowledge claims were identified by Reid with the principles of common sense, and because the Germans were not very clear about common sense, while at the same time invoking it, the Scots can be seen to be very important in this regard as well. They could help the Germans to move away from their understanding of common sense as good judgment, or opinion of the majority in a certain society.

By describing common sense as a set of principles necessary for all knowledge and action the Scots might have called attention to the Quixotic character of the philosopher's quest for *absolute* certainty. For the Scots had clearly understood that the method of psychological analysis and reliance upon common sense cannot give any ultimate justification. In fact, they had called attention to their belief that such justification of our basic principles of knowledge could not be obtained, and that any attempt to supply it would necessarily lead to scepticism. For Reid all we can do is *describe* the way in which the mind works, but not show why it necessarily must work in the way in which it does. We can exhibit the kinds of principles we rely on, but we cannot show why we have the principles we have. All that can be said is that they are *facts*. To the German enlightenment philosophers who still wanted justification, this should have been an important objection and an occasion to clarify their own project.

But all this should not obscure the fact that in a certain sense Reid's most valuable suggestions were lost or misconstrued—and this in a fashion often painful to observe. German philosophers went on to philosophize either very much in the same way as they had done before, or in almost the same way as the British philosophers criticized by the Scots. Many of the changes in terminology and method occasioned by the Scots turned out to be half-hearted. And the reason for this was usually that the Germans wanted to be more "thorough" (*gründlich*) than the Scots. This is why they finally rejected both Reid's fundamental criticisms of the theory of ideas and his critique of philosophy as justification. What makes this rejection so painful is not the fact of rejection but the way in which it took place.

Neither Feder, nor Lossius, nor Eberhard; not Tetens, not Kant, nor indeed any Kantian, offered any explicit arguments for rejecting the most fundamental tenet of Reid's critique of the theory of ideas. They did not seem to feel the force of Reid's objections to mediating mental entities, and they simply reasserted the validity of the principle of "ideal philosophy" that "all external objects are only judged in accordance with their representation within us." Feder thought that this principle "could very well be correct, even though we can easily go wrong in its interpretation and employment." In any case, the disagreement between Berkeley and Reid was probably only a verbal one. Tetens claimed that the principle was "certainly innocent" of causing idealism, and that Reid should not have rejected it "in accordance with his usual insight." Kant baldly stated that it could be "assumed and granted without detriment to the actual existence of external things."

But these assertions by themselves do not constitute satisfactory arguments against Reid's criticism, as Hamann, Jacobi, and Aenesidemus Schulze were to point out later. The fact remains that the theory of ideas or representations was never specifically argued for by Feder, Lossius, Eberhard-Mendelssohn, or Kant. The theory always remained an *unexamined* presupposition of their philosophical thinking in very much the same way that it is a presupposition for most modern philosophers. Whether the ideal theory is indeed a Trojan horse, as Reid claimed, need not be decided here. What is interesting to note is that *no one seems to have offered any significant arguments* against Reid's critique. And it is interesting and philosophically rewarding to speculate about *why* these philosophers failed to offer arguments. Could anyone have accepted Reid's fundamental critique of the ideal theory and still have developed a philosophical system of the kind that Kant put forward? Is philosophy in any form compatible with the rejection of mediating mental entities? Or does the rejection of ideas or representations of any kind spell the end of all philosophy and involve naive realism? Is Hume correct when he says that the "slightest reflection" destroys our belief that we perceive the things themselves?[5] In any case, many Germans seem to have believed Hume, accepting what Reid called the principle of ideal philosophy as one of the *fundamental* principles of all philosophy. For them Reid's refusal of this principle was a rejection of all philosophy.

A number of more recent philosophers think differently. According to them, philosophy need not involve the acceptance of a theory of ideas or representations. In fact, it need not even involve the inquiry into the human mind, simply because there is no mind. This view has been put forward most vigorously by Richard Rorty, in his *Philosophy and the Mirror of Nature*. And a central part of his argument, the attack on the "'idea' idea," is very similar to Reid's criticism of the "ideal theory."[6] For Rorty the rejection of the principle that we must judge external objects according to their representations within us, or, as he might call it, the principle that forces us to do philosophy with mirrors, is not a basic presupposition of all philosophy. But then again, his own conception of what philosophy is about would have been impossible for Kant and his contemporaries to accept just as it is for many of our contemporaries.

5. Hume, first *Enquiry*, p. 152.

6. Rorty, *Philosophy and the Mirror of Nature*; see especially pp. 139–148, and 192ff. He is obviously influenced by Reid, and some aspects of what he has to say have affinities to the "popular philosophy" of Kant's contemporaries. Let me add that I do not accept most of his conclusions about the nature of "mind" and philosophy.

But perhaps matters are not quite so simple. Those who try to show that Kant was not a "phenomenalist" in the modern sense of that term seem to imply that Reid's critique of the theory of ideas does not apply to Kant, and that Kant's repeated assertions that his "critical idealism" is entirely different from that of Berkeley (which degrades bodies to mere illusions) do actually lead the way to an answer to both the traditional empiricists *and* Reid.[7] It is only too bad that Reid is never mentioned in these discussions and that his philosophy is not considered by them to have been a "live option" for Kant. To put the argument concerning Kant's opposition to "phenomenalism" into its immediate historical terms would certainly be desirable.

The other important point to which the German (and most later interpreters) fail to address themselves is Reid's views concerning the impossibility of justification. Kant applied the word "naturalism" to the view that holds that "scientific" justification or foundation of our knowledge claims is impossible, and seems to have thought name-calling was a sufficient argument against naturalism. He simply insists that the necessary principles of the human understanding need justification and that naturalism is unscientific. Most of his German contemporaries were in agreement with Kant on this.

While Reid, Oswald, and Beattie had argued that first principles *qua* first principles neither need nor can be justified, and that all we can do is to exhibit their existence and to describe their functioning, Kant is usually understood as claiming that justification of a special kind is absolutely necessary. Indeed, he is seen as claiming that his philosophy can only be understood if this necessity for justification is seen.[8] But since he does not make any effort to convince those who believe that such justification is impossible or who do not believe it to be necessary, he is often accused of begging the question. Most often this is framed as the question of whether he has answered Hume or not.[9]

But here again, Kant may be closer to Reid *and* Hume than has been seen. For careful attention to Kant's text shows that he is not concerned with the justification of any and all knowledge claims. Rather, he is intent upon justifying a very special type of knowledge claim, namely,

7. This has been argued most recently and most vigorously by Henry Allison in his *Kant's Transcendental Idealism*. But see also Nagel, *The Structure of Experience*. Neither work takes into account Kant's relation to Reid and his German followers.

8. See, for instance, Axvi.

9. For a discussion of this approach see my "Kant's Conception of Hume's Problem."

those of the metaphysicians. He offers not a justification of knowledge, but a justification of metaphysics. Whether he thought the former to be necessary or even possible must, at this point, be considered an open question.[10]

His contemporaries all wanted to be "more thorough" than the Scots. And they tried to give a further foundation to the principles of common sense. Feder thought he could do this by tracing them to their occasions in sensation. Lossius thought he could supply them with their materialistic "*Unterbau*" in human physiology. The early Mendelssohn and Eberhard were confident that they could reduce them to more basic truths of reason. And Tetens also seems to have thought that if he could show how they were related to thought, he would make them "objective." It is to Kant's credit that he pointed out that these physiological and rational deductions ultimately cannot justify knowledge and the principles which give rise to it. But it has been objected against him that he himself failed to show how his own transcendental justification is possible. Hamann, Herder, Jacobi, and Hegel argued that Kant's *Critique* calls for a *Metacritique*. Perhaps they are right. But it may very well be that this Metacritique is entirely different from anything they conceived as such.

If Kant meant to justify the principles of common sense, Hegel correctly showed that Kant's justification needed itself a justification, and thus raised the spectre of infinite regress. If he showed anything, Hegel showed that if one begins the process of justification one cannot stop at any one point, but is lost in the "revel" of speculation. Justification seems to be radically opposed to common sense. The latter might be the starting point of the process of justification, but it is neither the tool of philosophical justification nor its necessary subject matter. They are not subservient to each other. Though philosophy might start out as an exercise in the justification of common sense, or experience, or science, it invariably seems to end up being concerned with justifying first and foremost itself and its justification. Critique leads to self-critique.

If Hegel is right, the German enlightenment, including Kant, set itself a self-contradictory aim. Philosophy per se can never be the justification of common sense. If philosophy is understood first and foremost as the enterprise of justification or foundation of all

10. See my "Kant's Transcendental Deduction" as well as Ameriks, "Kant's Transcendental Deduction as a Regressive Argument."

knowledge, then "common-sense philosophy," like "popular philosophy," is a contradiction in terms. The question might even be raised whether "common-sense philosophy" is not self-contradictory from any strictly philosophical point of view. Has there not always been something like an "intramural warfare between thought and common sense," as Hannah Arendt observes in *The Life of the Mind?*[11]

I do not know whether common sense and philosophy must engage in such an intramural warfare. But I do know that the contradiction between common sense and philosophy in the eighteenth century was closely connected with both these issues. It can already be observed in the works of the so-called popular philosophers, the moderate sceptics and indifferentists, who tried to do justice to both. In Kant's critical philosophy the struggle (or dialectic) between common sense and philosophy emerged as an important formative influence. And Kant's thought, like that of most of his contemporaries, may be considered as a sustained attempt to balance the aspirations of both common sense and critical reason. He explained why common sense, as giving rise to natural illusions (the antinomies), was in need of justification, and he made clear that the theory of representation allowed only an empirical realism, while necessarily implying a transcendental idealism. Though Kant's contemporaries were quite unwilling to accept it, what they considered to be Kant's scepticism (the doctrines developed in the Transcendental Dialectic) as well as what they tried to discredit as his idealism (the conclusions of the Transcendental Analytic) were the consequences of their own basic position as well. It appears that in Kant's thought critical reason and (transcendental) idealism won the upper hand. But the so-called philosophers of faith rejected all justification and chose common sense (even if they did not always call it by that name), saying that its principles are "revelations" that have to be believed blindly; arguing against any form of the theory of ideas as leading necessarily to idealism or nihilism; and advocating a "radical realism." With Hegel philosophy re-asserted itself very strongly, and ever since Hegel common sense has played a quite insignificant and negligible role in German thought. At the same time, Hegel rejected the theory of representation, arguing that our "representations" do not represent things in themselves, independent of the representations, ridiculing the enlightenment philosophers' fear of idealism as well as their half-hearted attempts towards realism.

11. See Arendt, *The Life of the Mind*, vol. 1, pp. 8off.

But be that as it may, Kant himself was clearly of the opinion that philosophy could not do without common sense—just as he believed that common sense could not do without philosophy. For Kant the disagreement of common sense and philosophy was far from inevitable. The two were essentially related to each other. Philosophy served common sense, and common sense could understand philosophy. There was, for him, no radical discontinuity between the one and the other, as there was for many others after him. His philosophy or science arose naturally, as it were, from common sense. In an open letter on Fichte's *Wissenschaftslehre* (7 August, 1799) Kant leaves no doubt about this:

> Since some reviewers maintain that the *Critique* is not to be taken literally in what it says about sensibility and that anyone who wants to understand the *Critique* must first master the requisite "standpoint" (of Beck or of Fichte), because Kant's precise words, like Aristotle's, will kill the mind, I therefore declare again the the *Critique* is to be understood in accordance with the letter, and is to be understood *exclusively from the point of view of common sense*, which only needs to be sufficiently cultivated for such abstract investigations.[12]

In this belief in the essential unity of reason and common sense, Kant is at one with most of his contemporaries.

One must ask why this has been realized so seldom. Kant is known for many things, but he is not often referred to as someone who valued common sense highly. Historians of philosophy have spent much time investigating his connections with Leibniz and Wolff, with Crusius and other Thomasians, with Hume, with the German idealists, and with the German irrationalists, but they have neglected to look at his connection with the Scottish and German enlightenment.

Perhaps this has to do with what the greatest successor of the European enlightenment, Friedrich Nietzsche, has called "the hostility of the Germans to the enlightenment." It seems to be true that "the whole great tendency of the Germans ran counter to the Enlightenment," and that Germans cannot appreciate their *philosophes* in the same way as other European nations.[13] Lessing, Kant, and Lichtenberg, who are usually characterized as already "transcending" the

---

12. Kant, *Correspondence*, ed. Zweig, p. 254. I have slightly changed Zweig's translation.

13. Nietzsche, *The Portable Nietzsche*, pp. 84f.

enlightenment, are most often interpreted in complete isolation from such figures as Feder, Lossius, Eberhard, Mendelssohn, Nicolai, Meiners, Garve, Platner, and Tetens. In fact, their friendship with these other enlightenment thinkers often seems to be considered as an embarrassment. But the fact is: they were friends, and the works of Kant, no less than those of Lessing and Lichtenberg, must *also* be seen against the background of their dialogue with their contemporaries. Indeed, they may perhaps be better understood as the best expression of what they *and* their contemporaries were about.

But their works not only arose from this dialogue and have their "*Sitz im Leben*" in it, they also owe some of their limitations to it. If, as Hegel claimed—and all studuies of influence presuppose—"no philosophy transcends its age," then a significant part of the meta-critique of Kant's critique must consist in the investigations of Kant's historical presuppositions. Scottish common sense figures greatly among these —and throws, I believe, a most interesting sidelight upon the problems of "transcendental idealism" and "transcendental justification." Therefore the investigation of the Scottish influence constitutes an important part of the "*Metakritik*" and "demythologization" of the *Critique of Pure Reason*.

Kant argued, possibly in anger, that because of the Scots "everything remained in its old condition, as if nothing had happened," that is, as if Hume had not attacked metaphysics. Apart from the fact that this claim of Kant's shows indirectly the very importance of the Scots—for he seems to say that *they* were the ones who could have made the difference—apart from this, he is clearly wrong. Exactly the opposite seems to be the case. It was because of the Scots that philosophy changed. Hamann said that without Berkeley there would not have been a Hume, and without Hume there would not have been a Kant. The present discussion of the Scottish influence suggests that, without the Scots there would have been no Kant.

Such a suggestion is, of course, unverifiable in any strict sense. But it does emphasize again that Scottish common-sense philosophy was of great importance to German thought. Kant's criticism in the *Prolegomena* shows the tip of the iceberg, as it were. For almost exactly a third of century it was one of the major philosophical forces in Germany.

Strangely enough, this third of a century was not only decisive for German thought, but also for the fate of Scottish common-sense philosophy. It appears that its reputation never really recovered after the blow dealt to it by Kant. But many of the ideas of the Scots survived "*aufgehoben*" in Kant's critical thought; others deserve to be revived, if only because of their importance for a "Meta-Critique of the Critique of Pure Reason."[14]

Goethe claimed that the German had "fully understood for many years the merits of worthy Scottish men." I believe it will be quite a long time before we can say again that we understand fully the merits of Scottish philosophy. But if German thought, as represented by Kant, played a most important role in the dismissal of Reid, Oswald, and Beattie, a better understanding of the developments that led to Kant's criticism can perhaps play a similar role in the re-evaluation of Reid and his followers.

14. See Beck, "Toward a Meta-Critique," and Walsh, "Philosophy and Psychology in Kant's *Critique*."

APPENDIX

Common Sense in the German Background

Neither the concept "common sense" nor its use in the critique of scepticism was an invention of the Scottish philosophers. When they began to make use of "common sense" in their arguments against Hume, it already had a long and distinguished tradition. While this is now often overlooked, they themselves were very much aware of it.[1] Beattie in his *Essay*, for instance, sees the history of his most important concept reach as far back as Aristotle's "*orthos logos*," "*koinai doxai*" and the Stoic conceptions of "*koinonoemosyne*" and "*sensus communis*."[2] But the related concepts of "*recta ratio*," "*notitiae communes*," "*instinctus naturalis*," "*naturalis ratio*" and "*consensus gentium*," all developed or brought into prominence by the Stoics in their fight against scepticism, also played an important role in the history of common sense. During the middle ages these concepts, though they were still found useful in discussions of natural theology and natural law, lost some currency. The early Humanists, however, made the appeal to common sense and the application of related concepts a central weapon against the Aristotelian tradition of the schools. Later they were also used to defend Humanistic values against the attacks of modern science.

1. Grave in his *Scottish Philosophy*, for instance, discusses only the immediate predecessors of Scottish common sense. For a concise but very interesting and suggestive, though not always accurate, account of the history of common sense, see Gadamer, *Wahrheit und Methode*, pp. 15–27. Gadamer believes that "*sensus communis*" constitutes one of the most central concepts ("*Leitbegriffe*") of the humanistic tradition. He considers it to be of the greatest importance for the self-understanding of the Humanities or *Geisteswissenschaften*. See also Ernesto Grassi, "Vorrang des Gemeinsinns und der Logik der Phantasie."

2. Beattie, *Essay*, p. 33ff.

Giambattisto Vico, for example, admitted that the *sensus communis* could not be considered as a source of absolutely certain truth, but he argued that as a source of probable and useful knowledge as well as in its social function of uniting the members of a common culture it could not be discarded without serious consequences.[3] Buffier in France used common sense to combat Cartesianism, while the earlier common-sense philosophers in the British Isles, most notably Shaftes-bury and Hutcheson, found it useful in the refutation of what they considered to be moral scepticism. Germany was no exception. Here common sense played a significant role in the thought of Christian Wolff and Christian Thomasius, "the two founders of the German enlightenment," and became increasingly important in the works of their followers.[4]

One might therefore wonder whether the German conceptions of common sense, as they are found in the works of Wolff and Thomasius, already contain everything that could have made the Scots significant for the philosophical discussion of the late eighteenth century. One might ask, whether the Germans really needed the Scots to tell them about common sense and basic principles, or whether they could find similar ideas among their immediate predecessors in Germany. In asking such questions one could, in support, point to nationalistic histories of philosophy and psychology, as they were written during the first half of the present century. For these argue that the British influence was, at best, of marginal importance. Max Dessoir, for example, tried to show in his *Geschichte der neueren Psychologie* (2nd ed., 1902) that "the basic direction of this development [of German thought in the eighteenth century] can be understood even without referring to England," by relating Kant to the later Thomas-ians and especially Crusius.[5] And Max Wundt argued that Kant's critical problem arose "from a connection of the subjective and psychological approach of Thomasius with the objective and ontologi-cal principles of Wolff," claiming that Kant's "transcendental logic must be derived from this tension within *German* philosophy and not from *foreign* influences."[6]

3. Vico, *On the Study Methods of our Time*, tr. Giantura.
4. For a general account of Wolff's and Thomasius's thought see Wundt, *Aufklärung*, and Beck, *Early German Philosophy*, pp. 243–75.
5. Dessoir, *Geschichte der neueren Psychologie*, 2nd ed., p. 53.
6. Wundt, *Aufklärung*, pp. 250 and 254. Some very interesting thoughts on the possibility of a national history of philosophy can be found in Beck's *Early German Philosophy*, pp. 1–15; especially pp. 13ff.

The study presented here is fundamentally opposed to such nationalism in the history of German philosophy. This opposition is not merely the expression of political preferences, but is based upon an examination of the historical evidence. I agree that, perhaps, one *can* indeed give an account of German philosophy without referring to British sources. Yet, even if it were possible (which I doubt), it is, quite clearly, neither necessary nor historically correct to do so. I can only agree with Collingwood on this point: genuine history "has no room for the merely probable or merely possible; all it permits the historian to assert is what the evidence before him obliges him to assert."[7]

In this Appendix I shall therefore examine the German background, and attempt to show that even the early German sources do not permit us to assert an autonomous development of German philosophy. More particularly, I shall try to show that the Wolffian and Thomasian conceptions of common sense, though they did influence the discussion of the Scottish theory in Germany, are by no means sufficient as an explanation for the changes that took place in German philosophical thought after 1755.

I

That Wolff, the "preceptor of Germany," was a thorough rationalist of Leibnizian persuasion is a stubbornly held prejudice in the history of philosophy. It is still not generally acknowledged that there is a decided tendency in his works to take experience and common sense into account. This tendency finds a significant expression in his doctrine of "the reduction to common sense" ("*reductio ad sensum communem*") which states that it is often very helpful to show the agreement of the notions of abstract thought with the concepts and sentiments of common sense and ordinary language.[8] However, this reduction is employed not merely as a pedagogical device to make the conclusions of his difficult arguments palatable, but also as an indirect demonstration of the truths of the abstract principles used in the "scientific" investigations of philosophers.[9] Through this reduction to common

7. Collingwood, *The Idea of History*, p. 204.

8. Christian Wolff, *Philosophia prima sive ontologia*, 1730, part I, section 2, chapter 2, section 125; *Philosophia moralis*, part 1, chapter 3, sections 241–46, part 3, sections 19–21.

9. Pinkuss, "Moses Mendelssohns Verhältnis zur englischen Philosophie," p. 450. Pinkuss argues that Wolff's *sensus communis* "has nothing to do with" the common sense of Reid and the German philosophers, since Wolff does not regard it as an "independent faculty of cognition." He also argues that Wolff uses the reduction to common sense only

sense it can be seen how the notions of ontology and logic, or the universal truths, also assert themselves in the common-sense distinctions of ordinary language.

Another, perhaps less obvious, expression of this tendency to take common sense into account is to be found in Wolff's distinction between natural and artificial logic ("*logica naturalis*" and "*logica artificialis*"). For him there exists a natural logic, which is expressed in ordinary language and the thoughts of uneducated people. This logic consists of "the rules which God has imposed upon our reason." He makes this natural logic the basis of his artificial logic. "Artificial logic explains the rules of natural logic and teaches us to use them perfectly."[10] Thus natural and artificial logic are for Wolff not opposed to each other, but the latter is the development and clarification of the former.

But this unity can be deceiving, for artificial logic not only clarifies and extends but also corrects and justifies natural logic and thus improves upon it. Whenever there is a disagreement between natural logic and artificial logic, artificial logic, which is considered to be based upon clear and distinct principles, takes precedence over the obscure and indistinct principles of natural logic. However much Wolff may have been concerned to reach agreement between metaphysics and common sense, rational thought and the method of definition and deduction are the only sources of absolutely certain truth, and they therefore have priority. While for Reid common sense and its principles have the final judgment in all matters philosophical, for Wolff it is pure reason which alone can serve this purpose. If common sense and natural logic did not conform with conclusions established by rigorous argument from pure reason alone (as, curiously, they always seem to do in Wolff's works), so much the worse for common sense and natural logic.

---

as a pedagogic device of clarification. While I agree with Pinkuss that there are fundamental differences between the common sense of Reid and that of Wolff, I do not think that it is correct to say that they are completely dissimilar and unrelated. The notion of common sense developed by the popular philosophers is determined by a struggle between more Wolffian and more Scottish conceptions of common sense. Further, that Wolff did not understand the reduction to common sense merely as a pedagogical device may be seen from section 125 of Wolff's *Ontologia*, a passage not referred to by Pinkuss.

10. See Wolff, *Vernunftlehre*, chapter 16, sect. 3; see also *Ontologia*, sect. 125. For the distinction between the two kinds of logic see also *Philosophia rationis sive logica*, 1728, sections 6–11.

The same holds for the other point of connection between philosophy and common sense in Wolff's thought, namely his distinction between "mother wit" and "school wit," which is analogous to that between natural and artificial logic. He expressly rejects all arguments which aim at establishing the priority of "mother wit" and natural logic, or which are intended to show that natural logic and an unadulterated understanding are "sufficient for all the operations of the understanding."[11] Since natural logic and "mother wit" have no clear and distinct knowledge of the rules according to which they operate, they can go amiss.[12] Though the rules are in the final analysis identical, since common sense and ordinary language are confused expressions of one and the same basic faculty, many prejudices and falsities are intermixed with correct judgments. Only when these false judgments have been discarded and when the correct ones have been brought into such a relationship that the more particular can be deduced from the more general can we be absolutely certain of their truth. Common sense, ordinary language, and natural logic in themselves can only mean accident and arbitrariness for Wolff and only pure reason and its artificial logic grant certainty and justified knowledge.[13]

Wolff's position with regard to common sense is thus almost as ambivalent as his position with regard to experience. Just as he wishes to be in agreement with common sense and even regards his logic as a kind of clarification and analysis of common sense, while relying in the final analysis on pure reason, so does he want, in matters epistemological, to take sense experience seriously. Ultimately, however, he cannot do this because of his rationalistic stance. He distinguishes, on the one hand, very clearly between "two ways of knowing truth," that is, sense experience, and rational thought proceeding from first principles; on the other hand, he hardly keeps to this distinction. It may even be argued that he cannot observe his distinction because of his failure to distinguish between "the ground of knowing" ("*ratio cognoscendi*") and

11. Wolff, *Vernunftlehre*, chapter 16, sections 3 and 4.

12. Ibid., p. 4.

13. The German term "*Gründlichkeit*," often taken to characterize Wolff's thought, is always translated as "thoroughness." This translation is entirely correct, but does not convey the connotation of "justification" and "foundation" which this term also has in German because of its close relation to "*begründen*." Thus when Kant speaks of the "spirit of *Gründlichkeit*," he does not simply have "thoroughness" in mind, but also the anti-naturalistic stance of wanting to justify and not simply explain. See also Cassirer. *Enlightenment*, p. 342.

"the ground of being" ("*ratio essendi*" or "*ratio fiendi*"). Since "reason" can mean for Wolff (i) a faculty of mind; (ii) an insight into the connection of truths; (iii) the *ratio* or *causa* of judgments about things; and (iv) the *ratio* or *causa* of the things themselves; there does not, for Wolff, appear to be any fundamental problem in our knowledge of objects.[14] And there is not much of interest with regard to epistemological matters to be found in his works. So his philosophy was not very helpful for the later Germans who considered the knowledge of objects to be a most serious problem. While he supplied much of the terminology and the framework in which this question originally was conceived, he did not contribute much to its supposed solution. As Lewis White Beck succinctly put it:

Wolff's philosophy is a confused mixture of rationalistic and empiricistic elements, and it is impossible to classify it as consistently one or the other . . . it is intellectualism with a vengeance, but it fails as rationalism. Unlike Leibniz's philosophy it is not even a good compromise between empiricism and rationalism . . . Seldom has a man tried harder to be empirical but remained a rationalist *malgré lui* or tried harder to be rational but found himself unable to leave the bathos of trivial experience.[15]

Something similar needs to be said about the relationship between philosophical analysis and common-sense beliefs in his work.

Wolff's followers, especially Alexander Baumgarten, were to shift towards the investigation of sensational knowledge and, in particular, to the aesthetic experience.[16] As true Wolffians, Baumgarten and his followers (Georg Friedrich Meier, for instance) tried to explain aesthetics as the "art of the analogue of reason." Baumgarten may be said to have made Wolffian principles in this way fruitful for the analysis of sensational knowledge and aesthetic experience, he also contributed unwittingly to showing the inherent weakness of the Wolffian position in regard to the non-rational sides of human nature. In showing the importance of the non-rational he may have hastened the demise of Wolffianism. In any case, in Baumgarten's work "the

14. I do not have to point out how much I am indebted to Beck's discussion of Wolff in his *Early German Philosophy*, pp. 261–71.

15. Ibid., p. 267.

16. For a more detailed account of Baumgarten, on whom Wundt is almost silent, see Cassirer, *Enlightenment*, pp. 338–60; Beck, *Early German Philosophy*, pp. 283–86; and Nivelle, *Kunst- und Dichtungstheorien zwischen Aufklärung und Klassik*.

ideal of 'God-like knowledge,'" which still dominated Wolff's search for absolute certainty, has given way to an investigation of "human knowledge."[17] In this way, the trend from "pure reason" to "common reason" (say "common sense") in German philosophy slowly began to assert itself. But this trend was, at the very same time, a trend away from Wolffianism.

II

For Christian Thomasius and his followers common sense was much more important from the beginning. He and his followers were deeply influenced by pietism and thus radically opposed to Cartesianism, Wolffianism, and indeed to all forms of rationalism in general.[18] For this reason their conception of "common sense" was also quite different from that of the Wolffians. Whereas the latter were continuing the secular tradition of "*sensus communis*" and were concerned to show the compatability of their "scientific" (or, perhaps better, rationalistic) philosophy with the conception of such a common sense, the Thomasians were very much part of a theological tradition

17. Cassirer, *Enlightenment*, p. 354.
18. These two characteristics serve better than any other to describe the general outlook of the Thomasian school. Since they were consciously eclectic in their philosophical approach and felt they should "accept truth wherever they found it," particular doctrines may differ very much in the works of different Thomasians. Giorgio Tonelli lists the following characteristic doctrines of Thomasianism (which, however, are immediate consequences of the characteristics given above): "the independence of revealed theology from philosophy; the psychologistic treatment of logic; the emphasis on the role of experience and of the limits of human reason in methodology; the close relation of essence and reality as well as the impenetrability of the essence of substance in ontology; moreover the dislike of the ontological proof, the *influxus physicus* between body and soul, the merely probabilistic value of the knowledge concerning nature; in ethics the independence of will from reason, psychologism and anthropologism, the dependence of the moral laws upon God's free will and the impossibility of their derivation from the mere concept of nature." See Tonelli, Introduction to Crusius, *Die philosophischen Hauptwerke*, vol. 1, pp. xvii–xviii.
The most important members of this school are Christian Thomasius, Johann Franciscus Budde, Joachim Lange, Andreas Rudiger, and very remotely A. F. Hoffmann and Christian August Crusius. Less important are Johann Jakob Lehmann, Johann Christian Lange, Johann Polycarp Müller, Konrad Friedrich Bierling, and August Friedrich Müller. Johann Jakob Brucker deserves perhaps special mention. His influential *Historia critica philosophiae* is supposed to have been the source of Diderot's articles on the history of philosophy in the *Encyclopédie*. See Gay, *The Enlightenment*, vol. 1, pp. 346–48.

reaching back to St. Augustine and Martin Luther, but having its sources in the epistles of St. Paul.

This is already revealed in the very name they adopted for common sense, namely the Latin "*recta ratio,*" which is translated into German as "*gesunde Vernunft.*" The phrase means "healthy reason" and can properly be understood only against the background of "sick," "corrupted," or "perverted" reason. This perverted reason is, according to the Pauline-Augustinian-Lutheran tradition, identical with our natural reason. It has been thoroughly corrupted by man's fall from God's grace. Because of original sin and man's sinful nature we are no longer capable of knowing anything with certainty. Indeed we are no longer capable of obtaining true knowledge of anything, as our knowledge is dimmed by prejudices and errors, unavoidable in the absence of God. Only through God's grace can man recover a true knowledge of the matters of this world and have his reason restored to a state of health.

However, many Thomasians are not willing to accept this theory in its most radical form. Thus Thomasius himself is arguing against more orthodox pietists.[19] And his theory of healthy reason plays an important role in this argument. For he tries to show that, in all matters concerning solely this life on earth, we can very well obtain true knowledge, as long as we follow "the *natural* impulse of healthy reason."[20] Our natural light is strong enough to remove all prejudices and errors concerning this world, and to *restore* reason in this way to its health.[21]

The reason for this is that the fall has not destroyed reason completely, nor even affected it directly. It is the will of man that is corrupt, and it is the influence of this evil will that corrupts reason. Accordingly, to make reason healthy means to eliminate the influence

19. Most orthodox German Protestants believed this. That Thomasius accepts the theory of original sin can be seen very clearly from the following passage: "in the state of innocence, in which man had no imperfections whatsoever, all people would have been learned; they probably would not even have needed any education. But since our understanding has been darkened so much through the Fall, and since it [now] has to be illuminated by different means, the distinction between the learned and the unlearned has arisen" (Thomasius, *Einleitung zur Vernunftlehre,* ed. Schneiders, p. 76).

20. Thomasius, *Ausübung der Vernunftlehre,* ed. Schneiders, p. 15 (emphasis mine).

21. See Thomasius, *Einleitung zur Vernunftlehre,* p. 90: "In some people the natural light is so strong that they are capable of removing clouds of prejudices without any education."

of the evil will.[22] It is therefore quite correct to say that for Thomasius "the obstacles which stand in the way of finding the truth are not epistemological but obstacles of the psychology or even morality of knowledge."[23]

In any case, Thomasius was not so much interested in philosophy and knowledge for their own sake, but almost exclusively in their usefulness for our daily life. He objected to mere school philosophy and did not want his philosophy to be taught at the universities and schools alone but to be practised by men of education in their private and public lives. Therefore it was one of his most important aims to show that his philosophy could be applied and that the philosophies of the Aristotelians, the Cartesians, and the Wolffians overrated the role of pure knowledge and abstract reasoning at the expense of usefulness.[24]

Heinrich Schepers has quite correctly called attention to the theological background of "healthy reason" in the Thomasian school. But when he argues that the Thomasians "have given new credence to the demand of philosophy precisely because these thinkers have placed the *recta ratio* between the corrupted reason with which man is endowed by nature and the reason to which we are restored by God's grace," he is quite misleading, even if he does not say anything that is directly false.[25] For Schepers tells only half the story. Pietism was only one movement among several in this period and not even the most powerful. In many respects it was not much more than a reaction to rationalism (represented by Wolff and his followers). But only in the context of pietism and its anti-rationalistic tendencies was it necessary to give such a defence of philosophy against theological doctrine. The enlightenment in general could only have ridicule for such a "defence" of philosophy against one of the consequences of the doctrine of original

22. Ibid., p. 177.

23. Schneiders, Introduction to Thomasius's *Ausübung der Vernunftlehre*. This is also the reason for his discussion of moral problems in logic. See also Beck. *Early German Philosophy*, p. 251.

24. Thomasius first proposed this view at great length in his *Introductio ad philosophiam aulicam* in 1688, but it remained his goal in his later works as well. See also Beck, *Early German Philosophy*, pp. 248f.

25. Schepers, *Andreas Rüdigers Methodologie und ihre Voraussetzungen*, p. 35. Though I disagree sharply with the conclusions which Schepers draws from his discussion, I have greatly benefited from his account of healthy reason. While he represents it only as a "digression" in his book (pp. 320–33n.), it is a detailed and thorough analysis of this concept in the Thomasian school.

sin, since, if it was united on any one issue, that issue was its rejection of the doctrine of original sin.[26] Thus the Thomasian enterprise makes sense only in a very esoteric context. From the point of view of the enlightenment in general the doctrine of healthy reason must have looked reactionary.

Schepers's characterization is even more misleading if we consider how limited the Thomasian "defence" of the claims of philosophy really is. In fact, Thomasius argues more against philosophy and its abuses than for its usefulness. His conception of a *recta ratio* is much more an attempt to reintroduce the claims of religion and to defend them against the "invasions" of speculation. He valued philosophy mainly in so far as it was helpful in practical life and could not appreciate the "useless" and abstract arguments of philosophy in general.[27] Accordingly, his conception of healthy reason is just as much the attempt to limit the pretensions of speculative philosophers with regard to religious truth as it is the attempt to save useful philosophical knowledge from the zeal of religious enthusiasts.[28]

In these circumstances we cannot expect, in the work of Thomasius and his followers, much original thought addressed to epistemological problems. Many of the traditional problems of perception and knowledge are regarded as sceptical quibbles of no consequence, or as the effects of the Fall upon man's faculty of knowledge. If the influence of the evil will is eliminated, everything will find its proper place and perspective. The Thomasian epistemology is accordingly meagre and

26. For a discussion of this issue see especially Cassirer, *Enlightenment*, pp. 137–60, especially p. 141: "The concept of original sin is the common opponent against which all the different trends of the Enlightenment join forces. In this struggle Hume is on the side of English deism, and Rousseau of Voltaire; the unity of the goal seems for a time to outweigh all differences as to the means of attaining it."

27. Thomasius often shows contempt for philosophy and philosophers. See, for instance, *Einleitung zur Vernunftlehre*, p. 154, where he ridicules the philosophers for wanting to establish the nature of first truths. He finds no difficulty in the matter: "We shall let the *philosophos* fight about it bravely and continue our way without stumbling over it. We cannot go amiss, if we say that the *primum principium* must be a concept which comprises all truths."

28. Thomasius shares this will to limit philosophy with most of the later popular philosophers as well as with Kant. But the late German enlightenment does not seem to know Thomasius well (see Wundt, *Aufklärung*, pp. 6of., and Beck, *Early German Philosophy*, pp. 255f.). Moreover, the theological background of Thomasius is almost entirely absent in the later Germans. They want to limit philosophy from the inside, so to speak, and they reject theological intrusions.

not overly interesting. Its most distinctive characteristics are: (i) an extreme sensationism, and (ii) a correspondence theory of truth. While it bears a great resemblance to the theory of Locke, everything that makes the latter interesting, namely the detailed investigations of particular epistemological problems, is completely absent from the works of Thomasius. These latter excel in general discussions of commonplaces.

But it is important for the purposes of this work to note that the doctrine of healthy reason in Thomasius's work goes hand in hand with a sensationist epistemology, a central feature of which is the rejection of innate ideas and principles. All thought begins from sense perceptions and, furthermore, all thought remains constantly dependent upon these sense perceptions and can again be reduced to the initial perceptions.[29]

Though, like all common-sense philosophers, Thomasius believes that there are certain fundamental truths which have to be taken for granted and cannot themselves be proved, he thinks that they are all really only different expressions of the same *primum principium veritatis*, that is, a principle that assures us of the reliability of sensation.[30] This principle is the only one needed to restore our reason to health. It prescribes limits to reason by showing that it cannot go beyond the evidence of the senses since all general concepts have their basis in sense perception. We have to be always on guard not to depart too far

29. This becomes very clear in Thomasius's formulation of the *primum principium*. To the question, whether external objects agree with our reason or with our senses, he answers: "My dear friend, this confusion is your own fault, since you oppose, misled by the heathen philosophy, the senses and the ideas to each other. But they both belong to the understanding. Therefore, truth must agree with the senses as well as with the ideas. The senses are the passive thoughts, but the ideas are the active thoughts of the understanding. The former have to do immediately with the *individuis*, the latter with the *universalibus*. Sensations are the beginning of all human knowledge, and the ideas follow them" (*Einleitung zur Vernunftlehre*, p. 156).

30. Ibid., pp. 152, 154f., 157. It has often been argued that Thomasius was fundamentally influenced by Locke in this and several other aspects of his thought (see Zart, *Einfluss*, pp. 33–44, for instance). Wundt, *Aufklärung*, pp. 31–32n., attempts to show that Thomasius had already developed the outlines of his theory before he read Locke. But nothing much depends on this, given the meagreness of Thomasius's epistemology. Beck quite correctly characterizes it as consisting of a "simple correspondence theory of truth based upon an uncritical belief in a natural conformity of the mind to its object. Nominalism, a sensationistic theory of the origin of ideas, a recognition of the importance of probability in life, and a belief in healthy common sense as a substitute for speculation were recommended" (Beck, *Early German Philosophy*, p. 249).

from the evidence of the senses in our speculations about the nature of the world. A healthy reason knows its limits as prescribed by sensation, and only a corrupted reason will attempt to reach farther.

However disappointing Thomasius's philosophical achievement may be, this does not detract from the importance of the man. For his achievements are to be found mainly in his practice as a professor of law and a moralist who was not afraid to speak out on the issues which concerned him. He was at the same time a very religious man, an individual who felt he owed it to himself to work for the improvement of society. Pietism did not lead him to quietism, as it did so many others.[31]

The doctrine of healthy reason must also be seen in the context of this struggle. With it Thomasius tried to achieve a lasting unification of elements taken from a particular tradition of German Protestantism and certain Humanistic ideals, or of pietistic thought and philosophical criticism. On the one hand, he wanted to hold that man can be independent and self-sufficient in all matters of this world, while, on the other hand, he did not want to reject the theory of original sin and salvation by God's grace alone.[32] But these two tendencies in his thought are often contradictory. For, the first implies the belief that reason and the senses are essentially trustworthy. It involves a mild form of rationalism, or, at least, a belief in the essential reliability of reason. But the other tendency goes to undermine the authority of reason altogether, and seems to lead towards a form of irrationalism.

Much of Thomasius's philosophy must be understood as the sustained effort to bring together these conflicting tendencies and to balance them. He wants to show that reason, though corrupted and dimmed by prejudice, can purify itself by its own power and reach some sort of certainty. And even if in the end his contribution to philosophical analysis is negligible, he is important in the history of common-sense philosophy for having attempted a solution to this problem. The tension between his secular concerns and his religious convictions also helps explain the interest his writings still hold today.

Thomasius is still being read, while most of his immediate followers

31. For an interesting and stimulating account of Thomasius, the man, see Ernst Bloch, *Christian Thomasius, ein deutscher Gelehrter ohne Misere.*

32. Beck notes this contradiction in Thomasius when he finds it "odd that Thomasius ever was a pietist and a *Naturphilosoph*" (*Early German Philosophy*, p. 300), and though he also describes Thomasius's religious struggles, he does not appear to realize how very much at the centre of all his philosophy this contradiction lies.

are virtually forgotten. One of the reasons for this is perhaps to be found in the fact that they were first and foremost theologians without any great concern for secular matters. Their audience was much more restricted from the beginning. Thus Johann Franciscus Budde, a friend and follower of Thomasius, considered *recta ratio* important only as the instrument which enables us to accept the message of the Bible.[33] The same also holds for Joachim Lange, a student of Thomasius and Budde, who remains known today as the first open enemy of Wolff. In his work healthy reason is pushed aside and much more space is given to the description of reason in its corrupted state.

Andreas Rüdiger, perhaps the most significant of these Thomasians, places perhaps even more importance upon *recta ratio* than Thomasius himself. But, like Budde and Lange, he is mainly interested in religious matters. Though, unlike them, he deals also with natural philosophy and secular issues, he does so from a thoroughly religious perspective. In some ways, he may even be characterized as a mystic. In him, the tension between the rationalistic and the irrationalistic tendencies within Thomasianism has given way to a thorough irrationalism.

Philosophically there is not much of importance to be found in Budde, Lange, or Rüdiger. Though their sensationist epistemology is perhaps somewhat more sophisticated than that of Thomasius, this does not show originality on their part. It is fully explainable as the result of the increased influence of Locke upon their thought.[34] In any case, apart from their religiously motivated criticism of Wolffian

33. For Budde a healthy reason is one for which it is "reasonable that there are things divine which cannot be comprised by human understanding" (Johann Franciscus Budde, *Historische und theologische Einleitung in die vornehmsten Religions-Streitigkeiten*, ed. Walch, pp. 83f.). "The most basic truths which lead to spiritual happiness . . . are contained and represented in the Holy Bible so distinctly that even the most simple person can grasp them in such a way that he is immediately convinced that they are truths. The only presuppositions are that he has a healthy reason and reads the word of God with proper attentiveness (Introduction). See also his *Institutiones Philosophiae Eclecticae*, 1703, p. 6: "Namque quae viam saltem ad Philosophiam paudunt animumque praeparant, disciplinae, *instrumentalis* Philosophiae nomine designo." Budde also tries to prove many theological doctrines by appealing to healthy reason. Thus the Lutheran teaching is the only true one because, among other things, it does not, for him, teach anything that would contradict our natural concept of God and his qualities (*Religions-Streitigkeiten*, p. 82).

34. This is shown by Zart, *Einfluss*, pp. 40–72. It is also more or less acknowledged by Wundt, in *Aufklärung*, pp. 62, 63, 72, 84, 85, 87, and 121. One may very well wonder what this does to Wundt's theory concerning the "ultimate roots of the increasingly strengthening spiritual movement . . . [which] reach down to the biological" (p. 4).

rationalism, they contributed nothing of importance beyond what they learned from the works of British philosophers or Continental Newtonians. But one may give them credit for having mediated to their followers some important impulses of the two latter groups.

Christian August Crusius, one of the last adherents of this school, is usually regarded as the most important of all the Thomasians. It is said that he helped Thomasianism to gain the upper hand in its relentless fight with Wolffianism. But the evidence upon which these claims are based is not as strong as one is led to believe. For one must remember that the "question concerning Crusius's *influence in general* has thus far remained virtually untreated."[35] Though he had some followers, he never appears to have played a role comparable to that of Wolff. Wolff continued to be very influential during the time that is said to be his most influential period (from about 1744 to 1770). Furthermore, British and French thought already began to exercise a considerable influence at that time. Indeed, it appears to me that Crusius himself was not unaffected by this. He did not offer an all-inclusive and decisive alternative to Wolff's system, but rather an eclectic approach to philosophy, and many of his doctrines can also be found in British writers such as Hutcheson.[36] Because he also incorporated much of Wolff's thought as well as the pedantic and thorough style of Wolffianism, many of the more conservative philosophers could follow Crusius in some respects, while still remaining Wolffians in their basic outlook. But many more appear to have rejected Crusius's school philosophy together with that of Wolff.[37]

---

35. See Tonelli, Introduction to Crusius's *Hauptwerke*, vol. 1, pp. xi–xxi. Tonelli himself gives a short account of Crusius's *Wirkungsgeschichte* and his relation to Kant as well (pp. xlvi–lii). But he does not succeed in showing that any significant philosopher of this period is fundamentally a Crusian. Johann Bernhard Basedow, who is characterized as an independent student of Crusius, for instance, was just as much (or more) dependent upon Rousseau and British philosophers. In fact, Basedow rejects one of the most important tenets of Crusianism. namely the importance of ontology. For Basedow ontology is no special discipline of thought at all. Riedel can only be understood against the background of British thought, and his inclusion of Aenesidemus Schulze as "continuing the Crusian direction" of thought is highly questionable. Schulze is much more dependent upon Jacobi, Hume, and Reid than on anything written by Crusius.

36. The sources of Crusius's eclectic philosophy would deserve to be investigated.

37. The best known and most important of these philosophers who followed Wolff *and* Crusius is Joachim Georg Darjes (see Wundt, *Aufklärung*, pp. 304–6). But Crusius never appears to have found general acceptance in Germany. As late as 1759 he was still regarded as an outsider by Mendelssohn, who felt that philosophy would reach its lowest

Following the earlier Thomasians, Crusius criticizes rationalism from a pietistic point of view, objecting strongly to the optimistic rationalistic faith in the omnipotence of reason. Reason has to be limited and shown to be dependent upon sense perception. But Crusius no longer accepts Thomasius's simple-minded sensationist account of the origin of knowledge. Instead, he hedges on the issue:

> At the occasion of external sensation the ideas of certain objects arise. We say at that time that we sense these objects. There are two possible explanations for this. Either the ideas themselves lie already beforehand in the soul, and are made lively by these concurring conditions . . . or there is only the immediate cause and the power to form them at the moment of the concurrent condition in accordance with it. We cannot know for certain which of these two possibilities is the true one. But one assumes less, when one assumes the latter.[38]

Crusius tends toward some sort of compromise between the Wolffian belief in innate ideas and principles and Thomasian sensationism. But he does not want to reject entirely the doctrine of innate ideas, and he leaves the matter undecided.[39]

The work of Crusius is also representative of the way in which the two conceptions of "common sense" in the early enlightenment, "*sensus communis*" and "*recta ratio*", developed during the fifties of the eighteenth century. As it already was in the work of his teacher A. F. Hoffmann, the sharp distinction between "*recta ratio*" or "*gesunde Vernunft*" (healthy reason) and "*sensus communis*," which was usually translated as "*gemeiner Menschenverstand*" is lost almost entirely.[40] Indeed, "*recta ratio*" no longer is a central term in the works of Hoffmann and Crusius.[41] Though Crusius does speak of "*gesunde*

---

low should Crusius become the philosopher in fashion. Hamann, whose religious outlook might have predisposed him favourably towards Crusius, does not think highly of him either. Nicolai's *Sebaldus Nothanker* of 1773 shows Crusianism to be very much out of style.

38. Crusius, *Weg zur Gewissheit und Zuverlässigkeit der menschlichen Erkenntnis* (Leipzig, 1747), vol. 3 of his *Hauptwerke*, p. 153. When he says, however, that sensation supplies us only with the material for knowledge, while the form is supplied by the laws of thought (p. 754), he appears to have made a decision, and he does sound like Lambert and Kant.

39. He is quite often as evasive on important issues as he is here.

40. See Hoffmann, *Vernunft-Lehre*.

41. The concept of healthy reason has lost so much in importance for Hoffmann that it is not even included in his "Register of Important Concepts" at the end of his work. Like Wolff, he distinguishes between natural and learned logic, and considers the latter

Vernunft," it is quite clear that he does not have the Thomasian conception in mind, but rather the Wolffian "*sensus communis*." And at times Crusius uses "*sensus communis*" itself.[42]

In Crusius the appeal to the corruptions of reason loses not only in importance, but is actually argued against. Though he admits that there are corruptions, reason itself is *essentially* uncorrupted and reliable in its natural state.[43] Accordingly, every attempt is made to show that appeals to the corruptness of human reason are not legitimate.

The opposition of Thomasians and Wolffians on the doctrine of common sense (and the related epistemology of rationalism and sensationism) more or less disappears in the works of Crusius and those close to him. "*Gesunde Vernunft*" and "*gemeiner Menschenverstand*" become synonyms in the philosophical language around the middle of the century. And this process was so quick and so thorough that many philosophers writing at the end of the century no longer knew of the theological background of "*gesunde Vernunft*" and its initial difference from "*gemeiner Menschenverstand*." Thus the historian of philosophy von Eberstein wonders in 1794: "To me the expression 'healthy reason' instead of common sense (*Gemeinsinn*) has always seemed peculiar: for

---

nothing but the development "of the reasons and rules upon which, without being aware of them, our understanding founds its judgments." Learned logic is "nothing but explained natural logic" (Hoffmann, *Vernunft-Lehre*, pp. 46f). Wundt is quite correct when he speaks of a synthesis of the Wolffian and Thomasian approach in the work of Hoffmann (see *Aufklärung*, pp. 245–54). For a short but substantial account in English see Beck, *Early German Philosophy*, pp. 300–305.

42. When Crusius says that he wants his philosophy to be compatible with the "*sensus communis*" as well as with Christian religion, he clearly cannot have anything close to the Thomasian conception of healthy reason in mind. (He makes this claim in the Introduction to the 2nd ed. of his metaphysics.) I quote in accordance with Festner, *Crusius als Metaphysiker*, p. 3. Compare also with his *Entwurf der nothwendigen Vernunftwahrheiten* (Leipzig, 1745), p. 450. Here he uses "healthy reason" to refer to "*sensus communis*" in expressing a similar thought: "it is known how boldly the doctrine of the Trinity is rejected by many immediately as though it would contradict healthy reason . . ." Incidentally, Thomasius also uses the expression "*sensus communis*." But he refers by means of it to outer sense in general (see *Einleitung zur Vernunftlehre*, pp. 105f.)

43. See Crusius, *Weg zur Gewissheit*, pp. 804f., 825, and *Dissertationis de corruptelis intellectus a voluntate penditibus* (Lipsius, 1740). (I have not seen the latter work.) There is no radical break between Thomasius and Crusius here. But whereas Thomasius often speaks of reason in general as being corrupted, Crusius tends to speak of (isolated and limited) corruptions which can be easily identified and removed.

it sounds as though cultivated reason, which judges in accordance with distinct knowledge, is not healthy."[44]

There is also much of importance to be found in the work of Crusius that appears to point to Kant. Thus he objects to Wolff's identification of the epistemological with the ontological.[45] Another important insight of his is considered to be his clear recognition of the difference between the relation of cause and effect and that of logical ground and consequence, and in his moral philosophy he develops views which have appeared to several commentators to be very similar to those of Kant.

However, there is hardly anything to be found in Crusius that could not be found equally well (and often better) in the works of other philosophers. To say, as Tonelli does, that Crusius is the most important philosopher "after Wolff . . . around the middle of the eighteenth century" in Germany appears to me a gross overestimation of his importance for both historical and systematic reasons.

Crusius's supposed influence upon Kant is, according to Tonelli, "a relatively frequently discussed topic." But it is also one that is characterized by a neglect of the actual facts. When and what exactly Kant learned from Crusius is not all that clear. And this is perhaps no accident.

Much of the discussion of Kant's relation to Crusius goes back to Heinz Heimsoeth's suggestions. He argued that "the philosophical interest in the history of philosophy aims at the coincidence or discrepancy of the motives of thought [expressed] in systematic conceptions," and that "the question of the historical connection is hereby only of secondary importance [*kann dabei zurücktreten*]." Accordingly, when he tried to establish some sort of "connection" between Crusius and Kant, he *compares* the two. Careful not to assert any actual dependence of Kant upon Crusius, he finds "the basic tendency is identical in both, "and that in "Crusius as in Kant a new demand for a critique of cognitive reason, of the determination of the

44. von Eberstein, *Versuch einer Geschichte*, vol. 1, pp. 336–37n.

45. See Beck, *Early German Philosophy*, pp. 396ff. It appears to me that Beck is somewhat too generous to Crusius when he suggests that Crusius actually succeeded in keeping the epistemological and the ontological apart. I do not see why his law of the inseparable ("Whatever two things cannot be thought apart from one another cannot exist apart [or be possible apart] from one another"), for instance, does not confuse thought and reality, or epistemological criteria with ontological ones.

limits of human knowledge, and of the review of its criteria in accordance with their universal or limited validity grows out of the *metaphysical recognition of the irrational.*"[46]

But it is far from clear whether Kant's philosophy must, or even can, be understood as "the metaphysical recognition of the irrational." To be sure, Kant was concerned to show the importance of sensation for limiting metaphysical knowledge, and thus "recognized" something essentially "non-rational" at the very foundation of knowledge. But presumably there is a difference between the non-rational and the irrational. It is true that *Heimsoeth* was interested in irrationalism, and that his *vorstossendes Problembewusstsein* must therefore have made it necessary for him to look for coincidences between Kant and irrationalism. Furthermore, given the general interest among Germans during the first half of the twentieth century in reducing everything considered important to German sources, it is understandable that Heimsoeth wants to relate Kant to a particularly *German* form of irrationalism. But whatever the interests of certain philosophers in the Germany of the twenties and thirties of this century may have been, they are certainly not binding for the understanding of German thought today.[47]

46. See Heimsoeth, *Metaphysik und Kritik bei Ch. A. Crusius,* p. 172; see also his *Metaphysik der Neuzeit,* p. 83. This wilful neglect of the factual connections appears to be an essential presupposition of the ontological school. In any case, it can be found in almost all of the learned historical scholarship produced by its members. See the following, as well as, for instance Schepers, *Andreas Rüdigers Methodologie,* p. 72. After having argued that there are many things in Kant that could have come from Rüdiger, Schepers notes that "the establishment of the connections between Rüdiger and Kant must be relegated to a later work . . ." Why? How important this *contempt* for "*mere* influences" still remains may also be seen from Heidemann's "Metaphysikgeschichte und Kantinterpretation," pp. 297f. To say that Heimsoeth was important both "as a historian of metaphysics and as a metaphysician of the historical" (Funke, "Der Weg zur ontologischen Kantinterpretation," p. 366), has to be taken *cum grano salis.* Perhaps *because* Heimsoeth was so much of a "metaphysician of the historical" we must be careful in accepting the results of his inquiries as a "historian of philosophy."

47. One may well wonder—though it is impossible here to argue this—whether such interests should ever be unquestioningly accepted as the basis for one's research. Perhaps they inevitably determine us to some extent. But does that mean that we should not resist them? Heimsoeth's stance is of course related to Heidegger's hermeneutics, and his interpretation of Kant is not too different from that of the latter's *Kant und das Problem der Metaphysik.* See especially pp. xiv and xviii of the 4th and enlarged edition. For a critique of the ontological approach see Lehmann, "Kritizismus und kritisches Motiv in der Entwicklung der Kantischen Philosophie." See also Gram. *Kant: Disputed Questions,* and

Therefore, it appears to me that it is safe to say that, when nationalistic historians of German philosophy say they are going to reduce the developments of eighteenth-century thought to tensions within German thought alone, they promise more than they deliver. Indeed, I would go so far as to say that they promise more than they can ever hope to deliver, given the historical evidence. When Wolffianism decreased in importance, it was not succeeded by Crusianism as the only alternative. Crusius was one among many alternatives; and—I think—he was far from being the most important one.

III

That the nationalistic view is wrong is also shown by other developments that took place around this time. Thus there were several philosophers who, for various reasons, rejected the approach of German school philosophy altogether and who, under the influence of British philosophers, developed their own theories of common sense in conscious opposition to the philosophy still taught at most universities. Some of the most important of these philosophers were Friedrich Christoph Oetinger, Johann Bernhard Basedow, and Friedrich Justus Riedel.

Oetinger, a mystically inclined cleric from the state of Swabia who is sometimes called "the Magus of the South," and who is unjustly neglected, used Shaftesbury's conception of a *sensus communis* to establish his own *Lebensphilosophie*.[48] Oetinger was a vehement enemy

---

especially Walsh, "Kant and Metaphysics," p. 376. Walsh concedes that the ontological interpretation may make sense as an account of Kant's "private thoughts," but finds it "to say the least wildly paradoxical" as an interpretation of Kant's published texts. I believe it is equally implausible as an account of Kant's prejudices. The ontological school, which argues so much against the Neo-Kantian evasion of opposing Kant's "private opinions" to his "public works," has in fact perpetuated this distinction and made it one of the corner-stones of its interpretation of Kant. Whereas the Neo-Kantians emphasized the public works, the ontological school speculates about metaphysical motives and intentions, and then tries to find them in Kant's texts. This often involves more "violence" to Kant's written word than Heidegger ever perpetrated.

48. Oetinger has long been forgotten. But there is a tendency today to acknowledge him as an important figure of the mid-eighteenth-century. The most important works about him are Herzog, *Friedrich Christoph Oetinger. Ein Lebens- und Charakterbild*; Herpel, *Friedrich Christoph Oetinger. Die heilige Philosophie*; Zinn, *Die Theologie des Friedrich Christoph Oetinger*; Schneider, *Schelling und Hegels schwäbische Geisteahnen* (important, but marred by national-socialistic propaganda); Hauck, *Das Geheimnis des Lebens*; Schulze, "Oetinger

of Leibniz and of rationalism in general. His own philosophy advocates irrationalism. Accordingly, his *sensus communis* is not to be likened to the usual *Menschenverstand* or human understanding of the German enlightenment, but is a sense in the true meaning of the word. It is implanted into us by God as the *"sensus tacitus eternitatis,"* or as the instinct that directs us to eternity. *Sensus communis* is what the Scriptures signify by "heart" and it has found its most perfect expressions in the Proverbs of Solomon.[49] Therefore it may also be considered as that which responds to the wisdom calling in the streets (*"id quod respondet sapientiae in plateis clamanti"*)[50] But, most importantly, *"sensus communis"* means for Oetinger our sense for life: "Nothing is more obvious to the *sensus communis* than life, and nothing darker to the understanding than life."[51] "In *sensus communis* kindred comes into contact with kindred, equal with equal, life with life, one could say, individual life with all-life (*All-Lebendigkeit*)."[52] As such a sense for life, his common sense can become the source of a mystical awareness or even mystical union of man and nature (and thus also of man and God). In this capacity it is called "central cognition" (*"cognitio centralis"*). But not everybody is capable of such an experience and only especially gifted persons can partake of it.

While Oetinger's philosophy was much too esoteric to have found many adherents,[53] Johann Bernhard Basedow, a student of Crusius, Reimarus, and Wolff, but also deeply influenced by Rousseau,

---

contra Leibniz." See also Gadamer's Introduction to Oetinger's *Inquisitio in sensum communem et rationem* (reprint of the edition Tübingen, 1753, Stuttgart, 1964), as well as his paper "Oetinger als Philosoph," and Fullenwider, *Friedrich Christoph Oetingers Wirkung auf Literatur und Philosophie seiner Zeitgenossen.* The importance of Shaftesbury for Oetinger is somewhat neglected in the most recent literature. Schneider, Hauck, and Schulze do not mention the Englishman, even though Oetinger himself not only acknowledges him (*Inquisitio*, p. 263), but even includes a translation of Shaftesbury's essay on the *sensus communis* in his *Die Wahrheit des Sensus Communis oder des allgemeinen Sinnes in den nach dem Grundtext erklärten Sprüchen des Prediger Salomo* (1753), "in order that everybody may see how this naturalist thought of the *sensus communis.*" See also Weiser, *Shaftesbury* and Zinn, *Die Theologie.*

49. See Herpel, *Oetinger*, pp. 185ff. Oetinger has indeed devoted a whole work to showing this (see previous footnote).

50. Herpel, *Oetinger*, p. 188.

51. Hauck, *Geheimnis*, p. 33.

52. Ibid.

53. Thomas Wizenmann, to some extent, appears to have been a follower of Oetinger. At least, he admired him very much, as his letters show. See A. Golz, *Wizenmann*, vol. 1, pp. 39 and 139.

Hutcheson, Hume, and Lord Kames, was very successful and even created something of a philosophical sensation with his *Philalethie* (1764) and his subsequent *Theoretisches System der gesunden Vernunft* (1765).[54] For Basedow, philosophy is nothing but the representation of useful knowledge. In fact, he argues that usefulness is perhaps the best criterion or test of truth we possess.[55] His healthy reason is constituted by certain basic truths derived from sense perception and by certain first principles to which "everybody gives just as immediate consent as to his own experience as soon as he understands [them]."[56]

However, since there are many propositions that are undoubtedly useful and should be accepted as true, but are neither perceptual truths nor first principles, Basedow feels he has to supplement the principles of healthy reason with principles which we have the duty to believe.[57] Thus he is fully convinced that natural and revealed religion are based to a great extent upon such a duty to believe. But it also applies to other aspects of human existence. We have to believe, for instance, many kinds of testimony by others in order to know anything about the past or about things of which we have had no experience ourselves. "Since doubt is against all the ends of individual human beings as well as against those of society," we have the duty to believe in these cases as well.[58]

54. For an indication of this see Buhle, *Geschichte*, vol. 6, p. 550. While Kant appears to have thought highly of Basedow as an educator. Herder and Goethe despised him. In addition, the two organs of the Berlin enlightenment, the *Briefe die neueste Literatur betreffend* (letter 300), and the *Allgemeine deutsche Bibliothek* (1766, vol. iii, 1. p. 69) reviewed his works unfavourably.

55. He rejects any formal definition of truth. Such a definition would be "superfluous." Everybody knows what "truth" means anyway. It is the "general quality of true sentences" (*System*, vol. 3. p. 69). The real difficulty lies not in the meaning of the concept. but in the determination of the criteria by which we determine truth or falsity. The correspondence theory of truth is rejected as "very confusing. For how does the warm oven, which gives me warmth, agree with my thoughts?" (p. 79). "*A true proposition is one that must be believed*" (p. 69). Reason gives such constant consent to some propositions because (1) it is aware that *all attempts to doubt are completely futile*, and because (2) it recognizes that it is naturally inclined to believe, and that the consent in accordance with such rules is the *proper means* to reach its aims. Doubt would lead to the wrong way, a way on which there would be danger without usefulness.

56. Ibid., vol. 1, p. 50.

57. Ibid., vol. 3, pp. 77f.: "Whenever a proposition is probable and practical, whenever the danger of doubt and consequently the advantage of belief is great, the duty to believe exists."

58. Basedow, *Elementarwerk*, vol. 1, p. 346. The relationship of Basedow's duty to believe and Kant's postulates deserves a thorough treatment. See also my "Kant's Transcendental Deduction of 'There is a God.'"

In the same way Basedow also tries to reinforce our belief in the first truths of healthy reason. For, he argues,

even if you could doubt the first truths, you still would have to recognize that this doubt is not useful, but harmful. In this case it would be your duty not to doubt with regard to these truths. You would have to reject the doubts as something despicable and pernicious and could not promote it but would have to hinder it.[59]

This last argument shows quite well how Basedow usually establishes his own views and how he discredits the objections of others. It should also be sufficient explanation of why his theoretical system of healthy reason remains so barren in philosophical respects.

While Oetinger was moved mainly by religious concerns and Basedow was a philanthropist interested in developing a more adequate pedagogic theory (and praxis), Friedrich Justus Riedel was almost exclusively concerned with literary criticism and aesthetic theory. In his *Theorie der schönen Künste und Wissenschaften* of 1767 and his *Briefe über des Publikum* of 1768 he attempted to provide the relatively new discipline of aesthetics with a fixed place in the systematic context of philosophy of equal right besides logic and ethics. He did this by trying to show that, like logic and ethics, aesthetic theory consists of the analysis of a special faculty of the mind. He was thus the first German to divide the human mind into three faculties, one concerning the true, another the good, and a third the beautiful, and to base the divisions of philosophy upon these faculties.[60] All three faculties are faculties of sensation for Riedel.[61] But they are governed

---

59. Basedow. *Elementarwerk*, vol. 1, p. 345.

60. For Riedel the soul has three kinds of laws, according to which it must function, namely for the true, for the good and for the beautiful (*Briefe*, p. 39; compare with *Theorie*, p. 6: "the True, the Good and the Beautiful. For each one, Nature has supplied us with a special faculty [*Grundkraft*]. For the True the *sensus communis* for the Good the conscience, and for the Beautiful the taste. Each of these three is based upon the necessary laws of action to which the soul, like any other substance, is subject.").

61. Kant could have been influenced by Riedel in the three-partition theory of the mind. This influence could have been direct or indirect (through Feder, perhaps). In any case, Riedel's theory is much more clear-cut on this subject than those of Sulzer, Mendelssohn, or Tetens who are usually mentioned as Kant's sources. Furthermore, in Kant's theory of the faculties there is a place for three forms "common-sense," corresponding to theoretical reason, practical reason and judgment. See Chapter IX below.

by certain laws which may be said to constitute the respective faculties of *sensus communis* (the sense of truth), conscience (the sense of good and evil), and taste (the sense of beautiful and ugly).[62] This differentiation of the mind into three basic faculties was to play an important role in the subsequent developments of German philosophy. Riedel himself, however, did not contribute much more than the bare outlines, and his name was forgotten soon.[63]

None of the German philosophers discussed here, including Kant, can be understood apart from Wolffianism and Thomasianism or Crusianism. So much has to be granted to the metaphysical and/or ontological school of Kant interpretation. But, and this is important, Wolff and Crusius are not *the* sources of Kant's criticism. Kant's younger contemporaries, as well as Kant himself, cannot be properly understood without these predecessors. By being the first to turn their eyes to British sources and to re-evaluate the German philosophical tradition in this light, they set the stage for a new German tradition, culminating in the work of Kant.

Riedel may have been important, and Basedow very clearly was. For Kant aligned himself with the latter's educational goals and methods, and his religious persuasion was perhaps closer to that of Basedow than

62. But they are, for him, all laws of feeling, as Riedel makes very clear. See, for instance, *Theorie*, p. 7.

63. Riedel was quite successful in the beginning. Lessing noted, for instance, with reference to his *Theorie*, that "Riedel promises to become an excellent thinker; 'promises' insofar as he has already shown to be such a thinker in many respects" (Lessing, *Sämtliche Schriften*, ed. Lachmann and Muncker, 3rd ed., vol. 10, p. 250. Herder, however, did not like the *Theorie* at all and in his fourth *Kritisches Wäldchen* reacted violently against the faculty psychology proposed by Riedel.

Riedel was not so much an original thinker as an eclectic. And he made no secret of this. Indeed, he seems to ridicule not only himself, but also his contemporaries, when he describes his approach as: "il compilait, compilait, compilait," and "there are more foreign thoughts than my own," then going on to give a list of "the writers whose work [he] ha[s] pillaged mostly" (a list which includes Home and Gerard as well as the writers of the *Literaturbriefe*, but not Crusius, by the way). And he remarks playfully that "everyone may take back his own, if he wants to" (*Theorie*, p. 9). Chapter III "Of the Great and Sublime" is called a "compilation of Longin, Mendelssohn, Gerard and Home" (ibid., p. 37). His reviewers took advantage of these remarks, and this is perhaps the reason why he left them out in the second edition (according to Wize, *Friedrich Riedel und seine Ästhetik*, p. 2n. I have only seen the first edition.) But the damage was done, and only now is the importance of his work seen again. Thus Rita Teras notes quite correctly in *Wilhelm Heinses Ästhetik* (München, 1972), p. 28 that "the two works of Riedel offered without doubt the most advanced ideas in aesthetic theory at the time of their appearance."

has been realized so far. His critical philosophy and Basedow's educational policies have a certain affinity that deserves to be investigated further.

However, there is an even richer field of investigation, namely, that of Kant's *early* relation to the German philosophers discussed here only from a rather limited perspective. It really comes quite close to being scandalous that these "popular philosophers," these "moderate sceptics," or "indifferentists," as Kant called them, are not merely neglected, but almost completely *disregarded* today. For to understand Kant's metaphysical intentions and motives without them is impossible. But that is exactly what the majority of Kant scholars seems to continue to attempt.[64]

64. It may well be that times are already changing. Kurt Röttger's "J. G. H. Feder—Beitrag zu einer Verhinderungsgeschichte eines deutschen Empirismus," and Walther Ch. Zimmerli's "'Schwere Rüstung' des Dogmatismus und 'anwendbare Eklektik,'" to name two exemplary papers, promise such a change.

Bibliography of Works Cited

PRIMARY SOURCES

Basedow, Bernhard. *Philalethie oder neue Aussichten in die Wahrheiten und Religion der Vernunft* 2 vols. Altona, 1764. Reviews: *Briefe die neueste Literatur betreffend* 22 (1765): letters 300 and 301.
— *Theoretisches System der gesunden Vernunft.* Altona, 1765.
  Reviews: *Allgemeine deutsche Bibliothek* 3 (1766): 69.
— *Elementarwerk.* 3 vols. Dessau and Leipzig, 1774.
Beattie, James. *An Essay on the Nature and Immutability of Truth in Opposition to Sophistry and Scepticism.* Edinburgh, 1770.
  Reviews: *Göttingische Anzeigen von gelehrten Sachen,* 1771, number 12 (28 January): 91–96.
  Bibliotheque des sciences et des beaux arts xxx (April, May, June, 1771): 429–31; xxvii (January, February, March, 1772): 110–46; (April, May, June, 1772): 444–64; (July, August, September, 1772): 1–22.
— *Versuch über die Natur und Unveränderlichkeit der Wahrheit im Gegensatz der Klügeley und Zweifelsucht. Aus dem Englischen.* Kopenhagen und Leipzig, 1772.
  Reviews: *Frankfurter gelehrte Anzeigen* lxxxiv (21 October 1772): 665–69; lxxxv (23 October 1772): 673–77.
  Allgemeine deutsche Bibliothek. Supplement to vols. 13–24 in 3 vols., vol. I (1776): 497–503.
— *An Essay on the Nature and Immutability of Truth in Opposition to Sophistry and Scepticism.* Reprint of the first edition, Edinburgh, 1770. Beattie, James. *The Philosophical Works.* Vol. 1. Edited by F. O. Wolf. Stuttgart and Bad Canstatt, 1973.
— *An Essay on the Nature and Immutability of Truth in Opposition to Sophistry and Scepticism; Poetry and Music, as they Affect the Mind; on Laughter, on Ludicrous Composition; on the Utility of Classical Learning.* 2 vols. Edinburgh, 1776.

Reviews: *Brittisches Museum für die Deutschen* 1 (1777): 63–68.
Musikalisch-Kritische Bibliothek 2 (1778) 341–55.
– *Neue philosophische Versuche.* 2 vols. Edited by Christoph Meiners. Leipzig, 1779.
Reviews: *Altonaischer gelehrter Mercurius.* 3. Stück, 3 February 1780, pp. 28–32.
– *Dissertations Moral and Critical.* London, 1783.
Reviews: *Neue Bibliothek der schönen Wissenschaften und der freyen Künste* xxix (1783) 182–84.
Göttingische Anzeigen 1784, number 165 (14 October): 1649–54.
– "Über das Erhabene" (Translation of one chapter of the *Dissertation*, author indicated with "J.B."). *Magazin für die Naturgeschichte des Menschen* 1 (1788): 35–70.
– *Recueil de pieces intéressantes concernant les antiquités, les beaux-arts, les belles lettres, la philosophie, traduites de different langues.* 2 vols. Paris and The Hague, 1787. Contains the French translation of two chapters by Beattie concerning the sublime and the difference of fable and romance from the *Dissertations* [?].
Reviews: *Journal Encyclopédique,* July 1788, pp. 245–67.
– *Moralische und kritische Abhandlungen. 3 vols. Translated by Carl Grosse. Göttingen, 1789–90.*
Reviews: Göttingische Anzeigen, 1789, number 143 (5 September) 1433–34; 1791, number 12 (20 January): 120.
Allgemeine Literatur-Zeitung, October 1789, pp. 6–8; October 1790, p. 14.
Allgemeine deutsche Bibliothek xciv (1790): 467–70; ci (1791): 136–37.
– *The Theory of Language.* London, 1788.
Reviews: *Allgemeine Literatur-Zeitung,* July 1788, pp. 286–88.
– "Etwas über die Sprache" (Extract from *The Theory of Language*), *Magazin für die Naturgeschichte des Menschen* iii, i (1790): 1–53.
– *Elements of Moral Science.* Vol. I. Edinburgh, 1790.
Reviews: *Intelligenzblatt der Allgemeinen Literatur-Zeitung,* 20 November 1790, p. 1268.
Allgemeine Literatur-Zeitung, January 1792, pp. 63–64.
– *Grundlinien der Psychologie, natürlichen Theologie, Moralphilosophie und Logik.* Vol. 1. Translated by Karl Philipp Moritz. Berlin, 1790.
Reviews: *Allgemeine deutsche Bibliothek* civ (1791): 220–23.
Brucker, Johann Jakob. *Historia critical philosophiae a mundi incunabilis ad nostram aetatem agitur.* 5 vols. Leipzig 1742–44.
Budde, Johann Franciscus. *Historische und theologische Einleitung in die vornehmsten Religionsstreitigkeiten.* Edited by Johann Georg Walch. Jena, 1724.
Buhle, Johann Gottlieb. *Geschichte der neuern Philosophie seit der Epoche der Wiederherstellung der Wissenschaften.* 6 vols. Göttingen, 1800–1805.
Campbell, George. *Die Philosophie der Rhetorik.* Translated by Dr. D. Jenisch. Berlin, 1791.
Reviews: *Allgemeine deutsche Bibliothek* cxi (1792): 98–101.

Crusius, Christian August. *Die philosophischen Hauptwerke*. 3 vols. Edited by Giorgio Tonelli. Hildesheim: Georg Olms, 1969.

– *Entwurf der nothwendigen Vernunftwahrheiten*. Leipzig, 1745.

– *Dissertationis de corruptelis intellectus a voluntate penditibus*. Lipsius, 1740.

Eberhard, Johann August. *Allgemeine Theorie des Denkens und Empfindens*. Berlin, 1776 (2nd ed. Berlin, 1786).

– *Von dem Begriff der Philosophie und ihren Theilen*. Berlin, 1778.

– *Vermischte Schriften*. Halle, 1784.

– *Neue vermischte Schriften*. Halle, 1788.

– ed. *Philosophisches Magazin*. 4 vols. Halle, 1788–92.

– *Handbuch der Ästhetik für gebildete Leser aller Stände*. 4 vols. Halle, 1807–20.

Eberstein, Wilhelm L. G. von. *Versuch einer Geschichte der Logik und Metaphysik bey den Deutschen von Leibniz bis auf die gegenwärtige Zeit*. 2 vols. Halle, 1794–99.

Feder, Johann Georg Heinrich. *Logik und Metaphysik nebst der philosophischen Geschichte im Grundrisse*. 2nd ed. Göttingen und Gotha, 1770.

– *Institutionis logicae et metaphysicae*. Göttingen, 1781.

– *Untersuchungen über den menschlichen Willen, dessen Naturtriebe, Veränderlichkeit, Verhältnisse zur Tugend und Glückseligkeit und die Grundregeln, die menschlichen Gemüther zu erkennen und regieren*. 4 vols. Göttingen and Lemgo, 1779–1793.

– *Über den Raum und die Caussalität zur Prüfung der Kantschen Philosophie*. Göttingen, 1787.

– ed. *Philosophische Bibliothek*. 4 vols. Göttingen, 1788–93.

– *J. G. H. Feder's Leben, Natur und Grundsätze*. Edited by K. A. L. Feder, Leipzig, Hannover and Darmstadt, 1825.

Ferguson, Adam. *Institutes of Moral Philosophy*. Edinburgh, 1769.

– *Grundsätze der Moralphilosophie, übersetzt und mit einigen Anmerkungen versehen von Christian Garve*. Leipzig, 1772.

Fries, Jakob Friedrich. *Tradition, Mysticismus und gesunde Logik, oder über die Geschichte der Philosophie. Studien* IV. Edited by Carl Daub and Friedrich Kreuzer. Heidelberg, 1811.

Garve, Christian. *Legendorum philosophorum veterum. Praecepta nonnulla et exemplum*. Leipzig, 1770.

Reviews: *Göttingische Anzeigen*, 1771 (8 November).

Reprint: *Beyträge zur Geschichte der Philosophie*. Edited by Gustav Fülleborn. Stück xi and xii, Jena, 1799, pp. 132–96.

– *Eigene Betrachtungen über die allgemeinsten Grundsätze der Sittenlehre*. Breslau, 1798.

– *Briefe an Christian Weisse und einige andere Freunde*. Theil 1.2. Breslau, 1803.

– *Popularphilosophische Schriften über literarische, aesthetische und gesellschaftliche Gegenstände*. 2 vols. Edited by Kurt Wölfel. Stuttgart 1974.

Goethe, Johann Wolfgang von. *Sämtliche Werke. Jubiläumsausgabe in 40 Bänden*. 40 vols. Edited by Eduard von der Hellen. Stuttgart, 1902–12.

Hamann, Johann Georg. *Schriften*. 8 vols. Edited by Friedrich Roth and Gustav Adolf Wiener. Berlin and Leipzig. 1821–43.

- *Sämtliche Werke*. 6 vols. Edited by Josef Nadler. Vienna: Herder, 1949–57.
- *Briefwechsel*. 8 vols. Edited by Walther Ziesemer and Arthur Henkel. Wiesbaden: Insel Verlag, 1955–75.
- *Hamann's Socratic Memorabilia, A Translation and Commentary*. Translated with commentary by James O'Flaherty. Baltimore: Johns Hopkins University Press, 1967.
- *Sokratische Denkwurdigkeiten/Aesthetica in nuce*. Edited by Sven Aage Jorgensen. Stuttgart: Reclam Verlag, 1968.
Hausius, K. Gottlob. *Materialien zur Geschichte der Critischen Philosophie*. 3 vols. Leipzig, 1793.
Herder, Johann Gottfried. *Verstand und Erfahrung. Vernunft und Sprache. Eine Metakritik zur Kritik der reinen Vernunft*. 2 vols. Leipzig, 1799.
- *Sämtliche Werke*. 33 vols. Edited by Bernhard Suphan. Hildesheim, 1967 (reprographic reprint of the edition Berlin, 1877–1913).
- *Essay on the Origin of Language*. In *On the Origin of Language: Rousseau and Herder*. Translated by J. H. Moran and Alexander Gode. New York, 1966.
Hissmann, Michael. *Anleitung zur Kenntnis der auserlesenen Literatur in allen Theilen der Philosophie*. Göttingen and Lemgo, 1778.
Hoffmann, Adolf Friedrich. *Vernunft-Lehre, darinnen die Kennzeichen des Wahren und Falschen aus den Gesetzen des Verstandes hergeleitet werden*. Leipzig, 1737.
Humboldt, Wilhelm von. *Gesammelte Schriften*. 15 vols. Edited by Albert Leitzmann. Berlin, 1903–18.
Hume, David. *Enquiries concerning Human Understanding and concerning the Principles of Morals*. Edited by L.A. Selby-Bigge. Oxford: Clarendon Press, 1970.
- *Philosophische Versuche über die menschliche Erkenntnis*. Ed. Johann Georg Sulzer. Hamburg und Leipzig, 1755.
- *Gespräche über die natürliche Religion von David Hume. Nach der zwoten Englischen Ausgabe. Nebst einem Gespräch über den Atheismus von Ernst Platner*. Leipzig, 1781.
  Reviews: *Göttingische Anzeigen*, 1782, number 18 (11 February): 143f.
Irwing, Karl Franz von. *Erfahrungen und Untersuchungen über den Menschen*. Berlin, 1772 (2nd and enlarged edition in 4 vols. Berlin, 1777–85).
Jacobi, Friedrich Heinrich. *Werke*. 6 vols. Edited by Friedrich Roth and Friedrich Köppen. Leipzig, 1812–25.
- *David Hume über den Glauben oder Idealismus und Realismus* (1787 edition with the Preface of the 1815 edition). Edited by Hamilton Beck. New York and London: Garland Publishing Company, 1983.
- *Friedrich Heinrich Jacobis Briefe an Friedrich Bouterwek*. Edited by W. Meyer. Göttingen, 1868.
- *Friedrich Heinrich Jacobis auserlesener Briefwechsel*. 2 vols. Edited by Friedrich Roth. Leipzig, 1825–1827.

Jacobi, Johann Friedrich. *Nähere Entdeckung eines neuen Lehrgebäudes der Religion nebst einer Prüfung desselben.* Zell, 1773.
Reviews: *Allgemeine deutsche Bibliothek* 25, 1 (1775): 75–96.
Jakob, Heinrich. *Prüfung der Mendelssohnschen Morgenstunden oder aller spekulativen Beweise für das Dasein Gottes.* Leipzig, 1786.
Kant, Immanuel. *Kants Gesammelte Schriften.* Published by the Preussische Akademie der Wissenschaften. Vols. 1–29f. Berlin: Walter de Gruyter, 1902—.
– *Vorlesungen über Enzyklopädie und Logik.* Vol. 1: *Vorlesungen über Philosophische Enzyklopädie.* Edited by Gerhard Lehmann. Berlin: Akademie Verlag, 1961.
– *Werke.* 6 vols. Edited by Wilhelm Weischedel. Darmstadt: Wissenschaftliche Buchgemeinschaft, 1966.
– *Selected Pre-Critical Writings and Correspondence with Beck.* Translated and introduced by G.B. Kerferd and D.E. Walford. Manchester and New York: Manchester University Press, 1968.
– *Critique of Pure Reason.* Translated by Norman Kemp Smith. New York and Toronto: Macmillan and Co., 1965.
– *Prolegomena to Any Future Metaphysics.* Edited by Lewis White Beck. Indianapolis, New York and Kansas City: Bobbs-Merrill Co., 1950.
– *Foundations of the Metaphysics of Morals.* Translated by Lewis White Beck. Indianapolis, New York and Kansas City: Bobbs-Merrill Co., 1959.
– *Critique of Practical Reason.* Translated by Lewis White Beck. Indianapolis, New York and Kansas City: Bobbs-Merrill Co., 1956.
– *Critique of Judgement.* Translated by James Creed Meredith. Oxford: Oxford University Press, 1952.
– *Kant, Philosophical Correspondence, 1759–1799.* Edited and translated by Arnulf Zweig. Chicago: University of Chicago Press, 1967.
Krug, Wilhelm Traugott. *Allgemeines Handwörterbuch der philosophischen Wissenschaften nebst ihrer Literatur und Geschichte.* 6 vols. 2nd ed. Leipzig, 1832–38.
Lessing, Gotthold Ephraim. *Sämtliche Schriften.* 23 vols. 3rd ed. by Lachmann and Muncker. Stuttgart, Leipzig, and Berlin, 1886–1924.
Lichtenberg, Johann Georg. *Schriften und Briefe.* 4 vols. and 2 vols. of commentary. Edited by Wolfgang Promies. München: Hanser Verlag, 1973—.
Lossius, Johann Christian. *Physische Ursachen des Wahren.* Gotha, 1774.
Reviews: *Göttingische Anzeigen*, 1775, number 62 (25 May): 525f.
– *Unterricht der gesunden Vernunft.* 2 vols. Gotha, 1776–77.
Reviews: *Göttingische Anzeigen*, 1777, number 54 (7 August): 751.
Meiners, Christoph. *Revision der Philosophie.* Göttingen, 1772.
– *Grundriss der Seelenlehre.* Lemgo, 1786.
– ed. *Philosophische Bibliothek.* 4 vols. Göttingen, 1788–1791.
Mellin, Samuel Albert. *Enzyklopädisches Wörterbuch der kritischen Philosophie.* 11 vols. Züllichau and Leipzig, 1797–1804.

Mendelssohn, Moses. *Gesammelte Schriften.* 7 vols. Edited by G. B. Mendelssohn. Leipzig, 1843–45.
– *Gesammelte Schriften. Jubiläumsausgabe.* 20 vols. Edited by I. Illbogen, J. Guttmann, E. Mittwoch. Continued by Alexander Altmann and others. Berlin, 1929—. (Now Stuttgart: Frommann and Holzboog) -*Schriften zur Philosophie, Aesthetik und Apologetik.* 2 vols. Edited by Moritz Brasch. Hildesheim, 1968.
– *Neuerschlossene Briefe an Friedrich Nicolai.* Edited by Alexander Altmann and Werner Vogel. Stuttgart: Frommann and Holzboog, 1973.
Newton, Sir Isaac. *Mathematical Principles of Natural Philosophy and his System of the World.* Translated by Andrew Motte. Edited by Florian Cajori. 2 vols. Berkeley, Los Angeles, London: University of California Press, 1974.
Oetinger, Friedrich Christoph. *Die Wahrheit des sensus communis oder des allgemeinen Sinnes nach dem Grundtext erklärten Sprüchen des Prediger Salomo.* 1753.
– *Inquisitio in sensum communem et rationem.* Tübingen, 1753. (Reprint, edited by Hans-Georg Gadamer. Stuttgart, 1964.)
Oswald, James. *An Appeal to Common Sense in Behalf of Religion.* 2 vols. Edinburgh, 1766, 1772.
Reviews: *Göttingische Anzeigen,* 1769, number 28 (6 March): 265–75; 1773, number 35 (22 March) 289–99, and number 44 (12 April), pp. 370f.
Bibliotheque des sciences et des beaux arts, April, May, June 1772, pp. 465–69.
– *Appelation an den gemeinen Menschenverstand zum Vortheil der Religion* 2 vols. Translated by F.E. Wilmsen, Leipzig, 1774.
Reviews: *Göttingische Anzeigen,* 1774, number 97 (13 August): 834–38; and 1775, number 8 (January 19), pp. 60f. *Allgemeine deutsche Bibliothek,* vol. 28, i (1776): 157–59.
Platner, Ernst. *Philosophische Aphorismen.* 2 vols. Leipzig, 1776, 1782.
– *Philosophische Aphorismen.* Vol. 1. 2nd ed. Leipzig, 1784.
– *Philosophische Aphorismen.* Vol. 1. 3rd completely revised ed. Leipzig, 1793.
– *Philosophische Aphorismen.* Vol. 2. 2nd ed. Leipzig 1800. Reviews: *Göttingische Anzeigen,* 1777, number 20 (15 February): 153ff.
– *Gespräche über die natürliche Religion von David Hume. Nach der zwoten Ausgabe. Nebst einem Gespräch über den Atheismus von Ernst Platner.* Leipzig, 1781. (The translator of this work is said to be Schreiter. Platner is only the editor.)
Priestley, Joseph. *An Examination of Dr. Reid's Inquiry into the Human Mind, Dr. Beattie's Essay on the Nature and Immutability of Truth, and Dr. Oswald's Appeal to Common Sense.* London, 1775.
Reviews: *Göttingische Anzeigen,* 1775, number 92 (17 August): 777–83.
Reid, Thomas. *An Inquiry into the Human Mind on the Principles of Common Sense.* Edinburgh, 1764.
Reviews: *Neue Zeitungen von gelehrten Sachen,* 1764 (14 June): 377–78.
Journal Encyclopédique, 1764 (December): 29–41.
Bibliotheque des sciences et des beaux arts 38 (July, August, September, 1767): 1–26.

– *Recherches sur l'entendement humain d'aprés les principes du sens commun.* Amsterdam, 1768.
Reviews: *Journal Encyclopédique*, 1768 (November): 29–37.
– *Untersuchungen über den menschlichen Verstand, nach den Grundsätzen des gemeinen Menschenverstandes.* Leipzig, 1782.
Reviews: *Allgemeine deutsche Bibliothek* lii (1783):417.
– *Essays on the Intellectual Powers of Man.* Edinburgh, 1785.
Reviews: *Journal Encyclopédique*, 1786, part ii, pp. 3–7.
Allgemeine Literatur-Zeitung, 1786 (April): 181–83.
Göttingische Anzeigen, 1787, number 63 (21 April): 625–32.
Philosophische Bibliothek 1 (1788): 43–62.
– "Versuch über den Geschmack" (German translation of Chapter VIII of *Essays on the Intellectual Powers*), in *Neue Bibliothek der schönen Wissenschaften und der freyen Künste* 31 (1786): 183–96.
– *Essays on the Active Powers of the Human Mind.* Edinburgh, 1788.
Reviews: *Philosophische Bibliothek* 2 (1789): 83–118.
Journal Encyclopédique, 1791, part 1, pp. 3–18.
– *Philosophical Works.* 2 vols. Edited by W. Hamilton, with an Introduction by Harry M. Bracken. Hildesheim: Georg Olms, 1967.
– *An Inquiry into the Human Mind on the Principles of Common Sense.* Edited by Timothy Duggan. Chicago and London: University of Chicago Press, 1970.
– *Essays on the Intellectual Powers of Man.* Edited by Baruch Brody. Cambridge, Mass. and London, England: MIT Press, 1969.
– *Essays on the Active Powers of the Human Mind.* Edited by Baruch Brody. Cambridge, Mass. and London, England, MIT Press, 1969.
Reinhold, Karl Leonhard. *Versuch einer neuen Theorie des menschlichen Vorstellungsvermögens.* Prag and Jena, 1789.
Resewitz, Friedrich Gabriel. *Erziehung des Bürgers zum Gebrauch des gesunden Verstandes.* 1773.
Reviews: *Allgemeine deutsche Bibliothek* 22, i (1774): 325ff.
Riedel, Friedrich Justus. *Theorie der schönen Künste und Wissenschaften. Ein Auszug aus den Werken verschiedener Schriftsteller.* Jena, 1767.
– *Briefe über das Publikum.* Jena, 1768.
Rink, Friedrich Theodor. *Ansichten aus Kant's Leben.* Königsberg, 1805.
Schopenhauer, Arthur. *Die Welt als Wille und Vorstellung.* 2 vols. Berlin and Wien, 1924.
Schubert, Friedrich Wilhelm. *Immanuel Kant's Biographie zum grossen Theil nach handschriftlichen Nachrichten.* Leipzig, 1842. (As vol. 2, part 2 of Immanuel Kant, *Sämtliche Werke*, edited by Karl Rosenkranz and Friedrich Wilhelm Schubert.)
Schulze, Gottlieb Ernst. *Kritik der theoretischen Philosophie.* 2 vols. Hamburg, 1801.
Schulze, Johann. *Prüfung der Kantischen Critik der reinen Vernunft.* 2 vols. Königsberg, 1789 and 1792.
Reviews: *Philosophische Bibliothek* 4 (1791), pp. 20f.

Storchenau, G. von. *Grundsätze der Logik.* Augsburg, 1774. Reviews: *Allgemeine deutsche Bibliothek* 25, ii (1775): 505–08.

Suabedissen, David Theodor. *Resultate der philosophischen Forschungen über die Natur der menschlichen Erkenntnis von Plato bis Kant.* Warburg, 1805.

Tennemann, Wilhelm Gottlieb. *Geschichte der Philosophie.* 11 vols. Leipzig, 1798–1819.

Tetens, Johann Nicolaus. *Über die allgemeine speculativische Philosophie.* Bützow and Wismar, 1775.

– *Philosophische Versuche über die menschliche Natur und ihre Entwicklung.* 2 vols. Leipzig, 1776–77.

– *Über die allgemeine speculativische Philosophie/Philosophische Versuche über die menschliche Natur und ihre Entwicklung.* Vol. 1. Edited by Wilhelm Uebele. Neudrucke seltener philosophischer Werke. Hrsg. von der Kantgesellschaft. Vol. 4. Berlin, 1913.

Tiedemann, Dietrich. *Untersuchungen über den Menschen.* 3 vols. Leipzig, 1777–78.
Reviews: *Erfurtische gelehrte Zeitungen,* 1777 (22 January): 57–62.

– *Handbuch der Psychologie.* Edited and supplied with a biographical and bibliographical account by Ludwig Wachler. Leipzig, 1804.

Tittel, Gottlob August. *Erläuterungen der theoretischen und praktischen Philosophie nach Feders Ordnung.* 6 vols. Frankfurt/Main, 1783–94.

Thomasius, Christian. *Einleitung zur Vernunftlehre.* Halle 1691. (Reprint edited by W. Schneiders, Hildesheim: Georg Olms, 1968).

– *Ausübung der Vernunftlehre,* Halle, 1691. (Reprint edited by W. Schneiders, Hildesheim: Georg Olms, 1968).

Ulrich, Johann August Heinrich. *Erster Umriss einer Einleitung zu den philosophischen Wissenschaften.* 2 vols. Jena, 1772, 1776.
Reviews: *Göttingische Anzeigen,* 1772, number 125 (17 October): 1070.

Vico, Giambattista B. *On the Study Methods of our Time.* Translated by Elio Gianturico. Indianapolis, New York and Kansas City: Bobbs Merrill Co., 1965.

Wolff, Christian. *Gesammelte Werke.* Edited by J. Ecole, J.E. Hofmann, M. Thomann and W. H. Arndt. 1. Abteilung: Deutsche Schriften. 1. Band: *Vernünftige Gedanken von den Kräften des menschlichen Verstandes und ihrem richtigen Gebrauche in Erkenntnis der Wahrheit.* Edited by W. H. Arndt. Hildesheim: Georg Olms, 1965.

– *Gesammelte Werke.* 2. Abteilung: Lateinische Schriften. 8. Band: *Philosophia prima sive ontologia.* Edited by Jean Ecole. Hildesheim: Georg Olms, 1962.

– *Gesammelte Werke.* 2. Abteilung: Lateinische Schriften. 12. Band: *Philosophia moralis sive ethica.* Hildesheim and New York: Georg Olms 1970.

SECONDARY SOURCES

Alexander, W. M. *Johann Georg Hamann: Philosophy and Faith.* The Hague: Nijhoff, 1966.

Allison, Henry E. *The Kant-Eberhard Controversy.* Baltimore and London: Johns Hopkins University Press, 1973.
- *Kant's Transcendental Idealism. An Interpretation and Defense.* New Haven and London: Yale University Press, 1983.
Altmann, Alexander. *Moses Mendelssohns Frühschriften zur Metaphysik.* Tübingen, 1969.
- *Moses Mendelssohn; A Biographical Study.* Alabama: University of Alabama Press, 1973.
Ameriks, Karl. "Kant's Transcendental Deduction as a Regressive Argument," *Kant-Studien* 69 (1978) 273–87.
Arendt, Hannah. *The Life of the Mind.* 2 vols. Edited by Mary McCarthy. London and New York: Harcourt, Brace, Jovanovich, 1977.
Aster, Ernst von. *Geschichte der neueren Erkenntnistheorie.* Berlin and Leipzig, 1921.
Barnouw, Jeffrey. "The Philosophical Achievement and Historical Significance of Johann Nicolaus Tetens." *Studies in Eighteenth-Century Culture.* Vol. 9. Edited by Roseann Runte. Madison: University of Wisconsin Press, 1979.
Bärthlein, K. "Zur Lehre der 'recta ratio' in der Geschichte der Ethik von der Stoa bis zu Christian Wolff," *Kant-Studien* 56 (1965): 125–55.
Bäumler, Alfred. *Das Irrationalitätsproblem in der Ästhetik des 18. Jahrhunderts bis zur Kritik der Urteilskraft.* Darmstadt: Wissenschaftliche Buchgesellschaft, 1967. (Reprographic reprint of the 1st. ed., Halle, 1923.)
Baum, Günther. *Vernunft und Erkenntnis. Die Philosophie F.H. Jacobis.* Bonn, 1969.
- "K.L. Reinholds Elementarphilosophie und die Idee des transzendentalen Idealismus." *Kant-Studien* 64 (1973): 213–30.
Barker, S. F. and Beauchamp, T., ed. *Thomas Reid: Critical Interpretations.* Philosophical Monographs. Philadelphia, 1976.
Beanblossom, Ronald E. Introduction. *Thomas Reid's Inquiry and Essays.* Edited by Ronald E. Beanblossom and Keith Lehrer. Indianapolis: Hackett Publishing Co., 1983.
Beck, Hamilton. Introduction to Friedrich Heinrich Jacobi, *David Hume über den Glauben oder Idealismus und Realismus (1787).* Edited by Hamilton Beck. New York and London: Garland Publishing, 1983.
- "Kant and the Novel. A Study of the Examination Scene in Hippel's 'Lebensläufe nach aufsteigender Linie.'" *Kant-Studien* 74 (1983): 271–301.
Beck, Lewis White. *Studies in the Philosophy of Kant.* Indianapolis, New York, Kansas City: Bobbs Merrill Publishing Co., 1965.
- *Early German Philosophy. Kant and his Predecessors.* Cambridge, Mass. Belknap Press, 1969.
- *Essays on Kant and Hume.* New Haven and London: Yale University Press, 1978.
Berlin, Isaiah. *Vico and Herder.* London: Chatto and Windus, 1980.
- *Against the Current.* Edited by Henry Hardy. New York, 1980.
Bernstein, Richard J. "Why Hegel Now?" *The Review of Metaphysics* 31 (1977): 217–74.

Blassneck, M. *Frankreich als Vermittler englisch-deutscher Einflusse im 17. und 18. Jahrhundert*. Bochum-Langendreer, 1934.

Bloch, Ernst. *Christian Thomasius, ein deutscher Gelehrter ohne Misere*. Frankfurt/Main: Suhrkamp, 1967.

Bollnow, F. O. *Die Lebensphilosophie F. H. Jacobis*. Stuttgart, 1933 (2nd unchanged ed. with a new Foreword, 1966).

Boutroux, Emil. "De l'influence de la philosophie ecossaise sur la philosophie francaise." *Transactions of the Franco-Scottish Society*. Edinburgh, pp. 16–36. (Reprinted in Emil Boutroux, *Etudes d'histoire de la philosophie moderne*. Paris, 1846–47.)

Bracken, Harry M. *The Early Reception of Berkeley's Immaterialism, 1710–1733*. Revised ed. The Hague: 1965.

– "Thomas Reid; A Philosopher of Un-Common Sense." Introduction to Thomas Reid, *Philosophical Works*. With notes and supplementary dissertations by Sir William Hamilton. 2 vols. Hildesheim: Georg Olms, 1967.

– *Berkeley*. Toronto, 1974.

Brentano, Franz. *Versuch über die Erkenntnis*. Edited by A. Kastil, F. Mayer Hildebrand. Hamburg: Meiners, 1970.

– "Was an Reid zu loben." *Grazer philosophische Studien* 1 (1975): 1–17.

Brody, Baruch. Introduction to Thomas Reid, *Essays on the Intellectual Powers of Man*. Cambridge, Mass., London, England: MIT Press, 1969.

– "Reid and Hamilton on Perception." *The Monist* 55 (1971): 423–41.

– "Hume, Reid and Kant on Causality." *Thomas Reid: Critical Interpretations* (ed. Barker and Beauchamp), pp. 8–13.

Cassirer, Ernst. *The Philosophy of the Enlightenment*. Princeton, N.J.: Princeton University Press, 1951.

– *Das Erkenntnisproblem in der Philosophie und Wissenschaft der neueren Zeit*. Vol. 2. Berlin, 1907.

Clark, Robert T. *Herder: His Life and Thought*. Los Angeles and Berkeley, 1955.

Collingwood, R. G. *The Idea of History*. Oxford: Oxford University Press, 1946.

Crawford, Donald W. *Kant's Aesthetic Theory*. Madison: University of Wisconsin Press, 1974.

Cummins, Phillip D. "Reid's Realism." *Journal of the History of Philosophy* 12 (1974) 317–41.

Daniels, Norman. *Thomas Reid's Inquiry: The Geometry of Visibles and the Case for Realism*. New York: Burt Franklin, 1974.

– "On Having Concepts 'By our Constitution.'" *Thomas Reid: Critical Interpretations* (ed. Barker and Beauchamp), pp. 35–43.

Deleuze, Gilles. *Kant's Critical Philosophy. The Doctrine of the Faculties*. Translated by Hugh Tomlinson and Barbara Habberjam. Minneapolis: University of Minnesota Press, 1983.

Dessoir, Max. *Geschichte der neueren Psychologie*. 2nd ed. Berlin, 1902.

– "Des Johann Nicolaus Tetens Stellung in der Geschichte der Philosophie." *Vierteljahresschrift für wissenschaftliche Philosophie* 16 (1982): 355–68.

Düsing, Klaus. Review of G. Baum's *Vernunft und Erkenntnis.*" *Philosophische Rundschau* 18 (1971): 105–16.

Duggan, Timothy. "Thomas Reid's Theory of Sensation." *Philosophical Review* 69 (1970): 90–100.

– Introduction to Thomas Reid. *An Inquiry into the Human Mind on the Principles of Common Sense.* Edited by Timothy Duggan. Chicago and London: The University of Chicago Press, 1970. *Encyclopedia of Philosophy.* Edited by Paul Edwards (1967), s.v.

– "Tetens, Johann Nicolaus." By Giorgio Tonelli.

– "Beattie, James." By Elmer Sprague.

Erämtsae, E. *Englische Lehnpragungen in der deutschen Empfindsamkeit des 18. Jahrhunderts.* Helsinki, 1955.

– *Adam Smith als Mittler englisch-deutscher Spracheinflusse.* Helsinki, 1961.

Erdmann, Benno. *Martin Knutzen und seine Zeit. Ein Beitrag zur Geschichte der Wolfischen Schule und insbesondere der Entwicklungsgeschichte Kants.* Leipzig, 1876.

– "Kant und Hume um 1762." *Archiv für Geschichte der Philosophie* 1 (1877–8), pp. 62–77, 216–230.

Festner. *Crusius als Metaphysiker.* Halle, 1892.

Finger, Otto. *Von der Materialität der Seele, Beitrag zur Geschichte des Materialismus im Deutschland der 2. Hälfte des XVIII. Jahrhunderts.* Berlin (Ost), 1961.

Flajole, Edward S. "Lessing's Retrieval of Lost Truths." *Proceedings of the Modern Language Association* 74 (1959): 52–66.

Forster, Robert, and Forster, Elborg. eds. *European Society in the Eighteenth Century.* New York, Evanston, and London: Harper and Row, 1969.

Fullenwider, Henry W. *Friedrich Christoph Oetingers Wirkung auf Literatur und Philosophie seiner Zeitgenossen.* Göppingen, 1975.

Funke, Gerhard. "Der Weg zur ontologischen Kantinterpretation." *Kant–Studien* 62 (1971): 364–68.

Gadamer, Hans-Georg. "Oetinger als Philosoph." *Kleine Schriften.* Vol. 3: *Idee und Sprache.* Tübingen: J. C. B. Mohr (Paul Siebeck), 1972.

– *Wahrheit und Methode.* 4th ed. Tübingen: J.C.B. Mohr (Paul Siebeck), 1975.

– Einleitung to Friedrich Christoph Oetinger, *Inquisitio in sensum communem et rationem.* Stuttgart, 1964.

Ganz, P. F. *Der Einfluss des Englischen auf den deutschen Wortschatz.* Berlin, 1957.

Gay, Peter. *The Enlightenment.* 2 vols. London, 1967, 1971.

George, Rolf. "Kant's Theory of Perception." *Proceedings of the Ottawa Congress on Kant in the Anglo-American and Continental Traditions, Held October 10–14, 1974.* Edited by Pierre Laberge, Francois Duchesneau and Brian F. Mortrisey. Ottawa: University of Ottawa Press, 1976.

"Kant's Sensationism," *Synthese* 47 (1981): 229–55.

Golz, A. T. *T. Wizenmann, der Freund F.H. Jacobis, in Mitteilungen aus seinem Briefwechsel und handschriftlichen Nachlass, wie aus Zeugnissen von Zeitgenossen.* Gotha, 1859.

Gram, Moltke S., ed. *Kant: Disputed Questions.* Chicago: Quadrangle Books, 1967.

Grassi, Ernesto. "Vorrang des Gemeinsinns und der Logik der Phantasie." *Zeitschrift fur philosophische Forschung* 30 (1976): 491–509.

Grave, Selwyn A. *Scottish Philosophy of Common Sense.* Oxford: Oxford University Press, 1960.

– "The 'Theory of Ideas.'" in *Thomas Reid: Critical Interpretations* (ed. Barker and Beauchamp), pp. 55–61.

Grenzmann, Wilhelm. *Georg Christoph Lichtenberg.* Leipzig, 1939.

Groos, Karl. "Hat Kant Hume's *Treatise* gelesen?" *Kant-Studien* 5 (1901): 177–181.

Guyer, Paul. *Kant and the Claims of Taste.* Cambridge, Mass. and London: Harvard University Press, 1979.

Habermas, Jürgen. *Erkenntnis und Interesse.* Frankfurt/Main: Suhrkamp, 1973.

Hammacher, Klaus. *Die Philosophie Friedrich Heinrich Jacobis.* München, 1969.

– Review of G. Baum's *Vernunft und Erkenntnis* in *Zeitschrift für philosophische Forschung* 24 (1970): 625–33.

Harris, H. S. *Hegel's Development: Toward the Sunlight, 1770–1801.* Oxford: Oxford University Press, 1972.

– *Hegel's Development: Night Thoughts (Jena 1801–1806).* Oxford: Oxford University Press, 1983.

Hartmann, Eduard von. *Geschichte der Metaphysik.* 2 vols. 1899–1900. (Reprographic reprint, Darmstadt: Wissenschaftliche Buchgesellschaft, 1969).

Hauck, Wilhelm-Albert. *Das Geheimnis des Lebens. Naturanschauung und Gottesauffassung Friedrich Christoph Oetingers.* Heidelberg, 1947.

Haym, Rudolf. *Herder nach seinem Leben und Werken.* 2vols. 1880–85.

Heidemann, Ingeborg. "Metaphysikgeschichte und Kantinterpretation." *Kant-Studien* 67 (1976): 291–312.

Heimsoeth, Heinz. *Metaphysik und Kritik bei Chr. A. Crusius. Ein Beitrag zur ontologischen Vorgeschichte der Kritik der reinen Vernunft im 18. Jahrhundert.* Berlin, 1926.

– *Metaphysik der Neuzeit.* Darmstadt: Wissenschaftliche Buchgesellschaft, 1967 (unchanged reprint of the ed. München and Berlin, 1934).

– *Studien zur Philosophie Immanuel Kants.* Vol. 1. Köln, 1956 (2nd ed., Bonn, 1971).

– *Studien zur Philosophie Immanuel Kants.* Vol. 2. Bonn, 1970.

– *Transzendentale Dialektik.* 4 vols. Berlin: Walter de Gruyter & Co., 1966–1971.

Heinsius, Wilhelm. *Allgemeines Bücherlexikon oder vollständiges Verzeichnis der von 1700–1810 erschienen Bücher.* 4 vols. Leipzig, 1812—.

Henrich, Dieter. "Hutcheson und Kant." *Kant-Studien* 49 (1957–1958): 49–69.

– "Über Kants früheste Ethik." *Kant-Studien* 54 (1963): 404–31.

Henry, J. "Le traditionalisme et l'ontologisme a Universite de Louvain, 1835–1865." *Annales de l'institut superieur de philosophie* 5 (1924).

Herpel, Otto. *Friedrich Christoph Oetinger. Die heilige Philosophie.* München, 1923.

Herzog, Johannes. *Friedrich Christoph Oetinger. Ein Lebens- und Charakterbild.* Stuttgart, 1902.

Hettner, H. *Geschichte der deutschen Literatur im 18. Jahrhundert.* 3 vols. Leipzig, 1928.

Hinske, Norbert. "Kant's Begriff der Antinomie und die Etappen seiner Ausarbeitung." *Kant-Studien* 55 (1966): 485–96.

Hoeveler, J. D., Jr. *James McCosh and the Scottish Intellectual Tradition: From Glasgow to Princeton.* Princeton: Princeton University Press, 1981.

Höhn, G. "Die sensualistischen Missverständnisse der Jacobischen Kant-Kritik, zu G. Baums *Vernunft und Erkenntnis.*" *Kant-Studien* 62 (1971): 113–20.

Holzhey, Helmut. *Kants Erfahrungsbegriff.* Basel and Stuttgart, 1970.

Immendorfer. *Johann Georg Hamann und seine Bücherei.* Königsberg and Berlin, pp. 245–256.

Immerwahr, John. "The Development of Reid's Realism." *The Monist* 61 (1978): 245–56.

Janitsch, Julius. *Kants Urteile über Berkeley.* Strassburg, 1879.

Jones, O'McKendree. *Empiricism and Intuitionism in Reid's Common Sense Philosophy.* Princeton, N. J., 1927.

Johnston, G. A. *Selections from the Scottish Philosophy of Common Sense.* Chicago, 1915.

Justin, Gale D. "Re-relating Kant and Berkeley." *Kant-Studien* 68 (1977): 77–79.

Kayser, Christian Gottlob. *Vollständiges Bücherlexicon, enthaltend alle von 1750 bis zum Ende des Jahres 1831 in Deutschland und angrenzenden Ländern gedruckte Bücher.* 6 vols. Leipzig, 1834—.

Kayserling, Meyer. *Moses Mendelssohn. Sein Leben und seine Werke. Nebst einem Anhang ungedruckter Briefe von und an Moses Mendelssohn.* Leipzig, 1862 (2nd. ed. 1888).

King, E. H. "James Beattie's *Essay on Truth* (1770). An Eighteenth-Century 'Bestseller.'" *Dalhousie Review* (1971–72): 390–403.

Kloth, Karen and Fabian, Bernhard. "James Beattie: Contributions Towards a Bibliography." *Bibliotheck* 5 (1970): 232–45.

Knoll, Renate. *Johann Georg Hamann und Friedrich Heinrich Jacobi.* Heidelberg, 1963.

Kuehn, Manfred. "Dating Kant's 'Vorlesungen über Philosophische Enzyklopädie,'" *Kant-Studien* 74 (1983): 302–13.

— "Kant's Conception of Hume's Problem," *Journal of the History of Philosophy* 21 (1983): 175–93.

— "The Early Reception of Reid, Oswald and Beattie in Germany," *Journal of the History of Philosophy* 21 (1983): 479–95.

— "Hume's Antinomies," *Hume Studies* 9 (1983), pp. 25–45.

— "The Context of Kant's 'Refutation of Idealism' in Eighteenth-Century Philosophy," in *God, Man, and Nature in the Enlightenment* (forthcoming).

— "Kant's Transcendental Deduction: A Limited Defense of Hume," in *New*

Essays on Kant, ed. Bernard den Ouden (New York and Bern: Peter F. Lang Publishing Company, forthcoming).

– "Rethinking Kant—Again," *Dialogue* 24 (1985): 507–514.

Lauth, Reinhard. Review of Baum's *Vernunft und Erkenntnis* in *Archiv für Geschichte der Philosophie* 54 (1972): 97–103.

Lehmann, Gerhard. "Kritizismus und kritisches Motiv in der Entwicklung der Kantischen Philosophie." *Kant-Studien* 49 (1957–58): 25–54.

Lehrer, Keith. "Scottish Influences on Contemporary American Philosophy." *Philosophical Journal* 5 (1968): 34–42.

Lovejoy, A. "Kant and the English Platonists," *Essays Philosophical and Psychological in Honor of William James.* London, 1908.

– "Kant's Antithesis of Dogmatism and Criticism," in Moltke S. Gram, *Kant: Disputed Questions.* Chicago: Quadrangle Press, 1967, pp. 105–30.

Löwisch, Dieter Jürgen. "Kants *Kritik der reinen Vernunft* und Humes *Dialogues concerning Natural Religion.*" *Kant-Studien* 56 (1966): 170–207.

Lorsch, J. *Die Lehre vom Gefühl bei Tetens.* Giessen, 1906.

Marcil-Lacoste, Louise. *Claude Buffier and Thomas Reid: Two Common Sense-Philosophers.* Kingston and Montreal: McGill-Queen's University Press, 1982.

Martin, Gottfried. *Gesammelte Abhandlungen.* Vol. 1. Köln, 1961.

Martin, T. *The Instructed Vision: Scottish Common Sense Philosophy and the Origin of American Fiction.* Bloomington, 1961.

Mautner, Franz H. *Lichtenberg, Geschichte seines Geistes.* Berlin, 1969.

McCosh, James. *The Scottish Philosophy.* London, 1875.

Merlan, Philip. "From Hume to Hamann." *The Personalist* 32 (1951): 11–18.

– "Hamann et les *Dialogues* de Hume." *Revue de Metaphysique* 59 (1954): 285–89.

– "Kant, Hamann-Jacobi and Schelling on Hume." *Rivista critica di storia filosofia* 22 (1967) 343–51.

Metzke, Erwin. *J. G. Hamanns Stellung in der Philosophie des 18. Jahrhunderts. Eine Preisarbeit.* Halle, 1934.

Miller, George. "Kant and Berkeley: The Alternative Theories." *Kant-Studien* 64 (1973): 315–35.

Mossner, E. C. "Beattie's 'The Castle of Skepticism': An Unpublished Allegory against Hume, Voltaire and Hobbes." *University of Texas Studies in English* 27 (1948): 108–45.

Mossner, E. C. and Todd, William, ed. *Hume and the Enlightenment.* Edinburgh and Austin, 1974.

Nagel, Gordon. *The Structure of Experience. Kant's System of Principles.* Chicago and London: The University of Chicago Press, 1983.

Neumann, W. *Die Bedeutung Homes für die Aesthetik und sein Einfluss auf die deutschen Aesthetiker.* Halle, 1894.

Nietzsche, Friedrich. *The Portable Nietzsche.* Translated and edited by Walter Kaufmann. New York: Viking Press, 1954.

Nivelle, Armand. *Kunst- und Dichtungstheorien zwischen Aufklärung und Klassik.* Berlin, 1960.

Norton, David Fate. "From Moral Sense to Common Sense. An Essay on the Development of Scottish Common Sense Philosophy, 1700–1765." Ann Arbor: University Microfilms, 1966.
— "Reid's Abstract of the *Inquiry into the Human Mind*" in *Thomas Reid: Critical Interpretations* (ed. Barker and Beauchamp), pp. 125–32.
— "Hume and his Scottish Critics." *McGill Hume Studies*. Edited by David Fate Norton, Nicholas Capaldi, and Wade L. Robison. San Diego: Austin Hill Press, 1979.
— "Thomas Reid's *Curâ primâ* on Common Sense," Appendix to Louise Marcil Lacoste. *Claude Buffier and Thomas Reid, Two Common-Sense Philosophers*. Kingston and Montreal: McGill-Queen's University Press, 1982, pp. 179–208.
— *David Hume: Common-Sense Moralist, Sceptical Metaphysician*. Princeton: Princeton University Press, 1982.
Noxon, James. *Hume's Philosophical Development, A Study of his Method*. Oxford: Oxford University Press, 1973.
O'Flaherty, James C. *Unity and Language: A Study in the Philosophy of Johann Georg Hamann*. Chapel Hill, 1952.
— *Hamann's Socratic Memorabilia, A Translation and Commentary*. Baltimore: Johns Hopkins University Press, 1967.
— *Johann Georg Hamann*. Boston: Twayne Publishers, 1979.
Oppel, Horst. *Englisch-deutsche Literaturbeziehungen*. 2 vols. Berlin, 1971.
Pascal, Roy. "Herder and the Scottish Historical School." *Publications of the English Goethe Society* 14 (1939): 23–42.
Peach, Bernard. "Common Sense and Practical Reason in Reid and Kant." *Sophia* 24 (1956): 66–71.
Peirce, Charles Sanders. *Collected Papers of Charles Sanders Peirce*. 6 vols. Edited by Charles Hartshorne and Paul Weiss. Cambridge, Mass., 1931–35 (vols. 7–8, ed. by Arthur Burks. Cambridge, Mass., 1958).
Peterson, R. "Scottish Common Sense in America 1768–1850, an Evaluation of its Influence." Dissertation, University of Michigan, 1972.
Pinkuss, Fritz. *Moses Mendelssohns Verhältnis zur englischen Philosophie*. Würzburg, 1929.
— "Moses Mendelssohns Verhältnis zur englischen Philosophie." *Philosophisches Jahrbuch der Görres Gesellschaft* 42 (1929): 449–90.
Piper, W. B. "Kant's Contact with British Empiricism." *Eighteenth-Century Studies* 12 (1978–79): 174–89.
Popkin, Richard H. "Hume and Isaac de Pinto, II, Five New Letters," in *Hume and the Enlightenment, Essays Presented to E. C. Mossner*. Ed. William Todd. Edinburgh and Austin, 1974.
Price, Mary Bell, and Price, Lawrence Marsden. "The Publication of English Humanioria in Germany in the Eighteenth Century." *University of California Publications in Modern Philology* xliv (1955).
Price, Lawrence Marsden. *The Reception of English Literature in Germany*. Berkeley, 1932.

Pringle Pattison (Seth), A. *Scottish Philosophy: A Comparison of Scottish and German Answers*. Edinburgh, 1890.

Raffaele, Ciafordone. "Über den Primat der praktischen Vernunft vor der theoretischen." *Studia Leibnitiana* 14 (1982), pp. 127–135.

Randall, Helen W. *The Critical Theory of Lord Kames*. Northampton, Mass.: Smith College Studies in Modern Languages, 1964.

Raphael, D. D. *The Moral Sense*. Oxford: Oxford University Press, 1947.

Rescher, Nicholas. "The 'Special Constitution' of Man's Mind; The Ultimately Factual Basis of the Necessity and Universality of A Priori Synthetic Truths in Kant's Critical Philosophy." *Akten des IV. Internationalen Kant-Kongresses* (1974). Part 2.1, pp. 318–37.

Röttgers, Kurt. "J. G. H. Feder—Beitrag zu einer Verhinderungsgeschichte eines deutschen Empirismus," *Kant-Studien* 75 (1984): 420–41.

Rollin, Bernhard H. "Thomas Reid and the Semiotics of Perception." *The Monist* 61 (1978): 257–70.

Rome, Sidney C. "The Scottish Refutation of Berkeley's Immaterialism." *Philosophy and Phenomenological Research* 3 (1942–43): 313–25.

Rorty, Richard. *Philosophy and the Mirror of Nature*. 2nd printing with corrections. Princeton: Princeton University Press, 1980.

Ryle, Gilbert. *The Concept of Mind*. Harmondsworth: Peregrine Books, 1963.

– "Ordinary Language." *Philosophy and Ordinary Language*. Edited by Charles E. Caton. Urbana, Chicago, and London: University of Illinois Press, 1970 (5th ed.).

Schepers, Heinrich. *Andreas Rüdigers Methodologie und ihre Voraussetzungen. Ein Beitrag zur Geschichte der deutschen Schulphilosophie im XVIII. Jahrhundert*. Köln, 1959.

Schlegtendahl, Walter. *Johann Nicolaus Tetens Erkenntnistheorie in Beziehung auf Kant*. Leipzig, 1888.

Schmucker, Josef. "Zur entwicklungsgeschichtlichen Bedeutung der Inauguraldissertation." *Kant-Studien* 65 (1975): 261*-82*.

Schneider, Robert. *Schelling und Hegels schwäbische Geistesahnen*. Würzburg-Aumühle, 1938.

Schneiders, W. Einleitung to Christian Thomasius, *Ausübung der Vernunftlehre*. Edited by W. Schneiders. Hildesheim, 1968.

Schöffler, Herbert. *Deutsches Geistesleben zwischen Reformation und Aufklärung*. Frankfurt/Main, 1956.

Schouls, Peter A. "The Cartesian Method of Locke's *Essay Concerning Human Understanding*." *Canadian Journal of Philosophy* 4 (1975): 579–601.

Schubert, Friedrich Wilhelm. *Immanuel Kants Biographie zum grossen Theil nach handschriftlichen Nachschriften*. Leipzig, 1842 (vol. 2, part 2 of Immanuel Kant, *Sämmtliche Werke*, ed. Karl Rosenkranz and Friedrich Wilhelm Schubert).

Schulze, W. A. "Oetinger contra Leibniz." *Zeitschrift für philosophische Forschung* 2 (1957): 607–17.

Sciaccia, M. F. "Reid e Gallupi." In *Studi sulla filosofia moderna*. Milano, 1964.

Seebohm, Thomas M. "Der systematische Ort der Herderschen *Metakritik*." *Kant-Studien* 63 (1972): 58–73.

Segerstedt, Torgny T. *The Problem of Knowledge in Scottish Philosophy*. Lund, 1935.

Shaw, Leroy R. "Henry Home of Kames: Precursor of Herder," *Germanic Review* 35 (1960): 116–27.

Sidgwick, Henry. "The Philosophy of Common Sense." *Mind* 14 new series (1895): 145–58.

Silver, Bruce. "A Note on Berkeley's *New Theory of Vision* and Thomas Reid's Distinction between Primary and Secondary Qualities." *Southern Journal of Philosophy* 12 (1974): 253–63.

Smith, Norman Kemp. *A Commentary to Kant's Critique of Pure Reason*. Atlantic Highlands, N. J.: Humanities Press, 1984 (reprint of the 2nd ed. of 1923).

– *The Philosophy of David Hume*. London, 1941.

Sommer, Robert. *Grundzüge einer Geschichte der Psychologie und Ästhetik von Wolff-Baumgarten by Kant-Schiller*. Leipzig, 1892.

Stäbler, Eugen. *Berkeley's Auffassung und Wirkung in der deutschen Philosophie bis Hegel*. Tübingen, 1935.

Störring, G. *Die Erkenntnistheorie von Tetens*. Leipzig, 1901.

Strawson, P. F. *Individuals. An Essay in Descriptive Metaphysics*. London, 1964.

Stroud, Barry. *Hume*. London and Boston: Routledge and Kegan Paul, 1977.

Süss, Theobald. "Der Nihilismus bei F. H. Jacobi." In *Der Nihilismus als Phänomen der Geistesgeschichte in der wissenschaftlichen Diskussion unseres Jahrhunderts*. Edited by Dieter Arendt. Darmstadt: Wissenschaftliche Buchgesellschaft, 1974.

Swain, Charles. "Hamann and the Philosophy of David Hume." *Journal of the History of Philosophy* (1967): 343–51.

Taylor, Charles. "The Opening Argument in the *Phenomenology*." In *Hegel: A Collection of Critical Essays*. Edited by Alasdair MacIntyre. Garden City and New York: Anchor Books, 1972.

– *Hegel*. Cambridge, London, New York, and Melbourne: Cambridge University Press, 1975.

Taylor, Richard. Review of S. A. Grave, *The Scottish Philosophy of Common Sense* in *Philosophical Review*, July, 1961.

Teras, Rita. *Wilhelm Heinses Ästhetik*. München, 1972.

Tonelli, Giorgio. Einleitung to Christian August Crusius, *Die philosophischen Hauptwerke*, vol. 1. Hildesheim: Georg Olms, 1969.

Turbayne, Colin M. "Kant's Refutation of Dogmatic Idealism." *Philosophical Quarterly* 5 (1955): 225–44.

Uebele, W. "Herder and Tetens." *Archiv für Geschichte der Philosophie* 18 (1905): 216–49.

– "Johann Nicolaus Tetens zum 100 jahrigen Todestag." *Zeitschrift für Philosophie und philosophische Kritik* 1908, pp. 137–51.

— *Johann Nicolaus Tetens.* Kant-Studien Ergänzungsheft. Vol. 24. Berlin, 1911.

Unger, Rudolf. *Hamanns Sprachtheorie im Zusammenhang seines Denkens.* München, 1905.

— *Hamann und die Aufklärung. Studien zur Vorgeschichte des romantischen Geistes im 18. Jahrhundert.* 2 vols. Halle, 1925.

Vaihinger, H. *Commentar zu Kant's Kritik der reinen Vernunft.* 2 vols. Stuttgart, 1881.

— "Zu Kant's Widerlegung des Idealismus." *Strassburger Abhandlungen zur Philosophie,* 1884.

Vernier, Paul. "Reid on Foundation of Knowledge." In *Thomas Reid: Critical Interpretations* (ed. Barker and Beauchamp), pp. 14–24.

Verra, Valerio. *Friedrich Heinrich Jacobi, 1743–1819.* Torino, 1967.

Vleeshauwer, H. J. *The Development of Kantian Thought.* Translated by A. R. C. Duncan. London: Thomas Nelson & Son, 1962.

Vorländer, Karl. *Immanuel Kants Leben.* Leipzig, 1911.

Wagner, Albert Malte. *Heinrich Wilhelm von Gerstenberg und der Sturm und Drang.* Vol. 1: *Gerstenbergs Leben, Schriften und Persönlichkeit.* Heidelberg, 1920.

Walsh, W. H. "Philosophy and Psychology in Kant's Critique." *Kant-Studien* 57 (1966): 186–98.

— "Kant and Metaphysics." *Kant-Studien* 67 (1976): 372–84.

— *Kant's Criticism of Metaphysics.* Chicago: University of Chicago Press, 1976.

Walz, J. A. "English Influences on the German Vocabulary of the 18th Century." *Monatshefte* (Madison) 35 (1943): 156–64.

Walzel, Oskar F. "Shaftesbury und das deutsche Geistesleben des 18. Jahrhunderts." *Germanisch-Romanische Monatsschriften* 1 (1909): 416–37.

Weber, Heinrich. *Hamann und Kant.* München, 1904.

Weiser, Christian F. *Shaftesbury und das deutsche Geistesleben.* Leipzig und Berlin, 1916.

Werkmeister, W. H. "Notes to an Interpretation of Berkeley." In *New Studies in Berkeley's Philosophy.* Edited by Warren E. Steinkraus. New York: Holt, Reinhart & Winston, 1966.

Wessell, Leonhard P. *G. E. Lessing's Theology; A Reinterpretation.* The Hague, 1977.

Winch, P. G. "The Notion of 'Suggestion' in Thomas Reid's Theory of Perception." *Philosophical Quarterly* 3 (1953): 327–41.

Windelband, Wilhelm. *Geschichte der neueren Philosophie.* Vol. 2. Leipzig, 1909.

Windelband, Wilhelm and Heimsoeth, Heinz. *Lehrbuch der Geschichte der Philosophie.* 14th ed. Tübingen: J. C. B. Mohr (Carl Siebeck), 1950.

Wize, Filip. *Friedrich Riedel und seine Aesthetik.* Leipzig, 1902.

Wölfel, Kurt. "Nachwort." In Christian Garve, *Popularphilosophische Schriften über literarische, aesthetische und gesellschaftliche Gegenstände.* 2 vols. Edited by Kurt Wölfel. Stuttgart, 1974.

Wohlgemuth, Josef. *Henry Homes Ästhetik und ihr Einfluss auf deutsche Ästhetiker.* Berlin, 1893.

Wolf, F. O. "General Introduction: Scottish Philosophy and the Rise of Capitalist Society — Some Remarks on the Relevance of a Study of Beattie and on the Methodology of the History of Philosophy." In James Beattie, *The Philosophical Works*. Vol. 1 (*Essay on Truth*, 1st. ed.). Edited by F. O. Wolf. Stuttgart and Bad Canstatt: Frommann and Holzboog, 1973.

Wolff, Robert Paul. "Kant's Debt to Hume via Beattie." *Journal of the History of Ideas* 21 (1960): 117–23.

Wreschner, Arthur. *Ernst Platners und Kants Erkenntnistheorie mit besonderer Berücksichtigung von Tetens und Aenesidemus*. Leipzig, 1882.

Wundt, Max. *Die Schulphilosophie im Zeitalter der Aufklärung*. Tübingen, 1945.

Yolton, John W. *Perceptual Acquaintance: From Descartes to Reid*. Minneapolis: University of Minnesota Press, 1984.

Zart, G. *Einfluss der englischen Philosophie seit Bacon auf die deutsche Philosophie des 18. Jahrhunderts*. Berlin, 1881.

Zinn, Elisabeth. *Die Theologie des Friedrich Christoph Oetinger*. Gütersloh, 1932.

Zimmerli, Walther Chr., "'Schwere Rüstung' des Dogmatismus und 'anwendbare Eklektik,'" *Studia Leibnitiana* 15 (1983): 58–71.

Index